LIBERATING LIBYA

British Diplomacy and War in the Desert

RUPERT WIELOCH

CASEMATE

Philadelphia & Oxford

Published in the United States of America and Great Britain in 2021 by
CASEMATE PUBLISHERS
1950 Lawrence Road, Havertown, PA 19083, USA
and
The Old Music Hall, 106–108 Cowley Road, Oxford OX4 1JE, UK

Hardback Edition: ISBN 978-1-63624-082-4
Digital Edition: ISBN 978-1-63624-083-1

A CIP record for this book is available from the British Library

Printed and bound in the United Kingdom by TJ Books

Typeset in India by Lapiz Digital Services, Chennai.

For a complete list of Casemate titles, please contact:

CASEMATE PUBLISHERS (US)
Telephone (610) 853-9131
Fax (610) 853-9146
Email: casemate@casematepublishers.com
www.casematepublishers.com

CASEMATE PUBLISHERS (UK)
Telephone (01865) 241249
Email: casemate-uk@casematepublishers.co.uk
www.casematepublishers.co.uk

Contents

List of Maps

Dedication

To the nine soldiers awarded the Victoria Cross in Libya between April 1941 and October 1942 and the only Libyan to be awarded the Military Cross.

Corporal John Hurst Edmondson, 2/17th Australian Infantry Battalion
14 April 1941 (posthumous)

Lieutenant Colonel Geoffrey Charles Tasker Keyes MC, Royal Scots Greys
18 November 1941 (posthumous)

Rifleman John Beeley, King's Royal Rifle Corps
21 November 1941 (posthumous)

Second Lieutenant George Ward Gunn MC, Royal Horse Artillery
21 November 1941 (posthumous)

Brigadier John Charles (Jock) Campbell DSO, MC, Royal Horse Artillery
21 November 1941

Captain Philip John (Pip) Gardner MC, Royal Tank Regiment
23 November 1941

Captain James Joseph Bernard Jackman, Royal Northumberland Fusiliers
26 November 1941 (posthumous)

Lieutenant Colonel Henry Robert Bowreman Foote DSO, Royal Tank Regiment
27 May 1942

Sergeant Quentin George Murray Smythe, Royal Natal Carabineers
5 June 1942

Mulazim Awal (Lieutenant) Sa'ad Ali Rahouna, Libyan Arab Force
23 April 1942

Foreword

When we look into the history of Libya, two aphorisms immediately spring to mind, the first is the realisation that: *"History is geography stretched over time."* The second, attributed to Mark Twain, is that: *"History never repeats itself; but it rhymes."*

No historian, used to finding that throughout history battles are constantly being fought over the same piece of ground, will dispute these truisms. However, in writing what will become the definitive work tracing the history of Britain's interest in and relationship with Libya, Rupert Wieloch has not only confirmed their accuracy but explained in detail just why they are true. Furthermore, and most importantly, both his historical and contemporary analyses also bear out another maxim—one which has fallen out of favour in the West in recent times, but which our authoritarian competitors are currently demonstrating is still valid—Frederick the Great's observation that: *"Diplomacy without arms is like music without instruments"*.

Armies do indeed play a major role in this story, as one might expect when the author is a first-rate military historian with a distinguished Army career behind him. But this is not just a military history. Drawing on his extensive knowledge of and deep feeling for the country, Rupert Wieloch has been able to use Libya as a stage, explaining the drama of Britain's long involvement with the country as a means to illustrate the role national security and defence have played in our foreign policy. It is this which is the real lesson the book imparts, and which gives it such resonance today, when we are in danger of forgetting this fundamental point.

The book is also distinguished from military and diplomatic histories by its style. Nowhere is the writing heavy, overly formal or excessively technical and detailed. Without sacrificing accuracy and balance, the author has told his story in an easily accessible and engaging way, with a great deal of personal human detail about—and by—many of the key characters involved. This human touch, which is one of the main characteristics of Rupert Wieloch's approach, not only brings out the lessons more effectively; it also acknowledges the contribution that individuals make to the way things turn out for good or ill, a fact denied by some schools of historiography.

The author starts his story in pre-Roman times, describing how, in Libya, European, African and Arabic influence and cultures have interacted over the centuries, thereby providing us with a basis for understanding the complexities of modern Libya and her relationships with other countries in today's world. The

English, and later British, involvement with Libya began in earnest in the mid-17th century, with efforts to stop piracy and the seizing of white Christian slaves which had begun to be a problem a century earlier and which continued well into the 19th century, ultimately goading even the infant United States into activity, providing the US Marine Corps with its first overseas military campaign and one of the opening lines in its Corps Hymn.

The book describes how, as the 19th century progressed, Libya became a playing field for the growing competition between Britain and France, both countries seeking to expand their empires and fields of interest. The emergence of modern Turkey is also illustrated, as it played out in Libya and the other subject territories of North Africa, interacting with Western powers in the process. As an added bonus, the book provides the reader with a particular understanding of how France's conflicted relationship with North Africa has evolved. A major part of the book is a description of the military and diplomatic history of the 20th century, including the conflicts fought on Libyan soil in World War I and World War II. Again, this explains why Italy's relationship with modern Libya is so awkward. Indeed, understanding the history of French and Italian involvement in North Africa explains why today's EU finds it so difficult to develop a balanced relationship with its close neighbours to the south but why, for the UK, the relationship with North Africa for much of the last century has been somewhat more relaxed and comfortable.

Students of the Desert Campaigns of World War II will find, in the six chapters that the author devotes to this period, not only an insightful exposition of the main aspects of that campaign and the birth of Britain's Special Forces, but a constant linkage of the military events to the underlying background of the rapidly evolving political process. Von Clausewitz' famous quotation: *Der Krieg ist eine bloße Fortsetzung der Politik mit anderen Mitteln* is usually translated as: *War is just a continuation of politics by other means*. But, as another reknowned military historian and strategist, Maj Gen Mungo Melvin, has pointed out, *Politik* in German means both *politics* and *policy*; and *mit* means *with*, ie *accompanied by other means*, not *by alternative means*. Politics and policy do not stop once war starts; indeed they speed up and become more acute. Rupert Wieloch does us great service by making this essential interaction very clear.

It is in continuing to make that crucial interplay clear in describing events since 1945 that the author makes his most valuable contribution to modern strategic thinking. This part of the book does not make for comfortable reading. Rather it is a litany of failure. In the post-war period, the path of British-Libyan relations is truly paved with good intentions, poor decisions and lost opportunities. What Rupert Wieloch demonstrates in analysing this period is that a successful foreign policy must always have defence and security at its heart, and that these forms of power invariably need to be woven into a truly coherent, pro-active strategy with all other forms of power. This has always been the case, although today it has become fashionable to term this *hybrid warfare*. But, just as with the mistranslation of Clausewitz, *hybrid* warfare is often taken to be an alternative to classic, kinetic warfare, whereas in fact classic weapons and violent battle are still an essential, integral part of the whole spectrum of modern hybrid conflict.

My own personal experience—and the reason why I was happy to be invited to write this foreword—is that the UK has, alas, lost this capability to make and implement joined-up national strategy. Nowhere is this loss more clearly evident than in our policy towards Libya. In early 2012 I was deployed to Libya as part of a team from the UK Government's Stabilisation Unit, to support our Ambassador's sterling efforts to help the Libyans gain control of the very chaotic internal security situation that had developed after the death of Gadhafi. My mission report drew attention to the lack of strategic thinking in Government, the failure to have a restoration plan to follow the military operation, and Whitehall's inability to understand the urgency of taking action. I wrote:

> The situation will not be improved by a series of tactical initiatives, however well intentioned and well funded. Unless … a process appropriate to the circumstances can be devised and introduced, then we must steel ourselves to sit back and wait for a renewal of the conflict and accept the loss of whatever influence and prestige in the region the UK had acquired as a result of our past military intervention.

The report was acknowledged, but too little was done too late; and after the murder of the US Ambassador and the attempted assassination of the British Ambassador, any remaining enthusiasm for action rapidly dissipated. What I had feared indeed came to pass.

The failures of our military interventions in the Middle East during the decade since our intervention in Libya have undermined our political will to contemplate intervention abroad in any operation that might be considered "discretionary". The run-down of our military strength has indeed made such operations difficult—perhaps well-nigh impossible—to mount and sustain with any credibility, especially if we face serious military opposition from a hostile state actor. Yet we are witnessing daily the, alas, effective actions of authoritarian regimes which have not lost sight of the truth of Frederick the Great's maxim and which understand only too well that economic levers, education in democratic practices and social justice programmes do not have the same strategic effect if they cannot be backed up by credible military diplomacy.

The world now faces the huge challenge of climate change which, coming on top of the pandemic, poses an irresistible threat to many countries with inadequate governance. There are many such countries in Africa alone. We are also just coming to understand that climate change is likely to be much more rapid and much worse that we have been preparing for. It is not impossible that, for example, we will soon see mass migration waves, greater than anything seen so far, flooding into North

Africa with the aim of finding safety and stability in Europe. If this happens, we will have a choice of three courses of action:

- We can welcome the migrants in;
- We can deploy our military to stop them physically from coming to our shores, or;
- We can go to where they are running from, whatever the violent environment, and we can help them fix things so that they can safely stay in their homes.

Whilst I acknowledge that, in practice, we may need a combination of all three options, the last proposal seems to me to be the wisest on which to concentrate. But, for that to be possible, we will need, as this book suggests, to be able to make and implement joined-up, cross governmental strategy which includes credible, appropriate military capabilities and capacity. We need to get moving.

Christopher Donnelly, Director, Institute of Statecraft and Emeritus Senior Fellow, UK Defence Academy, July 2021

Acknowledgements

My gratitude to the many Libyans who have helped me to write this book begins with members of the National Transitional Council, who I met in London in March 2011, and includes hundreds of officials, revolutionaries and ordinary citizens who I encountered in the vibrant country, from Tobruk to Ghadames. In England, I am particularly indebted to David Cameron and Lord Ricketts, who were the prime minister and national security advisor during the operation to protect civilians under United Nations Resolution 1973. I am also profoundly grateful to the three British ambassadors who served in Tripoli from 1999 to 2010 (Sir Richard Dalton, Anthony Layden and Sir Vincent Fean) for their help and advice.

The 2021 national lockdown proved to be an obstacle to researching important government documents at the National Archives, so I greatly appreciate the help of Russell McGuirk with the section covering the early 20th century and the support of several members of the excellent Great War Forum, who filled in some of the World War I gaps. I pass special thanks to the Duke of Westminster and to Captain Andrew French, the curator of the Berkshire Yeomanry Museum, for their generous help and photographs to illustrate the Sanussi Campaign, as well as to Francis Gotto and Richard Higgins at the University of Durham's Special Collection, for sending such evocative images from the Newbold Archive.

I have cross-checked over 100 of the histories and memoirs that relate to the Western Desert Campaign that freed Libya from Italian rule and am beholden to the Commonwealth War Graves Commission and to the meticulous Hans Houtermann, who clarified details of individual soldiers, as well as Christopher Chant for his intriguing website on operational code-names. I offer my utmost appreciation to David Jamieson, whose father was the padre of 5th Green Howards during their courageous stand at the battle of Gazala, and to The Hon. Philippa Weatherly for allowing me access to the private papers of Patrick McCraith, the first commander of the Long Range Desert Group's Yeomanry Patrol, who led the advance of the Sherwood Rangers Yeomanry at the second battle of El Alamein.

Piecing together the post-war reconstruction, I accessed dozens of fascinating websites which reveal the birthing pangs of a new country and the anguish of the Jewish community that was evacuated when Israel declared its independence. I acknowledge the colourful internet sites and international bloggers who describe what life was like in Libya during the time of King Idris and I heartily thank Lieutenant Colonel The Reverend Christopher Walker and Captain Richard Wilkin for their generous help and recollections about the watershed moment in Libya's history, when Colonel Gadhafi came to power in 1969.

Finally, I pay tribute to the two inspirational academics who have generously contributed the Foreword and Afterword. Professor Chris Donnelly has an unsurpassed reputation for his work at the Soviet Studies Research Centre and later at the Advanced Research and Assessment Group in the UK Defence Academy. The prescient report that he wrote for the government, after visiting me in Tripoli in 2012, succinctly identified the strategic risks in Libya and made important recommendations, which sadly Whitehall did not act upon. Jason Pack has an equally formidable reputation as a leading writer on modern Libya and appears to be one of the few academics who understands the need for an integrated diplomatic, economic and military approach to help Libya overcome its current problems. His gracious help and sound advice across the whole book have been invaluable.

Prologue

Writing history in a post-feminist era, when readers are especially alert to issues of social and racial justice, requires a sensitive approach to modern opinions. Authors today have to accept that many influential academics are highly critical of government authority and that public organisations are responding to the so-called "culture wars" by revising attitudes to the past. For example, the National Trust has produced a *Report on the Connections between Colonialism and Properties now in the Care of the National Trust* and has invited "teams of children into its properties to lecture staff volunteers about the horrors of colonialism".[1] It is therefore more vital than ever that archives are scrutinised through a watertight lens and the deeds and letters of ordinary men and women are considered equally with the affairs of high-ranking officers.

Fortunately, the Anglo-Libyan relationship falls into a unique category because it was founded on humanitarian interest, not imperial expansion. It began after the Restoration when white slavery was rife in North Africa. The Tripoli trade continued through the Napoleonic era, when the United States of America fulfilled its first overseas military intervention, and did not end until long after the abolitionist movement was established in London.

For unknown reasons, historians have only addressed the subject of British diplomacy and war in Libya in a piecemeal fashion. The help provided during the 19th century to resist French colonialism is largely forgotten. The Western Desert Campaign against Rommel is described in most histories with scant reference to the campaign that covered much of the same ground 25 years earlier. Significant interventions, such as during the Italo-Ottoman War, when British and Irish journalists reported breaches of the Hague Conventions and changed international opinion about the Italian invasion, have been neglected. This book aims to fill the gap in knowledge, by tracing the hidden links that connect Britain's long friendship that twice liberated Libya from repressive regimes.

The author recognises that certain unfiltered passages from the works of 19th-century British explorers and authors may appear to reinforce colonial stereotypes. For those who might take offence at outdated terminology, the author confirms that he is not agreeing with these controversial views, but considers that their inclusion is essential because they provide vital evidence about the continuum of Anglo-Libyan friendship. Likewise, tributes to soldiers of all backgrounds who fought and died in the desert, are not intended to glorify war, but to commemorate those individuals who paid the ultimate price in the cause of today's freedoms.

For those who are unaware of the significance of the Victoria Cross, a word of explanation is necessary. The VC is the only Commonwealth gallantry medal that can be awarded posthumously and is so rare that recipients either have to be killed in action or have a probability of certain death to The VC is the UK's highest level operational gallantry award in the face of the enemy and is so rare that recipients either have to be killed in action or have a 90% probability of death. For example, only two were awarded during the Falklands conflict—both were posthumous. Of the nine awarded in Libya, five were posthumous and the others were all cases were the individual was either very seriously wounded or lucky to be alive. The historical significance of this is in the way armies create fighting spirit to overcome overwhelming odds. Since the world is still divided between democracies and totalitarian states, the significance remains relevant today. The political considerations increase the interest in these awards as readers will discover in the stories of Hugh Souter and Geoffrey Keyes. It is also worth highlighting the geographical dimension; the VCs in Libya were spread among Australia, South Africa, Scotland, Ireland and England at the same time as Indian and New Zealand soldiers received the highest gallantry awards in Abyssinia and Crete.

Turning to the main theme of the book, it is important to recognise that the benign Anglo-Libyan relationship was built as much on science and exploration as shared security interests. In the 19th century, the astounding ancient sites in Cyrenaica and Tripolitania captivated proponents of the new discipline of archaeology, while the daunting expanse of the Sahara challenged young geographers (10 French and Royal Geographical Society gold medals have been awarded for Libyan exploration). This sympathetic relationship was tested to exhaustion during World War I, but through the friendships developed by officers such as Leo Royle and Milo Talbot, Britain established the foundations of a long collaboration with the Arab population in Libya.

However, in World War II, the Desert Rats were poorly informed about previous British involvement in Libya. Myles Hildyard, who fought with the Sherwood Rangers Yeomanry throughout their campaign in North Africa, wrote to his brother Toby on 16 February 1943: "I don't really know who there was in Libya for the Italians to pacify. We have been a long way and you could count the Arabs we have seen on two hands. I believe in the last war we had a large force tied down in Libya, defending Egypt from 30,000 Sanussi, but after the war (and one action when the Duke of Westminster charged some Arabs in armoured cars) it was discovered that the Sanussi was a myth."

Apart from the lack of knowledge about the rich Anglo-Libyan history, this letter demonstrates a deeper problem concerning the part played by Libyans in the war effort. Of course, many Tripolitanians were in the pay of the Italian army, but in Cyrenaica, the majority the population supported the Allies and where they could, helped Special Forces to raid Rommel's supply lines. Perhaps more importantly, many Libyans living in the rugged mountains and harsh desert assisted thousands of disorientated soldiers as they attempted to rejoin their units after the rapid armoured advances left them behind enemy lines. By offering bread, water and eggs from their own meagre supplies and helping with directions and alerts about enemy locations, they made a significant contribution to the victory, which is acknowledged in Part 3.

This is not the only example of collective amnesia revealed in this book. In 1967, the American consul in Benghazi, John Kormann, was forced to barricade himself with his staff of nine in the consulate and began to destroy secret US documents. After a 10-hour siege, he was rescued by British soldiers who also collected his anxious family from their diplomatic quarters. This pivotal month, which proved to be a watershed in the relationship between Libya and the West, was subsequently obscured by tumultuous events, including the coup that brought Muammar Gadhafi to power.

It is especially sad that the 1967 lessons were neglected because they might have prevented the death in Benghazi of Kormann's successor, Christopher Stevens, 45 years later. The murder of the US ambassador on 11 September 2012 has proved most costly to Libya's transition to a stable country. A peaceful outcome remains elusive, but by learning the lessons of the past, we can avoid previous mistakes and identify what works well, which in the case of Libya, is an integrated diplomatic-military-economic solution. Unfortunately, the UN Mission, which has been responsible for reconstruction since November 2012, has failed repeatedly in the second of these fundamental levers of national power.

In a similar way, memories of the 9,336 casualties buried in Libya are fading and the story of Britain's post-war assistance is at risk of being submerged by a media narrative of a failed state that is "a crucible of terror" and a source for illegal migration. This book aims to redress the balance and provide a firm foundation for anyone interested in this poorly understood country. It does not shy away from the difficult moments such as the post-war anti-Jewish riots and modern terrorism, which continues to be seen in tragic events such as the Manchester Arena bombing. However, as the 80th anniversary of the Siege of Tobruk, the 70th anniversary of independence and the 10th anniversary of Gadhafi's death approach in 2021, the time seems right for a new perspective on Britain's involvement in Libya, which twice freed the country from brutal tyrannies.

PART 1

A HARD PLACE TO LIVE
(631 BC–AD 1880)

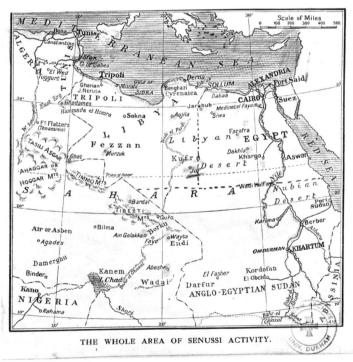

THE WHOLE AREA OF SENUSSI ACTIVITY.

Libya and its neighbours in World War I. The frontiers of Libya were not settled until after World War I. The two biggest disputes have been Egypt's claim to Jaghbub oasis and Chad's claim to the Aouzou Strip which led to the Toyota War in 1987. (Reproduced by kind permission of Durham University Library and Collections—Newbold Archive)

CHAPTER I

Greek Settlement to Arab Invasion

It has been said that any invader who conquered Egypt would find the occupation of Libya little more than child's play.

GLUBB PASHA, 1963

The suffocating Saharan heat could not prevent a sliver of ice from piercing Berenice's heart. The young queen felt an aching in her stomach when she learned that her husband, King Demetrius, had humiliated her so completely by having an affair with her mother.

Berenice realised that her 35-year-old consort was much closer in age to the 42-year-old dowager Queen Apama; but for them to cavort so brazenly after the royal wedding magnified the emotional and physical pain coursing through her body. She wondered whether her seductive mother had planned this all along and resolved to regain her honour.

Berenice's father, King Magas, had ruled Cyrenaica, in what is now part of Libya, for 25 years. Soon after he died in 250 BC, his widow invited her uncle Demetrius the Fair to visit her in Libya. She was keen for the country to remain independent from Egypt, but this Macedonian prince was nothing compared to his illustrious predecessor Alexander the Great, who had made Greece the pre-eminent power in the Middle East. Tempted by the easy pickings in a wealthy North African kingdom, this vain narcissist with bonny looks readily accepted the queen's offer of the hand of her daughter.

Berenice was only 20 years old, but she was not willing to tolerate "three of us in this marriage". Her swelling anger led to a path of revenge and she plotted her way ahead with support from those who were outraged by the interloper's behaviour. Unaware of his wife's intentions, the lustful king was caught in bed with his mother-in-law and killed by a hired assassin, less than a year after arriving from Greece.

The people of Cyrenaica had little sympathy for the philandering king and the Senate agreed that he deserved his fate. Berenice was not challenged and, in turn, allowed two senators to rule in her stead until she made peace with her cousin, the young Egyptian heir to the throne, who was so impressed with her character that he married her in 246 BC and unified the kingdoms of Egypt and Cyrenaica.[1]

Thereafter, Ptolemy III and Berenice II heralded a new era of prosperity that lasted until Rome seized North Africa. Berenice was so loved by the population that she was worshipped as a goddess in her own right and a constellation was named after her, or rather her hair (Coma Berenices), which she cut as a votive offering.

The final Ptolemaic ruler in Libya was Kleopatra Selene, the fearless daughter of Antony and Cleopatra. Her parents' suicide in 30 BC brought uncertainty to her life, but she travelled to Rome and married the king of Mauretania, thus becoming one of the most important women in the Augustan age. Through her daughter, Drusilla, she extended the Ptolemaic line by marriage with Roman nobility.

Cyrenaica was united with Crete in 27 BC and placed in the diocese of Egypt within the Praetorian Prefecture of the East (Constantinople), whereas Tripoli was included in the Prefecture of Italy. After 40 years of prosperity, a crisis arose with the extinction of the plant that created Cyrenaica's wealth, silphium.[2] Its disappearance was caused by a combination of climate change and over-harvesting, with one of the last plants allegedly presented to Emperor Nero.

Nero was opposed by the humanitarian activist and poet Marcus Annaeus Lucanus, known as Lucan. Tragically, he was forced to commit suicide for treason when he was only 25 years old, but in his unfinished masterpiece, *Pharsalia*, he established Cyrenaica's place in history with a tale about Pallas Athena:[3]

> Pallas, who springing from her father's head
> First lit on Libya, nearest land to heaven,
> (As by its heat is proved); here on the brink
> She stood, reflected in the placid wave
> And called herself Tritonis.

Throughout this era of classical antiquity, when the North African coast was occupied by foreign settlers, the interior of Libya remained firmly in the hands of the Berber (or Amazigh)[4] tribes, who resisted all invaders and retained their culture and customs. However, after the fall of the Roman Empire, a new threat arrived, which was to permanently change the regional balance of power.

* * *

Before the Prophet Muhammed was born, the north coast of Africa was part of the same world as Europe. The decline of pagan civilisations allowed Christianity to spread through Roman and Eastern Orthodox colonies for nearly 500 years. In the west, Vandals from Western Silesia ruled Mauretania for 100 years until it was incorporated into the Byzantine Empire. However, in the interior, the nomadic tribes continued to resist conversion and retained control of the mountains, valleys and desert.

That all changed in the tumultuous 7th century. It took no more than 11 years from the death of Rasūl Allāh in AD 632 for an army led by the restless Amr ibn al-As al-Sahmi (described in Gibbon's *Decline and Fall* as Amrou) to invade Libya and extend Arab dominion over the province of Cyrenaica. He occupied Barqa (Cyrenaica in Arabic) without opposition and established a forward operating base known as Barce.[5] The local Louata and Ausurii tribes appeared ready to adopt Islam and welcomed the Arabs, but the Byzantine garrison at Tripoli resisted their advances until AD 643.

The Arab army did not have the same success further south. Amr's nephew, Uqba ibn Nafi, led a large force that was defeated swiftly by Sudanese archers. This did not stop Uqba's ambitions and when his first patron died in Egypt in AD 663, he made a plan to extend the limit of Arab control across Libya and appealed to the founder of the Umayyad Caliphate, Mu'awiyah. The ambitious caliph allowed Uqba to lead an army into the Sahara where he defeated the Berbers and in AD 670, he established a new cantonment 100 miles south of Carthage, named Qairawa (now Kairouan).

Uqba may have been a great soldier, but he was no diplomat and in the three-cornered contest between the Byzantines, the Berbers and the Arabs, he was unable to forge long-standing alliances. Before venturing further west, the caliph replaced him with Dinar abu al-Muhajir who put his predecessor in chains and won enough support from the Berber tribes to reach Tlemcen, near to the Algerian border with Morocco.

A frustrated Uqba travelled to Damascus and, after the death of Mu'awiyah, managed to persuade his frivolous son, Yezeed, to reinstate him as commander-in-chief in *Ifriqiya* (Africa). Returning to Libya in AD 681, he placed Dinar in chains, but his arrival alienated the charismatic Berber leader, Kusaila, who ended his co-operation with the Arabs.

Uqba launched another military expedition and this time, he captured Tangier and continued along the Atlantic coast to the river Sus. Riding into the Atlantic at what is now Agadir, he proclaimed: "Allahu Akbar! If my course were not stopped by this sea, I would still go on, to the unknown kingdoms of the West ... "[6]

Returning to Qairawa after this extended raid of 1,500 miles, Uqba was ambushed at Tahuda by King Kusaila. The Arab army was put to the sword and at this news, other Berber tribes rose up and overthrew their overlords who retreated to Barqa, which again became the limit of Arab exploitation. For a decade, their expansion was put on hold as the Second Fitna (civil war) was fought in Syria and Arabia for leadership of the Islamic world.

The third Arab invasion of North Africa began after Abd al-Malik ibn Marwan reunited the caliphate in AD 692. The new expedition was led by Hassan ibn al

Nu'man al-Ghassani, who raised an army of 40,000 Saracens and advanced west along the coast. Hassan captured Carthage, but was defeated by the Berber warrior queen al-Kahina (Dihya) at Meskiana.[7] Retiring to Tripoli, he waited for reinforcements from the caliph, while the Byzantine Emperor Leontios retook Carthage.

Queen Kahina had succeeded Kusaila in AD 688, but her scorched-earth policy, accepted initially "with unanimous applause",[8] alienated many of the oasis-dwelling Berbers. Several tribes defected to Hassan and these reinforcements allowed him to resume his campaign. He killed the warrior queen in battle at Tabarka and destroyed Carthage before establishing Tunis as the main Arab port on the coast of *Ifriqiya*.

The diplomatic Musa ibn-Nasayr completed the Muslim conquest of North Africa. He became the first independent ruler and captured Tangiers in AD 707, before turning his attention to the southern coast of Spain and the Balearic Islands. Thus, in the 65 years from 643 to 708, the face of the Mediterranean changed profoundly, and the Koran became the dominant holy book in North Africa.[9]

It would be an oversimplification to suggest that the reign of the Arabs led straight to the dominion of the Barbary Coast. In reality, the political situation in Islamic territories during the period between the 8th and 16th centuries witnessed constant power struggles. The Umayyad Dynasty lasted less than 100 years before it was overthrown by an Abbasid Caliphate in AD 750 when the second caliph, al-Mansur, heralded a golden age of Islam centred on the new capital he built at Baghdad.

This focus on Mesopotamia meant that outlying territories were ceded to tribes such as the Aglabids, who ruled *Ifriqiya* from their base at Qairawa. Obeid Allah united the land west of the Nile as "Mahdi" in AD 908, but the Shia Fatimids seized Egypt 60 years later. After the Berber tribes attempted to reinstate Sunni orthodoxy in 1049, the caliph sent the Ibn Hilal and Ibn Salim tribes from the Nile valley to crush the rebellion. During the following months, a quarter of a million Arabs migrated into Tripolitania and forever changed the social character of Libya. The upheaval continued for 100 years as the rival Berber dynasties competed with the Arab tribes. The oppressed looked for salvation through the arms of a warrior leader and the decline of the Fatimids allowed the youthful Saladin to become Vizier and establish the Ayyubid Caliphate in 1169.

Meanwhile, Sicily had fallen into the hands of the Normans who crossed into Africa in 1146. Roger II captured Tripoli and established the Kingdom of Africa, but in 1159 Abd al-Munen drove out the Christian inhabitants. Almost a century later, Louis IX of France took up the Cross, but was defeated in Egypt at the battle of Mansurah in 1250. His capture by the Mamluk army coincided with their dynasty supplanting the Ayyubids.

After paying a fortune in ransom, Louis tried once more to defeat the Muslim armies in Africa. Leading the Eighth Crusade, he arrived at Carthage in 1270, but died of dysentery six weeks later and the campaign petered out. Edward Longshanks, the future king of England, joined this force and was the first British military commander to land in North Africa, but he did not stay long because his focus was on the Holy Land and Jerusalem. With the failure of these crusaders, European countries gave up their claims on the north coast of Africa that stemmed from the Byzantine Empire[10] until 1510, when a Spanish resurgence defeated their Muslim neighbours and captured Tripoli.

CHAPTER 2

American Hostages on the Barbary Coast

He had a large order from the Dey of Tripoli.

LORD BYRON, 1819 (DON JUAN C.III V.XVI)

At the beginning of the 16th century, when Michelangelo was sculpting his statue of David, Leonardo da Vinci was painting the Mona Lisa, Copernicus was creating a model of the universe and Martin Luther was paving the way for the Reformation, Europe was coming to terms with improvements in the manufacture of gunpowder. France and England used this Chinese invention to establish absolutist monarchies and fight their neighbours, whilst Spain and Portugal forged empires in the New World and the Indian Ocean.

In the Middle East, the Ottomans under Sultan Selim I defeated the Mamluk Empire in 1517 and assumed control of their extensive dominions. Sultan Mehmed had already captured Constantinople after a 53-day siege in 1453, but gaining Syria, Egypt and Arabia not only "catapulted the Ottomans into a position of leadership within the vast Muslim community"[1] but also gave them vast resources for their advance to the gates of Vienna.

The North African territories were consolidated by Hayreddin Barbarossa, grand admiral of the Ottoman Navy, who secured dominance in the Mediterranean. Controversially, he joined forces with France under a Franco-Ottoman Alliance. This was the first pact between a Christian and Muslim state and was criticised by many zealots as a "sacrilegious union of the lily and the crescent".[2]

In Libya, Spain ceded Tripoli to the Knights of St John who lost their home on the island of Rhodes in 1522. However, Christian dominion lasted only until the middle of the century when the Ottoman Empire ejected the Holy Order and established the Vilayet of Tripolitania.[3] This new rule followed the course of previous occupations. A corps of janissaries, answering only to their own laws, governed a multitude of impoverished people from their fortified castles.

Meanwhile, Cyrenaica again became a forgotten land. In his slanted treatise, Leo Africanus suggests that in 1550 there was "no citie or towne of account between

[Tripoli] and Alexandria".[4] He further describes the area around Barce as containing three castles with plenty of dates, but no corn.

The governor of Tripolitania, who was afforded the title "pasha with three tails",[5] kept the country in check, whilst encouraging Barbary corsairs to continue their state-sponsored piracy at sea. From the 16th century, the fleet sailing from Tripoli, along with those harboured at Algiers and Tunis, earned a fearsome reputation for capturing human cargo, who were ransomed or sold as slaves. Samuel Tooker was appointed as the first British consul in Tripoli in 1658 and his primary duty was to save British captives from this gruesome fate.

Unfortunately, he did not satisfy his masters in London and King Charles II authorised his imprisonment for serious breaches. The historian Nabil Matar suggests this was due to Tooker inflating the ransom price for British captives, in order to increase the percentage he received from each deal.[6] A huge amount of money was exchanged in the ransom and slave trade business. In 1675, Britain's second consul, Nathanial Bradley, paid £985 pounds to rescue 11 men captured on the *Grace*, which included buying clothes for them, settling their debts and providing them with allowances. Ironically, one of the passengers was Henry Capel, who took over from him two years later as Britain's third consul in Tripoli.

In January 1676, Rear Admiral Sir John Narborough conducted an early example of gunboat diplomacy by forcing the dey, Ibrahim Pasha, to sign a treaty "in favour of English traders over the French".[7] Paris brooded on this for nine years and then ordered its fleet to sail into the harbour and bombard the port in April 1685. A pilgrim who was travelling from Morocco to Mecca, Ahmad ibn Muhammed ibn Nasir, described the attack:

> Whenever their cannons fired a bomb, we thought it would hit us. Sometimes the bomb fell near us, sometimes it passed above us; more often it fell inside the city or in the sea outside the city walls. All that night, we raised our helpless hands in despair to God almighty, our eyes unable to sleep.

The dey at that time, Bosnak Ismail Pasha, turned to Britain for help. The new British consul, Nathanial Loddington, brokered a treaty based on defence and security that was eventually signed on 21 January 1692. At the time, Louis XIV of France was the most powerful monarch in Europe and was asserting French dominion through military means. After, he crossed the Rhine, a Grand Alliance had been formed between the Holy Roman Empire and England (ruled by William and Mary), Sweden, Portugal and Spain to counter French hegemony. By effectively joining this Alliance, the dey laid the foundation stone for the geo-strategic partnership between Britain and Libya. When the French fleet returned in September, British military advisers were ready and provided the Libyans with modern arms to defend themselves.

Economic hardship resulted in a period of political turbulence and in 1711, a popular cavalry officer, Ahmed Qaramanli, whose father was a janissary and mother a Berber, seized power in Tripoli. Ruling as an independent monarch, he established a hereditary dynasty that lasted until 1835. He paid a nominal tribute to the Ottoman sultan in Constantinople, while expanding his power south into the Fezzan and east to Cyrenaica.

The economy improved, but it was still based on tribute won by the corsairs at sea. According to Nancy Dornbush, Ahmed's grandson, Ali I, surrounded himself with opulence and made Tripoli the "most civilised" of the Barbary States. Dornbush lived in Tripoli for 10 years with her brother-in-law Richard Tully,[8] who published her writing under his name in 1816.

Dornbush's keen eye for detail offers a remarkable insight into life in Tripoli. She provides an interesting if somewhat distorting account of the manners, customs and political intrigues of society, including the lives of the royal harem. She also records major events, such as the plague that swept through Libya in 1785, forcing the Tully family to remain quarantined for more than a year. Her elegant prose impressed Lord Byron, who admitted to his publisher John Murray that descriptions of furnishings and clothing in *Don Juan* were "taken from Tully's Tripoli":

> Haidee and Juan carpeted their feet
> On crimson satin, border'd with pale blue;
> Their sofa occupied three parts complete
> Of the apartment—and appear'd quite new;
> The velvet cushions (for a throne more meet)—
> Were scarlet, from whose glowing centre grew
> A sun emboss'd in gold, whose rays of tissue,
> Meridian-like, were seen all light to issue.[9]

The strict Muslim world did not approve of the influence that Tully's women wielded in Tripoli. British soft power was frowned upon in Constantinople and Ali's authority was undermined by his scheming sons, Ahmed, Hamet and Yusef. The Ottomans decided to act and the execution of Louis XVI in January 1793 provided them with a catalyst for change.

The crisis erupted when Ali Burghul Cezayrli arrived off the coast with an invasion fleet. Dornbush provides an intimate description of the chaos that swept through the palace and the narrow escape they had in Tajura, which forced Tully to evacuate all the British citizens from the city with the help of the Royal Navy:

> Ali Ben Zool [sic] was still on board and messengers were passing continually from the castle to and from him. At seven in the evening, it was thought quite necessary for us to take advantage of the commodore's offer and go on board the frigate…[10]

A bitter civil war lasted for 18 months until Ahmed II wrested the throne for the Qaramanlis. However, less than six months later, on 11 June 1795, he was murdered by his brother Yusef, who was backed by the rival dey in Tunis. Sealing his succession, Yusef exiled his other brother Hamet, who later moved to Cairo.

* * *

Libya was generally unaffected by the Napoleonic wars, but the plucky governor of Derna did refuse a French landing after the turn of the century.[11] Corsairs could not challenge a 74-gun ship-of-the-line of the First Republic, but they were able to maintain a constant income from the plunder of international merchantmen, including the light schooners that flew the Stars and Stripes of America.

Troubled by the loss of its ships, the United States government signed a series of pacts with the Barbary States beginning with a treaty to pass through the Straits of Gibraltar. The payment to Tripoli of $56,000 in 1796 was just over half what they paid to Tunis in 1797 ($107,000). However, American trade with Spain and Italy reached almost $12 million by 1800 and, jealous of the amount received by Tunis and also Algiers, Yusef captured the merchant ship *Betsy* and held the American sailors as hostages. With this surety, he issued a demand for a new treaty to the American consul James Cathcart, including tribute of $250,000 and an annuity of $20,000. For good measure, he declared war on the United States in May 1801.[12]

The demand was refused by President Thomas Jefferson, who responded by sending a flotilla to blockade Tripoli. The sparring continued for two years until disaster struck in November 1803 when the 36 gun USS *Philadelphia* ran aground. The ship's captain William Bainbridge threw the guns into the sea and surrendered to the pasha, who now held a further 307 American hostages under guard.

The corsairs managed to refloat the frigate, but in February 1804, Lieutenant Stephen Decatur led a daring raid into Tripoli's harbour and under the noses of his enemy, destroyed the frigate before it could be used against its former owners. Commodore Edward Preble, in charge of the US naval forces, called for reinforcements and continued to attack during the summer months with some success. Unfortunately, an operation to send a bomb ship into Tripoli on 4 September backfired and he had to return to Malta for resupplies and await augmentation from Washington.

It was not naval power that brought the recalcitrant pasha to heel, but a land operation led by 41-year-old William Eaton, the former consul at Tunis, who had been given the title of naval agent to the Barbary States. He and James Cathcart had the idea of replacing Yusef with his surviving elder brother, Hamet Qaramanli, who was still living in Cairo. Eaton travelled with a small detachment of US marines to Egypt in November and on the promise of $40,000, the "pretender" agreed to the proposal.

The marines were commanded by 29-year-old Lieutenant Presley O'Bannon from Virginia. Together with two midshipmen, he raised a force of 400 mercenary

Greeks and Arabs. This multinational battle group assembled west of Alexandria at Borg el-Arab, before setting forth on the long march to Libya on 6 March 1805.

Their destination was Derna, an important Ottoman port in Cyrenaica. The 521-mile trek took six weeks of hard toil in the desert. Rations were sparse and several times during the early weeks, the Arabs attempted to mutiny, but the officers managed to keep control. In fact, Eaton's army swelled with 650 local recruits and this expanded force reached Sollum on 7 April, spending a full day climbing the escarpment at Halfaya on a track that became known to future British soldiers as Hellfire Pass.

The pace quickened on the higher ground and they did not linger as they passed the "pretty port of Toubrouk [sic]"[13] on 14 April. The following night Eaton pitched his camp by the Gulf of Bomba and made contact with the US frigates *Argus*, *Nautilus* and *Hornet*.[14] To his great relief, the ships provided fresh supplies and sufficient money to pay the army.

During the following week, Eaton approached Derna and prepared for the historic operation that was launched on Saturday 27 April 1805. He divided his forces into two groups and began the attack at 2.45 p.m. In the east, O'Bannon advanced with his marines and Greeks against the fortress, while Hamet cut the road to Tripoli and approached from the west.

Maneuvering *Argus* into the harbour, Captain Isaac Hull led the bombardment from the sea, ensuring that he did not fire on the marines as they advanced towards the fort. Resistance was fierce and the attack was petering out when Eaton seized the initiative and ordered a desperate charge, despite being shot in the wrist. The marines passed through "a shower of musketry from walls of houses" and reached the battery in good order. Victory was swift and for the first time ever, the American flag was raised over a captured city on foreign soil. Meanwhile, Hamet captured the city centre and by 4 p.m., the local governor surrendered.

When he heard of Hamet's return to Libya, Yusef sent reinforcements to Cyrenaica. This force took two weeks to travel around the Gulf of Sirte and on 13 May, it overwhelmed the perimeter in the south of the city. However, as it advanced towards the battery, *Argus*'s guns and Eaton's troops beat back the attackers and when night fell, the sides were back in their original positions. Several more attempts were made to retake the city, but the American artillery swept each one away and protected Hamet in the castle.

In Tripoli the American emissary Tobias Lear was under instructions to negotiate a deal, irrespective of Eaton's plan. The contrite pasha agreed to end his attacks and return the crew of the *Philadelphia* for a payment of $60,000. On 4 June, he released the hostages and six days later, he signed a peace treaty, while the USS *Constellation* carried the news to Derna. Overall, the historian Ronald Bruce St John suggests that the outcome "represented a significant achievement for the [Q]aramanli regime".[15]

Hearing about the pact, Eaton was livid at the "sell-out" and having to abandon Hamet. However, when he and O'Bannon returned to America, they became national heroes as their victory on foreign soil was acclaimed by a jubilant population and the phrase "To the shores of Tripoli" was added to the flag of the US Marine Corps. This seminal operation did not compare to the battle of Trafalgar later that year, but it did confirm to the Washington government that if America wished to be a successful trading nation, it would need a powerful navy to protect its ships and also a strong army because political decisions are made on the land among the people, not at sea. Little did they realise how frequently the US Navy would deploy on operations off the Libyan coast in the future.

CHAPTER 3

British Consuls and Explorers

The physical condition of the country, owing to the absence of rivers or any large artificial reservoirs for water, is not adapted to the requirements of a settled sedentary population.
MURDOCH SMITH 1862[1]

Anglo-French rivalry in the fields of science and exploration did not end with the battle of Waterloo. If anything, competition intensified as the two powers built on the Age of Reason and the Industrial Revolution to be the first to claim new discoveries. Backed by wealthy patrons and inspired by explorers such as the Comte de Bougainville and Captain James Cook, many aspiring young men and women travelled to uncharted regions, in order to extend the limits of human knowledge.

The Western Desert and Cyrenaica offered exciting potential to those interested in geography and the new discipline of archaeology. In the 18th century, the French consul, Claude Lemaire, had written a report about the relics at Cyrene[2] and King Louis XIV's antiquarian, Paul Lucas, had followed this up.[3] However, the French were more interested in the Roman ruins at Leptis Magna close to Tripoli and had agreements to take marble columns inserted into their treaty of 1720.[4] Conscious of this Gallic precedence, the British government commissioned a survey of Libya six years after Napoleon's surrender.

The idea originated with William Smyth, captain of the survey ship HMS *Aid*.[5] He had visited the North Coast of Africa in 1817 and at Tripoli had, with the help of the consul, Colonel Hanmer Warrington,[6] secured an agreement with Pasha Yusef Qaramanli to survey the whole tract of country between Tripoli and Derna. Returning to London with 37 marble columns from Leptis, he submitted a proposal to the Admiralty, suggesting that while he charted the coastline from the ship, now renamed HMS *Adventurer*, a land party should survey the historical sites.

Robert Dundas, 2nd Viscount Melville, who had been first lord of the Admiralty since 1812 and Henry Bathurst, secretary of state for war, commissioned a joint military and civilian team led by Lieutenant Frederick Beechey of the Royal Navy, the son of the official portrait painter to Her Majesty Queen Charlotte. They brought in Beechey's brother Henry, who had gained a solid reputation copying ancient murals in Egypt for Henry Salt, to examine the antiquities. The party also included a surgeon, John Campbell, a young midshipman, Edward Tyndale, and another volunteer, Lieutenant Henry Coffin.[7]

* * *

Beechey intended to travel all the way to Alexandria and return via the oasis at Siwa. He held reports from previous consuls such as Richard Tully and British explorers who had set out from Tripoli to other destinations, such as Captain George Lyon, who was with the naturalist Dr Joseph Ritchie, when he died at Murzuk in 1818. He also had a fine understanding of classical history and made special reference to Strabo's *Geographica*, James Rennell's *Geographical System of Herodotus* and the "ingenious" report by Dr. Paolo Della Cella who had accompanied the pasha's army to subdue Barce in 1817.[8]

Libya was still under the rule of Yusef Qaramanli when HMS *Adventurer* cast its anchor in Tripoli harbour on 11 September 1821. The British party was welcomed heartily because the groundwork had been laid by Colonel Warrington. This Peninsular War veteran was a larger-than-life character, who was fiercely partisan and fanatically patriotic.

He strutted around wearing a red coat with blue facings and gold embroidery and his cocked hat was decorated with ostrich feathers. He built a resplendent villa two miles outside the city, known as the English Garden, where he and his wife Jane-Eliza entertained lavishly. The French complained that he was "a sore trial to the other consuls" and his indiscretions earned rebukes from Whitehall. However, he developed a close relationship with Qaramanli and for more than 30 years prevented the French from overshadowing Britain in Libya.

Using the consul's help and influence, Beechey completed the final preparations for his expedition. His time in Tripoli overlapped with the ill-fated Doctor Walter Oudney and Lieutenant Hugh Clapperton, who were preparing to make the second British attempt to reach Bornu. Little did the Beecheys realise that their friends would both die in Nigeria before their report was published.[9]

Beechey wished to avoid the mistakes made by Joseph Ritchie, who had cut himself off from local people and died of fever before reaching his objective. He decided to wear Turkish robes rather than European clothes and spoke with several of Warrington's Berber friends, who held liberal views on Europeans. In particular, he received help from Sidi Muhammed d'Ghies and approvingly noted in his diary the Muslim's charitable giving and tolerant teaching of the Koran.

On 4 November, the party of 18 departed from Tripoli. Other than the British members of the group, Beechey hired three Europeans to act as interpreters as well as a *tchaous*, or janissary, named Massoud, who was loaned from the pasha, and

Sheikh Muhammed el Dúbbah with five Bedouin and three Arab grooms to look after the horses.

The sheikh was head of the Maràbut tribe and "presided over the district of Syrt [sic]". He was assigned by Pasha Yusef to ensure the British had safe passage to Benghazi, where they would come under the supervision of Sheikh Hadood of Barka, who held sway over the land to Bomba. This was the limit of Tripoli's dominion and crossing Marmarica would need the support of the Egyptian pasha, which was being arranged through Henry Salt in Cairo.

The sheikh was nearly 60 years old. He wore a turban rather than a skull cap, but otherwise was clothed as all the other Berbers. An ample *baracàn* covered a white cotton shirt, with a belt holding two decorated pistols and pouches for powder and money. On his feet were sandals of camel hide, with thongs of leather. His beard had flecks of grey and his large flashing eyes did not rest. He had a lean frame, a wide smile and a wild and daring spirit. As a young man he had earned a fearsome reputation and the name el Dúbbah (the hyena), but now he held great authority, so the British were delighted to come under his protection.

It did not take long for Beechey's leadership to be tested. At Sidi Abdellati, while he was looking at an ancient tomb, one of the camel drivers allowed their beasts to graze over cultivated land. The owners demanded payment, which was refused, and the antagonists came to blows. The sheikh's trusty servant overreacted and after his pistols were wrested from him, he pulled out a blade which he was about to plunge into a Berber's heart before the janissary put a musket to his head and disarmed him. El Dúbbah settled the dispute, but it was an important test that set the tone for the remainder of the journey.

On the way to Leptis Magna, they met Colonel Warrington, who warned them of marauding Arabs planning to ambush them south of Misuratah. They did not dwell at the ruins because these had already been surveyed by Smyth, and Beechey was concerned that he needed to cross the marshy ground of Syrtis Major before the heavy rains arrived.

At Misuratah, where they purchased camels for the desert, the locals heard about John Campbell's medical skills, so he was besieged by people needing aid. During their stay at this important city, they were entertained with green tea and sherbet by the flamboyant Sheikh Belcàzi and acquired many friends through their humanitarian work. Two days before their departure, the sky darkened with a plague of locusts, but this did not delay them unduly.

Beechey was right about the marshy conditions around the Gulf of Sirte. They passed many fragments of wrecks along the shore and found evidence of *La Chevrette*, that had recently completed a French coastal survey. Further on, there were traces of a landing by HMS *Adventurer* and then more treacherous marshes, where two riders just managed to avoid a deep chasm that opened in the ground. The camel drivers were spooked by this and mutinied, but the British officers called their bluff and loaded the camels themselves.

Reporting on the coastal ruins, they paint a fascinating picture of the ancient inhabitants and silted harbours such as Marsa Zafran (Saffron Harbour, which later became the city of Sirte where Colonel Gadhafi was captured and killed). They investigated abandoned forts and the Ptolemaic boundary between Carthage and Cyrene marked by the Castle of Euphantres, as well speculating about the previous location of the Philaenes Altars. Their most significant discovery was Charax, a town at the centre of an illegal trade between Cyrene's silphium and Carthage's wine.

* * *

One morning before setting off, el Dúbbah entered Beechey's tent and after a long-winded preamble asked Campbell for a draught to help him be more attractive to his young wife. The sympathetic doctor made up a phial that the sheikh placed in his pouch before mounting his mare and galloping away with a huge smile on his face.

They celebrated Christmas Day at Hudia in a valley with wild geraniums and a pungent species of leek. There was fresh rain water, but the Arabs decided to wash their clothes before the British could taste the sweet drink. The next day they camped at a desolate place and once again, the camel drivers attempted to extort money from Beechey. Weapons were drawn and threats were made, but the British avoided stepping over the line and eventually, after el Dúbbah's timely intervention, they continued as if nothing had occurred.

Heading north, they passed the port of Brega (the scene of an important battle in March 1941) and suffered more mischief. The wily sheikh tried to trick the British group by selling them some lambs, but the shepherd, who he was swindling, stole three of his camels. There were several other cases of perfidy, but Beechey never lost his temper and dealt with each of these incidents in a calm, resolute and fair way.

The whole party arrived at Benghazi on 12 January just before the "heavy rains arrived". Signor Rossini, the British agent, had rented a substantial house where Beechey drew charts and compiled his notes. The Georgian governor's entourage doubted "the sanity of a government which could concern itself with science and research"[10] without pecuniary benefits, but nevertheless allowed them to use Benghazi as a base for their survey.

The day after they arrived, a rebel leader in Greece, Alexandros Mavrokordatos, proclaimed the First Hellenic Republic in the war of independence against the Ottoman Empire. This increased tension among the population and the British party was constantly asked what part they "should take, in the event of the arrival of any Greek vessel off their port".[11] Of course they expressed their support for the pasha, and this seemed to satisfy the authorities, who referred to them as "Sahab [sic] or ally".[12]

Unfortunately, this did not allay the fears of the local citizens and following reports of Greek maltreatment of Muslims, the population became nervous about an invasion and the slaughter of their families. The appearance of HMS *Adventurer* combined with Beechey drawing charts of the ports somehow made the people believe the British might be supporting the Greek infidel. It only took a strange cloud formation out to sea, which resembled an armada, for panic to spread through the city with the men fetching their firearms and the women screaming that the Christians were coming to murder them.

A mob assembled outside the British house and attacked the agent, who was outside wearing European clothes. Tension rose to fever pitch as the chants against Nazarines increased and these caused the British to load their guns and barricade the house. However, at this moment Sheikh el Dúbbah arrived and after a protracted negotiation, he prevented a full assault.

Soon afterwards an alarm went around that the Greeks were landing in the harbour and the mob moved away. Muskets were discharged in the dark, but after several hours with no sign of an enemy, the crowd dispersed. The next day dawned as if nothing had happened and life returned to normal, albeit with a worry that never quite disappeared.

The rain slowed the survey of the ancient sites and the British had to make use of the hoods on their *burnouses* as they rode along the coast and through the mountains. Completing their plans of Benghazi and the nearby sites, they journeyed to Cyrene, arriving at the beginning of May and approaching through the southern Necropolis. At that time of the year the ground "springs to life with flowers flourishing in footholds in the naked rock and silent tombs".[13] They pitched their tents by the fountain in the Apollo sanctuary, but had to be careful because the jackals and hyenas were active in this neglected area. Here, the Beecheys spent several weeks documenting a huge amount of detail, describing the tombs along the sides of the road with dozens of busts and statues scattered on the ground.

Moving their base to Derna, they were hosted by the British agent, Signor Regignani, "with the greatest attention and kindness". The town was suffering from the after-effects of a plague that had arrived during the previous year. The progressive ruler, who was the son of the pasha, had contained the disease by ordering anyone affected to burn their clothes and ventilate their houses and by ensuring the streets were cleared of anything that might spread infection.

At Derna, they reunited with HMS *Adventurer* and said farewell to Edward Tyndale whose "joyous disposition had so often enlivened the frugal board of our company". Captain Smyth informed Beechey that he had managed to complete the coastline to Alexandria and so it was decided that Derna would be the limit of their expedition. This was also due to the continuing war in the Eastern Mediterranean and because the Cyrenaican sites offered more than those to the east in Marmarica.

The reduced party returned to Benghazi via Cyrene and other ancient sites. However, news arrived of their premature recall and on 25 July, they embarked for Malta. From there, Beechey wrote about his disappointment at not completing the surveys in a letter to Earl Bathurst: "[N]otwithstanding the reluctance with which I left so interesting a field of research, I hastily embarked the expedition, on receiving the order to return, under the influence of feelings, which I would have given whole empires to be spared".[14]

Returning to much acclaim,[15] the brothers continued to catalogue their discoveries at home in Harley Street, but before they completed the report, the Admiralty appointed Frederick to command HMS *Blossom* and explore the Bering Strait from the east. This voyage lasted three years and, in the summer of 1826, he reached Point Barrow, which he named along with several islands in the Pacific. It was only when he returned to London in 1828 that the 600-page record of his expedition to Libya was finally published.

* * *

Meanwhile in 1824, the French *Société de Géographie,* hearing of the British progress, offered a substantial prize of 3,000 francs to the explorer who provided the best account of Cyrenaica. The society was no doubt irritated that Claude Lemaire's report on Cyrenaica would soon be superseded by Beechey and wished to finesse the British study and maintain Gallic primacy in this area.

The prize was won by 32-year-old Jean-Raymond Pacho. Arriving in Cairo to stay with his brother on 12 February 1822, his initial focus was in Egypt, but he had trouble raising funds. After a short excursion, he was eventually sponsored by Celestine Guyenet, the Swiss founder and director of the viceroy's calico textile business.

On 17 November 1823, Pacho set out to visit the five great oases, beginning with Siwa,[16] and returned with a wealth of material in August the following year. In Cairo, he heard about the prize and quickly organised an expedition to Libya. Departing from Alexandria with a small caravan and an assistant named Frédéric Müller, he followed the 1805 coastal route of William Eaton and entered Cyrenaica from the opposite direction to Beechey.

On the way, he made the first studies of Marmarica and wrote about the Bedouin whose customs he observed with fine detail. He continued through Cyrenaica and all the way to the Gulf of Sirte, noting and drawing the monuments and scenes of everyday life. He returned to Cairo with another extensive collection, which he took straight to Paris, arriving there in November 1825.

When he presented his work to the society, the committee did not take long to award him the prize of 3,000 francs. He was then in a race to publish his report before the Beecheys produced theirs in London. However, he invested the money badly and while concentrating on the manuscript, he fell on hard times.

Pacho had suffered from bouts of depression earlier in his life. He now cut himself off from his friends, working night and day to convert his notes and drawings into a formidable *magnum opus*.[17] The constant anxiety of the work combined with his poverty and misanthropic lifestyle to deepen his depression.

He believed he was unappreciated and unrewarded by the authorities in Paris and lost his friends when he accused them of unfaithfulness. His churlish character was built on a frailty that spread like cancer. His health began to fail, and he took drugs, which lifted him briefly out of his depression before abandoning him to melancholy thoughts. In this isolated state, he began to despise himself as his haunted mind spiralled into a slough of misery.

Finally, he published the first volume in 1827, but rather than feeling elation and seeing the opportunities this would open for him, he worried unnecessarily about rejection and the Beecheys' report. Despondency set in and soon after his 35th birthday, on 26 January 1829, he took his own life.[18]

In many ways, the heartbreaking story of Jean-Raymond Pacho is sadder than the deaths of the many adventurers who died whilst exploring Africa. The tragedy of his suicide is compounded by the fact that his "sumptuous" book of 400 pages complements the equally superb report by the Beechey brothers that was published the following year. According to the renowned archaeologist, Farley Goddard, they "mutually correct and supplement each other, and together constitute almost all that is known of the modern Cyrenaica".[19]

* * *

The scientific world moved on. If gold or diamonds had been found in Cyrenaica, perhaps avaricious eyes might have considered its colonisation. However, Benghazi's reputation for "famine, plague and civil war",[20] instigated by the famous 18th-century explorer James Bruce, was not improved by the ground-breaking studies of Pacho and Beechey.

Colonel Warrington did collect antiquities, including a fine statue of Aesculapius that his son later donated to a Scottish museum, but no serious archaeology was seen for 20 years. Learned societies in London were more interested in exploring the route to the Niger Basin and so Warrington assisted both his son-in-law, Major Alexander Gordon Laing, on his expedition to Timbuktu in 1825 and the anti-slavery campaigner James Richardson on his expedition to Ghat. After Laing was murdered, the British consul accused the French of interference and illegally keeping his diary. However, to make amends the *Société de Géographie* posthumously awarded Laing their gold medal in the year after it was instigated.

Warrington's greatest contribution was to persuade the Qaramanlis to end the slave trade in Tripoli. However, the economy suffered as British and French ships policed the seas to prevent the return of piracy. Yusef abdicated in favour of his son Ali II in 1832, but civil unrest continued and the sultan sent troops to restore direct rule from Constantinople.

The fragile state of security in Libya at this time was matched in Europe as the Congress of Vienna's peace unravelled. The restlessness of people demanding reform in the 1830s built to a wave of revolutions in the 1840s, while in Britain, foreign policy was dominated by the liberal interventionism of Lord Palmerston. Despite his disagreements with Queen Victoria about the role of the Royal Family in foreign policy, he supported Prince Albert when he paved the way for German researchers to join British expeditions abroad.

One of the first to accept this opportunity was an aspiring young explorer from Hamburg, Dr Heinrich Barth, who visited London to study Arabic before travelling to North Africa. He had no problems securing permission for his proposal and in 1846, spent several months in Cyrenaica, afterwards writing a celebrated account of his journey.[21]

Barth was in Libya during Warrington's hand-over to another of Wellington's heroes. Colonel George Crowe had served with the 27th Enniskillings in the Peninsular War, but it is not known whether he was present when the regiment earned its nickname of the Skins for being surprised by French soldiers when swimming in the sea and having to fight with musket and bayonet, but no clothes. After the battle of Waterloo, he served with the occupying force in Paris and subsequently joined the diplomatic corps. Initially, he was posted to Greece[22] before his promotion as consul in Tripoli.

During his service in Libya, Crowe helped three pashas between 1846 and 1852 and witnessed a renewed international interest in the ancient Greek sites of Pentapolis. The French agent at Benghazi, Joseph Vattier de Bourville, conducted the first underground searches of Cyrenaica in 1848 and transported an important collection of antiquities to the Louvre. He was followed by Edmond Pellissier de Reynaud, who added 200 more objects from excavations in eastern Libya to the Louvre during the following three years.

James Hamilton lamented the "ruinous state" of these violated sites when he visited them in 1852.[23] By then, Crowe had handed over to Colonel George Herman[24] of the Rifle Brigade. He was the third ex-military consul to have served with distinction in Spain, but in his case it was with the British Auxiliary Legion during the first Carlist War.[25] After earning the gratitude of the Spanish crown, he was appointed vice-consul in Benghazi in March 1848. There, he witnessed the French appropriation of antiquities, before his promotion to consul in Tripoli when the British government downgraded the post on 1 January 1852.

During the Crimean War, an attempt was made by Libyan insurgents to seize power from their Ottoman overlords. Sheikh Ghoumer, who had returned from prison in Constantinople, gathered the support of many Berber tribes and began a military campaign against Pasha Mustafa Nuri. Ghoumer won several victories in battle, but after the pasha sought Colonel Herman's military advice, the tide turned, and the insurgency was eventually defeated.

The astute consul[26] followed the example set by his gallant predecessors and secured the close confidence of Tripoli's ruler. Britain again became Libya's international partner of choice, much to the chagrin of France, which was expanding its empire in North Africa under the direction of the recently crowned Napoleon III. The London government recognised Herman's work and upgraded the post to consul general again in 1856.

Frederick Beechey, who had been promoted to rear admiral and appointed president of the Royal Geographical Society, sadly died that year on 29 November. One of the last books he read was Hamilton's *Wanderings in North Africa* and he would have been delighted that four years later the British Museum sponsored another major survey of Cyrenaica. This was the idea of 44-year-old Captain Robert Murdoch Smith of the Royal Engineers, who was drawn, like his Scottish predecessors Clapperton and Laing, to North African exploration.

Smith had made his name on Charles Newton's archaeological investigation in Anatolia and with his help and the support of the foreign secretary, Lord Russell, he organised and funded the expedition. His companion was an experienced surveyor, Edwin Augustus Porcher, who had accompanied the artist Harden Melville on board HMS *Fly* during the first hydrographic survey of north-eastern Australia in 1842, where he became a skilled draughtsman. He was commissioned into the Royal Navy in 1846 and spent 10 years recording his visits to the Far East and Mediterranean. He met Smith in Malta, where he was first lieutenant on HMS *Hibernia* and together they hatched the plan "to examine Cyrene and the Pentapolis".[27]

In his report, Smith explains the motives for exploring the rich history of Cyrene, including the absence of modern towns and likelihood of significant remains still being in existence. He also hints at the main reasons why Libya had not attracted as much attention as Egypt and Greece: the mountainous terrain that made transportation of large statues problematic in terms of "time, labour and costs", as well as the fanatical Bedouin, feared for their "rapacity and violence",[28] and the Turkish officials, who controlled the ports where objects had to be checked.

Reaching Benghazi on 30 November 1860, Smith and Porcher were persuaded by the vice-consul to base the expedition there rather than at Derna because "there was not a single European at Derna" to assist and make up a caravan. However, it appeared that Benghazi had changed little in 40 years. The incessant flies that swarmed and settled on every part of the body, including mouth, nostrils, ears and eyes, covered the food and followed people in the streets were still as incessant as when Beechey visited. The fleas and mosquitos that replaced them at night were almost as bad.

The vice-consul secured permission to collect objects from the sites and organised the group's protection through his contacts with local sheikhs, who were more effective than the Turkish troops. The explorers hired Amir ibn Abdi Seyat and his brother, as well as an Italian merchant who helped them purchase supplies, such as reed sleeping mats and *girbehs* (goat skin containers) for carrying water.

They set off on 12 December as a party of five on horseback with their workers following in a caravan of 10 camels. Two Arab guides joined them as they journeyed across the plains, woods, *marj* (meadows) and through the "rugged ravines" in cold, wet and windy conditions.

Eleven days later, they arrived in Cyrene at midday. Visibility was poor, but they pitched their camp in a tomb, 250 yards from Apollo's Fountain. The caravan arrived in the middle of the afternoon and the handlers dumped their possessions on the ground before turning around and leaving before dark. That night, bags and boxes lay on the muddy ground in their tomb and it took the whole of Christmas Eve to make their "quarters as comfortable as possible".

It was not difficult to understand why this site had been chosen by Battus for his citadel. The sweet water of the fountain and the natural defences provided by the steep ravines made this the perfect location for an aspiring ruler. There was so much to investigate that Murdoch Smith was delighted that the Duke of Cambridge, as head of the Army, had given him indefinite leave for the duration of the expedition.

Using the reports by Beechey and Pacho, they were able to concentrate on the key areas without wasting time and commenced excavations on 27 December. It took them almost a week to make their first major discovery, a life-size statue of Bacchus "lying four or five feet underground" in the western end of a temple. At the end of the month, they started work in the temple and immediately found an unbroken statue of a girl over a metre tall. A few days later they made their most important discovery, a colossal statue of Apollo about 10 feet below the surface of the ground. It took Smith several days to find the head and all 121 pieces of marble which were eventually put together and restored at the British Museum.

That month, Smith visited the representative at Derna, Mr. De Fremaux, who had already sent food and supplies to their camp. En route, he passed Labrak, the location of a great battle fought 30 years before when the Barassa tribe, led by Sheikh Abubakr ibn Haddouth,[29] routed the Hassa. It was said that 700 Hassa were buried at the site and as a result of his victory, the sheikh was appointed as bey over all the Harabi tribes, including the Ubaidat, Drissa and Aulad-Hamad. However, the Ubaidat resented his appointment and in 1860 they began a war that was to last 30 years. Although the British took no sides in this conflict, the tension made the Bedouin more suspicious than they might have been in a time of peace.

Smith and Porcher were also troubled by the Achwani tribe during their nine-month stay. Sheikh Sidi Mustapha had recently joined the Sanussi sect and was particularly indignant that Nazarines were living next to the enclosure for his wives that overlapped Cyrene. He frequently threatened the work parties, but Smith and Porcher gained much goodwill for their medical work with the local community, so they managed to keep the peace.[30]

Peace was an important concept to the tribal people. Smith observed that the Bedouin form of salutation included a torrent of questions "regarding each other's welfare, but to which answers are never given".[31] The conversation he recorded could have occurred at any time in the past 500 years: "Peace. Peace be with you. How are you? How are you? Peace. How are you? Are you very well? Thanks be to God. How are you? Are you very well? What is your colour?" This can continue for five minutes before the conversation turns to another favourite subject, the price of food and shopping.

At Derna, Smith wrote to Lord Russell in London about transporting the treasures to England, but the response did not arrive until May when HMS *Assurance* arrived at Marsa Susa (also known as Apollonia) with supplies and a letter from the British Museum containing a grant of £100. The challenges of moving the sculptures from Cyrene to the ship were immense. Commander Charles Aynsley provided a party of 30 blue jackets and marines under command of Lieutenant Philip Luard to carry two wagons by hand up the mountain and build a road, so they could be driven down with the marble statues loaded on top.

They started on 14 May, and it took three days to reach Augubah, where they reassembled the wagons. The midday heat was impossible, so they rose each day at daybreak and started work before sunrise. At nine they rested in the shade until three in the afternoon when they continued their labour until sunset. In the meantime, two of the marines carried the tents forward, set up camp and cooked supper for the exhausted party. After the meal, the sailors would tell stories and sing shanties around the fire until late at night.

They arrived at Cyrene on 24 May. It had taken 10 days to complete a journey that normally took 12 hours on a horse. They lifted the statue of Bacchus and some smaller relics onto one cart and on the other, they loaded Apollo in three boxes, made by the ship's carpenters. The party began the return journey on 29 May, and it took six days to reach Augubah, where the final descent proved the greatest challenge of all.

Smith used his engineering skills to construct a tackle system to lower the carts down the mountain. All went well with the Bacchus as it descended to a track halfway down the elevation, but the same anchor used for the Apollo lost its hold and the load slipped. To Smith's horror, the wagon careered away "at a tremendous pace" and the destruction of the statue seemed inevitable as it headed straight for a 300-foot precipice. Fortunately, there was a large ditch in the ground and before calamity struck, it came to an abrupt halt.

This was not the end of the problem for there was another 400-yard cliff face that required all the ropes the ship could provide and a team of men with hand spikes to steer the loads as they were carefully lowered to the bottom. Finally, they dragged the transports onto the beach by hand and set up a haulage system in the sea to transfer the loads into a boat, which took the statues to the ship anchored more than a mile away. Early the next morning, 8 June, the *Assurance* left for Malta with 22 wooden cases of statues and carvings, while Smith and Porcher returned to their solitary residence at Cyrene.

Except that it was not that lonely. Nine days later a large party of naval officers arrived at their tomb having spent all day climbing from Marsa Susa where their ship, HMS *Scourge*, was anchored. They brought a telegram informing Smith that the British Museum had granted a further £500 and sent a carpenter named William Dennison. This money enabled Smith to hire more help, but he had to pay an inflated rate of five Turkish piasters, about four pence, a day because it was difficult to keep the workers so far from their families.

After the initial tension, relations with the Bedouin improved. Smith and Porcher formed a close relationship with the tribal elders and were invited to the celebration of *Mawlid*, the birth of the Prophet, on 18 June. After a long prayer, duelling horsemen demonstrated their fabulous equine skills in a tournament that lasted all day. The British pair were allowed a privileged insight into tribal affairs and discovered that important issues were settled by a *Majli* or council, at which all men could speak. After much discussion, the general opinion seemed to be understood and a decision was taken accordingly. The British observers noted that in these deliberations, the "sheikhs do not seem to possess the power or influence usually attributed to them".[32]

The intrepid pair continued to excavate promising sites in the city. Unfortunately, Smith suffered from a fever after a visit to Benghazi and this stayed with him for two months. He was too ill to supervise the final recovery, when HMS *Melpomene* collected the last statues and explorers in September. However, Porcher together with a naval party of 90 men provided by the ship's captain, Charles Ewart, managed to repeat the previous operation, albeit with a hostile sheikh, who wished to extort *bakshish*, constantly interfering with the transport.

They loaded a further 63 cases of antiquities onto the ship, which had to stay two miles away because the winds and tide prevented it coming closer. Smith and Porcher said farewell to their helper, Amir, who had been "naturally quick-witted, active and courageous". Thanking him for his work, they gave him two horses and their gunpowder for his loyal nine months' support. The next day, 14 October, the ship weighed anchor and sailed for Malta, just before the breeze turned into a gale.

In England, the explorers were acclaimed for their discoveries. Porcher was promoted to commander and later given command of HMS *Sparrowhawk* in which he discovered an island off British Columbia that is named after him. Smith was posted to Persia, where he rose to the rank of major general and was knighted for his work for the shah.

In their majestic volume with 16 photographs by Francis Bedford, the British explorers hint at a secret mission to advise the government whether the region should be secured as a colony. Counselling against this course of action, Smith describes the innumerable difficulties they experienced and suggests that the population was totally unsuitable for "achieving the public works" necessary, illustrating this by explaining that the road he built between Cyrene and Marsa Susa was regarded with "considerable suspicion" by the local tribes.[33]

* * *

Three years later, the Ottomans renamed the colony "Vilayet of Tripolitania". While George Herman continued as consul general in Tripoli, Lord Russell appointed the renowned historian George Dennis as vice-consul at Benghazi[34] where he made further discoveries in 1865. In the same year, a German medic, Gerhard Rohlfs, set out from Tripoli on the route that had seen the death of Ritchie, Oudney, Clapperton and Laing. His Arab disguise, which included circumcision, helped him become the first explorer to reach Lagos via Lake Chad and the Niger River.

For his achievement, Rohlfs became the second German to be awarded a gold medal by the Royal Geographical Society for an expedition launched from Tripoli. In 1868, he returned to Libya and while he visited Siwa on the way to Alexandria, another German explorer named Gustav Nachtigal and the wealthiest woman in the Netherlands, Alexandrine Tinné, headed south from Tripoli. At Murzuk, they separated because the German wished to explore the Tibesti Mountains, while Tinné was determined to become the first woman to cross the Sahara. Unfortunately, she lost control of her caravan and was murdered on 1 August 1869 before reaching Ghat.

From then until 1880 Rohlfs made several pioneering expeditions into the Western Desert, providing his recently unified country with an important knowledge base for the future. His report to a sceptical Chancellor Bismarck[35] in 1879 concludes with "a plea for colonisation by the German government". However, this potential threat to Libya was not the only security concern the Ottoman rulers faced, because the religious order of Sanussi was now spreading its influence among the Bedouin tribes.

Apollonia, now Marsa Susa, was the main port of Cyrene in the ancient world and one of the five cities built by King Battus I that formed Pentapolis. Lieutenant Colonel Geoffrey Keyes landed near here on his way to earning the Victoria Cross. It was excavated by the University of Michigan in 1965. (Picture courtesy of The Hon. Philippa Weatherly)

Sabratha, in the north-west, was founded by the Phoenicians and rebuilt by the Romans during the time of Emperor Septimus Severus, who was born along the coast at Leptis Magna. Mussolini visited the excavations of Renato Bartoccini in 1937 and Donald Sinden filmed *The Black Tent* there in 1955, but in the past ten years the area has earned notoriety as a launch base for illegal migrants attempting to cross the Mediterranean. (Picture courtesy of Anthony Layden)

Ghadames, known as the Pearl of the Desert, pre-dates Greek and Roman settlements and has been an important trading oasis for 4,000 years. The British consulate opened in 1850 after the anti-slave campaigner James Richardson had completed his fact-finding mission. It was the capital of French-administered Fezzan before independence and the old town was inscribed as a World Heritage site in 1986. (Author)

Tadrart Acacus, home to prehistoric cave paintings near Ghat, is a World Heritage site in Libya. The force of nature that is the Sahara may look like a wonder of the world when at rest, but in the midday sun, or during a *ghibli* sandstorm, it is, according to Bill Kennedy-Shaw, "as good an imitation of Hell as one could devise". (Picture courtesy of Anthony Layden)

PART 2

RELUCTANT COLONY
(1880–1940)

CHAPTER 4

British Journalists on the Fourth Shore

We are not well served in Tripoli.

GERALD FITZMAURICE, CHIEF DRAGOMAN TO THE OTTOMAN EMPIRE, 31 AUGUST 1911

The noble Sharif Muhammad ibn Ali as-Sanussi, who was descended from the daughter of the Prophet, founded his exoteric order in 1837. To begin with, this was a wholly peaceful undertaking, but it was not the only orthodox Islamic movement in North Africa during the 19th century. Further south in the Sudan, Muhammed Ahmad ibn Abd Allah, proclaimed as the mahdi[1] by his devout Ansār followers, led the oppressed Nubian tribes to rebellion against their Ottoman overlords in 1881.

Within four years, his army of dervishes created an Islamic state that extended from the Red Sea to central Africa. They overwhelmed a British-led force of 8,000 at the battle of Shaykan in November 1883 and followed this with the siege of Khartoum where General Charles Gordon died as a martyr in January 1885. By the end of that year, the mahdi controlled Sudan and Darfur, which bordered the Sanussi land in Libya.

Winston Churchill understood the power of the mahdi. He was 10 years old when Gordon was killed and would have read about his heroic sacrifice at Harrow School. After leaving the seat of his education, young Winston joined the Army and cut his teeth in the Northwest Frontier. Drawn to action, he volunteered for Kitchener's expedition to reconquer Sudan and found himself on the outskirts of Khartoum with the 21st Lancers[2] on 2 September 1898.

He arrived in time to charge with the regiment at the battle of Omdurman. As a 23-year-old, he witnessed the carnage when 400 courageous men galloped against a force of 3,000 dervishes as well as the heroism of Raymond de Montmorency, Paul Kenna and Thomas Byrne, who were all awarded the Victoria Cross for their bravery.

Lieutenant de Montmorency earned the highest gallantry medal for returning to the *mêlée* to assist a brother officer, Lieutenant Robert Grenfell, who was surrounded by a large group of enemy. Finding that Grenfell was dead, he placed his mutilated body onto his horse, but it bolted, and he was left alone with only his revolver as a weapon against a closing foe.

Captain Kenna, who had already rescued Major Walter Crole-Wyndham after his horse was shot from under him, saw the stricken officer and together with Corporal Fred Swarbrick, helped him to rejoin the regiment, which was now dismounted and firing at the enemy. Swarbrick was awarded the Distinguished Conduct Medal (DCM) for his part in the rescue along with five other soldiers in the 21st Lancers and Squadron Sergeant Major William Blake of the 17th Lancers.[3]

Thomas Byrne's award was no less deserving. Despite being shot in the arm, the 33-year-old from Dublin turned back in the middle of the charge to assist Lieutenant Richard Molyneux of the Royal Horse Guards, whose horse was shot from under him. Dismounted, disarmed and disorientated, the wounded young officer stood little chance as he was attacked by a group of dervishes. Churchill described the rescue in his book, *The River War*:

> Private Byrne, although already severely wounded by a bullet which had penetrated his right arm, replied without a moment's hesitation… and turning, rode at four Dervishes who were about to kill his officer. His wound which had partly paralysed his arm, prevented him from grasping his sword and at the first ineffectual blow it fell from his hand and he received another wound to the chest. But his solitary charge had checked the pursuing dervishes.[4]

From this campaign, Churchill learned about the nature of desert warfare and Islamic culture. His natural instinct for "defending human values"[5] led him to sympathise with the oppressed Sudanese and to admire their leader as a "great reformer". Resigning from the Army, he wrote his bestselling book, in which he compared the mahdi favourably with the heroic General Gordon: "Both were earnest and enthusiastic men of keen sympathies and passionate emotions… The Arab was an African reproduction of the Englishman…"[6]

This controversial publication gave credit to Kitchener for his victory, but also criticised his character and some of the brutalities of the campaign, such as the disproportionate killing by the Gatling machine-gunners. It also provided powerful insights into how the war affected British politics at home and the rivalry with France, as well as the impact on Britain of suddenly taking control of the largest territory in Africa.

* * *

The European scramble for Africa had begun soon after the Franco-Prussian War. It was not just Germany that wished to join England, France, Spain and Portugal with colonies in the continent. Italy took Eritrea in 1882 and coveted the Horn of Africa. The Kingdom of Belgium also aspired to an empire and at the Berlin Conference of 1884, was granted the Congo.

In Libya, Ottoman power was declining. The rulers in Constantinople, who relied on Britain to halt Imperial Russia in the Crimea and to govern Egypt and the Sudan, were struggling to keep their empire intact. As the 19th century drew to a close, the sultan's hold in Tripoli was still strong but in Cyrenaica, it was loosened by the followers of the Grand Sanussi.

His modest message of earning a living through hard work, rather than charity, appealed to the Bedouin, whose subsistence in the desert was a matter of daily survival. Although the Turks closed his mosque at Bayda and forced him to move to Jaghbub, this did not diminish the fervent support he garnered among the people who lived in the oases.

When the Grand Sanussi died in 1859, the authorities hoped this would be the end of his sect. However, his eldest son, Muhammad al Mahdi ibn Sayed Muhammad as-Sanussi, who was born in Bayda, took up the baton and founded mosques and *zawiyas*[7] across the Islamic world from Morocco to India, maintaining his father's peaceful message. The Sanussi doctrine was popular in the Hejaz[8] and more importantly with Sultan Abdul Hadid II, who was a keen follower and influenced by the Libyan, Sheikh Muhammad Zafir al-Madani, whose lessons he attended in disguise.

By 1880, the revered Grand Sanussi held the authority of a sovereign in Libya's interior and the mahdi in Sudan wrote to him asking if he would become one of his four caliphs. However, Sanussi refused to ally himself to the cause of violence and managed to steer clear of military confrontation with the Ottoman Empire and Britain, only taking up arms when French colonialists invaded his domain in 1901.

* * *

The situation changed after the death of Queen Victoria. Tension in Europe increased significantly with the Anglo-German arms race and the shifting alliances where Britain signed the *Entente Cordiale* with its old enemy, France. The Russian defeat by Japan also changed the global balance of power as the imperial government in St Petersburg switched its priority to the Balkans. The atmosphere of suspicion that pervaded foreign relations between the European powers found its release in 1905, during what became known as the Morocco crisis,[9] when France sought to take control of one of the remaining independent countries in Africa, while Germany attempted to secure a naval base for its ships.

In the Middle East, Britain lost patience with the sultan for the massacres of Christians and the border dispute with the Sinai Peninsula.[10] Corruption in Constantinople increased as the Ottoman Empire continued to split. To obtain concessions, diplomats were forced to pay a price, which was to say nothing about Armenian massacres and protect the sultan from criticism by the Great Powers. The foreign secretary, Edward Grey, wrote that: "No British Government could pay this price." However, the German government was willing to overlook the atrocities and "became dominant at Constantinople"[11] while British influence declined.

In the summer of 1908, the Young Turk movement rose up and this led to the overthrow of Sultan Hamid. His successor, Mehmed V, attempted to strengthen the Ottoman defences, but internal intrigues weakened his hand, and the "Sick Man of Europe" continued its decline. Alert eyes in the Balkans and Italy saw an opportunity, but before these countries acted, Germany's belligerence resulted in another confrontation in Morocco.

Britain was not in a stable position in 1911. A constitutional crisis had led to two general elections and then the Parliament Act, which reduced the power of the House of Lords. The militancy of the rapidly growing labour and suffrage movements and the death of King Edward VII concentrated the government's attention on domestic issues. Where there was time for discussion about foreign affairs, the overriding worry was German naval expansion.

A month after the coronation of King George V on 22 June 1911, the Agadir crisis erupted, when the German gunboat SS *Panther* arrived to stake a claim on the North African coast, causing a run on the banks in Berlin. Preparations were made for a continental war after the Chancellor of the Exchequer, David Lloyd George, speaking at a Lord Mayor's dinner on 21 July, fulminated about the German menace: "peace at that price would be a humiliation, intolerable for a great country like ours to endure".[12]

On 23 August, the future chief of the Imperial General Staff, Brigadier Wilson, successfully persuaded the British government to commit itself to sending an army to France in the event of war with Germany.[13] Winston Churchill took over as first lord of the Admiralty in October and issued precautionary orders to the fleet, but the crisis was not averted until 4 November, when France and Germany concluded an agreement, a month after Italy had invaded Libya.

* * *

Edward Grey includes Italy's conquest of Tripoli in "the chain of events that began with the Turkish revolution and led straight to the catastrophe of 1914".[14] The day before the declaration of war on 29 September, Sultan Mehmed sent a despairing telegram to King George V begging him to intervene and bring about a settlement. The king followed the accepted protocol and immediately referred this plea to the Foreign Office.

He was briefed by Sir Arthur Nicolson, who had been British ambassador to Russia from 1906 to 1910 and was now permanent undersecretary to the foreign secretary. This senior diplomat explained that the government had been aware of Italy's plans for some time and was worried the attack on the Ottoman Empire would have severe repercussions in Muslim parts of India and Egypt. He also correctly predicted that this would "excite the appetites of smaller countries" and that "the Balkans will begin to move".[15]

However, the invasion should not have been a shock to Turkey. Edward Grey had recorded after a meeting with the French prime minister, Georges Clemenceau, as far back as 28 April 1908 that France and Britain were "inconveniently pressed by Italy about the Tripoli frontier". Grey had declined to sign a proposed agreement because he didn't wish Turkey to "give us trouble in Egypt". However, he did assure the Italians that Britain would not put forward a claim to the place to which they attached most importance.[16]

The Italian press had been lobbying their government to seize Libya since March 1911, depicting the country as full of riches and with a population that hated their Ottoman overlords. This was fake news. Economic surveys conducted by the Great Powers suggested that Libya had little potential as a colony. Britain had sent a five-man team with an engineer and agriculturist under the renowned geologist Professor John Walter Gregory to see whether it would make a homeland for Jews, but they wrote a pessimistic report, and the Jewish Territorial Organization declined the offer.[17]

However, this did not put off a new generation of Italian imperialists, who played down the challenges of conquest and exaggerated the opposition to Constantinople. In fact, Libya had been relatively stable during the reign of Hamid, who had allowed a multicultural population to coexist in peace. Tribal tensions did exist, but a sign of the stability was that eminent scholars were able to follow in the footsteps of Smith and Porcher and visit Pentapolis safely. These academics included: Herbert Weld-Blundell, who created a photographic record of Cyrene in 1894; Charles Clermont-Ganneau (Collège de France) in 1895; David Hogarth (later the Keeper of the Ashmolean Museum) in 1904 and the American Richard Norton in 1910.[18]

The quality of archaeologists was not matched by the standard of the consuls in Tripoli, which had declined since the era of Warrington and Herman. The independent observer Francis McCullagh reports that the national representatives were "mainly a weak-minded crew of diplomatic derelicts, who were originally sent to Tripoli as to a quiet backwater out of harm's way by their respective governments".[19] The British chief dragoman in Turkey, Gerald Fitzmaurice, agreed with this description when he was asked to trouble-shoot in Tripoli before the invasion.

Italy's representative, Signor Berardini, was the most able and worked hard to remove French influence because he was worried that after Morocco, France would sweep into Libya from Tunisia. Further encouragement from the Italian consulate helped persuade Prime Minister Giovanni Giolitti that the conquest would be easy and that his troops would be welcomed. After his token ultimatum issued on 27 September ran out, he declared war two days later and launched the invasion force, under the leadership of *Generale* Carlo Caneva.

A naval squadron commanded by Admiral Luigi Faravelli arrived at Tripoli before the Army left Italy. The admiral was not keen on attacking the port and tried to persuade the Ottoman pasha, Ahmed Bessim, to surrender without fighting. He knew that the Turkish garrison had been weakened because it had sent troops to assist the counter-insurgency operation in Arabia and the experienced military commander, General Vali, had been recalled. However, a new Turkish leader, Colonel Neshat (Nesciat) Bey, took up the gauntlet and used the delay to withdraw his troops beyond the range of naval gunfire and to begin recruiting an army of Libyan Arabs and Berbers.

Rome ordered a frustrated Faravelli to start the invasion before the Army arrived. After a long bombardment against empty forts, a naval party under the renowned Arctic explorer *Capitan* Umberto Cagni landed without opposition and raised the Italian flag on 5 October. For a few days, they were unhindered, but then on the night of 9 October, the first action took place at Bou-Meliana.

The Turkish assault was not successful, but the incursion hastened the Italian Army's arrival. By 23 October, 25,000 troops were positioned around Tripoli within a protective zone provided by the fleet.[20] Lulled into a false sense of security, the Army established a poorly sited perimeter that was easily approached under cover. Their complacency in neglecting the key principles of all-round defence and mutual support was about to be exposed by a disaster that would change the face of the war and how it would be perceived forever.

* * *

International reaction to the invasion was mixed. The Muslim world was outraged and there was rioting in Alexandria and Tunis. Germany disliked Italy's action due to the awkward position in which it placed them with their Ottoman protégé. France had their hands full with Morocco, but protected their interests on the Libyan border by occupying Djenat. London also moved to protect their interests and ordered the Mediterranean Fleet to the Egyptian frontier. With the agreement of Sultan Mehmed in Constantinople, the Royal Navy helped Egypt to annex the Bay of Sollum, much to the Italian government's indignation.[21]

On the ground, a plethora of British war correspondents travelled to North Africa to report on the first ever land, sea and air war.[22] Ernest Bennett, a Member of Parliament who lost his Woodstock seat in 1910, journeyed to Tripoli via Tunis and wrote about his time with the Turkish Red Crescent as the official correspondent for the *Manchester Guardian*. He was joined by Allan Ostler, the *Daily Express* reporter,

Henry Seppings-Wright, who sketched images for the *Illustrated London News*, and Captain Henri "Beetle" Bettelheim, who had led General French's scouts in South Africa. They also shared experiences with George Abbott, who was embedded in the Ottoman forces, having been the *Daily Chronicle*'s special correspondent in Southeastern Europe.

Bennett took a P&O steamer to Tunis and then arrived at the Libyan border by means of rail and road. He paid 12 francs for the hire of a camel and travelled 34 miles in a day but was so uncomfortable that he completed the last seven miles to Zuwarah on foot. The price of horses and camels fluctuated throughout the country. Captain Bettelheim bought a sound horse for £26 which was considered a bargain because at Gharian it was 1,000 francs, or £40, for a decent mount.

Food was scarce on their journey and sometimes they had to make do with bread dipped in a can of fortifying Nestlé milk, but Bennett particularly enjoyed the occasional fried *galettas* for breakfast. When they eventually reached the Turkish troops, the officers looked after the British journalists extremely well. At Zuwarah, Captain Hassan loaned Bennett his bed and slept on the floor. The commandant *Bimbashi* (Major) Muhammad was equally helpful and when the former MP visited the 38th Cavalry Regiment, the paymaster provided a sumptuous desert feast.[23]

On the other side, the Italian government accredited Francis McCullagh, who accompanied the invading force. Thomas Grant wrote for *The Daily Mirror* and Ellis Ashmead-Bartlett was the Reuters correspondent. Initially, McCullagh stayed in the Minerva hotel rather than the Astoria, which accommodated 40 Italian journalists. The owner, Chevalier Julius Caesar Aquilina, a Maltese who claimed to be descended from the Roman emperor and the Knights of Malta, left abruptly with his family when the Italians arrived.

McCullagh initially saw the invasion as a "civilising mission".[24] However, he returned his accreditation papers to General Caneva after the watershed events at Shar al-Shatt, or Sciara Sciat, which began on 23 October. The battle commenced with Italian Air Force biplanes[25] flying the world's first combat mission, as *Capitan* Carlo Piazza manoeuvred over the Turkish lines on an aerial reconnaissance mission.

This technological advantage did not help their troops in the trenches, who were defeated decisively.[26] More than 500 soldiers were killed, including a high number of officers who stood upright with their distinctive uniforms, rather than taking cover. Although the Turks took prisoners, the Arab irregulars slaughtered many of the 11th Bersaglieri Regiment soldiers, who were surrounded.

The defeat shattered any illusions the Italians had about local support. *Generale* Caneva was shocked by the loss and considered the Arabs living in the oases to be traitors. He ordered his commanders to disarm and punish the offenders, but the next day, the vengeful troops began a systematic massacre of the civilian population living in the Mechiya oasis. The indiscriminate killing continued for four days with the bodies of 4,000 men, women and children left on the ground for the grateful vultures and rampant flies.

Meanwhile Neshat Bey decided to attack again. On 2 November, *Capitans* Piazza flying a Blériot and Riccardo Moizo in a Nieuport reported about 6,000 Turkish and Arab soldiers, in three columns, approaching from the south. The next morning at 5 a.m., Francis McCullagh was woken by the sound of naval gunfire and made his way from his hotel along the coast to Shar al-Shatt. He noted the emptiness as he passed through the oasis:

> This suburb, so filled with noisy life four days earlier, was now as uninhabited as Pompeii... The stillness was hostile; the very air was dense with unutterable menace. The shattered doorways and windows gaped like the mouths of dead men. Black with blood and pitted with bullets, the naked walls exhaled the quintessence of malignity and hate.[27]

Whilst capturing the images with his pen and camera, he was appalled to see four women and three children tied together with their necks cut. The great newspaper editor at the time, W. T. Stead, who died the next year on the *Titanic*, lavished praise on McCullagh's writing from Libya and described him as having "a potent influence on the policy of Great Britain". He wrote: "Francis McCullagh... whose ready pen, whose fearless spirit and whose presence in the firing line has made it possible to make the great public realize the criminality of the plunder-raid on Tripoli."[28]

The Italian consul, Signor Berardini, told Ernest Bennett that: "he could not understand how it was that while the Government in England was correct and even sympathetic in the attitude to Italy, the general tone of the Press was distinctly hostile."[29] However, by then, Italy had lost any moral authority it might have had at the outset.

The British consul was a Spaniard named Justin Alvarez. He was suddenly thrust into the limelight when McCullagh informed him about the return of his accreditation. Alvarez had witnessed the exemplary behaviour of the Turks when dealing with the Europeans before they evacuated the city. Now, he saw the opposite from the Italians, who shot several British subjects "owing to them not having given the password, or for some other reason".[30]

When the reports of the massacres were published in London, Berlin and New York, they were categorically denied by those who were sympathetic to Rome, such as Lord Roberts, Richard Bagot and James Garvin, the editor of *The Observer*. The outbreak of the war had already given Sir James Rennell Rodd, the British ambassador in Rome, "a great deal of work".[31] Now, he had to placate the Italians who attacked the character of McCullagh, suggesting he hadn't even been to Tripoli. Alvarez was consulted by the Foreign Office and replied with a statement confirming the stories and the scale of the war crimes. In response, four Italian journalists entered the consulate to complain vigorously and sent a report that was published in Rome, justifying the killings by claiming that their soldiers were provoked.

This was taken up by Italian representatives in London, who used their influence to increase the pressure. On 5 December, Henry Cowan stood up in Parliament and asked whether the secretary of state for foreign affairs would: "consider the desirability of appointing thereto a British-born member of our Consular service with experience gained by actual service in some similar position in the near East?"[32] As a result, Edward Grey acceded to Italian protests and replaced the honest consul in Tripoli with an official who was more favourably disposed to Rome.

In the longer term, the foreign secretary reduced his tacit support for Italy after the atrocities. The riots in Alexandria, combined with the hostility generated by the media, drove him to vacillate between the two sides. Professor Massimiliano Cricco suggests that many MPs who knew Ernest Bennett in the House of Commons "assumed an openly pro-Turkish stance which added to the growing irritation of the British government against Italy for reopening the Eastern Question".[33]

This animosity had an impact on the proposed Anglo-Italian Mediterranean agreement that Churchill wished to pursue, in order to loosen Italy's ties to Austria and Germany in the Triple Alliance. As first lord of the Admiralty, Churchill was supportive of Italy, but also saw the risks to British interests: "The reactions of this Italian adventure threaten to be deep, and we stand both to gain and to lose by it. But clearly we must prefer Italy to Turkey on all grounds…". His opinion was shared by Sir Arthur Nicolson, who felt the press was being unhelpful: "I am exceedingly vexed at the tone of our press here towards Italy… I should far prefer having Italy as a neighbour to Egypt than the Turks…".[34]

* * *

In fact, it was not Francis McCullagh who informed London of the massacre, but a British officer serving with the Turkish Army. Herbert Gerald Montagu had been educated at St Paul's and was commissioned as a second lieutenant in the Northumberland Fusiliers, known as the Fighting Fifth, on 1 April 1911. At the outbreak of the Italian war, he took leave from his militia posting and travelled to Libya, not realising that King's Regulations forbade any serving officer from fighting for another country.

He met Seppings-Wright at Sfax but was stranded for three days and survived on a diet of octopus. Arriving at Neshat Bey's headquarters, he was given the rank of captain, with a command of 3,000 Turkish troops and Arab irregulars comprising the right flank of the Turkish forces. He was so successful that Alan Ostler, who witnessed his gallantry and leadership of irregular Arab troops, described him as a

"Paladin of the Desert". On 26 October, he led part of the successful attack at Sidi Mersi and afterwards, he described the preparations:

> On the night before [the attack] six Arabs sallied out of the city with a quantity of cord, with which they secretly looped up a dense plantation of prickly pear bushes, joining up the cords to the main rope, which they entrusted to an Arab urchin of 11 years. During the night the urchin, acting on instructions, pulled the rope vigorously for some time, causing the bushes to rustle. This scared the Italian troops in the vicinity, and they fired on the bush for six hours, literally blowing the jungle away and leaving themselves without ammunition.[35]

Entering the oasis, Montagu saw the bodies of the women and children in the mosque and was so angry that he sent a cable, on 2 November, to London exposing the massacre:

> I feel it is my duty to send you the following telegram, and I beg you, in the name of Christianity, to publish it throughout England. I am an English officer and I am now voluntarily serving in the Turkish army here…
>
> Imagine then my feelings when on entering and driving the Italians out of the Arab houses which they had fortified and were holding, we discovered the bodies of some hundred and twenty women and children, with their hands and feet bound, mutilated, pierced and torn. Later on… we found a mosque filled with the bodies of women and children mutilated almost beyond recognition…
>
> The idea of the Italians when they slaughtered these innocents was obviously one of revenge… Hoping you will do all you can to bring the barbarous atrocities before the British public and authorities.[36]

The story was verified by other correspondents such as Thomas Grant, who wrote: "The two-mile ride to the cavalry barracks was a perfect nightmare of horrors. To begin with one had to pass a huddled mass of some 50 men and boys who were yesterday herded into a small space enclosed by three walls and there fired upon until no one was left alive."[37]

* * *

In a state of panic, the Italian prime minister proclaimed sovereignty over Libya on 4 November. The British ambassador in Rome unofficially expressed his doubts about the "wisdom of this policy in Italy's own interests",[38] and proposed an interim stage of protectorate which might have avoided a debilitating conflict with Turkey. Meanwhile, the Italian advance from Tripoli was "delayed by torrential rain which converted the trenches and rifle pits into pools and made the movement of guns and ammunition carts almost impossible".[39]

When Montagu was severely wounded in December, he was treated by the Egyptian Red Crescent that had been founded by the owner of the *al-Mu'ayyad* newspaper, Sheikh Ali Youssef and earned a magnificent reputation in Libya.[40] However, after he returned to England, the War Office demanded Montagu's resignation for communicating with the press, despite him joining the exalted company of Admiral Horatio Nelson and General Charles Gordon[41] when the sultan awarded him the prestigious Order of the Medjidie.

In Libya, the focus of the fighting switched to Marmarica and the battle for Tobruk. Rome was keen to develop the natural harbour into an important naval base and according to Francis McCullagh, the first troops sent from Genoa were "destined for Tobruk".[42] The Italian fleet, commanded by Vice Admiral Augustus Aubry, entered the port on 3 October and landed without opposition the following day.

Ernest Bennett suggested that Tobruk "would be shorn of half its importance if within 80 miles the powerful ships of the Royal Navy can harbour in Sollum".[43] Heeding this advice, Winston Churchill as first lord of the Admiralty and Viscount Haldane as secretary of state for war worked together to ensure Britain secured the Western Frontier and coast of Egypt and pre-empt any attempt by Italy to seize Sollum.[44]

In the first week of December, there were 5,000 Italian troops at Tobruk and after a few trivial clashes, they occupied the hill at Nadura overlooking the Mureyra Valley. For the Turks, Captain Mustafa Kemal (later Ataturk), was placed in charge of the Tobruk region by Brigadier Edhem. Kemal noticed that the Italian fortifications would jeopardise his position and on 21 December, he issued orders to Sheikh Yasseen, head of the Meryem tribe, to attack the high ground.[45]

The Ottoman and Libyan force approached the hill before dawn on 22 December and launched a surprise attack after a short bombardment. The Italian soldiers had no artillery support and the position was captured after two hours' fighting. When reinforcements mounted a counter-attack, Kemal was ready with 1,000 men and drove the Italians back into Tobruk. The valiant sheikh was killed in the battle, but his men continued to resist the invaders for another month.

Following this success, the renowned Turkish leader, Enver Pasha, promoted Kemal to command all the forces around Derna. He was greatly helped in the middle of January, when Ahmed Sharif as-Sanussi, who had taken over the Order after the death of his uncle, issued a proclamation inscribed on a silk banner, urging everyone to continue the struggle.

On 3 March 1912, Kemal's force comprised eight officers, 160 regulars, an artillery company and 7,742 tribesmen. He continued to besiege the Italians who unhappily remained in their enclaves throughout the summer. Waging war in Libya was much harsher than the occupying soldiers had expected. The tribal customs of the locals contrasted with their lives at home and very few spoke Arabic. Women all wore heavy veils and one soldier complained, "we lead ascetic lives like the monks on Mount Athos".[46]

* * *

Despite the Italian campaign descending into a quagmire, several British journalists remained through the winter. Bennett woke up on Christmas Day in an empty harem at Gharian and spent the day interviewing five Italian prisoners of war. They had been captured in October, but did not complain about their treatment. He then visited the Troglodytes living in the nearby caverns and was loudly abused by the *viragoes* from their deep holes in the ground.[47]

George Abbott, who later published a book about his time in Libya, was one of the last British journalists to leave. He describes the arrival at al-Aziziyah, 25 miles south-west of Tripoli, of a brown-bearded "soldier of the Crescent" on 25 February, "who regarded this last encroachment of Christian Europe on Moslem Africa as the beginning of the Great Jehad [sic] of which he dreamed all his life".[48] His name was Mohammed el-Kiani and he spoke Arabic, Turkish, English, French, German and Modern Greek.

Hailing originally from Albania, Baba, as he was also known, was armed to the teeth and carried a banner that read "Victory is from God and conquest near". It had taken him 94 days to walk from Alexandria to Aziziyah, stopping to fight and preach at Derna, Benghazi and Khoms. He claimed that he had been a political prisoner for 12 years and had travelled from Morocco to Afghanistan preaching Pan-Islamism. He explained his vision to Abbott:

> I have spent years trying to bring all the Moslems together and this war will help to unite us… it will not stop at Tripoli. We hate the Italians, but we hate the French no less.[49]

When he was not exalting the Holy War, Kiani was a man of very refined manners, with a keen sense of humour and a quiet charm that fascinated Abbott. He offered to escort the Cambridge Exhibitioner, disguised as an Arab, to Kufra to meet the Grand Sanussi, but an abscess from the Turkish artillery saddle and the pangs of hunger dampened Abbott's enthusiasm. After a few days, the jihadist said farewell, fortifying the spirit of the Arabs with his words of "faith and fire" and hopes for an Islamic re-birth before disappearing into the desert.

* * *

Some histories suggest that the Italians defeated the Turks easily and as a result, the Balkan League decided to wage war in 1912. However, the evidence provided by British reporters demonstrates conclusively that the victory was neither easy nor swift. It is certainly true that Italian forces captured the important coastal cities, but its army failed to advance into the interior and although the Italian troops established a bridgehead in October, they failed to exploit this advantage and became bogged down in a long and bitter struggle.

It was not so much the ease of victory that encouraged Balkan leaders as the fact that none of the Great Powers supported the Ottoman Empire, even after the brutality of the Italian troops was exposed to the world. Britain's lengthy procrastination centred on the implications for its Mediterranean Fleet. Italy had been a member of the Triple Alliance with Germany and Austria since 1882. An aggressive Italian fleet could deny access to Egypt and the Suez Canal, but London also knew the Italian Navy was opposed most strongly against Austria in the Adriatic.

The key question was whether Britain should hold the balance of power against Austria and Italy as she did against the German Fleet in the North Sea. Just after the battle of Tobruk, Lord Esher recommended an increase to Britain's naval power in the Mediterranean, but Churchill resisted, telling the House of Commons on 18 March that "the 4th Battle Squadron based on Gibraltar could act eastwards, or westwards as required".[50]

This issue was so important that Prime Minister Herbert Asquith and Churchill travelled to Naples and consulted with the former chief of the Naval Staff, Admiral Fisher, on board the Admiralty Yacht. For five years, the Royal Navy's plans in the event of a war with Germany had been to abandon the Mediterranean. This was succinctly summarised by Churchill in May 1912, when he wrote: "it would be very foolish to lose England in safeguarding Egypt".[51]

After discussing the issue with Fisher in Naples, the British politicians sailed to Malta and met the commander-in-chief in Egypt, Lord Kitchener. They reached a compromise, which Churchill put before the Committee of Imperial Defence in a detailed memorandum that outlined five war contingencies, the worst of which was Britain alone against the Triple Alliance.[52] The priority Churchill set the Royal Navy of facing Germany in the North Sea upset many people who called for a strong fleet in the eastern Mediterranean, including his predecessor Reginald McKenna. However, Churchill's view prevailed when the decision was made on 4 July, although the committee did ameliorate the consequences by binding the first lord of the Admiralty into maintaining a strong naval presence at Malta.[53] A far-reaching decision that would have a vital impact in the Second World War.

* * *

On 11 September, a force of 16,000 Italians launched a major offensive from Derna against the Libyan troops in Cyrenaica. However, Kemal managed to blunt this attack and was only stopped after a peace treaty was signed at Ouchy in Switzerland, on 18 October. When Italy eventually agreed terms, more than a year after declaring war on Turkey, its troops were effectively besieged in seven enclaves under the protection of its navy's guns. The largest zone at Tripoli extended barely 10 miles from the coast.

Turkey might have continued its resistance if Montenegro had not declared war 10 days earlier. When they did sign, the Ottoman war minister, Şevket Pasha, exclaimed that aid was continuing to flow into Libya from Islamic countries and that "the whole world knows that victory remains with our soldiers in Tripoli and

Cyrenaica and that the breasts of our soldiers, both Turk and Arab alike, are still filled with enthusiasm".[54]

The treaty made little difference on the ground. Turkey did transfer some troops to fight in the Balkans, but "a skeletal Ottoman force"[55] remained to organise the insurgency in the west under Sulayman al-Baruni and in the East under Ahmed Sharif. In spite of this reality, the perception of an easy victory did contribute to the Balkan League's decision. Professor Christopher Clark suggests that when Italy launched its war of conquest, it triggered "a chain of opportunistic assaults on Ottoman territories across the Balkans" and the "system of geographical balances that had enabled local conflicts to be contained was swept away".[56]

Apart from the costs of the invasion in terms of blood and treasure, questions of the war's legality and the lingering war crimes issue continued to haunt Italy. Sir Thomas Barclay, the distinguished authority on international law, who had been a Liberal MP with Ernest Bennett, promptly published *The Turco-Italian War and Its Problems,* in which he referred the dispute to the Permanent Court of Arbitration. In addition, several of the British correspondents published books in 1912 condemning the massacres in the strongest words. Italy responded with the apologist William McClure, who wrote a book that was "wholly favourable to Italian diplomacy and military and naval operations",[57] but by then they had lost the propaganda war.

Francis McCullagh's publishers, Herbert and Daniel, included a disclosure that they were "not necessarily committed to the views on the war expressed by the author". Sensitive to the controversy, they refused to include some of his more gruesome photographs, deeming them "unsuitable" for general circulation. Ernest Bennett's book provided important corroboration and also condemned Italy's crimes. Alan Ostler was less moralistic, but just as reproachful, accusing the Italian soldier of being "chicken-hearted" and explaining: "it was because they were mad with terror that the Italian soldiers (and sailors) ran amok and butchered every defenceless person on whom they could lay their hands".[58]

The unhappy occupation and the Balkan wars were not the only legacies of the conflict. A longer-lasting contribution was felt in the nature of warfare itself with the development of new technologies. Italy changed the battlefield forever by introducing the air component, with the first ever bombing raid by Giulio Gavotti in an Etrich Taube aircraft on 1 November.[59] Together with the network of wireless telegraphy stations and Marconi's experiments with the Italian Corps of Engineers, the Italians made a profound step that was copied by all the belligerents in World War I.

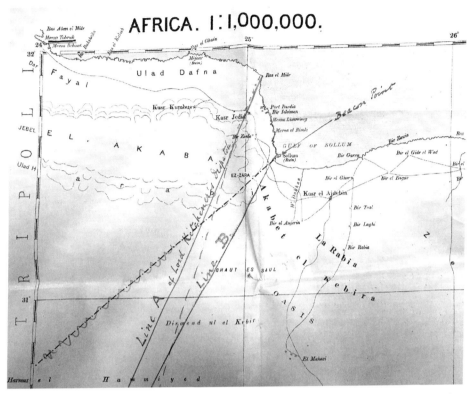

Kitchener's Line 1911. When Italy invaded Libya and landed troops at Tobruk the British commander-in-chief in Egypt, Lord Kitchener, decided to settle the long-standing disputed border. His proposed line for the frontier is marked clearly as Line A on this map compiled in the Topographical Section, General Staff, Cairo 1905 (TSGS 1539). The key difference between the eventual border and Kitchener's line is the inclusion of the whole of the Gulf of Sollum and further south, the oasis of Jaghbub, both of which became vital ground in the two World Wars. Crown Copyright (expired)

CHAPTER 5

Sanussi Jihad

Allah is high and the desert wide!

LIBYAN PROVERB TRANSCRIBED BY ERNEST BENNETT

The name Bir Hakeim is synonymous with the gallant resistance of the Free French against Rommel in 1942, but 26 years earlier it was a desolate prisoner-of-war camp, where 100 British sailors and a dog named Paddy were held by the fearsome Sanussi.

These crew members were from HMS *Tara* and HMT *Moorina*, both sunk by the world's most successful submarine commander, Lothar von Arnauld de la Perière, in *U-35*.[1] The *Tara* survivors were towed to Bardia on 5 November 1915 and, because they had seen the German's secret submarine cave, he passed them to the Sanussi who marched them deep into the desert. There, they were joined by men from the horse transport *Moorina*, including two naval officers, two Indian grooms, a cook named Joe and Lieutenant Thomas Seth Apcar.[2]

The captain of the *Tara*, Rupert Gwatkins-Williams, had a chequered career in the Royal Navy. He was an outstanding cadet at Dartmouth and was present at the capture of the Taku forts during the Boxer Rebellion. However, he was severely reprimanded for not reporting the grounding of a ship and relegated to the coast guard, where he languished for four years. At the start of World War I, he was appointed to command the passenger ship SS *Hibernia*, which was converted into an armed boarding steamer and renamed HMS *Tara*. His crew was drawn mainly from Holyhead and included the ship's former captain, Edward Tanner.

After a year patrolling the North Sea, they received orders to join the Egyptian coastal patrol. In Alexandria, Gwatkins-Williams welcomed two important additions to his complement. The first was a Greek-Syrian interpreter named Vasili Lambridimis, known to everyone on board as Basil. The second was Paddy "whose special qualification was cheerfulness under all circumstances". This plump hound was a blend of fox terrier and pug.[3]

Completing the short journey to Sollum, the captain met the British commander, Lieutenant Colonel Cecil Snow, who ran an effective spy network across the frontier. His small force was outnumbered by thousands of Sanussi camped on the high ground in Libya. Tension was high as Turkish agents fomented trouble and sniping across the border increased in the autumn. The plan for HMS *Tara* was to patrol the coast, enforce the blockade and call in daily at Sollum, being prepared to evacuate the British subjects, if the enemy attacked.

Twelve of the crew were lost when the enemy torpedo struck the ship on its second patrol. Two officers and eight ratings were presumed to be in the engine room when the ship went down.[4] The ship's carpenter, 60-year-old Owen Williams, died when a meat safe landed on his head while he was attempting to board a lifeboat, and Cook Walter Jackson also drowned, but the survivors brought his body ashore and buried him on the beach.

To Paddy the torpedoing of the ship was "a delightful and unexpected event that added to his enjoyment of life". Edward Tanner fished him out of the water and landed him with the disorientated crew close to Bardia. Their anxiety was palpable, but Gwatkins-Williams was encouraged by his interview that evening with the aesthete Captain Nouri Bey, half-brother of the Ottoman Army commander and veteran of the war with Italy, Enver Pasha.

Nouri Bey had arrived at Bardia earlier in the year with a chest full of gold to organise the Libyan opposition to the Italian occupiers. He was a slightly built, gentle-looking man with a straggling beard and a "dreamy appearance". Captain Tanner and Basil joined the meeting along with two Turks who supplied soap and chocolates and were "kind and compassionate" to the prisoners.[5]

The interview was clearly a test, which the Royal Navy captain passed. Over the next week, the prisoners were visited by a holy man carrying a Mauser rifle, reported to be a relation of the Grand Sanussi, and the commander of the Ottoman Army in Libya, Ja'far Pasha al-Askari (who later became the prime minister of Iraq). Deciding their fate, the Sanussi separated them from the Italian prisoners in Libya and escorted them to an isolated camp south-west of Tobruk, to be held as hostages.

Before they were marched into the desert, there was a moment when they were nearly rescued. After the *U-35* had sunk the *Abbas* at her moorings in Sollum, Colonel Snow learned about the plight of the *Tara*. He sent a signal alerting the Royal Navy and the 250-foot minesweeper, HMS *Jonquil*, captained by George Bevan, responded rapidly. Steaming up the coast, he entered Port Bardia on 14 November and tried to land a party close to one of the broken lifeboats on the shore but was greeted by a fusillade of rifle fire. At that time, the fleet had strict instructions not to retaliate against the Sanussi, so Bevan had to make an awkward withdrawal without using any of his guns.

* * *

The next day, the *Tara*'s crew was marched 15 miles into the desert. The seamen had not received their promised boots, so many of them were barefoot. The wounded struggled badly and the 65-year-old quartermaster, William Thomas, who was suffering worst of all, was carried on a makeshift stretcher. As the ship began to sink, he had gone below to fetch a mate, sleeping in his bunk. By the time they reached the deck, there was only one lifeboat remaining and, in his attempt to board it, he had trapped his leg, which fractured in two places.

The injured leg became infected with gangrene and while sheltering in some caves, the Turkish doctor Béchie Fouad decided to amputate. Unfortunately, he had no anaesthetic and only a pair of scissors and a sharp rock to complete the operation. Two of Thomas' mess mates held the old sailor's hands as he bravely bore the agony, but the loss of blood proved too much for him and later that night, he died.

After burying him in a shallow grave the next morning,[6] the crew were forced to continue their journey. The desolation of the country "beggared belief". For 10 days, they grimly trudged into the desert and became increasingly anxious about their destination. The days were blistering hot and the nights bitterly cold. Several of the sailors were over 60 years old and had little experience of trekking, but incredibly none were lost during this ordeal.

As the torment continued, there was one member of the complement who did not suffer. Paddy was in "paradise" as they crossed the barren terrain. His little round body "became more shapely and his short legs sturdier" as he chased an indolent hare, or a twitching lark. The faithful hound's home was with his friends, and he did his best with bright and never-ending optimism to lift the prisoners' spirits and instil some faith into the brooding minds of those who feared for the future. Occasionally, he fraternised with the guards, but this was only temporary because he knew that he was an "infidel dog" and played this role well, often barking at their approach.[7]

On 24 November, they turned south and for another 48 hours stumbled across the desert with lacerated feet. Their meagre rations were served out before each forced march. During night marches, the stones were pitiless and, in the dark, the slower sailors fell blindly and fretted that they would lose touch with the camels carrying the water.

Eventually, the straggling column of sick, feeble and lame reached Bir Hakeim. Unfortunately, there were no tent supports, so that night they huddled together wrapped as best they could against the cold. The next day they started to build their camp and make the best of their situation.

Their neighbour, who controlled the well, was a whip-carrying, 60-year-old Ethiopian with twisted legs, who the sailors named Holy Joe. He looked after a herd of goats and lived with his extended family in a bell tent. He remained aloof from both the prisoners and the 20 Sanussi guards, who were commanded by Achmed, an Egyptian convert who had once been in the pay of the British in Cairo.

Dining on starvation rations became a ritual. Everyone wanted to cook because it was too serious a business to leave to one person. No grain of rice was ever wasted and the delicate ceremony of dividing the food, presided over by the chief officer, Mr. Leslie Dudgeon, was watched suspiciously with jealous eyes, quick to accuse someone of taking more than their portion. Despite this, Paddy always received sufficient to keep him healthy. If the majority of prisoners only gave him half a teaspoonful of rice, this was ample for his needs, and he was in the best condition of anyone in the party.[8]

With the arrival of December, the weather worsened, and the wind and rain deepened the pervasive gloom. The prisoners were allowed to write some letters, but they heard no news about what was happening on the border. Little did they realise that their capture had begun a series of events that would become known forever as the Sanussi Campaign.

* * *

The roots of this desert war were not deep. Relations between Britain and the Sanussi had remained amicable before Italy joined the Allies in World War I. Although Lord Kitchener took care to remain neutral in the fight for Libya, he understood the geostrategic importance of the disputed frontier from both a military and an economic viewpoint. As a result, he sent his most trusted officer, Captain Oswald Fitzgerald, who had worked personally for him for many years and saved his life during an assassination attempt at Cairo railway station,[9] to reconnoitre the area. In his historic letter, dated 1 January 1912,[10] Fitzgerald assesses the "sufficiency of the forces in Egypt" in the event of a "European conflagration" and includes a summary of border negotiations since 1844, as well as a map showing Kitchener's intended boundary line (see page 45) and a report of the Turkish troops' evacuation from Sollum on 21 December 1911.

The Turks in Libya "protested to Constantinople" about the British proposal and as a result, the frontier was redrawn with the Sanussi oasis at Jaghbub and the escarpment overlooking Sollum placed in Libya. These changes were to have a profound effect in both World Wars, when the two locations were used as mounting bases for invasions into Egypt. It can only be imagined what might have happened if the sultan had agreed to Kitchener's boundary line and the vital ground was controlled by Cairo.

The porous Egyptian frontier was policed by the Coastguard led by Colonel George Hunter, who had his hands full with the extensive smuggling routes (he later styled himself as Governor of the Western Desert). A network of agents reported on the movements at Jaghbub and trade along the coast. Fortunately for the Awlad Ali tribes, 1912 was a "good year" because there was a high demand for their camels from the war in Libya. Meanwhile, Kitchener maintained his scrupulous neutrality and had to write to the foreign secretary in London to explain that he would not authorise Italian troops onto Egyptian territory because "the Arabs in the neighbourhood would... most probably oppose such a landing and we could not allow hostilities to take place within our undisputed frontier".[11]

When the Grand Sanussi invited Leo Royle, in charge of the detachment that monitored the tribal traffic across the frontier, to visit him at Jaghbub, a cautious Kitchener forbade the British officer from making the journey. He did, however, encourage further communication and so the 30-year-old Royle, who had spent more than a decade chasing smugglers in the desert, became the official British intermediary with Ahmed Sharif.[12]

Their eventual meeting took place in November 1914. By then Kitchener was in London, having become Herbert Asquith's secretary for war, a week after the assassination of Archduke Franz Ferdinand in Sarajevo. However, his long shadow continued to dominate the lands of the Nile, as his successor, General Sir John Maxwell, regularly reported to London and the energetic Kitchener could not resist offering a guiding hand to his long-term friend.

At the outset of World War I, Italy was a member of the Triple Alliance with Germany and Austria. However, since this was a defensive agreement and Austria was deemed to be the aggressor, the Rome government stalled before entering the war. Meanwhile, the Ottoman Empire, which still supported the Libyan tribes fighting the hated occupiers, joined the Central Powers and launched a surprise attack on Russia's Black Sea Fleet on 29 October 1914.

Italy negotiated for territories with both sides and finally revoked the Triple Alliance by signing a pact with the Allies in London. On 23 May 1915, a month after a column of 4,000 of their soldiers were defeated in Tripolitania, Rome declared war against Austria and mobilised along their 400-mile border. The Italian Army's chief of staff, *Generale* Luigi Cardona, was a staunch advocate of the frontal assault, but his tactics resulted in heavy losses and very soon the front-line trenches resembled the quagmire in Flanders.

Meanwhile, agents from Berlin dusted down Baron Max von Oppenheim's decade-old, three-pronged strategy against the British in Egypt. This encompassed a simultaneous strike on the Suez Canal from the east, a Sanussi invasion from Libya and a nationalist uprising along the Nile Valley. Setting this in motion, Sultan Mehmed V sent envoys to the sharifs at Mecca and Siwa asking them to join the Holy War that he declared in Constantinople, but neither of these noble leaders were inclined to support the axis of German-Turkish militarism.

On the night of 2 February 1915, the Ottoman Army launched an attack across the Suez Canal, but the defenders easily repelled this isolated assault and without the support of the religious orders, the strategy seemed to be doomed to failure. Leo Royle, who had by now established friendly relations with the Grand Sanussi,[13] managed to secure Ahmed Sharif's re-affirmation of his "friendship and esteem for the British".[14] Just as importantly, the new British high commissioner, Sir Henry

McMahon, held positive meetings with the Grand Sanussi's cousin, Muhammad Idris as-Sanussi, who passed through Cairo after the attack, on his way home from a year-long pilgrimage to Mecca.

What changed everything was Italy's entry into the war and the Allies' failed landings at Gallipoli. These pivotal events provided the German agent Otto Mannesmann and the two Ottoman military advisors, Nouri Bey and Ja'far Pasha, with an opportunity to stimulate the avarice of the Sanussi leaders and they in turn persuaded Ahmed Sharif to revoke his friendship with Royle and assemble a force of 5,000 irregular troops in Marmarica, overlooking Sollum.

The audacious General Ja'far Pasha led this army. He had a distinguished record in the Dardanelles, where he had been awarded the Iron Cross, and twice had smuggled gold, weapons and ammunition to Libya under the noses of the British authorities (even posing for a studio photograph in Alexandria on 27 April). Now, he set about preparing the Grand Sanussi's army, with help from German military advisors, to invade Egypt and began by sending intelligence-gathering patrols across the frontier at night.

In Egypt, the deployment of the 42nd (East Lancashire) Division to Gallipoli had weakened General Maxwell's hand. Although the commander-in-chief was confident about the Suez Canal's security, he was still worried about a civilian uprising in Cairo. He felt it would not take much for the Muslim population to join the Holy War and required a large military force to police the country and prevent a major insurrection.

A doubt remained about the depth of loyalty of the Egyptian Army, which meant that it operated mainly in the Sudan. Maxwell's force was therefore made up of colonial regiments and British garrison battalions that comprised soldiers who were too old or unfit to serve in the A1 infantry. The Devonshire and Northamptonshire regiments both sent their garrison battalions to Egypt in October 1915, and they were joined by the Royal Scots and Royal Warwickshire battalions a few months later.

By November, the Allied situation in the war was not good. In France, the British Army had lost twice as many soldiers as Germany at the battle of Loos and failed to gain any significant territory. To add to this disappointment, King George was thrown from his chestnut mare on 28 October while visiting troops and suffered two fractures to his pelvis, from which "he was never quite the same man again".[15]

In the Balkans, the Serbian Army was losing ground to the Bulgarian Army, which was assisted by Austro-Hungary and Turkey. Greece was in turmoil, with the monarchy supporting Germany and the prime minister leaning towards the Allies. The British 10th Division was pinned down at Salonika defending the approaches, but it was exhausted from Gallipoli. There was talk about a Russo-Rumanian force attacking from the north, but the tsar's losses on the Eastern Front prevented this from happening.

In Tripolitania, the Italians were still licking their wounds after Colonel Miani's defeat at Misuratah and in Cyrenaica, the occupiers failed to control any territory beyond their chain of five fortified strongholds at Benghazi, Barce, Cyrene, Derna and Tobruk.[16] The British government was well aware of Italy's failings because the elegant and well-connected British ambassador in Rome, Sir James Rennell Rodd, regularly updated the Committee of Imperial Defence. On 24 October 1915, he sent a telegram, informing London that there were only "30,000,000 to 40,000,000 rounds of ammunition in Italy, which must be kept to supplement the supply in Libya, where the position was menacing".[17]

The attempted landing by HMS *Jonquil* at Bardia on 14 November gave Ja'far Pasha the excuse to launch incursions into Egypt and that night the Sanussi captured weapons from a guardpost at Sollum. Three nights later, 300 elite *Muhafizia*[18] occupied Sidi Barrani and attacked the Egyptian Coastguard detachment that was commanded by *Bimbashi* Mohamed Saleh Harb, a graduate of the Cairo military academy. The company of 135 men deserted their posts and later transferred their allegiance to the enemy, handing over 176 camels,[19] weapons and supplies in the process.

This attack 60 miles behind Colonel Snow left him in an untenable position and on 23 November, he evacuated the Sollum garrison on the SS *Rasheed*. This move to Mersa Matruh was so rushed that he had to leave behind his artillery and vehicles, which were disabled so the enemy could not use them. That afternoon, the Sanussi walked into Egypt unopposed and advanced in a chaotic move towards Sidi Barrani.[20]

The humiliating British withdrawal, together with Sanussi's occupation of the coastal area and the related unrest in Alexandria, led General Maxwell to recognise that a state of war now existed with the Sanussi. In response, he created the *ad hoc* Western Frontier Force and gave its command to 57-year-old Major General Alexander Wallace.

Hundreds of men assembled at Matruh from an extraordinarily broad spectrum of cultures. The composite infantry brigade under Brigadier Lord Lucan comprised a Royal Scots battalion, two Middlesex battalions and the 15th Sikhs.[21] Later on, they were joined by the fledgling New Zealand Rifles.

The cavalry brigade under Brigadier Julian Tyndale-Briscoe comprised three yeomanry regiments and a composite Australian Light Horse regiment, all of which were made up of reserves and reinforcements diverted from Gallipoli work. The Nottinghamshire Royal Horse Artillery provided the guns and the Egyptian Military Works force provided the engineers. A number of orphan units also joined the Force, including a battery of the Honourable Artillery Company, a Royal Marine detachment with two 4-inch guns, two Royal Flying Corps BE2c aircraft from 14 Squadron and a six-car detachment of Royal Naval Armoured Cars.

About 30 of the Australian regiment had fought in the Boer War, but many were novices who knew nothing about warfare let alone the technical aspects of operating as a cavalry force in the harsh desert.[22] The yeomanry regiments were made up of troopers from no less than 20 different regiments (there are 55 yeomanry regiments in the Army List of 1914), some of whom had fought as dismounted infantry at Gallipoli.[23] A few of the commanders had operational experience of the North West Frontier, but hardly any had seen action in a multinational, joint, combined arms grouping.

The journey to Matruh was no holiday. The insanitary railway box cars in which the soldiers travelled were full of fleas and the ride along the road was grim, with sweaty days and bitter nights. The bully beef and biscuits were old and the water was foul. Many soldiers were taken ill and the conditions did not improve when they arrived at Matruh. Squadron Sergeant Major Bill Cox from Reading wrote about life with the Berkshire Yeomanry on 30 November:

> We have been at this place since last Friday and it is about the most desolate spot one could imagine. We have nothing else except what we stand up in... the camp is surrounded by hills of sand and rock, and bushes of scrub. There is a little grove of palms to the east to relieve the desolation. There is only our regiment here, and we had to dig wells for water, which is the only means of getting it, and is like milk in colour. We have some tents now but had to sleep behind our horses before we got them, and we have been having awful weather for the last two days. Yesterday it started with a dust storm, which nearly blinded all of us; my eyes are awful, and then it started raining, and it is very cold; we want all our warm clothing.[24]

In the lull, both sides built up their capability. Ja'far Pasha organised the Sanussi into four brigades, each of four regiments comprising 400 men. At the front, he ordered the *Muhafizia* to close in on the British camp. As they approached Matruh in early December, the senior air observer, Brevet Major Arthur Ross, spotted their movement and reported it to General Wallace, who began offensive operations on 11 December.

His first plan was to send an infantry column west along the telegraph road to clear the enemy 15 miles away. This battle group was led by the commanding officer of the Sikhs, Lieutenant Colonel Jack Gordon. A second column, commanded by Major John Tyson Wigan, followed the Khedivial Road that had recently been built by the sultan. Wigan, who had recovered from severe wounds he received at Gallipoli, led 2nd Composite Yeomanry Regiment, with four armoured cars, two artillery guns and the Bikaner Camel Corps in tow. He had orders to sweep the enemy north towards the infantry and at dawn, his column set off with each man carrying 200 rounds of ammunition. Their guide was the veteran commander at Sollum, Lieutenant Colonel Cecil Snow.

After three hours without incident, the three squadrons stopped to water their horses. Wigan, who was originally commissioned in the 13th Hussars, sent the Royal Navy's armoured cars to the head of the column with the Buckinghamshire Hussars. He deployed the Berkshire Yeomanry on the right and the Queen's Own Dorset Yeomanry on the left.

The regiment spread out in the broken ground, but the pace of the horses meant that they missed the enemy and were ambushed in the flank at about 11 a.m. The Berkshire squadron, commanded by Major Edward Foster, hooked around the enemy and charged at what they believed was a section position. Unfortunately, they repeated the mistake of the 21st Lancers at Omdurman and tumbled into a much larger force in the dead ground that led straight into the waiting Sanussi battalion at Wadi Majid.

Cavalry tactics had changed after the Boer War and horsemen were now expected to dismount and use their firepower, rather than stay in the saddle. Trapped in the gully, the yeomen had to fight for their lives as they were engaged by a well-organised adversary. They were severely outnumbered and began taking heavy casualties. Corporal Thornhill from Wantage was wounded in the leg and wrote afterwards: "When we got to the top we charged and as soon as they started we came under a hail of bullets on all sides. We got to within about 10 yards of the enemy who were in another gully and would not move. I moved to the right and got mine."[25]

One of the troop leaders, John Ressich, was shot in the chest and arm and through his shin. As his unflappable troop sergeant, Sam Chanel, assumed command, Ressich was helped to shelter behind some rocks by two dismounted yeomen, whose horses had also fallen from under them. Before passing out, he gave one of the soldiers his revolver and ammunition and told them to use it like a rifle. Three times he woke up to hear them defend the position with accurate fire against approaching enemy. Somehow, he survived and was stretchered from the battlefield into an ambulance and evacuated to hospital in Alexandria.

John Wigan, who after the war became the Member of Parliament for Abingdon, saw the plight of his regiment. He directed the armoured cars to support Foster and sent the Dorset Yeomanry to turn the flank of the enemy. No quarter was given in the hand-to-hand fighting, which continued for four hours, but eventually, with the Royal Navy's fire support, Foster was able to extricate his troops from the gully.

Meanwhile, the Buckinghamshire squadron, reinforced by the Australian Light Horse, fought a running battle with the Sanussi as it withdrew from the area. By 3 p.m. the battle was over, the dead were being buried and the wounded were returning to Matruh in ambulances. Sadly, the valiant Colonel Snow was killed when he attempted to talk with a Bedouin hiding in the wadi. Almost all the other 16 who died were in Foster's squadron, including 11 Berkshire, two Warwickshire and two Surrey yeomen.[26] The dead included 30-year-old Bill Cox whose last words, remembered by his successor William Bond, were: "Stick it youngster. Ride straight and let them have it." The youngest soldier to die was 18-year-old Trooper Fred North from Hungerford whose possessions, including a wallet slashed by a sword, were presented to his parents on Christmas Day.[27]

With 50 per cent casualties and incredible acts of courage and sacrifice, it is curious that the Berkshire Yeomanry were not recognised officially for their exploits. Their war record was exemplified by Trooper Fred Potts, who earned the first Victoria Cross awarded to a yeoman for "most conspicuous bravery in rescuing a comrade under heavy fire" at Gallipoli. However, the deeds of their squadron in this first battle of the Sanussi Campaign seem to have been unfairly neglected.

The only decoration earned by a soldier was awarded to Trooper Constable from the village of Faringdon, who though wounded twice refused to leave the battlefield and attended to the horses. This was a deserving award, but what about the soldiers who saved the life of their troop leader, John Ressich? Only three months earlier, on 5 September, Shoeing Smith Charles Hull of the 21st Lancers was awarded the Victoria Cross for rescuing his adjutant, whose horse had been killed during a battle in the Khyber Pass, and three Distinguished Conduct Medals were awarded in the same action to soldiers rescuing comrades under fire.

The fact that no journalists accompanied the Western Frontier Force when the fighting began possibly contributed to the lack of recognition. Eventually, two war correspondents attached to the Mediterranean Expeditionary Force joined the fray and the awards began to flow. One of the reporters was William Massey, who later wrote a book about the campaign that criticised the neglect and "lack of knowledge of the Army's work in Egypt".[28]

By then, the Berkshire Yeomanry had been withdrawn, but it used its hard-earned experience at the second battle of Gaza in April 1917, when John Wigan, who had been promoted to lieutenant colonel and awarded the Distinguished Service Order (DSO), led the regiment in a decisive charge and one of the officers who faced the Sanussi, Major Philip Wroughton, the much-loved commander of D (Wantage) Squadron, was fatally wounded by Turkish shellfire.

* * *

Meanwhile, Colonel Gordon established a secure base at Umm er Rakham, where the yeomanry bivouacked for the night. The next day they rested the exhausted horses while a local patrol captured 25 prisoners. One of the Royal Flying Corps aircraft spotted a large force of Sanussi seven miles south-west, so Gordon, who was now reinforced by two companies of Royal Scots, gave orders for an advance to Wadi Hasheifat.

In the morning, the cavalry led the battle group out of camp with a company of Sikhs in the vanguard. Forty-five minutes later, after crossing Wadi Shaifa, Gordon saw the Scots platoon on the left flank retreating under fire from the fearsome *Muhafizia*. The Sikhs bravely blunted the enemy's advance but lost four of their soldiers in the process and as the situation became perilous, Gordon called for reinforcements from his base camp.

A makeshift reserve formed by the Australian Service Corps and the Royal Scots machine-gun section responded courageously to prevent the enemy from overrunning the position. The battle now became a stalemate as the two sides settled into an artillery and machine-gun duel that lasted for most of the day. The turning point came when HMS *Clematis* arrived in the afternoon and one of their shells exploded among a group of Sanussi on the high ground.

Ja'far Pasha began to thin out his forces and withdraw into the desert. Colonel Gordon did not have enough men to pursue the enemy, so he returned to camp with the nine dead and 56 wounded, who were loaded onto HMS *Clematis*. The next day, the British force marched back to Matruh and reported on their expedition to the waiting commander.

They had learned that the Sanussi were an effective, well-drilled foe. If the overall result was a draw, the fierce hand-to-hand fighting destroyed any complacency and shattered the perception that this would be a cake-walk against a primitive enemy. The lack of a decisive victory failed to boost the prestige of the British, but General Wallace could take comfort in the performance of the Sikhs, yeomanry and Australians as well as the Royal Navy's guns.

Fighting patrols and sniping continued for 10 days as the wet weather turned the low ground into a sea of mud. Ja'far Pasha established a brigade-sized base with mountain guns and machine guns on Jebel Medwa about six miles from Matruh. He had 2,000 regulars and another 3,000 auxiliaries, which included women and children camp followers. Wallace realised he had to strike before the Sanussi became too strong and early on Christmas Day he launched another expedition, but this time with two brigades in the field.

In the absence of Lord Lucan, Colonel Gordon again commanded the infantry column on the right, which comprised Sikh, New Zealand and Middlesex battalions, while Brigadier Tyndale-Biscoe commanded the mobile column on the left. Lieutenant Douglas Newbold, who later explored the Libyan desert with Ralph Bagnold and was knighted for his work in the Sudan, saw his first military action as the commander of the machine-gun section of the Dorset Yeomanry. After a rough night when the camp was kept awake by frequent enemy sniping, Newbold saddled his guns and moved off with the left-hand column at 4.45 a.m.

While the infantry headed straight to the enemy position, the cavalry climbed the escarpment through Wadi Toweiwia, but were delayed as their artillery had to be dragged with ropes up the steep sides. The day belonged to Gordon who took the heights and routed the Sanussi with more effective gunfire from HMS *Clematis* and the Royal Horse Artillery under the 48-year-old Olympian, Major Joe Laycock.[29] The two columns did not link up until late afternoon and with the problems of weather, terrain and water, Gordon decided not to pursue the enemy.

Newbold, who spent 14 hours in the saddle, describes rare examples of war crimes in his diary when he later found the stripped body of a captured New Zealand soldier, who was "one bruise from head to foot" after had been "evidently flogged to death".[30] He also reports on the significant haul of arms, ammunition and barley, as well as "proclamations in Arabic, printed in Constantinople, urging all Mohammedans to combine against the British". This loss of food, more than the weapons, led Ja'far Pasha to move south, out of range of the naval guns and establish a base deep in the desert, while the exhausted Allied troops recovered in Matruh.

* * *

Meanwhile at Bir Hakeim, the British prisoners of war had suffered for almost a month trying to survive the gales, sandstorms and meagre rations. The sailors had supplemented their food with snails that trailed around the well, but the refined captain could not bring himself to indulge in this delicacy. The officers saved some of their rations and did their best to celebrate Christmas with a special dinner. The highlight was a 20-pound suet pudding that took five hours to cook and kept them quiet for 20 minutes.

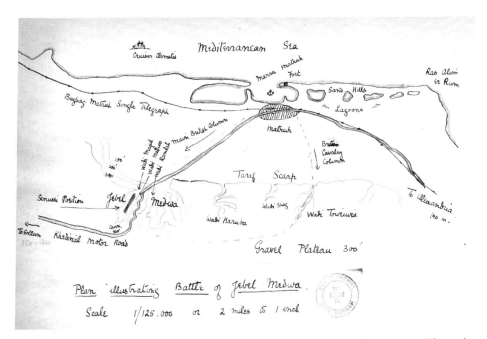

Battle of Jebel Medwa 1915. Douglas Newbold's sketch of the battle fought on Christmas Day. The result was in the balance until the accurate gunfire of HMS *Clematis* gave victory to the Allies. (Reproduced by kind permission of Durham University Library and Collections—Newbold Archive)

In the evening, they sang uplifting carols led by the melodious voice of Captain Tanner, who had an infinite memory of songs and hymns. Later that night, Gwatkins-Williams was woken by the sound of howling women in the Sanussi tents. A messenger had arrived with news of the casualties from the first battle and in response to the losses, their dependents began a customary mourning.

On Boxing Day, the sullen guards looked menacingly at the prisoners, but took no action. None of the prisoners had died since William Thomas, but many suffered from dysentery and malnutrition. Discipline was upheld quite simply with the threat of handing over any guilty man to the Sanussi, whose punishments escalated from the lash to the severing of a hand.

Morale was harder to maintain. They survived through faith and friendship, satire and song, and of course Paddy. Prisoners were allowed to wander about a mile from the camp to collect brushwood for the fire and anything that might be useful. In the evening, they dumped this outside their accommodation, but by the morning, the pile had usually shrunk.

At first, they believed their guards were pilfering the supply. Paddy had caught one of them red-handed and sunk his teeth into the offender's fingers. However, it turned out that the chief culprits were the two donkeys belonging to Holy Joe. Paddy was on friendly terms with the equines and allowed them to eat the daily collection, but to add insult to injury, the donkeys tried to knock down the officers' tent when the pile of brushwood was moved inside.

Very heavy rains arrived on 3 January, and this precipitated the demise of the weakest sailors. The first to die was 57-year-old Artificer George Cox on 5 January, followed five days later by 49-year-old Seaman John Hodgson. Gwatkins-Williams worried that they had been abandoned, but on 17 January, two Indians from HMT *Moorina* arrived and gave them news of the Christmas Day victory at Jebel Medwa. They had been employed as camel drivers by the Sanussi; however, after 31 of the company escaped, these two Rajputs were marched to Bir Hakeim. News of the Allied success lifted the prisoners' spirits, but they would have been heartened even more had they known that General Wallace had responded to the enemy's peace overtones by exclaiming there will be "no peace until *Tara* prisoners are released".

* * *

At Matruh, the army camp resembled a quagmire as the tents were flooded and the mud oozed into the food and water. The navy's armoured cars could not cope and were withdrawn to Alexandria, but the BE2c aircraft continued to search for Ja'far's base and finally on 19 January, Lieutenant Reggie Rowden and Leo Royle, who had transferred from the Egyptian Coastguard to the Royal Flying Corps, discovered a large tented camp at Halazin.

Royle reported that there were 250 Bedouin and 100 European tents in the enemy camp. General Wallace waited until he was reinforced by a South African battalion and the Hong Kong and Singapore Mountain Battery before he launched another large multinational force on 22 January, with Scots and Sikhs, Aussies and Kiwis, Egyptian and British Yeomen.

The weather was bad, and the going was soft. The sea of mud made the job of hauling the artillery and supplies even more demanding than in December. For the third time, Jack Gordon commanded the infantry column and Brigadier Tyndale-Biscoe again led the cavalry, which had to camp four miles from the objective, due to the slow progress of the main column.

At 9 a.m. the next day the yeomanry were in the field and soon came under fire on the left of the British force. They had learned from the mistakes in December when the columns were too far apart and now in the open ground, they co-ordinated their actions more effectively. The Sikhs again bore the brunt of the fighting and formed the backbone of the formation, but the 1st New Zealand and 2nd South African battalions both fought well, with accurate fire support provided by Laycock's guns.

The critical moment arrived when the Sanussi launched a counter-attack on the right and pushed the Royal Buckinghamshire Hussars and Queen's Own Dorset Yeomanry squadrons back towards Wallace's headquarters. Fortunately, two companies of New Zealanders steadied the line and repelled the enemy with "invincible dash and resolution".[31] For five hours the intense fighting continued until at last, the Sikhs broke through the lines and caused a general retreat. It was another decisive victory, but the general could not pursue the enemy because the horses were exhausted, and the troops were at the limit of their supply line.

With 31 dead and 291 wounded, it took another two days for the column to return to Matruh. Each stretcher was carried by 12 men, who rotated regularly and laboured through the clawing mud for six miles before they reached the ambulances.

Back on the coast, another reorganisation took place with the replacement of the Sikhs[32] and New Zealand Rifles by the 1st South African Brigade, commanded by Brigadier Henry Lukin. The appearance of 2,000 camels to carry supplies also extended the range of operations beyond their previous radius of 25 miles. Another arrival was Major Hugh Grosvenor, 2nd Duke of Westminster, who had taken over the Royal Navy's armoured cars with a group of yeomanry and cavalry volunteers.

General Maxwell travelled from Cairo to congratulate the troops and decide on the next course of action. He was offered two options; the first was an amphibious landing and the second was an overland expedition. Both had significant drawbacks. The port at Sollum was mined and overlooked by Hellfire Pass; whereas the debilitating march along the coast would require a huge logistic tail because there was little water and forage available locally.

The Royal Navy offered full assistance to Maxwell, but the commander-in-chief chose the land option and agreed with the ailing Wallace that he would hand over to Major General William Peyton. As a former commanding officer of the 15th Hussars, who had led the 2nd Mounted Division at Gallipoli, 49-year-old Peyton was well acquainted with the yeomanry regiments in the Western Frontier Force.

He also knew how to manoeuvre cavalry on the battlefield, so he was ideal for the next phase of the campaign.

The situation became more complicated when the Sanussi launched an advance in southern Egypt and captured Bahariya oasis two days after Peyton arrived at Matruh. General Maxwell was forced to create a new command under Major General John Adye, but nevertheless maintained his main effort in the north, where Peyton began his advance along the coast.

On the same day that Germany launched one of the longest and bloodiest battles of World War I at Verdun, air reconnaissance reported a large Sanussi position at Agagia. On 26 February, the steadfast Brigadier Lukin engaged the forward elements of the enemy and advanced against the main force. Ja'far Pasha used the same tactics as before and launched a counter-attack on the right, but Lukin was ready for this and easily blocked the move. Ja'far decided to withdraw and gave orders for a move towards Sollum; this provided Peyton with the opportunity to release the Dorset Yeomanry under Lieutenant Colonel Hugh Souter.

Souter was originally commissioned into the Manchester Regiment and then served with the Jat Lancers in Tibet. On 26 February he had taken up a position on high ground to the right of Peyton's force and at about 1 p.m. received a message from the general "to pursue and cut off the enemy if possible".[33] He decided not to intercept the column immediately, in case there were wire and obstacles in the broken ground around their camp.

For two hours he tracked their movement until he could see the whole array which stretched for about a mile with a depth of 300 to 400 yards. He dismounted the regiment to rest the horses while he examined the ground. In front of him lay a "slightly undulating plain of firm sand with low tufts of scrub about six or eight inches high".[34]

It was a bold but calculated decision to gallop with swords drawn against an overwhelming enemy of 3,000 troops, wielding four Maxim machine guns. The regiment rode in two ranks with eight yards between each mount in the front file. Souter gave the order to charge about 50 yards from the enemy "and with one yell the Dorsets hurled themselves upon the enemy".

Frenzied yeomen slashed left and right with their swords as the enemy fired at them at close range. Lieutenant Cedric Tamplin, who was born in St Petersburg, needed all his experience riding with wolves in the Russian forests to stay on his horse as he galloped through the Turkish-led flank guard. He only just managed to hold onto his sabre as it bent double when he thrust it into a huge rifleman. Turning back into the carnage, he drove away a group of Sanussi that were threatening the wounded yeomen, who had fallen from their mounts.

Lieutenant John Blaksley was a troop leader in B Squadron, which took the greatest punishment on the right. He had two horses shot from under him and in the *mêlée* was joined by Trooper William Brown in the same predicament. Blaksley had to use his revolver at close quarters, but suddenly found that a group of senior officers were surrendering to him, including Ja'far Pasha, who was wounded in his right arm from a sabre slash.

Colonel Souter also had his horse shot from under him and after he recovered saw Ja'far kneeling before Blaksley. He dashed over and thrust his revolver in the enemy's face, telling him to wave away the other Sanussi. Calling for an escort, he sent the captive commander, under guard, to General Peyton's headquarters.

Blaksley's troop was particularly hard hit. Out of his troop of 17 men, 11 were killed and one was wounded. This was more than a third of the total deaths suffered by the regiment (which included General Peyton's aide de camp, Captain John Bengough of the Royal Gloucestershire Hussars).[35]

After the battle, the South African Brigade occupied Sidi Barrani and for the next three days the Allied soldiers saw large groups of Arabs returning to their homes, carrying white flags, many of them with their heads and arms bandaged. The Dorset Yeomanry recovered their dead and built a cairn on the battlefield to commemorate their fallen comrades.

Whereas the Berkshires had received no recognition in December, Peyton wrote up the Dorsets well. Sixteen members of the regiment were mentioned in General Maxwell's next despatch to Lord Kitchener. Souter was awarded the Distinguished Service Order, while George Dammers, Reginald Gordon and John Blaksley all received the Military Cross. There were also eight Distinguished Conduct Medals awarded to soldiers ranging from Squadron Sergeant Major Gibbs to young Private Ashley.

Peyton did not wish to pause, but before he could continue the advance, he needed to replenish his troops and establish a logistics base, which took the best part of two weeks at Sidi Barrani. He knew all about the dangers of an over-watched position from his experience at Gallipoli and that he needed to clear the high ground to the west of Sollum as a preliminary operation before its capture. While building up his strength, he was delighted to welcome the Cavalry Corps Motor Machine-Gun Battery, with 17 light armoured cars and 21 motorbikes.

It was not feasible to assault up Hellfire Pass and so on 9 March, Peyton instructed Brigadier Lukin, with the South African infantry, to march 20 miles south and ascend the Median Pass. The Duke of Westminster provided an armoured car escort up the steep slope and by 14 March, Lukin was in control of the fort at Capuzzo with the Hong Kong guns and a company of the Camel Corps providing close support. The yeomanry held the lower part of Hellfire Pass and this enabled General Peyton to enter Sollum unopposed.

On finding the port empty, he instructed the Duke of Westminster to pursue the enemy into Libya. Driving at speeds up to 40 miles per hour, the duke's force found the main body 20 miles west of Sollum near to Sidi Azeiz. The appearance of the British armour was too much for the enemy, who fled into the desert, allowing the duke's raiding party to capture all the artillery and machine guns, as well as 40 prisoners.

Back in Sollum, Captain Leo Royle (who was the nephew of Colonel Snow) had taken over the intelligence section and interviewed the Sanussi captives. He discovered that the *Tara* prisoners were still being held in the desert and after deliberating for some time, General Peyton decided on a rescue attempt. However, the problem he faced was that no one knew the location of Bir Hakeim.

* * *

While the British were fighting 200 miles to the east, the prisoners of war were wilting fast. The strong did their best to look after the weak, but on 28 January, a 52-year-old engineer, Lieutenant Robert John Seaborn Williams of the Royal Naval Reserve, died of dysentery and on 19 February, the youngest so far, 28-year-old Owen Roberts died of the combined effects of starvation, dysentery and consumption.[36]

On 20 February, Rupert Gwatkins-Williams made an attempt at escape, but he was captured and returned a week later. He suffered a public beating from the guards and a lashing by Holy Joe; even the women were allowed to throw stones at his face as he was thrown into solitary confinement in a sheep pen. After dark, however, the guards took pity on him and provided mats to sleep on, as well as clothes, water and dates. An hour later, "a bright-eyed merry little boy" named Mahmood held out a huge bowl of rice and a guard offered him a cigarette.

As March unfolded, the food store emptied for the prisoners and their keepers. Promised supplies failed to materialise and on Sunday 12 March, they all "felt the end was very near. The spectre of death by starvation stared us in the face, and I think we looked back unafraid."[37]

About 30 of the men were sick, so a mass attempt to reach Tobruk was out of the question. They were all barefoot and too weak to trek more than 10 miles in a day. A message came through to fetch supplies from El Zebla, so on the morning of 15 March, Leslie Dudgeon and Basil left by camel. Two days later, the prisoners woke on St Patrick's Day and set about their normal routine. In the afternoon at 3 p.m. Gwatkins-Williams was catching up on his diary when he heard someone shout: "There's a motor car coming!" At first he believed it was Dudgeon with the long-promised supplies, but as he walked out of the tent, he saw to his astonishment that there were dozens of vehicles driving into camp.

* * *

The rescue operation was entrusted to the Duke of Westminster. Captain Royle volunteered to join the attempt and found as a guide, a one-eyed Sanussi named Achmed, who appeared to be the only person in Sollum to have been to Bir Hakeim.

Every wheeled vehicle that worked in the port was requisitioned into a fleet of ambulances that was manhandled up Hellfire Pass by hundreds of volunteers, who heard about the rescue mission. On 16 March, they toiled all day, hauling petrol, water, medical equipment, food and clothing up the steep slope, and by midnight had loaded everything aboard the ambulances, which were joined by the Duke's armoured cars.

The convoy of 43 vehicles set off three hours later and drove to Sidi Azeiz, where they waited for the first streaks of sunlight to heat their backs. The course was set along the Trigh Capuzzo, which would see thousands of tanks fighting along its dusty track 25 years later. Royle estimated that it was 65 miles to Bir Hakeim, but as a precaution, they had loaded sufficient fuel for almost twice that distance.

About 65 miles down the road, beyond Sidi Rezegh, they passed the amenable Doctor Fouad travelling in a camel caravan, but did not take him prisoner. By this point, their progress had slowed to 12 miles per hour due to the stops for punctures and navigation checks. The doubtful drivers were becoming anxious about the fuel when suddenly Achmed jumped from a moving car and shouted to the duke to stop.

Their one-eyed guide had recognised a lone fig tree marking an old well and knelt at its base to thank Allah. Ten miles further, Cyclops spied what no one else could see: five tents on the horizon. The duke sent a reconnaissance party to check for enemy and hearing their yells, the whole convoy accelerated into Bir Hakeim, causing the guards to flee from the camp.[38]

Tears of joy! Are we free? Smiles which wouldn't "come off"; tins of chicken and bully-beef; cans of milk; bread and marmalade; prayers answered; faith restored; hope rewarded. The naked were clothed in blue hospital suits and the sick were carried carefully to the vehicles.

That evening, the freed prisoners were driven to Sidi Azeiz, where they slept soundly. The following day, General Peyton welcomed them to Sollum, which they had not seen for over four months. However, their loudest cheer was saved for the moment they boarded the boats that ferried them to the SS *Rasheed*.

Before departing for Alexandria, where they were reunited with Basil and Dudgeon who had been freed at Tobruk, there was one final sad task for Gwatkins-Williams to complete. It was decided that their faithful fox-terrier-pug, who had helped them so cheerfully throughout the ordeal, could not accompany them home. However, the Duke of Westminster's armoured car brigade needed a mascot and so, with much hugging and patting, the heavy-hearted captain said farewell to Paddy and handed him over to their saviours.

The duke was awarded an immediate DSO, which was published in the *London Gazette* on 28 March. Other gallantry decorations for the Sanussi Campaign were announced on 3 June in the King's Birthday Honours. About 20 members of the rescue party were awarded medals, including Military Crosses for Royle,[39] the Duke's deputy Ernest Bald (who later earned notoriety for his involvement in the Prince of Wales' affairs)[40] and the first-class cricketer, Lieutenant John Leslie of the 12th Royal Lancers.[41]

The soldiers were not forgotten either. Sergeant Sam Roshier of the 17th Lancers, attached to 3rd Light Armoured Car Battery, was awarded the Distinguished Conduct Medal. He was later commissioned as a lieutenant in his regiment and commanded in both 3rd and 4th Light Car Patrols. Eleven other DCMs were awarded to soldiers in the cavalry, light armoured car batteries, or Army Service Corps.[42]

General Peyton was livid that his Victoria Cross citations for Colonel Souter and the Duke of Westminster were down-graded and subsequently wrote several letters that revealed the secrets of the War Office honours committee. He later commented to Souter: "I appealed personally both to Lord Kitchener and His Majesty when they were good enough to give me audience. Both agreed that your performance was a good VC case but gave the same reason about the standard in France… Apparently, the Army in France is very jealous of honours given elsewhere."[43]

It was well known that there was World War I snobbery that suggested the "real war" was fought against the German strongholds on the Western Front and that all the side shows were somehow easier. The "six Victoria Crosses before breakfast" awarded to soldiers of the Lancashire Fusiliers at Cape Helles in April 1915 might have earned grudging respect, but there were many other deserving cases that did not receive their due recognition, including the two Hughs, Souter and Grosvenor.

On 19 March 1916, General Maxwell handed over command in Egypt to General Sir Archibald Murray who had instructions from London to combine the Cairo Headquarters with the Mediterranean Expeditionary Force. In writing his final despatch to the secretary of state, Maxwell claimed that he was confident that Peyton had eradicated the menace of the Sanussi from the coast. However, although the north was clear, the threat to the south had increased and the first tasks the new commander-in-chief had to address were the enemy-held oases and the spiritual influence of the Grand Sanussi, who was still active in Siwa.

* * *

Placed within the historical context of events in France, the four battles against the Sanussi during the winter of 1915-16 may seem no more than an isolated "little war" (as suggested in a letter by T. E. Lawrence). However, in his *magnum opus* on World War I, Professor Hew Strachan concludes: "the tactical ingredients which brought success in the eastern desert and Syria in 1917-18 found their origins in the Western Desert and Libya in 1915–16".[44] There was certainly a strong link, if not a continuum between the two campaigns as Peyton's staff compiled a huge amount of relevant advice that was used by General Allenby in Palestine. However, understanding the value of aircraft and armoured cars, which Lawrence called "more valuable than rubies", was not the only inheritance from this campaign.

Looking at the war from the strategic perspective of Anglo-Libyan relations, there are two important aspects that can help those looking to assist Libya move forward in the 21st century. The first stems from the practical nature of the relationship, which was based on freedom, defence and security. After defeating the Sanussi, Britain had no interest in occupying Libya, but by earning their respect (despite the over-exuberance of some of the *Tara* rescuers) laid the foundation for their allegiance in World War II and the Treaty of Friendship that was signed in 1953. These same elements formed the basis of the successful Anglo-Libyan alliance in the 21st century and should be at the heart of any future relationship.

The second aspect is in the way Leo Royle developed a unique friendship with the Grand Sanussi. By sharing the hardships of the desert, displaying the skills that impressed the Bedouin and understanding the cultural and religious nuances of the Senussi, he should be held up as an outstanding model for those who wish to live and work in Libya. However, Royle was not the only British exemplar in this respect, as a renowned Royal Geographical Society gold medal winner was about to embark on a secret peace mission to woo the Grand Sanussi's cousin, the future King Idris.

Khedivial Road: the Sanussi Campaign was characterised by the alliance of old and new mobility with armoured cars fighting alongside camel troops. (Reproduced by kind permission of Durham University Library and Collections—Newbold Archive)

Sidi Barrani: unloading stores for the Western Frontier Force in 1915. HMS *Clematis* is the ship on the right of the picture. (Reproduced by kind permission of Durham University Library and Collections—Newbold Archive)

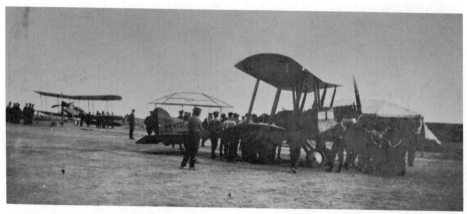

Air War: this pair of 14 Squadron's BE2c aircraft, flown by officers of the Royal Flying Corps, proved indispensable to the commander-in-chief for identifying where the Sanussi camped in the desert. (Reproduced by kind permission of Durham University Library and Collections—Newbold Archive)

Memorial: the cairn built by the Queen's Own Dorset Yeomanry after their decisive cavalry charge at Agagia. The left-hand cross commemorates John Bengough of the Royal Gloucestershire Hussars, aide de camp of Major General William Peyton. (Reproduced by kind permission of Durham University Library and Collections—Newbold Archive)

Ja'far Pasha, the wounded commander of the Sanussi army, following his capture at the Battle of Agagia on 26 February 1916. (Reproduced by kind permission of Durham University Library and Collections—Newbold Archive)

Sollum, looking towards Libya. This port changed hands nine times in World War II. (Reproduced by kind permission of Durham University Library and Collections—Newbold Archive)

The armoured Rolls-Royce of the 2nd Duke of Westminster, after his daring mission to Bir Hakeim that rescued the Royal Navy prisoners of war. (Reproduced by kind permission of the 7th Duke of Westminster)

Squadron Sergeant Major Bill Cox of the Berkshire Yeomanry, who died in the first cavalry charge of the campaign on 11 December 1915. His final words were: "Ride straight and let them have it." (Reproduced by kind permission of the Berkshire Yeomanry Museum)

John Tyson Wigan earned a DSO for leading the 2nd Composite Yeomanry Regiment in the Sanussi Campaign. He was originally commissioned into the 13th Hussars and was wounded at Gallipoli, but later commanded the Berkshire Yeomanry in a decisive charge at the Second Battle of Gaza. After the war, he was elected Member of Parliament for Abingdon. (Reproduced by kind permission of the Berkshire Yeomanry Museum)

Major General William Peyton was the commander of the Western Frontier Force in February 1916 and led it to victory at the decisive battle of Agagia. He was livid that his two citations for the Victoria Cross were watered down by the Honours Committee in London and appealed to the king and Lord Kitchener, but the only result was his posting as General Haig's military secretary in Flanders. (Picture courtesy of the Light Dragoons)

CHAPTER 6

Talbot of Tobruk

Colonel Talbot's personality and wise counsel have sensibly influenced the attitude of Sayed Idris to the proposals of our Allies and have contributed very materially to the successful issue of these negotiations.

SIR REGINALD WINGATE, HIGH COMMISSIONER FOR EGYPT, WRITING TO THE
FOREIGN SECRETARY ARTHUR BALFOUR IN 1917[1]

After the rescue of the *Tara* prisoners and the capture of Ja'far Pasha, the elders of the Awlad Ali tribes, who lived along the Egyptian coast, made their peace with the British victors and pleaded for food for their families. Meanwhile in Cairo, General Murray produced a plan to defeat the Sanussi in the south. The new commander-in-chief had been at the centre of the war in France with the British Expeditionary Force and briefly became chief of the Imperial General Staff, before handing over to General "Wully" Robertson, the main advocate of the "single front" policy that relegated the campaigns in Egypt and Mesopotamia to "side shows".

Murray's critics (including Field Marshal Haig) suggested he was not practical, but had a studious mind and, after Robertson ordered him to send a quarter of a million soldiers from Egypt to France, he realised that he had to use an indirect approach to defeating the Ottoman Empire. Before authorising Captain T. E. Lawrence to assist the Arab Revolt in the east, he agreed to a similar mission to win over the Sanussi leadership in the west. But first he had to contain the incursion in the south and recapture the four oases that were in enemy hands.

The general had to look after HRH The Prince of Wales as a staff captain in his headquarters from 18 March until his departure on 1 May 1916.[2] The prince was friends with several heroes of the Sanussi campaign, including the Duke of Westminster, and spent a lot of time luxuriating in Cairo, but he was also there when the Western Frontier Force was split into two halves, with the boundary drawn east to west through Deirut, 350 miles south of the coast.

In the northern sector, Murray sent raiding parties into Libya to capture arms and ammunition. On 7 April a detachment of four armoured cars and the machine-gun section of 2nd/7th Middlesex Regiment crossed the frontier and attacked a platoon of *Muhafizia* at Moraisa, 18 miles from Sollum. After a brief battle, the British captured 21 boxes of artillery shells and 120,000 rounds of small-arms ammunition.

British diplomats persuaded the Italians to occupy Bardia, in order to strengthen the blockade on the Sanussi. Meanwhile, British soldiers driving armoured cars captured two camel convoys with weapons at El Alamein and British administrators set up food markets in Mersa Matruh and other Bedouin villages to win the hearts and minds of the local population.

In the south-west, Murray reoccupied Khargah oasis without a fight on 15 April and established a line of blockhouses along the Darb-el-Rubi camel track in May. In the heat of the summer, he undertook a gruelling project to extend the railway line to Bahariya, while the Imperial Camel Corps patrolled the desert between the oases "under especially trying conditions".[3]

General Peyton's dubious reward for making a fuss about the Victoria Cross demotions was to become Sir Douglas Haig's military secretary in Flanders. Unfortunately, his successor in the Western Frontier Force was invalided home with severe sunstroke and after a succession of short-term placements, Major General Arthur Watson took over on 4 October 1916.

Watson set about concluding the campaign and before Christmas, his light armoured car and camel patrols retook the oases. As the Grand Sanussi retreated with his devout followers to Siwa, the British conducted conciliatory *durbars* with the tribal elders and offered food and supplies. Ahmed Sharif still maintained authority over the vast Libyan desert, but by now many of his supporters were transferring allegiance to his 27-year-old cousin, Muhammad Idris bin Muhammad al-Mahdi as-Sanussi.

* * *

At the political level, the high commissioner for Egypt, Hugh McMahon, was collaborating with Reginald Wingate, who had returned from the Sudan to head the Hejaz operations. Wingate had previously been director of Military Intelligence and in this role, he had established a good relationship with Idris' father, the former Grand Sanussi, through British agents at Jaghbub and Kufra.

When he died in 1902, the title of Grand Sanussi had passed to his nephew, Ahmed Sharif, because 12-year-old Idris was considered too young to lead the Order. However, Idris had now grown to be a dignified leader and favoured a rapprochement with Britain having established good relations with McMahon on his way back from the Hajj. He maintained a secret dialogue with Wingate throughout his cousin's campaign after he was approached to mediate when the *Tara* prisoners were captured.[4]

After the successful rescue operation, McMahon and Wingate pursued this relationship and gave an experienced Arabist, Colonel Milo Talbot of the Royal

Engineers, a mission to entice Idris to the peace table. Talbot was an outstanding surveyor, who had spent many years mapping two of the most inhospitable countries on Earth, Afghanistan and Sudan. As a renowned explorer and diplomat, he was awarded the Royal Geographical Society's Patron's Medal in 1909 for his topographical work and the government used his "exceptional ability" on several commissions before and during the war, for which he was made a Companion of the Order of the Bath (CB).[5]

On 25 May 1916, he boarded an Italian ship in secret at Alexandria accompanied by an Oxford-educated Egyptian nobleman, Hassanein Bey. Avoiding the German submarine threat, they circuitously travelled to Rome because Wingate knew the British ambassador, Rennell Rodd, from their successful Abyssinian mission together in 1897 and understood that Italy was the key to ending the Sanussi war. In Rome, Talbot obtained the services of a Royal Naval Reserve officer, William Heywood Haslam, and together they travelled to the Gulf of Sirte and set up quarters at Zuwetina, an Italian fort 60 miles south of Benghazi.

Idris had his camp 20 miles away at Ajdabiya and during the next month, he developed a cordial friendship with Talbot. These negotiations resulted in an Anglo-Italian Agreement that established six main provisions, of which the most important were that neither Britain nor Italy would make a separate peace with the Sanussi and that Idris would be recognised as the spiritual head of the "confraternity".[6]

The agreement that was signed in July avoided the most contentious issue between Italy and Britain, which was the question of the Libyan-Egyptian border that had festered for many years.[7] This spirit of co-operation had positive results. Apart from the Italian move into Bardia, the Royal Navy conducted a number of combined patrols along the coast and in October, attacked Nouri Bey's camp at Agheila, 32 miles west of Tobruk.

Talbot provided Cairo with details of Idris' letter to the Grand Sanussi, criticising him for the strategic mistakes and blaming Ja'far Pasha's campaign for the blockade that was crippling the country, so that fellow Muslims were cursing the name of Sanussi. His wide-ranging epistle exposed the weakness of the Turks and their puppet in Tripoli, Sulayman al-Baruni:

Sir, look at the Sheriff Husein, Emir of Mecca, who was made by the Turks. He saw that his interest and the interest of his country required him to go against them. He proclaimed his independence, and asked the approval of the Allied Governments (which he obtained), and now he is the King of the Arabs. He is now arranging his Government, such as the formation of Cabinets and other things. If he had entered the war with the Turks, the Allies would have been occupying his country as they now occupy Basrah and other towns...

How can the Turks enter Egypt after they have failed to retake Hejaz? After being near the Canal, they have today retired from el-Arish, and the English have occupied Rafa, and are striking at the Hejaz railway to cut it, as those who can read maps will inform you if you do not know. Don't you see the Seyyid [sic] of the Yemen who is still independent and did not commit himself, though the English tried to convince you to fight...You might have done like him before the affair of Sollum. The government and the English were in your hand. Regret is now useless. I draw your attention to the Islamic world, which desires to know you. You must look for what is to our advantage and that of our country, so that we may not be sacrificed for others.[8]

This letter was a crucial piece of intelligence that helped to persuade General Murray that a strike at Siwa was feasible, but first, he had to consider the strategic viewpoint in London.

* * *

In Britain, 1916 was a year of ever-increasing strain, danger and disappointment. While the battle of Verdun was "bleeding the French Army white", the Easter Rising in Dublin on 26 April changed the assumption that the Irish would support the Allies. Three days later, the disaster at Kut, where 13,000 British soldiers were marched into captivity, altered perceptions about the "side show" in Mesopotamia. On 1 June the Royal Navy's losses at the battle of Jutland shocked the government and four days later, the country went into mourning after the secretary of state for war, Lord Kitchener, was drowned *en route* to Russia, when HMS *Hampshire* hit a mine in the North Sea.

The second half of the year was even worse for Prime Minister Herbert Asquith. On 1 July the British Army launched its summer offensive on the Somme, but instead of hastening victory, it became synonymous with the waste of life that embodied the war in France. The Middle East provided no succour and by the autumn, the Arab Revolt, launched in Mecca on 10 June, was on the verge of collapse. The rate at which British merchant vessels were being sunk by submarines increased dramatically, with 41 ships and 176,248 tonnes lost in October. In the aftermath of these calamities, rumours reached the British government that German "emissaries in the United States were angling for intervention by President Wilson with a view to an early and favourable peace".[9] These were followed by a controversial memorandum by Lord Lansdowne in response to an invitation by Asquith to express their views on peace terms. The prime minister's hesitancy fractured the coalition and David Lloyd George took over, "kissing hands" with King George V on 8 December.

The new government was desperate for some good news at the beginning of 1917. Lloyd George suggested the capture of Jerusalem, but General Murray knew this was beyond the capability of the British Army in Egypt without massive reinforcements. In January, as T. E. Lawrence was beginning his work in Arabia, Milo Talbot returned to Cyrenaica to negotiate a peace treaty with the Sanussi. Apart from Hassanein Bey, he also took with him the son of the British ambassador in Rome, 21-year-old Francis Rodd, who was fluent in Italian and had recently graduated from Balliol College, Oxford. They travelled by motor-car to Sollum and then an Italian torpedo-boat ferried them to Tobruk on 25 January.[10]

Talbot reported that the Grand Sanussi was planning on leaving Siwa and this provided General Watson with an opportunity to attack the Sanussi stronghold. He originally intended to launch a joint armour and camel expedition, but due to the slowness of the quadrupeds, he sent only the armoured cars. He allocated three batteries each with four Rolls-Royces and three Light Car Patrols, with a total of 18 Fords, to the commander, Brigadier Henry Hodgson. This 48-year-old, battle-hardened cavalry officer had commanded the same regiment as William Peyton (15th Hussars) and also led a yeomanry brigade at Gallipoli.

The key components of the Siwa operation were the Light Car Patrols (Numbers 4, 5 and 6), commanded by Major Llewellyn Partridge of the Pembroke Yeomanry. There were also 82 support vehicles allocated for the signallers, medics and logisticians. An Italian military attaché, *Capitan* Mario Caccia of 28th Cavalry, accompanied the expedition and the ever-ready Leo Royle worked as Hodgson's interpreter and advisor.

The plan was to attack with the main force and with one battery and one Light Car Patrol, cut off the escape route some 16 miles to the west at Garet el-Munasib. This was the only pass between Siwa and Jaghbub that was suitable for camels. A substantial sandstorm delayed the heavy vehicles assembling at Matruh, but the Model T Fords were ready to move and departed on 31 January, making good time along the desert trails.

Brigadier Hodgson set off with the main force at dawn on 1 February and arrived at the agreed concentration point, 15 miles north of the escarpment, at noon on the following day. Partridge briefed him on a reconnaissance he had made and reported that the road had been mined, but he had found an alternative pass through the hills.

The Light Armoured Cars moved off at first light the next morning and, descending by the new pass, completely surprised the enemy. The Sanussi force of about 800 held a very strong position at the foot of the escarpment on the south-west side of the oasis. They brought two mountain guns and two machine guns into action and would not yield an inch. The British were subjected to a heavy fire and owing to the nature of the ground, it was not possible for the cars to advance closer than 600–800 yards from the enemy line.

The Sanussi commander, Mohammed Saleh Harb, who had been promoted from a major in the Egyptian Coastguard to a general in the Sanussi army, took control of the battle. All day long, his troops kept Partridge's force at bay, but that night, the crews heard the distinctive noises of departure as the enemy decamped, leaving some 50 dead behind when the British soldiers took the position during the following morning.

The Grand Sanussi had earlier withdrawn with his bodyguard of *Muhafizia*. As predicted, he left on a southerly bearing heading into the sand dunes for a few miles before turning north towards the Munasib pass. The detached Light Armoured Car Battery and Light Car Patrol were waiting to intercept him and hit the Sanussi hard in a well-planned ambush. After suffering further losses, the enemy turned south again and slowly made their way west towards Jaghbub.

After their victory, the British were welcomed into the holy site by the local population. They raised the Union flag and held a short parade, firing a nine-gun salute with a Krupp gun brought from Matruh. The yeomen spent the day at the oasis sorting out their vehicles and equipment and the next day, they returned to Matruh, arriving on 8 February with only three minor casualties.

Reporting to the secretary of state, General Murray praised the "dash and enterprise" of the armoured car officers for their pivotal role in driving the Sanussi back into Libya.[11] Partridge was awarded a DSO for his "inexhaustible resource" and "dashing" leadership and Captain Claud Williams and Captain Roy Davidson of the Denbighshire Hussars, who commanded 5 and 6 Light Car Patrols respectively, were both awarded the Military Cross.

* * *

Talbot's patient negotiations with Idris took nearly four months, but he had the advantage that the blockade was having a devastating effect on the Libyan economy. The Arab Bureau, headed by Major Kinahan Cornwallis, suggested in their weekly bulletin: "There is great misery, because the blockade leads to frequent cattle-raids amongst the various tribes. The immediate prospects of food are also bad, since, owing to insufficient rainfall, much less barley was sown than usual, and a poor crop is expected."[12]

The key to Talbot's success was to secure the release of 45 Italian prisoners held in a desert camp. He persuaded Idris' brother Muhammed al-Rida to ride out with an armed escort to prevent any interference with the prisoners and bring them to the coast. Idris further stated that he personally would deliver the final four, who were being held at Jaghbub and Kufra.[13]

While Talbot was in Tobruk, the Foreign Office persuaded the French government to accede "to the Anglo-Italian agreement for action against the Sanussi" and the arrangement for no separate peace agreements.[14] On 28 March, the foreign secretary, Arthur Balfour, signed the draft tripartite agreement with the French and Italian ambassadors "respecting the Sanussi"[15] and thereby conferred official diplomatic recognition on Idris.

The arrangement included a proposal to open the coastal markets at Benghazi, Derna, Tobruk and Sollum to the Sanussi "on the understanding that they would be closed again on the first sign of danger."[16] Balfour asked Wingate, who by this time had taken over from McMahon as the high commissioner, to relay to Colonel Talbot a request for him to stay with Idris and negotiate the final details of this agreement.

The most important condition was that any Sanussi or Libyan merchant who wished to buy goods in Sollum had to hold a pass authorised by Idris. General

Murray objected to the opening of Sollum[17] to the Sanussi, but Wingate overruled him as the Egyptians were particularly keen on Libyans bringing their sheep to the port.

Idris needed to visit the Sanussi heartland to assume the leadership of the Order. However, before he departed from his base close to Tobruk, Talbot persuaded him to sign the ceasefire pact with the Italian government. This treaty recognised Idris' authority in Cyrenaica, without exceeding Italian sovereignty. It allowed the Sanussi to control most of inland Cyrenaica but was ambiguous about their autonomy. The Grand Sanussi was allowed to keep his title but had to cede day-to-day control to his cousin and leave the country, eventually settling at Medina, where he died in 1933.

Wingate wrote effusively to the foreign secretary about Talbot's achievements in Tobruk in his dispatch of 28 April 1917: "To his patience, tact, and clear foresight are due, I consider, not only the signature of our Treaty with Sayed Mohammad Idris, but also in a very considerable degree, the satisfactory arrangements made between the latter and the Italian authorities." Later, he added: "The manner in which these difficult and delicate negotiations were conducted showed him to be possessed of statesmanlike qualities of no mean order, which merited the highest consideration."[18] Given this recommendation, it seems extraordinary that Talbot received no public reward, or recognition, for this service when he returned to England and was struck of strength from the Army on 31 August 1917.

Italy's good relations with Idris resulted in another accord signed in October 1920. This increased his autonomy and awarded him the title of Emir of Cyrenaica and a monthly stipend of 63,000 lira. The Rome government agreed to take responsibility for policing areas under Sanussi control and stipulated that Idris must disband the *Muhafizia*; however, the new leader was neither willing nor able to comply with this condition.

* * *

After Talbot departed from Libya, contact was maintained with Idris and he was helped to assert his authority and clear the country of Turkish "intriguers". In the summer he captured the "redoubtable Musa Pasha el-Yemeni" and his Turkish contingent at Adjabaya, 90 miles south of Benghazi,[19] but he did not find governing Cyrenaica easy with the continued presence of Turkish opponents and Italian occupiers.

Wingate did not wish to interfere in Libyan affairs and Cairo had enough on its hands with the campaign in Sinai and Palestine to administer. However, the Light Car Patrols based at Siwa continued to travel into Libya several times to provide support. Captain Claud Williams, who rose to command the whole unit, was instructed to plan for a major expedition to Benghazi in January 1918 and wrote:

On a journey of this description, there is no end to the mass of detail that has to be personally supervised and inspected. Our column is 22 cars and a possible journey of 1200 miles means an infinity of spares, tools, tyres, petrol, oil, food and a million or two other matters that don't worry anyone when there is a garage and a petrol store every few miles.[20]

This secret journey to escort Major Mervyn MacDonnell and Captain Leo Royle to meet Idris eventually left Sollum on 17 July 1918. It made excellent progress and three days later, the crews reached Benghazi, where they were welcomed by the head of the Italian mission, *Generale* Moccagatta, and spent three days reviewing his military facilities and troops.

On 23 July they travelled south and met the Sanussi leader at the small port of Zuwetina. The key discussions began on the following morning and while the British intelligence officers satisfied their concerns about Idris' relationship with the leaders of the budding Tripolitania Republic, Williams looked around the area that changed hands five times during World War II and became the front line during the 2011 revolution. After two weeks at Adjabaya developing a British strategy in the event of an Ottoman armistice (which was signed on 30 October), the skilled and astute Williams led the convoy safely back to Sollum, arriving in Egypt on 8 August.

* * *

The situation in eastern Libya was relatively simple compared with the west. In Tripolitania, Arabs who supported the Italians included those who had been alienated by the Young Turk revolution, such as the Muntasirs, and those who were "bribed" by the policy of *Politica dei Capi*. On the Ottoman side, the most prominent leader was Sulayman al-Baruni, an Ibadi Berber from the Nafusa Mountains. Farhat Bey, an influential commander from Zuwarah, close to Tunisia, was originally in this camp, but his preference for a French-style protectorate led him to transfer his allegiance to Italy after the treaty of Ouchy was signed.

The second main opposition was in Misuratah, where Ramadan al-Suwayhli held court. This port on the north-west corner of the Gulf of Sirte was the base for Nouri Bey when he lost influence with the Sanussi in 1916. It became an important German U-boat harbour, and effectively a provincial capital, raising taxes and printing its own money.

Ramadan had made his name as a military leader when he defeated Colonel Miani at the battle of Qasr Bu Hadi in April 1915, which effectively ended Italian hopes of control beyond their coastal hubs. His nearby neighbour at Bani Walid was Abd en-Nebi Bilkhayr, head of the influential Warfalla, and together they won another important battle, which ended the Senussi's brief incursion into Tripolitania.

The fourth power base was south-east of Tripoli at Tarhuna, where Ahmed el-Murayid built another strong army. Of the four leaders, he was the closest to the Italian front line and therefore the most vulnerable to attack. He was also at loggerheads with the Misuratans due to his allegiance to the Sanussi.

British Intelligence monitored the situation closely and reported that Baruni landed in Tripolitania on 15 October 1916 "with a firman from the Sultan of Turkey appointing him Governor General of the Vilayets of Algiers, Tunis and Tripoli". Unfortunately, his first operations near to Zuara proved to be a disaster as he was defeated by General Latini at the oasis of Agilah. In February 1917, Major Cornwallis warned General Murray:[21]

> Two distinct campaigns are being prepared in Tripoli. In the east, the Tarhuna appear to be joining forces with the Sanussi in order to crush Ramadan Shitewi [sic], who is doing all in his power to collect an army. Two thousand Sanussi, with three guns were reported to have left Cyrenaica for Sert, [sic] and a simultaneous attack on Shitewi may be made from north and south.
>
> In Northern Tripoli, Baruni's forces are anxious to avenge their defeat at Agelat (east of Zuara), where the Italian force, which consisted of Erythreans and Somalis,[22] lays claim to 820 killed and 1,200 wounded, whereas its own losses were light. Baruni admits heavy losses, but is anxious to organize attacks on Nuail (Nalut) and Zuara, saying that no help can be expected from Turkey until Zuara is taken. Baruni has among his following: Sheikh Sof, Mahdi el-Sunni, Mohammed Figheni (Fekini), Khalifa ben Askar, Mohammed el-Shellabi, Abeda ben Zikri and Zaki el-Maghegh, and their forces at the battle of Agelat were rather over 4,000. They would, therefore, seem to have lost about half of their effectives.

Encouraged by President Wilson's declaration of support for national self-determination and Italian acquiescence to Sanussi co-leadership in the east, the leaders of the four main groups in the west met at Misuratah and agreed to form the *Jumhuriyyah al-Tarablusiyyah*, or Tripolitanian Republic. The American political scientist Professor Lisa Anderson suggests that the choice of name was "less a reflection of the republican sentiments of its founders than of their inability to agree on a single individual to act as its head of state".[23] Unfortunately the Turkish pasha, Uthman Fuad, declined the role of leader, so Baruni, Ramadan, en-Nebi and Murayid ruled as a council of four with a cultured Egyptian, Abdul Rahman Azzan Bey, appointed the secretary.

As the first of its kind, the Tripolitanian Republic did not have a long or happy life. The idea was not supported by the delegates at the Paris Peace Conference. Rome was unwilling to yield autonomy in the west, as it was compelled to do in Cyrenaica by Britain. In April 1919, Italy signed an agreement with the republicans, but later instigated a divide and rule policy within the *Legge Fondamentale*.

The anthropologist Edward Evans-Pritchard, who worked in the British Administration of Cyrenaica in 1942, suggests that the Italians at this time "were, in fact, bribing the whole country to be quiet".[24] However, they also worked to dispose of the two most educated republican leaders. Ramadan was killed in 1920 at Bani Walid by the Italian-armed en-Nebi and Abdul Qadr Muntasir. The Italian military commander wrote: "So died the fiercest of all those who hated the name of Italy. And it was a lucky day for us, because he possessed to an excellent degree every quality of the barbarian chieftain, along with exceptional organizational and military skills, and a profound religious leadership."[25]

Turning their attention to Baruni's heartland, Italian agents fomented an Arab-Berber civil war that resulted in the Berbers seeking sanctuary on the coast and Baruni's departure in self-exile to Tunisia. Without these two charismatic leaders and the counterweight of the Ottoman Empire, the Republic disintegrated and looked to the Emir of Cyrenaica for salvation. Idris' advisers were divided and he realised this was a poisoned chalice, but eventually he agreed to the proposal, preferring the notion of Libyan unification to the demeaning status of Italian minion.

Everything changed on 31 October 1922, when Benito Mussolini grasped power in Italy after he marched on Rome at the head of 30,000 Blackshirts. The Emir was acutely aware of the implications of a military dictatorship for his country. As the nationalists dusted down their plans for domination of the central Mediterranean region, Idris knew that he could not continue. He was unwilling to be a Roman puppet, but neither was he persuaded by the fundamentalist viewpoint. With a heavy heart, he went into self-imposed exile in Egypt while the Fascists eyed their prey on the Fourth Shore.

CHAPTER 7

Lion of the Desert

War is a duty for us and victory comes from God.

OMAR MUKHTAR

Now, we come to the dark pages of Italian history. The tragedy of how a wondrous, enticing place and a vibrant, enchanting people could produce the vicious political party that came to power in 1922 is worthy of a Verdi opera and provides a salutary lesson to reject intolerance and opportunistic populism.[1]

Part of the blame lies in the Paris Peace Conference. Italy did relatively little to defeat the Central Powers, but demanded much in the way of victor's spoils. The Roman elite's frustration at their representatives' "inept and damaging diplomacy"[2] manifested itself in disappointed industrialists unable to expand into the Balkans and thwarted imperialists, who were blunted by a French buttress named Clemenceau.

The cost of the war to Italy, in terms of blood and money, was huge. More than 700,000 men died in the trenches and on battlefields along the Austrian border and elsewhere. The financial bill of 26.5 billion lira and the debt, above 10 billion lira, led to economic destitution and revived demands for an active foreign policy after the 1921 election. Responding to this, the new prime minister, Ivanoe Bonomi, launched a campaign to regain control in Tripolitania, but this was not enough to satisfy the Fascists, who spread their influence through violence and intimidation.

With loud rhetoric, they berated the government for their "subservience to France in Europe and to Britain in the Mediterranean".[3] In fact, the British prime minister did favour Italy in his anti-Turk stance, but he had little time for their Adriatic expansion, or the list of territorial demands that included the land between Sollum and Siwa taken in 1911. Reacting to this disappointing outcome, Mussolini seized control of Milan in a three-hour battle and in October marched on Rome, but before the situation descended into civil war, King Victor Emmanuel invited him to become prime minister on 29 October 1922.

The new government revoked Italy's treaties with Emir Idris and the Council of Four and accelerated the military campaign in Tripolitania conducted by the governor, Giuseppe Volpi. He had already extended the Italian zone to most of northern

Tripolitania by supporting the Arab-Berber civil war that undermined al-Baruni, but he could not win over Mohammed Khalifa Fekini and some of the other Arab sheikhs, who continued their resistance in the rugged hills south of Tripoli.

Fekini was head of the Rojeban tribe and initially welcomed the Italians against the Ottomans in 1911. However, he reverted after the Tripoli massacres and was appointed *Mutasarrif*, or governor, of the Fezzan (southern Libyan province) during the brief life of the Tripolitanian Republic. With over 2,000 men at arms, he waged a tenacious insurgency throughout the 1920s, using tactical ingenuity to compensate for the Italian technological advantages.

Initially, he defended the impenetrable Nafusa mountains, but after the military commander, General Rodolfo Graziani, assaulted the jebel with an overwhelming air and land force, he withdrew to the barren Fezzan, where his raiding was highly successful for another six years. He operated in partnership with the Sanussi brothers Ahmed and Mahdi es-Sunni, and the Tuareg sheikh Sultan Ahmud, as well as Ahmed and Mukhtar Rasem Koobar from Gharian.

Volpi referred to him as "our unyielding enemy" and tried flattery and bribery to turn him around, without success. The next governor, Emilo de Bono, was no more effective, so in February 1929 Mussolini handed the job to Marshal Pietro Badoglio, the "most merciless of all the long series of Italian governors that had been sent to Libya".[4]

Badoglio was given a budget of 21 million lira to finally conquer the Fezzan. When he arrived in Tripoli, he issued an uncompromising proclamation to the population that he posted in the towns and dropped from the sky: "We also know how to be implacable and merciless toward those few outlaws who, in their folly, delude themselves into believing that they can oppose the invincible power of Italy."

Fekini wrote to him on 22 February 1929 seeking a restoration of the original statute, but there was no negotiation and the battle of Umm el-Melha made him realise that the cause was lost. After 10 years of fighting with honour intact, but ailing health, he crossed the "invisible desert frontier" and surrendered to the French garrison at Fort Tarat in Algeria. Having lost two sons in battle, he settled in Gabes with his remaining family and lived for another 20 years, until 28 March 1950.

His revelatory biography, published in 2011, changed perceptions about the intensity and longevity of the insurgency in Tripolitania. His letters reveal the lack of unity in the resistance movement; a crucial factor in its defeat. The American academic Ruth Ben-Ghiat writes about the "corrosive effects of inter-tribal and regional factionalisms on Libyan resistance to Italian rule"[5] and how these feelings are part of the national identity (the abiding strength of Libyan tribal rivalry resurfaced in the rebellion against Colonel Gadhafi and is arguably the primary cause of the civil wars that have plagued the country since 2011).

* * *

When Volpi returned to Rome, General Graziani moved across as deputy governor of Cyrenaica. It was there that the worst of the Italian war crimes were committed during the euphemistically named "pacification". The founding principles of the *Risorgimento*, or Italian unification, were tolerance and liberalism, but somehow these were distorted when Italy became a colonial power.[6] Although the wrongdoing had its precedent in the era of the liberal regime of 1911, the criminality was vastly multiplied by Mussolini's henchmen and their behaviour only increased the hatred of the occupiers and added support for the insurgents.

After Emir Idris went into exile, the Sanussi found an inspiring leader, who took command of the military struggle in 1923. Omar al-Mukhṭār Muḥammed bin Farḥāṭ al-Manifī was born close to Tobruk at Janzur. He became a teacher after studying at the Sanussi university at Jaghbub and travelled with the Grand Senussi's son as he spread the influence of the Order in the 19th century.

Omar learned his military skills against the French in Chad. His strategy, which would be replicated by the Long Range Desert Group 20 years later, was to attack outposts, ambush convoys and cut supply-lines with small groups of riders on fast horses. He avoided pitched battles where Italy's technological advantage would result in unsustainable losses. His guerrilla tactics were highly effective in the close country and rugged valleys of the Green Mountains (Jebel Akhdar), where the terrified Italian soldiers proved incapable of defeating the troops under his command.

An impatient Mussolini railed against the slow progress of the counter-insurgency and when General Graziani transferred from Tripoli, he gave him a free hand to hunt down the leaders of the suppressed Order. However, the Sanussi hold on Cyrenaica was too strong and their support from the Muslim world, through the porous Egyptian border, was too plentiful. The Italians attempted to bring al-Mukhṭār to the negotiating table, but the compromise did not provide the population with their previous autonomy and once again, the 71-year-old Lion of the Desert took up arms in the cause of freedom.

Badoglio, who was now governor of all Libya, and Graziani "responded with ever growing levels of brutality designed to eliminate support for the rebels".[7] They erected the "frontier wire" along the Egyptian border to cut their supply line. This comprised four lines of six-foot stakes laced with barbed wire running 200 miles from the Gulf of Sollum, past Fort Capuzzo and deep into the desert. It was patrolled by aircraft and armoured cars, which fired at anyone attempting to cross the border illegally.

They also resorted to the barbaric use of chemical weapons and concentration camps to cut off the rebels from their support base. The forced deportations of families, who were marched 300 at a time to squalid camps, began in 1930. Close to Benghazi at Abyar, a medium-sized camp held 3,123 prisoners, but the main detention centres were located on the Gulf of Sirte. The two largest, each with over 20,000 people, were at Suluq and Brega. Three others at Adjabaya, Agheila and

Magrun each held over 10,000 men, women and children, many of whom died of starvation and disease.

By the end of the year all the Bedouin and Libyans who lived in tents had been rounded up. Estimates of the total number of civilian deaths vary, but in his book *Cyrenaica Today*, Dr. Todesky, who in 1931 was the director of the Italian Army Health Services, states that 55 per cent of the Libyan civilians died in the camps.

Mukhtar's struggle of nearly 20 years came to an end on 11 September 1931, when he fell from his horse south of Bayda and was captured by the Italian Army. Five days later, he was hanged before thousands of his followers in the Suluq prisoner-of-war camp. Before the end of the year, Graziani laid siege to the Senussi's final stronghold at Kufra and after starving the population and bombing them from the air, his armoured cars entered the oasis.

As with many war crimes, a survivor's tale came to light. In his autobiography, Muhammed Asad, who was born in the Galician capital of Lemberg and became a correspondent for the *Frankfurter Zeitung*, describes the capture of Kufra through the eyes of a man who escaped on a camel after hiding for two nights in the oasis and told his story while sitting on his haunches with his ragged *burnous* around him.

> They came upon us in three columns, from three sides, with many armoured cars and heavy cannon. Their aeroplanes came down low and bombed houses and mosques and palm groves. We had only a few hundred men able to carry arms; the rest were women and children and old men. We defended house after house, but they were too strong for us, and in the end only the village of Al-Hawari was left to us. Our rifles were useless against their armoured cars; and they overwhelmed us. Only a few of us escaped. I hid myself in the palm orchards waiting for a chance to make my way through the Italian lines; and all through the night I could hear the screams of the women as they were being raped by the Italian soldiers and Eritrean *askaris*. On the following day an old woman came to my hiding place and brought me water and bread. She told me that the Italian general had assembled all the surviving people before the tomb of Sayyid Muhammad al-Mahdi; and before their eyes he tore a copy of the Koran into pieces, threw it to the ground and set his boot upon it, shouting, "Let your Bedouin prophet help you now, if he can!" And then he ordered the palm trees of the oasis to be cut down and the wells destroyed and all the books of Sayyid Ahmad's library burned. And on the next day he commanded that some of our elders and *ulama* [scholars] be taken up in an aeroplane—and they were hurled out of the plane high above the ground to be smashed to death.[8]

Hearing this tale and other reports of war crimes, the Libyan diaspora appealed for support from Arab and North African countries. Nationalist parties such as the al-Muthana in Iraq organised protest marches[9] and during the 1930s, British and French governments watched in dismay as the people in the mandated countries rose against their administrators.

* * *

Meanwhile, in 1934, Rome announced that the separate provinces would be merged into Italian Libya. The *Quarta Sponda*, or Fourth Shore, had become reality and brought with it the importation of Latin customs and culture. Italian businesses jumped at the opportunity as hoteliers and shopkeepers, agriculturists and industrialists established their trade on the coast. Cinemas were opened; vineyards were planted; music, opera, theatre and literature were all introduced.

In Cyrenaica, Mussolini resettled Italians into the vacant farms and built new infrastructure, including an impressive naval base at Tobruk, where he began his imperial tour on 12 March 1937. As a former newspaper journalist, he knew the power of the media and did not stint on rewarding the conquerors and proclaiming the virtues of the Italian Air Force and Army. One of the biggest projects, built on the backs of Libyan labourers, was the *Strada Litoranea*, completed in 1937, that linked Tunisia with Egypt.

This communication artery enabled the first governor general of Italian Libya, Air Marshal Italo Balbo, to promote tourism on a wider scale. He established the Libyan Tourism and Hotel Association, which was responsible for 18 government-owned hotels and had a major part to play in the annual Tripoli Trade Fair.[10] He also catered for the academic coalition, building on the 15-day archaeological conference organised by his predecessor[11] and establishing protective institutions for ancient Roman and Greek sites.

Italian archaeologists, led by Frederico Halbherr, had benefitted from the colonial enterprise. During the first decade, they discovered the Venus of Cyrene and the base to a great statue of Zeus in the Pentapolis. In the west, Renato Bartoccini excavated Leptis Magna and Sabratha. In the east, the superintendent of antiquities between 1923 and 1935, Gaspare Oliverio, established the Italian Archaeological Mission and focused attention on the Sanctuary of Apollo.[12] Mussolini emphasised the importance of this work when he visited both Cyrene and Sabratha in 1937.

Entertainment was provided for the masses. Football leagues were set up in Cyrenaica and Tripolitania, with the inaugural competition in 1928 won by Genio.[13] The other sporting obsession of the Italians, motor racing, was catered for in Tripoli. Governor Volpi had already instigated a Grand Prix that was held on 18 April 1925. The winner in 1929, Gastone Brilli-Peri in a British-made Talbot, sadly died in an accident the following year and the bad publicity created by this and the concentration camps meant there were no more races until 1933. By then, Governor Badoglio had built the fastest circuit in the world at Mellaha Lake, close to Suq al Ju'mah.

Governor Balbo raised the profile of this Grand Prix by increasing the purse and treating the participants like royalty. He entertained them at his palace and provided accommodation at the luxurious Hotel Uaddan. The British driver Dick Seaman, who was seventh in the 1937 race, driving for Mercedes-Benz, described Mellaha as the "Ascot of motor racing circuits".[14]

Meanwhile, Britain had its hands full in Egypt with the Saad Zaghlul revolution that developed immediately after the Armistice, without having to interfere in the troublesome Libyan Desert. However, below the political level, British explorers maintained a keen interest in Egypt's neighbour. Between 1924 and 1941, the Royal Geographical Society awarded four of its prestigious gold medals to men who added to knowledge about the Libyan Desert.[15]

The first of these was Ahmed Hassanein Pasha, who had helped Milo Talbot with his peace mission in 1916. His expedition to Kufra with Rosita Forbes earned her the French Gold Medal in 1923. During his second trip, which extended into Sudan, he discovered unknown water sources at Jebel Uwainet and Jebel Arkanu that opened new Sahara routes from Kufra. He was awarded the Founder's Medal in 1924 and went on to be a key ally of Britain when he became chamberlain to King Farouk of Egypt.

The second recipient was the son of the ambassador to Rome in World War I. Major Francis Rodd, who was also introduced to Libya by Milo Talbot, travelled into the Fezzan and made studies of the Tuareg people in 1922 and 1927, at the same time as reporting on the state of the Italian counter-insurgency. He was awarded the Founder's Medal in 1929 and was later elected president of the Society in 1945.

Immediately after the Sanussi were defeated, Major Ralph Bagnold completed the first recorded east-west crossing of the Libyan Desert and established new geological processes that were later used by the US Space Agency. He was awarded the Founder's Medal in 1935 after publishing his book *The Physics of Blown Sand and Desert Dunes*, but perhaps he is more famous for founding the Long Range Desert Group in 1940 (see Chapter 12).

Bagnold's friend Pat Clayton, who worked in the Egyptian survey department, was the fourth recipient. He spent much time in the Western Desert confirming heights of the mountain features. In 1931, while surveying Jebel Uwainet, he rescued groups of starving refugees fleeing from the Italian massacre at Kufra and for his extensive work in the Libyan Desert, he was awarded the Founder's Medal in 1941.

Although Britain did not intervene in Libya, the British people were outraged at the horrific stories of Italian brutality and war crimes. When Mussolini decided to extend his empire into the Horn of Africa by attacking a respected member of the League of Nations, there was an outpouring of condemnation. Winston Churchill, commenting about this, wrote: "Mussolini's designs upon Abyssinia were unsuited to the ethics of the twentieth century. They belonged to those dark ages when white men felt themselves entitled to conquer yellow, brown, black or red men, and subjugate them by their superior strength and weapons... such conduct was at once obsolete and reprehensible."[16]

It is doubtful whether Mussolini ever had a moral compass, but other people who claimed to hold the high ground of civilisation in the League of Nations, also seemed to deviate when exposed to his magnetism. In particular, the French and

British governments did not pass this test of their international leadership. France did not wish to push Mussolini towards a pact with Germany and signed a secret convention with him on 7 January 1935 that gave the Duce a free hand in Ethiopia.[17] Meanwhile, Prime Minister Stanley Baldwin was fully occupied with domestic issues, including the dire economy and a vocal pacifist movement, so he too turned a blind eye to Italian aggression.

Many British politicians shared the view of Winston Churchill, who was "most reluctant to see Italy estranged and even driven into the [German] camp".[18] In a letter dated 25 August to the foreign secretary, Sir Samuel Hoare, he pointed out the deficiencies in the Mediterranean Fleet and its weakness compared with Mussolini's Navy.[19] The crisis continued for 10 months before the foreign secretary went to the League of Nations Assembly in Geneva determined to bring Italy back from the brink.

Hoare's stirring address on 11 September drew a line in the sand: "In conformity with its precise and explicit obligations the League stands, and my country stands with it, for the collective maintenance of the covenant in its entirety, and particularly for steady and collective resistance to all acts of unprovoked aggression."[20] However, Mussolini called the League's bluff and "launched a full-scale invasion on 3 October, when the rainy season in Ethiopia came to an end".[21] In response, the league imposed a few tame sanctions while the British Fleet slunk away from the Eastern Mediterranean much to the disdain of Churchill, who lamented the loss of the "opportunity of striking a decisive blow in a generous cause with the minimum of risk".[22]

A general election was announced in London, but according to A. J. P. Taylor, the Labour Party was "landed in an awkward predicament".[23] The Trades Union Congress pronounced a clear message: "restraint of Italy even at the risk of war", but the resolution passed at the Labour Party Conference diluted this to "all the necessary measures provided by the Covenant".

The Conservative leader, Stanley Baldwin, won a large majority on a "peace at all costs" mandate, but his government laid out contradictory policies of arms reduction and forcible resistance to aggression that could not be reconciled. A pact arranged with France by the foreign secretary to carve up Abyssinia drew instant condemnation in the House of Commons. Professor Taylor claims the outcry against this plan was the "greatest explosion over foreign affairs for many years".[24] A chastened Hoare resigned, and an apologetic Baldwin withdrew the plan.

In Abyssinia, Mussolini deployed the two military commanders who had so ruthlessly pacified Libya. Badoglio and Graziani used the same brutal methods they had employed in Cyrenaica, including widespread poison gas attacks, and by 5 May 1936 they had captured the capital Addis Ababa and forced King Haile Selassie into exile. The International Commission for the Red Cross highlighted the war crimes their medics witnessed. These reports brought further international condemnation and the popularity of Fascism in Italy declined, but the die was cast and Mussolini's prestige was strengthened among his fanatical followers.

Historians on both sides of the political divide agree that the conquest of Ethiopia "fatally damaged" the League of Nations.[25] The view in Germany of this affair was contemptuous of Britain's impotence and the failings of the covenant. In contrast, Berlin acclaimed Mussolini's efficient use of force and Italy's stock rose in Hitler's government. The Duce was invited to meet the Fuehrer and in October 1936, they signed the Rome-Berlin Axis Agreement while the British prime minister was occupied by the constitutional crisis that led to King Edward VIII's abdication.

Stanley Baldwin retired two weeks after the coronation of King George VI, but his successor as prime minister, Neville Chamberlain, continued to follow the path of appeasement and in October 1938 signed the infamous agreement in Munich. In the final judgement, blame for the beginning of World War II lies squarely with Adolf Hitler's policies, but Mussolini played an important part through his brutal adventures in Libya and Ethiopia. His role is perhaps best summarised by the historian Esmonde Robertson, who suggests that the Duce acted as an icebreaker for Hitler by "using terrorism as an instrument of policy".[26]

PART 3

NINE VICTORIA CROSSES (1940–1942)

CHAPTER 8

Churchill, Wavell and O'Connor

I only need a few thousand dead so that I can sit at the peace conference as a man who has fought.

MUSSOLINI 1940[1]

The shimmering heat on the Mellaha track added to the excitement for the 14th running of the Tripoli Grand Prix on 12 May 1940. Until two days before the race, World War II had hardly affected Libya because Mussolini had hesitated after Britain and France declared war against Germany on 3 September 1939 and kept his cards close to his chest.

The Duce had made his move into Albania five months earlier, but the news about Italian military preparedness did not embolden his advisors. His foreign minister, Galeazzo Ciano, suggested that Italy needed "a long period of neutrality in order to enter the war later".[2] He was also aware that the German people's "hatred" of Italy was a barrier to a profitable partnership, so Mussolini remained detached, hoping to enter the game as "a mediator".

Poland's capitulation preceded a phoney war when strategic leaders drafted military plans and civilian populations worried about chemical weapon attacks. The Soviet invasion of Finland in November focused minds on Scandinavia. At the instigation of Winston Churchill, who was appointed first lord of the Admiralty at the beginning of the war, the Royal Navy prepared to invade Norway and mine the sea route used by ships carrying Swedish iron ore to Germany. However, this was pre-empted by Hitler, who launched the invasion of Denmark and Norway on 9 April 1940.

The ill-fated British campaign in Norway[3] led to the collapse of support for Prime Minister Neville Chamberlain. On 8 May, the former war leader, David Lloyd George, made his last decisive intervention in the House of Commons: "It is not a question of who are the Prime Minister's friends. It is a far bigger issue. He has appealed for sacrifice. The nation is prepared for every sacrifice so long as it has leadership, so long as the government shows clearly what they are aiming at, and so long as the nation is confident that those who are leading it are doing their best." He concluded: "The Prime Minister should give an example of sacrifice, because there is nothing which can contribute more to victory in this war than that he should sacrifice the seals of office."[4]

Chamberlain duly resigned and by the evening of 10 May, Churchill had "acquired the chief power in the State".[5] An indifferent Mussolini met this change with "irony"[6] because he was more interested in the events unfolding in France. At 5 a.m., the German ambassador in Rome, Hans-Georg von Mackensen, had handed to him a letter from Adolf Hitler explaining why at that moment his airborne troops were landing in Holland and Belgium and would soon be followed across the frontier by 10 panzer divisions and 63 infantry divisions.

That night, while the Pope wrote supportive letters to the Allies and Churchill began to form his war cabinet in the National Coalition Government, Mussolini decided to join Hitler. However, this was against the advice of the king, the Italian General Staff and the Libyan governor, Italo Balbo, who told the foreign minister that Italy could not "go into the field before two months and before having received a definite quantity of arms and ammunition".[7]

Two days later, a pensive but exuberant Balbo welcomed the Maserati and Alfa Romeo drivers to the grid of the Tripoli Grand Prix. The crowds watching from the enormous shaded grandstand had plenty to talk about other than the absence of the Mercedes team. The questions on everyone's lips were: when would Italy declare war and where would Mussolini attack?

The race itself was sufficiently exciting to hold everyone's attention. During the first seven laps the lead changed twice, but by lap 10, the future Formula One world champion, Nino Farina, led in his Alfa Romeo 158 Voiturette. The key moment arrived on lap 17, when the Alfa team's slick pit stop gave him a boost and he was never threatened again.[8]

That evening, the leading elements of General Erwin Rommel's 7th Panzer Division created a bridgehead on the western bank of the river Meuse near to Dinant. The way into the heart of France was now open and led rapidly to the capitulation of the Paris government. Despite the miraculous evacuation of the British Expeditionary Force from Dunkirk on 4 June, the outcome of the war now looked certain.

Sensing an opportunity, Mussolini declared war on France and Britain six days later. The devious Duce invaded France just as her leaders were negotiating an armistice; thus gaining for Italy a few colonial concessions and economic control of the south-east of France, up to the river Rhône. His conceited eyes now focused on the bigger prize of Britain's African possessions.

* * *

The British Army's commander-in-chief in the Middle East was 57-year-old General Sir Archibald Wavell. He was a distinguished soldier described as "too clever for the Army class" at Winchester, who spoke Russian and wrote poetry in his spare time. His span of command touched three continents, stretching from the northern shores of the Mediterranean to the Equator and from the Nile to the Afghan frontier. During the phoney war and the fighting in France, he was left to his own devices, but when Churchill decided to take the fight to Mussolini, his plans came under close scrutiny in London.

At 65, Churchill was older than both Hitler and Mussolini and had vastly more experience of high office than the Axis leaders. He also had a much wider understanding of military affairs, but he admitted that the lessons of the Dardanelles "had sunk into [his] nature". As the war leader, he had not given himself extra powers, except for the undefined role of minister of defence, which allowed him to personally direct the Chiefs of Staff Committee and select and remove "all professional and political personages".[9] By excluding the first lord of the Admiralty and secretary of state for war and air from the War Cabinet, he effectively cut them out of the formulation of strategic plans and the day-to-day conduct of operations.

Early in his premiership, he established a morning routine of dictating written directives while eating breakfast in bed. He met the Service Chiefs at 10.30 a.m., when these were considered and any changes made. The staff work was completed in the afternoon and between 3 and 5 p.m., his orders and telegrams were issued to the commands.

As prime minister, he always had in his mind the need to broaden the conflict into a global war and Italy's entry gave him the opportunity to begin offensive operations in North Africa. In July, he sent a series of probing questions via his military assistant, General Hastings Ismay, with a view to forming a strategy for Egypt and the Middle East. However, he became frustrated by the passive resistance to his big ideas, which were to cut the Italian supply line in Libya with an amphibious operation and to reinforce the army in Egypt with 20,000 men by taking a risk in Kenya and using Polish and French volunteers.

Wavell was summoned to London and arrived on 8 August. Churchill's probing questions covered all levels from the strategic to the tactical. He was dissatisfied with Wavell's dispositions and annoyed about British Somaliland, which was lost while the general was in London. On 12 August, he gave him a long list of demands to be answered that evening.

Wavell responded calmly to the prime minister and they "thrashed out" a directive to build a mobile defensive force in Egypt of 56,000 men by 1 October. Churchill promised a brigade-sized armoured force from England and gave Wavell tactical instructions how to fight the impending Italian invasion. Wavell, in turn, suggested that a Cabinet minister should join him in the Middle East to provide the political interface between London and the military. Churchill refused, but later admitted that: "It took more than a year of ups and downs for me and my colleagues to learn the need of dividing the responsibilities of the Middle East between a commander-in chief [and] a Minister of State…"[10] Eventually he asked Oliver Lyttleton to provide political guidance and run the information and economic campaigns, but this was not until 28 June 1941, when the situation in Libya had changed dramatically.

Unfortunately, Wavell and Churchill parted on bad terms. After Mussolini made much of the Italian victory in British Somaliland, the prime minister demanded that General Godwin-Austen should be suspended. He believed the low casualty rate of 260 killed, wounded or missing was a sign of capitulation, not an orderly planned evacuation. Wavell replied by signal that the British troops fought well, as could be seen by the 10-fold Italian casualty rates, and that he would not suspend a competent general. He concluded: "A big butcher's bill is not necessarily evidence of good tactics." According to the chief of the Imperial General Staff, Sir John Dill, he never saw the prime minister so angry as when he read this message.[11]

It would be wrong to conclude that Wavell did little to prepare for war in Egypt before Churchill's intervention. Under his guidance, Lieutenant General Henry "Jumbo" Wilson, commander of British troops in Egypt, energetically dealt with the huge logistical problems caused by a 75 per cent reduction in British military bases following independence. Tactical deficiencies were addressed by the irascible Brigadier Percy Hobart, who had been sent to Egypt in September 1938. "Hobo", as his troops affectionately called him, built an effective armoured force at Mersa Matruh from scratch, despite the antipathy of many staff officers in Cairo. His troops had to relearn the lessons that the Light Car Patrols had mastered so well, including how to drive on soft sand, navigate by sun and stars and maintain axles and suspensions.

Although he emphasised the role of the tanks, he also advocated the integration of infantry, artillery and air support into the battle. Just as he achieved his goal, Jumbo Wilson sacked him in November 1939 over an argument that began after a test exercise. There is no doubt that Hobart split opinions; a fellow commander, General Richard O'Connor, said that his force was the "best trained division I have ever seen", but a resentful adjutant general wrote, "he does not get the willing best from his subordinates and has not welded them into a happy and contented body".[12] The truth is that he laid the foundation for the Desert Rats' success and when he drove the mile and a half to the aircraft waiting to return him to England, "the route was lined by the men of his division, gunners, rifle, cavalry and tankmen, all cheering their general in a spontaneous and unforgettable farewell".[13]

The saying "amateurs talk about tactics, but professionals study logistics" is highly relevant to desert warfare. The problems begin and end with supplying drinking water, food and fuel to soldiers and vehicles, but in between there are dozens of maintenance and storage questions that need to be answered. Soldiers require accommodation; vehicles require roads and maintenance; ammunition requires storage bunkers and security. There are also a host of civil engineering projects that accompany these requirements, from bore holes and water purification plants, to infrastructure. The need for medical facilities to treat, cure and heal disease and injuries adds another level of complexity to all these requirements.

Wavell ensured these challenges were met and also drafted ideas for raids into Libya to capture Bardia and Jaghbub using airborne troops and support from the sea. In his determination to seize the initiative, he was helped by the commander of the Eastern Mediterranean Fleet, Admiral Andrew Browne Cunningham, known as ABC, and the Air Force commander, Air Chief Marshal Arthur Longmore.

Immediately after Italy declared war, they began their attacks. The fleet bombarded Bardia and destroyed 10 enemy submarines; the Royal Air Force attacked the Italian port of Tobruk and sank the cruiser *San Giorgio*; and the 11th Hussars, known fondly as the cherry-pickers, crossed the frontier wire and captured 70 Italian prisoners of war during a night raid.

By the end of June, Hobart's former command had distinguished itself in the first armoured confrontations. The British were operating freely in Libya and captured several Italian bases, including Fort Capuzzo. They had also encountered the oppressive dust storms, known in Egypt as *Khamsin* and in Libya as *Ghibli*, which combined oven-like Saharan heat with 60-mile-an-hour winds blasting sand into every crack and crevice. This hot air, which originates in the Sahara, is pulled northwards by low pressure and can last several days, creating turbulence in the Mediterranean where red sand falls in its wake. Its wall of sand sucked the life out of everything it met, like a swarm of locusts. The correspondent Alan Moorehead described it as "the most hellish wind on earth"[14] and Bill Kennedy-Shaw, who suffered from it in the Long Range Desert Group, wrote: "You don't merely feel hot, you don't merely feel tired, you feel as if every bit of energy had left you, as if your brain was thrusting its way through the top of your head and you want to lie in a stupor till the accursed sun has gone down."[15]

Meanwhile the Libyan governor, Italo Balbo, who had opposed Mussolini's war, died on 28 June, when his plane was shot down by jittery Italian anti-aircraft gunners at Tobruk. Marshal Graziani returned as governor general to command the planned invasion, but he too realised that this was moving "towards a defeat which, in the desert, must inevitably develop into a rapid and total disaster".[16]

The motorised troops had no transport; the Italian Air Force had lost 290 of their 350 aircraft and the Italian Fleet refused to leave port. Churchill, who had vetoed the Admiralty's plan to withdraw its fleet from the Eastern Mediterranean, now encouraged the first sea lord, Sir Dudley Pound, to build up the defences of Malta: "The immense delay involved in passing… ships round the Cape cannot be accepted."[17]

The Admiralty resisted, but Churchill would not take no for an answer. In another letter to the first sea lord, he pointed out the flaws in the Royal Navy's logic and insisted that the Admiralty find a way of taking the much-needed tanks to Egypt through the shorter, but more dangerous route. The chiefs continued to defy the prime minister on the basis that an invasion by Italy was not considered imminent. However, Churchill never let this go and later complained to Pound: "The course of Operation *Hats* makes me quite sure that it was wrong to recede from the idea of passing the armoured vehicles through the Mediterranean…"[18]

* * *

On Friday 13 September 1940, the Italian Army finally advanced across the Egyptian frontier and occupied Sollum, nearly 25 years after the Sanussi had made the identical manoeuvre (see page 52). Wavell also adopted the same tactic that General Maxwell had used in 1915 and fell back to the well-fortified base at Mersa Matruh, in order to extend the Italian supply lines.

The British headquarters staff worried about the overwhelming number of Italian divisions they faced. However, the chaos as the infantry descended Hellfire Pass (which also resembled the 1915 invasion) and the lack of flank security reassured them that the soldiers in the Italian Tenth Army were not first rate. Brigadier William "Strafer" Gott, in charge of a harassing group that stayed behind on the plateau, struck a debilitating blow with the support of the Royal Horse Artillery. The psychological effect was so great that the Italian command came to an abrupt halt 10 miles beyond Sidi Barrani, much to the disgust of Lieutenant General Richard O'Connor, who was ready with the Western Desert Force for a fight at Matruh.

O'Connor was the opposite of Jumbo Wilson not only in size, but also in his temperament and speed of thought. He had what Napoleon described as *coup d'oeil*, an insight that set him apart from less imaginative officers. After a distinguished Great War when he was awarded the Military Cross and Distinguished Service Order in France, he became the chief of staff to General Fuller in the Experimental Brigade and an instructor at Staff College before he was posted to Palestine as a divisional commander. He had also earned one of the highest Italian gallantry awards in World War I, when he captured the island of Grave di Papadopoli while commanding 2nd Infantry Battalion of the Honourable Artillery Company in October 1918.

O'Connor was alive to new ideas in the battle for Libya. British policy had always been to recce by stealth, but in October, the 11th Hussars, which had been in constant action since June, were being targeted by an Italian air squadron created especially to hunt them down. In response, O'Connor created an *ad hoc* force with infantry and artillery to protect the Hussars and fight for the vital information that he required about the Italian defences.

These groups, known as Jock columns after their commander Lieutenant Colonel John Campbell, were out most nights probing and harassing Italian defences. The valuable intelligence they provided for O'Connor helped him identify a gap in the Italian defences, which could be used to insert a large, armoured force behind the Italian position. A plan was conceived for a five-day raid and approved by Wavell without reference to the prime minister in London, who was still sending his own tactical ideas to the commander-in-chief.

Churchill was delighted when he was informed, but slightly exasperated when Wavell tried to dampen expectations in a cable, he sent to Sir John Dill: "We are greatly outnumbered on ground and in air, have to move over 75 miles of desert and attack enemy who has fortified himself for three months. Please do not encourage optimism."[19] The key bone of contention was that Wavell wished to exploit any success with a campaign in East Africa, whereas Churchill's focus was in Europe after Mussolini invaded Greece at the end of October.

* * *

Operation *Compass*, known in Italy as *La Battaglia della Marmarica*, began early on 9 December 1940. There is no knowing whether O'Connor considered the Sanussi Campaign, but his manoeuvre was remarkably similar to General Wallace's forays in December 1915 because the geography dictated the tactics. The detailed planning was much more thorough, the use of the Royal Navy and the Royal Air Force more deliberate and the technology more modern, but Jack Gordon and John Wigan would have recognised the same ground, the same weather and the same grim determination to overcome the odds.

Everything was scaled up. A mixed column under Brigadier Arthur Selby hugged the Khedivial road. This comprised 3rd Battalion Coldstream Guards and companies from four other infantry regiments, together with a troop of 7th Hussars (the only cavalry regiment in World War II to fight against German, Italian and Japanese armies). Meanwhile the mobile 7th Armoured and 4th Indian Divisions deployed south-west and hooked around through a gap in the line identified by the cherry-pickers. Dummy tanks positioned by Selby added to the deception that the main thrust was along the coast. The guns of the South Nottinghamshire Hussars combined with bombardments from the air and sea to distract and pin down the forward elements of the Italian Army at Maktila.

The first assault was on the isolated camp at Nibeiwa, 10 miles south of Sidi Barrani. This honour was handed to 11th Indian Infantry Brigade, commanded by 46-year-old Brigadier Reggie Savory. He had earned a Military Cross as a subaltern in the 14th Ferozepore Sikhs in 1916 and was one of Churchill's volunteers, who served in Vladivostok in 1919.[20]

His brigade comprised 2nd Queen's Own Cameron Highlanders, 1st/6th Rajputana Rifles and 4th/7th Rajput Regiment. However, before they dismounted, the Matilda tanks of 7th Royal Tank Regiment crushed the defensive perimeter and caused havoc among the enemy. The Italians had no time to recover from this shock before the Highlanders, played in by their pipers, poured through the breach and set to work with their bayonets. They were followed by the Rajput Rifles and within an hour 4,000 prisoners had been captured, together with 23 tanks and scores of lorries and guns.

Having lost the element of surprise, they found the next position on the route north, Tummar West, was defended more stoutly. It did not help that a brutal sandstorm rose from the desert and made navigation almost impossible. This time, 5th Indian Infantry Brigade, commanded by Wilfred Lloyd, assaulted the camp with 1st Royal Fusiliers in the vanguard and 3rd/1st Punjab Regiment following up and capturing another 2,000 prisoners.

Tummar East was engaged by the brigade's reserve battalion, but with the return of the sand storm, the divisional commander, Major General Noel Beresford-Peirse, called a halt and bivouacked for the night. The bitter winter conditions did little to inspire the Italian defenders and at dawn, the entire garrison surrendered without another shot fired.

A delighted General O'Connor visited his two divisional commanders that night to satisfy himself about the state of the troops and to provide guidance for the following day, setting the first objective as the capture of Sidi Barrani. Orders were passed to 16th Infantry Brigade under Brigadier Cyril Lomax, who moved his three battalions forward to launch a dawn attack without knowing where his artillery or tanks were located.

At 0600 hours they advanced from their assembly area, but a mile before the position, the fog cleared and accurate Italian artillery fire forced the leading vehicles to halt and the Argyll and Sutherland Highlanders to take cover. The battalion, led by Lieutenant Colonel Robert Anderson, suffered badly, losing nine officers and 144 other ranks, but just as the situation became desperate, 10 Matildas swept through and took the initiative. Anderson called his men for a bayonet charge, but before the Highlanders closed with the Blackshirt Divisions, the Italian defenders dropped their weapons and raised their arms in the air.

There were further battles to clear isolated pockets, but the victory was completed early on 11 December, with 30,000 prisoners captured by British and Indian forces. When he was woken that morning, O'Connor received a message from General Wavell that 4th Indian Division was to return to Alexandria for the planned East African campaign. This was a "tremendous shock" and meant that he had to change his plan for the "fullest possible exploitation" that Churchill had encouraged from London.

It was obvious that the Italian enthusiasm to fight had diminished since the invasion. Alex Gatehouse later wrote that: "No defeated army has ever co-operated with its opponents to the extent that the Italians did on this day."[21] O'Connor realised what this meant and immediately ordered a rapid advance to the Libyan frontier.

The Italian loss of fighting spirit stemmed from the commander, Marshal Graziani, who made no plans for a proper defence of Libya. According to Ciano in Rome, Mussolini became "more and more calm" when he received the reports of the capitulation, but when they met on 12 December, he was "very much shaken".[22] Together with the ignominious defeats in Greece and Albania, the hollow house of cards that the Duce had built was collapsing everywhere.

* * *

General O'Connor's successes continued throughout December. The frontier post at Sidi Omar, with its guns facing Egypt, surrendered when British tanks circled the camp and attacked from the west. The troops at Sollum and Capuzzo withdrew to Bardia without a fight. This key port, where the British crew of HMS *Tara* was captured in 1915, now became the focus of the whole campaign. While the British closed on the garrison, Mussolini exhorted *Generale di Corpo* Annibale Bergonzoli to defend Bardia to the last: "I am certain that Barba Elettrica and his brave soldiers will stand at whatever cost…".

In London, Churchill read the hourly signals that were transmitted via the Royal Navy listening base at Winchester, HMS *Flowerdown*. In the House of Commons, he gave credit to Wavell and Wilson, not realising that O'Connor was the battlefield genius responsible for the victory. He sent ebullient telegrams to President Roosevelt in America and to Prime Minister Menzies in Australia and when the Italians were pushed out of Egypt, he sent another felicitous message to Wavell, encouraging him to continue along the coast, but not forgetting his pet obsession "about amphibious operations and landings behind the enemy's front".[23]

On 23 December, the British prime minister addressed the Italian people in a broadcast from London. In a conciliatory tone, he was unequivocal where the blame for the calamity facing Italy lay:

> One man and one man alone has ranged the Italian people in deadly struggle against the British Empire, and has deprived Italy of the sympathy and intimacy of the United States of America… It is one man who, against the Crown and Royal Family of Italy, against the Pope and all the authority of the Vatican and of the Roman Catholic Church, against the wishes of the Italian people, who had no lust for this war, has arrayed the trustees and inheritors of ancient Rome upon the side of the ferocious pagan barbarians.[24]

Preparations at Bardia continued over Christmas as 7th Armoured Brigade encircled the Italian perimeter. Although Bergonzoli was running out of water, he still provided wine and rich fare for his soldiers on Christmas Day. Among the besiegers, each Australian soldier was issued some beer and received a comfort parcel containing plum pudding, tinned cream, fruit and cheese. However, the British Tommie had to be content with another delivery of fuel and ammunition and a warning that food shortages would continue.

Supporting this campaign was a regiment made up primarily of the Sanussi. The exiled Emir Idris had made contact with Wavell's headquarters as soon as Mussolini entered the war and offered to raise a regiment from those of his followers who had fought the Italians with Omar al-Mukhtar. This Libyan Arab Force provided tremendous support and was gratefully thanked by the foreign secretary, Anthony Eden, in the House of Commons on 8 January, when he said: "The Government are determined that at the end of the War, the Sanussi in Cyrenaica will in no circumstances again fall under Italian domination."[25]

* * *

As the British Army paused, Bardia was softened up by the Royal Air Force and the 15-inch guns of HMS *Terror*. The weather remained vile; torrential sleet and rain filled the trenches and turned the tracks into glue. When it wasn't raining, the wind picked up the sand and blasted any exposed hands and faces.

General O'Connor's assault began on 3 January, two days after the Western Desert Force was renamed XIII Corps. Soldiers of 2nd/1st Battalion, part of 16th Australian Brigade, began moving forward at 0430 hours. The Italians were mentally defeated before these imposing giants came through the pre-cut wire, firing machine guns from the hip and lobbing grenades as if they were cricket balls.

The 16th Brigade faced little opposition, but in the southern sector, 17th Australian Brigade had a much harder time, coming up against the only effective part of the Italian Army, their field artillery. The bitter fighting in this area resulted in most of the 456 Australian casualties, but the gallant resistance only delayed the inevitable and by the end of 5 January, the port was in Allied hands along with another 40,000 prisoners.

Before the collapse of Bardia, O'Connor was already probing the next major objective, the pride of Italian Libya, Tobruk. Sweeping through El Adem, the tanks of 7th Armoured Brigade cut the western road to Derna while 19th Australian Brigade blocked the Bardia road in the east. By 9 January, 25,000 defenders were under siege with British and Australian patrols trying to determine where to launch a decisive assault.

O'Connor was conscious that even though Bardia had fallen quickly, the capture of Tobruk might be more costly. He was especially frustrated about the supplies provided by Jumbo Wilson and the confusion caused by his interference in the planning. At an intense, front-line meeting Wavell agreed to change the command arrangements, putting O'Connor on an equal footing to Wilson and handing to him the complete control of XIII Corps' activities.

Heartened by this outcome, O'Connor launched the attack on Tobruk with a pulverising salvo at 5.40 a.m. on 21 January. The engineers advanced first to fill in the tank ditches, clear the line of booby traps and create four gaps in the wire. The infantry waited as the flares and explosions gave away the element of surprise, but when called forward, they charged through the gaps alongside 18 Matilda tanks and assaulted the concrete sangars occupied by the Italian infantry.

Most of these posts surrendered immediately, but the 2nd/8th Australian battalion had to overcome dug-in tanks with machine guns and then faced a rare counter-attack at Fort Pilastrino. The surprised Aussies suffered badly, but when they were joined by British tanks, they rose from the ground and "with wild yells and fixed bayonets, the troops went for the sangars from which rifles, machine-guns and small mortars were still firing".[26] Continuing their advance, the troops were pinned down by anti-aircraft guns firing shrapnel, but were rescued by the Royal Horse Artillery, whose accurate fire left the enemy guns in a mangled ruin.

To the north-east, Fort Solaro was captured as dusk descended by 2nd/4th Battalion. Almost the final act of the day was to deal with a machine-gun position on the edge of the escarpment that was protecting an entrance to some caves. Suddenly, from under the ground, another large batch of prisoners emerged and much to the surprise of the victors, the Italian commander, *Generale* Petassi Mannella, tearfully surrendered to a young Australian officer, John Copland.

That night, orders were passed to clear the harbour. There was some uncertainty about how much fighting would be needed, but in the end, the Italian naval commander offered no resistance and Brigadier Horace Robertson accepted the surrender of the well-stocked and elegantly constructed port.

Meanwhile, the riflemen of Brigadier Gott's Support Group were still in action in the west. He had established a cordon across the Derna Road and was now dealing with groups of Italian soldiers attempting to escape along the coast. There were also a few isolated pockets of resistance that 16th Australian Brigade mopped up, but the biggest challenge was in the overcrowded prisoner-of-war cage that had to cope with 20,000 demoralised Italians.

The sanitary conditions were sickening and there was no shelter from the harsh conditions. When water arrived, it caused pandemonium and one observer wrote: "I had not thought that a crowd of men could so resemble a stampeding herd of cattle."[27] This perpetual problem caused considerable humanitarian heartache and troubled General O'Connor throughout Operation *Compass*.

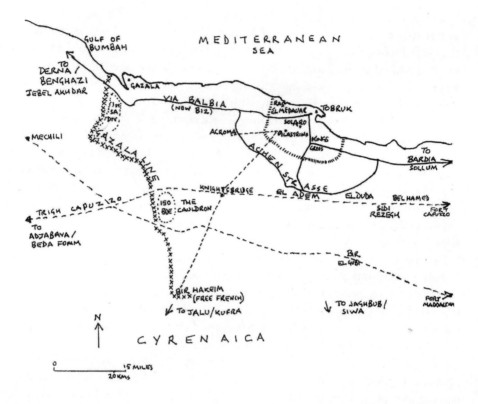

Gazala Line and Tobruk Perimeter 1942. After the siege of Tobruk was lifted in November 1941, many of the mines that were so effective in blocking the Afrika Korps were re-laid along the Gazala Line in 1942. However, when Rommel broke through the Allied position, this meant that Tobruk could not be defended so effectively and was one of the reasons for its surrender on 21 June.

CHAPTER 9

Siege of Tobruk

If anybody had predicted on October 15 what later actually happened, I would have had him shot.

MUSSOLINI TO CIANO, 18 JANUARY 1941

At the beginning of 1941, Winston Churchill was already intent on denuding the forces available to General O'Connor in Libya. From a global perspective, it is easy to see why Greece and Abyssinia took a higher priority for their control of vital sea routes, but the consequences of dispatching Royal Air Force squadrons and Army divisions seriously undermined his previous direction to "rip [Italy] off the African shore".[1]

In hindsight, it might have been best to follow the advice of the South African veteran General Smuts, who wrote to the prime minister on 8 January: "Magnificent victories in the Middle East open up a field of speculation regarding our future course. Flowing tide will soon carry Wavell to Tobruk. Should he go further? Tripoli is much too far. Even Benghazi is as far beyond the frontier as the frontier is from Alexandria… In the absence of good and special reasons Tobruk seems to me the terminus. Beyond it lie risks not necessary to detail".[2]

Two days later, Churchill issued a new directive to Wavell: "Nothing must hamper capture of Tobruk, but thereafter all operations in Libya are subordinated to aiding Greece."[3] Wavell flew to Athens, but the Greeks declined his offer and so Churchill changed his mind again and agreed to the push to Benghazi, for good measure asking Wavell also to seize the Italian islands in the Dodecanese.

The adaptable General O'Connor faced many challenges after capturing Tobruk. The terrain dictated that he had to split his formation into two. In the north, he allocated the formidable Green Mountains (Jebel Akhdar) to Major General Iven Mackay's 6th Australian Division. Mackay was a former school teacher, who was awarded the Distinguished Service Order in Gallipoli and a Bar in France, before studying Physics at Cambridge under Ernest Rutherford. He had already proved himself to be a first-class commander at Bardia and Tobruk.

The Australians' immediate objective was Derna, but 60th Sabratha Division established a strong defensive position and fought with steely determination. Bardia had taken two hours to crack, Tobruk a whole day, but Derna was still in enemy hands four days after the infantry launched their assault. It was not until 30 January that a party of Libyans climbed the wadi to offer a welcome sanctuary from the vile weather to their liberators.

After enjoying the first fresh vegetables they had seen for months, the Aussies set off into the daunting mountains that reached up to 2,500 feet. Their progress was slow because curtains of rain had turned the rich soil into a morass and the close country was ideal for the Italian defenders, who covered their well-placed booby traps with machine guns, causing a high casualty rate among the advancing troops.

Meanwhile, O'Connor released 7th Armoured Division under Major General Michael O'Moore Creagh, who had returned to the battlefield after treatment for an abscess, to strike south-west and turn the flank of the retreating Italian tanks. The discomfort faced by the Australians in the jebel was matched in the boulder-strewn desert, where the British crews had to contend not only with breakdowns to overworked vehicles that desperately needed a base overhaul, but also with thermos bombs (the AR-4 mine, dropped from aircraft, that superficially resembled a Thermos vacuum flask).

The biggest challenge facing XIII Corps was the supply line from Egypt. The most well-trained and courageous army can be defeated in the desert by a lack of food, water, ammunition and spare parts. Fortunately, the rapid opening of Tobruk harbour by the Royal Navy allowed O'Connor to establish two field supply depots close to Bomba and a third was constructed at Mechili, which was captured after a brief tank battle at the end of January.

As news came through about the Allied victories in Eritrea, the British regiments concentrated at the new depot and began to mend and re-stock their tanks. The exhausted troops expected to remain at Mechili for two weeks. However, this proved to be an illusion because O'Connor hatched a plan to cut off the Italian Tenth Army south of Benghazi and on 3 February, he launched 4th Armoured Brigade on a 150-mile dash to the Gulf of Sirte.

Two days later, the depleted Australian division entered Barce at the western end of the jebel. They found the ancient sites of Cyrene and Apollonia totally deserted but did not have time to appreciate the carefully preserved antiquities because their commander gave orders to push on to Benghazi the next day.

The Italians under *Generale* Bergonzoli fled south, without realising that the forward elements of 7th Armoured Division, led by Lieutenant Colonel John Combe of the 11th Hussars, had reached the coast. The long column of Italian vehicles closed up to the road block and was caught in the flank at Beda Fomm late on 5 February.

There was a complete contrast between the two sides that night. The outnumbered British, who had more or less run out of supplies, busily transferred ammunition to those who had none and siphoned fuel from captured vehicles. The inactive Italians huddled together, complaining about the lack of support from their commanders.

The failure to recce the British positions led to a half-hearted early morning attack that was repelled by Combe's force. Bergonzoli ordered some of his tanks to drive to the front of the column, but they were destroyed by Cruiser tanks of 2nd Royal Tank Regiment, perfectly positioned 600 yards to the east on a feature known as the Pimple. The Italians incorrectly concluded that they were surrounded by a prodigious force, not realising that it was only a thin line of British armour.

The fighting continued all day and at dawn on Friday 7 February, the Italians launched another surge into John Combe's position. Artillery shells crashed down on 2nd Rifle Brigade's trenches. Italian M13/40 tanks motored through the front line, followed by infantry with machine guns. The battle was ferocious and the outnumbered British were slowly being worn down, watched from afar by the tanks on the Pimple.

The situation required desperate measures and the gun commanders in 4th Royal Horse Artillery received permission to fire their 25-pounders[4] at the enemy tanks among the British position. The result remained on a knife edge as Major Burton of the Lancashire Yeomanry took over an unmanned gun and with his batman and cook drove it to the flank where he destroyed the final five Italian tanks. Just as the British ran out of ammunition, the demoralised Italians laid down their arms and much to the disbelief of their opponents, surrendered *en masse*.

Victory was completed with the capture of Adjabaya, where a young officer of 11th Hussars took the surrender of the Italian garrison. The British established a base at Agheila, from where patrols reported that the enemy had withdrawn into Tripolitania. At this stage, O'Connor's force had advanced 500 miles in two months, destroyed an army of nine divisions and captured 130,000 prisoners, 400 tanks and 1,290 guns. However, Wavell ordered no further advance because Churchill's focus had returned to Greece.

The prime minister confirmed this in a 10-point directive on 12 February: "We are delighted that you have got this prize three weeks ahead of expectation, but this does not alter, indeed it rather confirms, our previous directive, namely, that your major effort must now be to aid Greece and/or Turkey. This rules out any serious effort against Tripoli, although minor demonstrations thitherwards would be a useful feint. You should therefore make yourself secure in Benghazi and concentrate all available forces in the Delta in preparation for movement to Europe."[5] With Wavell thus occupied in Abyssinia, Mesopotamia and the Peloponnese, it is no wonder that little notice was taken that same day when a German Heinkel 111 landed at Castel Benito (now Tripoli International airport) and out stepped 49-year-old *Generalleutnant* Erwin Rommel.

* * *

There is nothing worse for a military officer who has built a successful team than having it broken up by higher command. The feeling is similar to that of an inventor who finds his designs being used by others, or a musician whose song is stolen by a rival band. It must have been extremely frustrating for Richard O'Connor to hear that the formations in Cyrenaica were being hollowed out and so many of his staff were to be redeployed. However, compensation followed swiftly. The *London Gazette* of 4 March 1941 announced that O'Connor was created a KCB and his three divisional commanders, Creagh of 7th Armoured, Mackay of 6th Australian and Beresford-Pierse of 4th Indian, were all knighted as KBEs.

Rommel, who had been equally honoured with Oakleaves to the Knight's Cross, took little account of desert reputations. Neither was he willing to adhere to the guidance of the German High Command, or Graziani's replacement as governor, *Generale* Italo Gariboldi, who both cautioned against an offensive campaign. Sensing an opportunity to turn the tables on the British, he allocated no time for acclimatisation, but dispatched his panzers to the front, together with the Italian Corps that was put under his direct command by Mussolini.

The first encounter occurred on 20 February when an eight-wheeler of 3rd Reconnaissance Regiment passed an armoured car patrol of the King's Dragoon Guards on the Via Balbia. Four days later, a German combat group captured three prisoners and left no one in any doubt that the Afrika Korps had arrived and was asserting its primacy at the front.

When Wavell visited the Gulf of Sirte on 16 March, he became aware of the appalling state of affairs. The two battle-hardened divisions that had defeated the Italians had been replaced by 2nd Armoured under Michael Gambier-Parry and Leslie Morshead's 9th Australian. Both formations were under-trained, poorly dispersed and ill-equipped. In particular, half the 52 Cruiser tanks were in workshops and the rest were breaking down because their tracks and engines were worn out. Apart from the reliability problems, the British tanks were no match for the 120 German tanks of 5th Light Division, which they would soon have to face.

O'Connor, who was rehabilitating after hospital treatment in Palestine, had been replaced in Cyrenaica by Lieutenant General Philip Neame, a Royal Engineer awarded the Victoria Cross in 1914, who had no experience of commanding armoured formations. To make matters worse, the Royal Air Force had lost most of its aircraft to Greece, while the Luftwaffe under *General der Flieger* Hans Geisler at Sicily was sending waves of bombers that made it impossible for the Royal Navy to provide much-needed supplies to Benghazi.

The fundamental problem, recognised by both sides, was that Cyrenaica offered few natural defensive barriers and given the mobility of modern forces, needed to be either fully occupied or totally abandoned. Secret intercepts from Bletchley Park about Rommel's deployment suggested to Wavell that Neame would have until 16 April to make his defences ready. This intelligence was supported by a report that

15th Panzer Division would not arrive until mid-May. By then, the Middle East commander hoped to redeploy a division from East Africa, where the British Forces were clearing the remnants of the Italian Army.

Rommel defied everyone and launched his first attack after consulting with Hitler in Berlin. The battle of Marsa Brega on 31 March marked a distinct swing in fortunes. The close co-operation between German Stukas, tanks and infantry contrasted with the feeble handling of Allied forces. By 3 April, Rommel was in Benghazi and on hearing about this success the Fuehrer granted him complete freedom of action in Libya.

When Wavell visited again on 2 April, he was so dismayed that he brought back O'Connor to replace the neophytic Neame. The effect on the headquarters was instantaneous. According to Wing Commander John Judge, it "was like a mother placing a cool hand on a feverish child."[6]

O'Connor refused to undermine Neame and take over in the midst of battle but stayed on to mentor his successor. However, this not only failed to stem Rommel's advance, but it also led indirectly to the capture of both generals, when their staff car drove into the forward elements of the Afrika Korps on the Derna Road (as well as Neame's aide de camp, Dan Ranfurly, whose wife Hermione wrote *To War With Whitaker*). They were not the only senior officers lost in the retreat. John Combe was captured with them in the car; Gambier-Parry and Brigadier Edward Vaughn, commander of 3rd Indian Brigade, were captured at Mechili and Brigadier Reggie Rimmington of 3rd Armoured Brigade died after his car overturned on the coast road.

It was not all misery on this road. The leader of the Yeomanry Patrol of the Long Range Desert Group, Captain Patrick McCraith, who was wounded on 1 April by a thermos mine south of Msus, recorded his fortunate rescue:

> My left arm was peppered with metal fragments (causing partial paralysis) and my mouth and front teeth damaged by striking the breech of my machine-gun. I was taken to an abandoned airstrip where I was handed over to a Free French rear-party about to withdraw. Next morning they got me somehow to Benghazi and, after reporting to Army HQ, I went to Benghazi Hospital, which was packed with patients and with its main drain blocked and overflowing…
>
> A few hours later we were told to leave our revolvers behind, take food (we had none), and enter an ambulance as the hospital was to be evacuated… We travelled all night and I slept the whole time. At dawn we stopped to find that we were towing another (broken down) ambulance filled with stretcher cases and that we were in an enormous traffic jam…
>
> I left the ambulance and found a derelict NAAFI and obtained a few bars of chocolate which I gave to the wretched stretcher cases and then sat at the back of my ambulance, smoking the last of my cigarettes and contemplating the prospect of becoming a POW…
>
> The door of the ambulance was ajar. Through it I suddenly saw the mudguard of a truck draw up outside. It had the green and yellow flash of the Sherwood Rangers Yeomanry. In the truck were the two people I most wanted to see at that time—Colonel Flash Kellett and Bob Stibbs! After a moment or two Stibbs said, "Would you like some breakfast Sir?"[7]

After a short pause to eat their rations cooked over a Benghazi fire, Lieutenant Colonel Edward "Flash" Kellett, who was the Member of Parliament for Birmingham Aston, used his rank to bully his way past the blockage and reach Tobruk, where the bulk of the Sherwood Rangers Yeomanry had been assigned to the role of coastal artillery. McCraith was evacuated to Alexandria by ship and thence by train to Cairo Hospital, before he re-joined the Long Range Desert Group at Siwa in May.

In 10 days, Rommel had swept the poorly led British forces out of the whole of Cyrenaica apart from the port of Tobruk and the oasis of Kufra, which had been captured by the Free French commander Philippe Leclerc on 1 March. The German commander was in a hurry to finish the job, but what he didn't realise was that Major General Leslie Morshead's 9th Australian Division, which had inherited the well-built Italian defences of Tobruk, would not capitulate as easily as the British 2nd Armoured Division.

* * *

Wavell flew to Tobruk on 8 April after conferring with Foreign Secretary Anthony Eden and General Dill, who were in Cairo attempting to pull together a Balkan Front. He was met by Brigadier John Harding, chief of staff of XIII Corps, who took temporary command when General Neame was captured. Both he and Morshead believed that it was possible to hold Tobruk, having inspected the Italian fortifications and water distilleries.

Wavell was accompanied by another Australian, Major General John Laverack, who was put in command of Strafer Gott's mobile force at El Adem. That evening, the commander-in-chief walked into the Officer's Mess and recognised the Earl of Ranfurly's butler, George Whitaker, who was working behind the bar. Wavell, who had a wonderful reputation for listening "to everyone carefully", shook his hand and said he was so sorry to hear His Lordship was missing and bought him and the other Mess stewards a whisky.[8]

When Rommel drove Gott's force out of Libya, Laverack returned to Egypt and Morshead was left in sole command of Tobruk. In many ways, his character was similar to that of Iven Mackay. Both had been school teachers before World War I; both had distinguished themselves at the battle of Lone Pine at Gallipoli and in France where they were both awarded the DSO; both remained active in the militia during the inter-war period, rising to the rank of brigadier and taking command of 5th Infantry Brigade before the start of World War II. And both were supported by Thomas Blamey, the only Australian to reach the rank of field marshal.

There was some resentment felt by professional soldiers when officers of Australia's citizen army were promoted to command divisions, but Mackay and Morshead proved this wartime policy was sound. Apart from their irreproachable war records, they both had incisive minds, flint-like characters and were the epitome of resolve and ruthlessness.

Wavell asked Morshead to hold out for eight weeks, by which time he hoped to assemble forces strong enough to return to Cyrenaica. Unfortunately, he still had to deal with a worrying revolt in Iraq and the calamitous situation in Greece following the German invasion of Yugoslavia and the capture of Salonika on 8 April. Churchill was sympathetic about the loss of Cyrenaica, but less understanding when the situation in Greece deteriorated. Writing to Wavell about Tobruk, he stated: "From here it seems unthinkable that the fortress of Tobruk should be abandoned without offering the most prolonged resistance."[9]

There was some good news with General Cunningham's victory in East Africa on 11 April, which enabled President Roosevelt to send American supply ships into the Red Sea. However, just as the commander-in-chief's concentration should have been focused on Marmarica, or Greece, the chiefs of staff in London hassled him about Iraq. One of the huge frustrations for General Wavell must have been the relentless suggestions from London that a military formation that was undertaking low-level security operations could be re-roled and sent without notice on rescue missions up to 500 miles away.

Apart from General Dill, there seemed to be little understanding in London about military preparedness and "robbing Peter to pay Paul". The difference between 800 recruits who have passed a basic military course and a trained regiment that is honed by battle experience is the difference between victory and defeat, or life and death. Military miracles do happen, but not by chance. Overcoming technical and numerical odds is primarily a result of careful planning, effective organisation and inspired leadership. Realising the importance of the latter, Wavell made an offer of a prisoner swap of six Italian generals for arguably the most gifted British commander of the war, General O'Connor, but the staff in London refused to countenance his proposal.

* * *

As Wavell was dealing with Iraq and Greece, Rommel was sealing Tobruk and pressing on to the Egyptian frontier. He launched his first assault on the enclave with 5th Light Division on 10 April along the Derna Road. However, a heavy sandstorm reduced visibility to 20 feet and when the weather cleared, the well-sited British artillery halted the advance and killed *Generalmajor* Heinrich von Prittwitz und Graffron, the newly arrived commander of 15th Panzer Division.

Tobruk's perimeter defence, or Red Line, was built by the Italians about eight miles from the town and stretched for twice that distance in an arc from Wadi Sehel in the west to Wadi Zeitun in the east. It comprised a series of 128 posts each of which was given a letter and number. The letter S indicated that the bunker was in the west, Z was in the east and between them were the R posts.

Each sangar was connected by telephone to the Fortress headquarters located in a series of caves and tunnels blasted into the foot of the Solaro escarpment. Engineers had cleared fields of fire in front of the posts that overlooked an anti-tank ditch, with barbed wire and mines increasing the obstacles. To the rear, a second position, known as the Blue Line, needed further enhancements to strengthen its defences.

The Desert Fox, who had nearly met his end on several occasions during the rapid advance, now switched his main effort from the west to the south. Aiming to drive straight up the El Adem Road, he ordered a mixed force under *Generalmajor* Johannes Streich to lead the attack on Good Friday, 11 April 1941. This German veteran, who was awarded the Knight's Cross in France, had successfully defeated 2nd Armoured Division, but criticised Rommel for his rash decisions that had caused the death of von Prittwitz. However, this did not stop Rommel from sending him into the attack without time for proper reconnaissance.

The result was a first defeat for the Afrika Korps. Their panzers were diverted by the effective anti-tank ditch and were mauled by the Cruisers of 1st Royal Tank Regiment and the guns of 1st Royal Horse Artillery. Either side of the road, the novice soldiers of Brigadier John Murray's 20th Australian Brigade pinned down *Oberstleutnant* Ponarth's battalion, which was caught in the open.

That night, German engineers came forward, but Murray, who had earned an outstanding reputation for night patrolling in World War I, sent out his aggressive Australians to prevent them clearing the obstacles. The morning battle followed the same trajectory as the previous afternoon. Soldiers of 2nd/17th Australian Battalion, supported in the depth battle by the Royal Air Force, fought magnificently to halt the advance. Rommel was furious with his troops and personally took charge of the third attempt which began at 1700 hours on Easter Sunday.

The intensity racked up as an Italian artillery barrage hit the area around posts R31 and R32 and Ponarth's men attacked towards R33. Four batteries of British 25-pounders responded in kind, but they could not prevent Ponarth from opening a breach in the Red Line. Sensing this critical moment, 22-year-old Lieutenant Austin Mackell in R33 took out a fighting patrol and stumbled on a major position with six machine guns, mortars and field guns.

The first hand-to-hand combat between Australia and Germany in World War II was a victory for the Southern Hemisphere, but it came at a cost. Mackell, who was involved with three enemy soldiers, called for help and Corporal John Edmondson, a giant of a man from Wagga Wagga who was already wounded in the neck and stomach, came across and killed two of the assailants. The last German retreated from the scene leaving the Australians to carry Edmondson back to the post where, sadly, he died of his wounds. For his conspicuous bravery and sacrifice in saving his officer's life, Edmondson was awarded the first Victoria Cross to be given to an Australian in World War II and the first to anyone fighting in Libya.

Mackell's intervention was vital for three reasons. First, it delayed the advance of German tanks through Ponarth's breach; second, it confirmed to Morshead where to assemble his main defence force; and third, it put a marker down for the 2nd/17th Battalion, who rose to their fire steps and opened a withering fire on the dismounted German infantry that was trying to join the panzers waiting in dead ground half a mile further on. Leading his men in this impossible mission, the courageous Ponarth paid for Rommel's mistakes with his life.

Meanwhile, the isolated German tanks still needed to be destroyed. Chestnut Troop, the senior battery in the British Army, and E Battery of 1st Royal Horse Artillery, blocked their path and fired over 100 rounds each as the panzers bore down on them. This was enough to turn the tanks away and with the support of 3rd Royal Horse Artillery and the Australian gunners they forced them into the sights of the British tanks. The German commander, *Leutnant* Joachim Schorm, described the carnage of their retreat: "Some of our tanks are already on fire. The crews call for doctors who dismount to help in this witches' cauldron. Enemy anti-tank units fall on us with their machine guns firing into our midst… the lane is in sight. Everyone hurries towards it… now comes the gap and the ditch… the vehicle almost gets stuck but manages to extricate itself with great difficulty."[10]

The wreckage of 17 tanks and many guns bore witness to the Afrika Korps' defeat, but this was not the only battle fought that day at Tobruk. In the skies above the harbour, Geisler's aircraft arrived in waves soon after dawn. Seventy Messerschmitts, Junkers, Heinkels and Italian G50s duelled with the anti-aircraft guns commanded by Brigadier John Slater and the eight Hawker Hurricanes flying from El Gubi airfield. The blitz was repelled, but sadly with the loss of three precious Royal Air Force fighters, whose pilots were buried that day by the tireless padre of 258 Wing, a 32-year-old chaplain from Worthing, Squadron Leader The Reverend James Cox.[11]

After the Germans retreated, Rommel turned to his Italian troops in the west, but they were easily repelled when they made several half-hearted attempts at Ras El Medauar over the next three days. This intervention was important, because Morshead realised that he needed to strengthen that part of the perimeter and so he laid a belt of mines stretching across two miles of country that would prove to be vital in the future.

* * *

After Easter week, two morale-lifting aspects became clear to the defenders of Tobruk. The first was the realisation that the so-called invincible German Army was beatable after all. The second was the mutual respect earned by all the various parts of the command. Everyone played their part, from the Australian infantry at the front to the Wiltshire yeomen manning the searchlights around the harbour.

There is nothing better for soldiers who have been ordered to fight to the last to know that the rear area shares their discomforts. In the case of Tobruk, the logistic hub was the port, which was the sole reason for the town. There was no other industry or agriculture and the population of 5,000 relied on the work it generated.

The men who ran the harbour were the Chief Control Officer, Major Charles O'Shaughnessy, and the 48-year-old naval commander, Captain Frank Montem Smith. Early on, they earned widespread fame for their heroics, described by Anthony Heckstall-Smith:

> Out in the harbour, one of the lighters inloading petrol alongside a merchant ship blew sky high. It was a ghastly sight. We could see the water burning all around and hear the dreadful cries of her crew, some of whom were burning like torches. A second later we saw smoke pouring from the forepart of the merchantman. O'Shaughnessy raced down the steps to the quay and old Smithy came rushing hell for leather from his office. Together they jumped into a launch and were off to the burning ship. I shall never forget how the two of them worked that night. Two of the oldest men in Tobruk, they were the first to board and last to leave. Unconcerned for their own safety, or the fact that at any moment the ship might blow up under them, they manned the hose and directed operations from the red hot deck…[12]

O'Shaughnessy, who already had the Military Medal, was awarded the George Medal for this rescue along with two Australians, Corporal Walter Brown and Sapper John Gleaves. He was also awarded the Military Cross and made an MBE for his Tobruk efforts. His partner-in-work was awarded the DSO and made a CBE, but sadly died in action on 21 June 1942 and was buried at Knightsbridge War Cemetery; as a poignant remembrance, the lantern with which he guided in the ships was placed on top of his grave.

Apart from fuel, the Royal Navy ships that Smith guided into the harbour brought military spares and 80 tons of chilled meat each month. On their return journey, they thinned out the garrison and by the end of April, Morshead had rid himself of 15,000 men and 5,000 prisoners of war. This left him 23,000 men at arms, ready to fight to the death.

The most important supply for these men was water. The garrison was fortunate to benefit from the wells sunk by Italian engineers, which pumped 600 gallons of water each day, and the two distilling plants that converted 100 gallons of sea water into fresh. These lifelines became targets for the Luftwaffe, which continued their relentless bombing throughout April.

For a month, the Royal Air Force faced up to this attack with additional planes sent by the commander of the Desert Air Force, Air Commodore Ray Collishaw. Initially, the crews lived in the Hotel Albergo, but the night raids forced them to move into tents in the desert after a bomb demolished the next-door warehouse.

Seeing the Hurricanes duelling with the Stukas was a huge boost to the morale of the garrison, but the attrition rate was unsustainable.

When the Luftwaffe established air bases close to Tobruk, they gained the advantage and by 25 April, only eight of Collishaw's original 36 fighters remained. Consulting with Arthur Longmore in Cairo, he reluctantly closed the Tobruk base and withdrew the fighters to Egypt with their honour intact. Three days later, the senior Royal Air Force officers departed in a Bristol Blenheim leaving behind a team of mechanics to recover precious spares from the crashed aircraft around the fortress.

This Blenheim should have taken off at dawn, but unfortunately, it was delayed and by the time it was in the air, six German fighters were approaching. The journalist Jan Yindrich described the moment when the plane fell from the sky: "One moment there was a Blenheim fleeing out to sea, the next there was nothing, except the Messerschmitt, which banked and flew inland again."[13] Apart from Wing Commander David Johnson from Cheltenham, the plane was also transporting Padre James Cox, who had given relief to so many wounded and buried so many airmen during the previous month.

* * *

The day before this tragedy, von Herff's troops seized Hellfire Pass from the Guards Brigade and this cleared the way for Rommel to return to Tobruk. For General Wavell on 30 April, the situation must have seemed overwhelming. He was in Crete discussing the defence of the island and at the same time, he had to help the besieged staff in the British embassy in Baghdad; then, that evening, Rommel mounted his strongest attack on Tobruk's perimeter.

It began with a deliberate break in battle by 115 Rifle Regiment in the Ras El Medauar sector. Since the Easter battles, the steely Australians had dominated no man's land at night by their expert patrolling, but that evening a heavy German barrage in the west followed by a determined attack kept them occupied in their posts. By dawn, the panzers of 15 Division were assembled inside the perimeter waiting to strike.

Facing the German threat was Brigadier Ray Tovell's 26th Brigade. He was another citizen soldier, awarded the DSO in World War I, who led a very successful civilian life until World War II. In his northerly front-line posts, he positioned 2nd/23rd and 2nd/24th Battalions and in reserve, 2nd/48th held the key ground of Wadi Glaida and the approach to the port.

There are four reasons why the May battle was harder for the Allies than the April encounter. First, the Germans were better prepared and instigated a longer artillery barrage before launching their assault. Second, the Luftwaffe was now totally dominant in the air. Third, Rommel was reinforced by 15 Panzer Division with many more tanks and battle-winning 88mm guns that outmatched the British Matilda tank. Finally, the sector that he chose to attack was harder to defend due to the dead ground and difficulty of interlocking the arcs of fire.

Despite these advantages, the crucial factor of fighting spirit and morale was evenly balanced. Yet again, the Australian infantry bore the brunt of the assault, but their will to win matched that of their fathers at Gallipoli. Every post was held with tenacious resolve and the most exposed, S7, held out for six hours, thus thwarting Rommel's plan to launch a dawn attack from a secure base.

On 1 May, German guns thundered, dive bombers screamed, and tank engines roared, but in an act of divine intervention, a blinding dust storm covered the whole area with a thick yellow cloud, reducing visibility to less than six feet. Rommel's initial point of attack was a large hill, known as Point 209, but his subsequent objective was the east-west track that ran from Macchia Bianca to Fort Pilastrino and thence into Tobruk.

Communications to several posts were cut, but the intermittent reports from 20th Brigade provided Morshead with a fair idea of Rommel's intentions. The Australian commander had insufficient reserves to cover every eventuality, but he was able to assemble a strong blocking force on the likely German approach. This was based around the Matilda tanks of 7th Royal Tank Regiment, with British and Australian artillery and Tovell's reserve battalion.

Soon after the weather cleared, two columns totalling more than 120 panzers advanced from the salient, expecting to drive straight into Tobruk. However, they stumbled at the minefield, where dozens of panzers blew up and the blocking force had a field day shooting at stranded vehicles. The intense fighting for the perimeter continued unabated. Hooded German soldiers wearing cowls and capes used flame-throwers against the stubbornly held posts, but the Boyes anti-tank rifle was effective at disabling this temperamental weapon.

A vital tank engagement did just enough to prevent 15th Panzer Division from widening the breach. One of the officers in this battle, who also fought in the April encounter, was Major George Hynes of 1st Royal Tank Regiment. Jan Yindrich's report of his Good Friday exploits, when he had three tanks blown up under him, was broadcast to the world by the BBC in London. After the May battle, they met over a cup of tea and Hynes explained how he had received a nasty burn to his left buttock.

On 1 May, his day had begun with a fight against 30 German panzers that were supported by a dozen Stukas dropping bombs from the sky. One of these landed six feet from his tank, but did not explode. After destroying three enemy tanks, an incendiary shell penetrated his Cruiser from the left and started to fizz on the floor. Hynes opened the turret to evacuate the crew and in the process, he was burned all over his back. As he was being rescued by another tank, a burst of machine-gun fire hit one of his crew in the wrist, but miraculously missed Hynes. Yindrich returned with another story of "the man they could not kill",[14] which further embellished the worldwide reputation of the Tobruk defenders.

Despite gaining a salient inside the perimeter, Rommel lost this pivotal battle for Tobruk. After a blitzkrieg that matched anything Germany had produced elsewhere, the "men who had suffered it and should by rights and all previous German experience have been queueing to surrender, had instead come out with their bayonets and thrown the blitzmakers on to a desperate defence".[15] More importantly, when the German High Command heard about the scale of Rommel's casualties (53 officers and 1,187 men), it refused to grant him any more forces because they were now focused on their invasion of Russia, Operation *Barbarossa*.

* * *

General Wavell heard about these plans from Bletchley Park, and this gave him the opportunity for an attempt to relieve Tobruk. On 15 May, he launched Operation *Brevity*, with Major General Gott leading three columns against the combined Italian and German defenders at Sollum, Fort Capuzzo and Hellfire Pass. The centre column, based on 22nd Guards Brigade, met stiff opposition from the Bersaglieri, who earned the emblem of the famous Cyrene plant, silphium, awarded to units that distinguished themselves in the Western Desert. However, their courage was not enough to prevent the British troops from capturing the top of Hellfire Pass by mid-morning. The southern column met little resistance and by midday, dominated the area around Fort Capuzzo. However, the bottom of the pass remained in Italian hands until the Rifle Brigade, with Australian reinforcements, captured it during the evening.

Although Gott achieved his objectives on the first day, a German counter-attack captured Capuzzo and due to the paucity of reserves, he had to withdraw to defend the pass. Wavell was unable to support the operation any further because he heard that Hitler was about to attack Crete and sure enough on 20 May, 3,000 parachute troops landed on the fifth largest island in the Mediterranean. Within a fortnight, the Army and the Royal Navy suffered devastating losses, including three cruisers and six destroyers sunk. To compound matters, Rommel launched Operation *Skorpion* on 27 May and recaptured Hellfire Pass.

* * *

Life for the defenders of Tobruk changed significantly in May. The signaller Frank Harrison suggests that: "Before the battle of May Day we neither thought nor felt that we were besieged. We were inside the wire and resisting an enemy who was outside it. After the battles… Rommel was forced to change his strategy from reduction by force to containment and slow strangulation and starvation."[16]

A straggle of Allied soldiers who had avoided capture made their way into Tobruk after it was surrounded. In April, Yindrich met a doctor who handed him his diary of an 11-day journey on condition that the journalist sent a cable to his pregnant wife in Rudgwick, West Sussex, informing her that he was safe and well.[17] He had become separated from his convoy when it was ambushed on the Derna Road and had to look after a wounded gunner, Harry Durkin, who was shot through the right arm with a compound fracture to his humerus.

The good doctor had cared for Harry until he died early on the third day. Unfortunately, a German plane landed nearby and this, together with a leaking water container, delayed his start until nightfall. Cautiously, he followed the rugged coast and was given water by a Libyan after asking: *"Attini mayyia min fadlak?"* He met a group of Indian soldiers escaping from Mechili, but they decided to try their luck on the road and were subsequently caught. Somehow, the doctor managed to avoid the enemy patrols and in spite of being bitten by mosquitos and suffering from paronychia, he reached the enclave after trekking 140 miles in 11 days.

This endurance record was broken when a 22-year-old Australian soldier arrived on 14 May. He had spent 39 days dodging German and Italian soldiers and was looked after by the Sanussi, who gave him food and water and steered him clear of enemy positions. He had been fighting near to Benghazi on 4 April and set out with 24 others, but was separated and then joined another group, finally coming through the wire wearing a towel on his head "to make anybody spotting me think I was a Sanussi".[18]

There were several ways of coping with the harsh conditions in the besieged garrison. Many Australians passed their time losing money in their "two-up" gambling sessions, tossing coins and throwing dice. Others occupied themselves by obsessively improving the holes in the ground in which they lived. In this endeavour, Frank Harrison and his signallers "sweated salt until we could scrape it from the armpits of our shirts".[19]

Discomforts such as fleas and flies, which were unaffected by the Army-issued insect powder, combined with the sand that found its way into every nook and cranny to cultivate rashes. Stout characters suffered alternately from diarrhoea, triggered by the brackish water, and constipation, induced by military rations. Despite these irritations, the fighting spirit remained high. Morale was not a commodity that could be brought in on a schooner like fuel on *The Pass of Balhera*. It was an intangible asset and depended on small things like mail from home and the NAAFI, which continued to operate despite its building being bombed.

Being informed about the outside world also helped. The daily newspaper, *Tobruk Truth*, which reproduced BBC news, did some good, but its nickname "Dinkum Oil" revealed a healthy scepticism for its content, along with its rivals, *Libyan News Bulletin* and the padre's paper, *Happy Valley News*. Perversely, one of the biggest boosts came when William Joyce, the British apologist for Hitler who broadcast on *Germany Calling*, taunted the garrison one evening and said: "When are you going to come out of your holes, you rats of Tobruk?" With this trite comment, Lord Haw-Haw, as he was known, gave the disparate groups a sense of shared identity and stiffened their resolve.

The chief drain on morale, according to Yindrich, was "the psychological effect of the presence of enemy planes constantly in the sky, without interference from the Royal Air Force... The noise of the exploding bombs and the spattering of machine-gun bullets induce a feeling of helplessness in the infantryman, who has to keep his head down while it is on. There are constant alarms and stand-tos in anticipation of attacks which do not materialise and this keeps the nervous tension at top pitch."[20]

This was a test of battlefield discipline as much as individual courage. Trenches were cut with zig-zags to deny enemy aircraft a clear run. Camouflage, take-cover drills and ensuring no vehicle was allowed to drive near to the headquarters because the tracks would give away its location to enemy air photography were all vital for survival.

However, the most important contribution to morale came from the performance of Morshead, affectionately known as Ming the Merciless, who showed he was more than a match for Rommel. His will to win was an essential ingredient in repelling the relentless attacks and this was reinforced by the outstanding brigade commanders, including John Slater, who dragooned everyone he could into firing anti-aircraft guns at the German bombers.

Other contributors included HMS *Ladybird*, a "Yangtse Gunboat" built in 1916 that regularly ran the gauntlet from Egypt to Tobruk, captained by Jack Blackburn from Harrogate. During the worst of the blitz, his crew brought down two Stukas and when Morshead heard about this success, he sent a message of congratulations: "You certainly played a great knock." By return, the Yorkshireman replied: "Well played Australia. Only Yorkshire could have done better. We will win by an innings."[21] The following day, HMS *Chakla* sank in the harbour, but the crew of HMS *Ladybird* saved everyone on board. Then on 12 May, she was hit badly and settled in 10 feet of water but continued to be an effective anti-aircraft platform.

* * *

After the catastrophe of Crete, Churchill sent tank reinforcements to General Wavell by sea and encouraged him to launch another attack against Rommel as soon as possible. This second attempt, named Operation *Battleaxe*, began on 15 June, one week before Hitler launched Operation *Barbarossa*. Hellfire Pass was again the scene of the initial moves by XIII Corps, commanded by Lieutenant General Sir Noel Beresford-Peirse.

The result was worse than Operation *Brevity*. Rommel had reinforced his defences on the high ground at Hellfire Pass and was given nine hours warning of the attack by 7th Armoured Division's insecure radio transmissions. A catalogue of mistakes was made by the British artillery, engineers and tanks. Guns became bogged in soft sand and failed to suppress the German 88mm guns on the escarpment. These in turn destroyed many of the new tanks that were poorly handled by 7th Armoured Division. Minefields were not cleared and these immobilised three Matilda tanks that blocked the route.

Meanwhile, the inspirational Pastor Major Wilhelm Bach and the Savona division commander, *Generale* Fedele de Giorgis, defended Hellfire Pass resolutely against Brigadier Savory's 11th Indian Brigade and this remained in Axis hands at the end of the first day. That night, German radio intercepts again allowed Rommel to know what was planned and redeploy his forces to key positions.

The performance of 7th Armoured did not improve on the second day. Neither O'Moore Creagh, nor Beresford-Peirse, both of whom did so well under General O'Connor's leadership, handled the battle well and Wavell had to take over in mid-battle because the corps commander was floundering. Hellfire Pass became the anchor for the counter-attacks by 5th Light and 15th Panzer Divisions, which by the end of the third day had recaptured all the lost ground. What added to the sense of disaster was the loss of 33 fighter aircraft and three bombers, which was blamed on a lack of pilot training.

When Churchill heard about the loss of precious lives and equipment, he made up his mind to replace General Wavell. This was a difficult decision because he was highly respected and his failings were very much caused by impossible political demands from London. His big successes, Operation *Compass*, East Africa, Tobruk, Iraq and Syria stand well above the misfortunes of Crete and *Battleaxe*, but the credit he held did not save him in the end.

The prime minister wrote three days after the defeat, on 21 June: "I have come to the conclusion that the public interest will best be served by the appointment of General Auchinleck to relieve you in the command of the armies of the Middle East. I have greatly admired your command and conduct of these armies both in success and adversity, and the victories which are associated with your name will be famous in the story of the British Army and are an important contribution to our final success in this obstinate war. I feel however that after the long strain you have borne a new eye and a new hand are required in this most seriously menaced theatre. I am sure that you are incomparably the best man and most distinguished officer to fill the vacancy of commander-in-chief in India..."[22]

When his chief of staff informed him of the decision the following morning, an unruffled Wavell appeared ready to go with good grace. Carrying on shaving, he calmly pronounced: "The Prime Minister's quite right. This job needs a new eye and a new hand."[23]

CHAPTER 10

Auk Arrives

Jealousies among generals are worse than among women.

GALEAZZO CIANO, 20 DECEMBER 1940[1]

Sunday 22 June 1942 was memorable not only for the dismissal of General Wavell as commander-in-chief, but also for the start of Operation *Barbarossa*. Churchill knew about Hitler's plans from Bletchley Park's code-breakers. Believing that Berlin would be distracted by the hefty demands of organising three million men to fight along a 1,000-mile frontage, he lost no time in urging his new commander in Cairo, General Sir Claude Auchinleck, to launch a rapid riposte in Libya. The prime minister needed instant results and had little patience for the rebuilding that was required to create an army capable of defeating Rommel.

As soon as he assumed command, the Auk realised that the Eighth Army was in no shape to attack and resisted the overtures from London to throw good money after bad. Concluding his assessment, he made three early decisions that had a profound effect on the campaign. The first was to appoint 54-year-old General Alan Cunningham as commander of Eighth Army (against Churchill's recommendation of Jumbo Wilson). He was the brother of the fleet commander and had just led the successful East African campaign, but had scant experience of armoured warfare.

The second decision was to add a second corps to Eighth Army. To do this, Auchinleck created XXX Corps and made it more mobile than XIII Corps by giving it 7th Armoured Division. The eminently qualified Lieutenant General Vyvyan Pope, a leading thinker on armoured warfare, arrived from England to take command, but unfortunately, on his way to Cunningham's first conference, the Hudson aircraft in which he was travelling crashed with no survivors.

Auchinleck's third decision was to replace 9th Australian Division that was stranded in Tobruk. This was foisted upon him by the government in Australia after the prime minister of a hung parliament was forced to resign over the conduct of the war. Auk was "so deeply affronted by the Fadden government's demand that he wished to tender his resignation on the grounds that he did not command the confidence of the Australian Government".[2] However, Churchill's, new minister in Cairo, Oliver Lyttleton, managed to smooth this over and for a substitute, the commander-in-chief selected 6th Infantry Division, which had defeated the Vichy French in Syria, but to avoid confusion with its Australian namesake, he renumbered it 70th Infantry Division.[3]

Meanwhile at Tobruk, Rommel intensified the siege. During the broiling summer, he used 3,000 Italian workers to build a bypass, known as the *Achenstrasse*, and constructed a ring of blockading posts beyond the range of the feared British artillery. He also planned another assault on the fortress, but before this was feasible, he needed General Geissler to destroy the Royal Navy ships that provided life-saving supplies to the besieged soldiers.

Morshead's brigades were equally busy strengthening their defences. To the west, Brigadier George Wootten cleared fields of fire and moved his trench line forward to create an "almost impregnable arc from S7 to R7".[4] Not content with passive resistance, the Australian commander launched an attack on 3 August to capture the salient with two battalions from 24th Brigade. On the northern side, Captain Conway led 2nd/28th and managed to capture S7, but the next day they were overwhelmed. On the southern side, Captain McCarter led 2nd/43rd against R7, but this was called off when only 23 fit men remained.

This was the bloodiest battle of the siege and was particularly memorable for a moment that characterised the mutual respect between the two sides and set the Western Desert apart from other theatres in World War II. When Father Tommy Gard led an attempt to recover the Australian casualties, the two stretcher bearers, William Tait and Keith Pope, were hailed by a German soldier with a Red Cross flag who proposed a truce. Informing them that they were entering a minefield, he brought out two engineers with mine-detectors and a doctor to help them recover the wounded and dead.

The courageous priest recovered 15 soldiers on the battlefield and another 13 in the minefield. Before departing, the German doctor announced, "We will send your four wounded men out", but in fact only three came across because the fourth had chosen to stay to try and find his brother, who had been captured earlier. The Australians were told not to engage until everyone was back in their trenches and taken down their flags. The German soldier then gave an old army salute[5] and disappeared into his post.

If the routine on the front line was all about night patrols, dawn raids, sniping and mortars, life in the fortress was no less stressful. During the first six months, Tobruk withstood 750 air raids and destroyed 150 enemy aircraft. There were of course some tranquil moments when the "Rats" emerged at the end of the day to stretch their limbs and enjoy "magnificent Ra" setting in the West. However, the noise and shock of the bombs continued to have a debilitating effect on the vast majority of men in the rear area.

The ferry service that supplied the garrison from Alexandria, known as the Spud Run, suffered as badly as anyone, with two destroyers, one mine-layer, three sloops and 19 smaller vessels lost. Several of the captains earned fame for their bravery, including an Australian Navy lieutenant known to everyone as Pedlar Palmer, who captained the 200-ton schooner *Maria Giovanni*. Palmer was wounded and awarded the Distinguished Service Cross for "courage, skill and devotion to duty in operations off the Libyan coast", before he was captured and sent to an Italian prisoner-of-war camp.

Morshead remained defiant, but his soldiers, who won fame as the first to blunt the German war machine, had earned their rest and recuperation. For Auchinleck, it also made sense to install a fresh formation at Tobruk, so it could participate fully in his autumn offensive.

The relief took place in three waves, dictated by the Navy's need for a moonless night. Between 19 and 29 August, a return journey, code-named *Treacle*, brought in the Polish Carpathian Brigade and took out Wootten's 18th Brigade. A month later, *Supercharge* brought in the advance party of 70th Division's headquarters, together with 16th Brigade and the vanguard of 4th Royal Tank Regiment, while removing Brigadier Godfrey's 24th Brigade.

The final Australian troops were due to come out during the third wave, code-named *Cultivate*, which brought in 70th Division's main party. This included 14th and 23rd Brigades, a Czech battalion and a field hospital. However, HMS *Latona* sank on the last journey to Tobruk on 25 October and although most of the troops were rescued,[6] the loss of this large ship depleted the numbers who could return to Alexandria. As a result, 2nd/13th Battalion drew the short straw and remained in the fortress.

* * *

The new commander, Major General Ronald Scobie, and his troops had much to do to match their Australian predecessors. Scobie had played for Scotland in a nail-biting Calcutta Cup match against England before World War I.[7] Influenced by Herbert Kitchener, he joined the Royal Engineers and was awarded a Military Cross in France before he was wounded and became a brigade major. It was unusual for a sapper with little command experience to be given a fighting division, but Tobruk needed a technical expert more than a combat leader and Scobie had come to prominence for his skills in the successful East African campaign.[8]

As soon as the British troops took over the front line, they were out patrolling no man's land. However, they were not as aggressive as their predecessors and during the handover, the Afrika Korps retook a number of the posts outside the perimeter, bringing forward concrete mixers to improve defences and linking them with wire and minefields.

Meanwhile, Rommel rebuilt his supply line and increased his command. The 5th Light Division was upgraded and renamed 21st Panzer Division and his special units were combined into 90th Light division, "strong in firepower and mobile infantry, but totally lacking in tanks".[9] Panzer Group Afrika now matched the Allied command with two corps. The much-improved Italian XX Corps, comprising the Ariete Armoured and Trieste Motorised Divisions, added to the Afrika Korps, now commanded by *Generalleutnant* Ludwig Crüwell.

Rommel tested the Allied defences with a frontier raid in September but failed to find any supply dumps and mistakenly concluded that the Allies were not planning an offensive. After satisfying Berlin about the risks, his higher command agreed to his plan for another assault on Tobruk on his 50th birthday, 15 November. However, after taking account of the moon's cycle, he changed this date to five days later.

On Rommel's birthday, Winston Churchill sent a message from the king to Auchinleck about the battle ahead, which concluded: "The Desert Army may add a page to history which will rank with Blenheim and with Waterloo. The eyes of all nations are upon you. All our hearts are with you. May God uphold the right!"[10]

Three days later, the Auk pre-empted Rommel's attack when he launched Operation *Crusader*. In the build-up, rain and poor visibility helped to camouflage the move of 500 tanks, but also prevented the Royal Air Force from softening up the Axis objectives. Nevertheless, Cunningham's Eighth Army passed through the frontier wire at dawn on 18 November relatively unhindered.

This was the third such venture since the siege of Tobruk began, but to those who had survived the previous failures, the "proceedings bore a close resemblance to... Battleaxe".[11] Initially all went well as XXX Corps, commanded by Lieutenant General Willoughby Norrie, advanced unopposed, but unfortunately, the brigade commanders had failed to learn their lessons and the first engagement, early on 19 November at Bir el Gubi, ended in defeat.

The battle was between 22nd Armoured Brigade, led by Brigadier John Scott-Cockburn, and the Ariete division. It began well enough with the Royal Gloucestershire Hussars' Crusader tanks (Cruiser Mark IVs) overrunning the Italian position. However, there were no ground troops at hand to take the surrender and the Italian soldiers retired to the gun line, where they destroyed 30 of the British tanks.

Both sides fought with courage and fortitude. For their outstanding leadership, Lieutenant Colonel Normand Birley of the 17th/21st Lancers was awarded the Distinguished Service Order and Captain Sandy Cameron of the County of London Sharpshooters earned a Military Cross, when he rescued his squadron commander from behind enemy lines.[12] However, the British could not shift the determined Bersaglieri soldiers, who had learned the importance of infantry-tank cooperation from their training with the Afrika Korps.

By now, the armoured brigades in Eighth Army had become so dispersed that they could not support each other in battle. The spearhead, 7th Armoured, had reached the airfield at Sidi Rezegh just south of Trigh Capuzzo. However, 40 miles back at the frontier, 4th Armoured, under Brigadier Alexander Gatehouse, was engaged by 21st Panzer Division in a point-blank duel that epitomised tank-to-tank battles in the Western Desert. By the evening of 19 November, Norrie's corps was deployed all over the desert like thinly spread jam.

While the two sides played blind man's buff on 20 November, an over-exuberant General Cunningham declared "Pop", the code-word for the breakout of 70th Division from Tobruk. General Scobie gave orders to the imaginatively named Tobforce and appointed Brigadier Arthur Willison, commander of 32nd Army Tank Brigade, as tactical leader of what became known as the Corridor, while retaining control of the three infantry brigades and supporting arms from the Fortress Headquarters.

In the dark, the Leicestershire Regiment secured the entry points into the perimeter minefield while a Polish diversion drowned the noise of the approaching tanks. The King's Dragoon Guards cleared a lane and the sappers constructed bridges across the tank ditch, which allowed 2nd King's Own Royal Regiment to launch an attack on the listening post named Butch and 2nd Black Watch to attack Jill. These battalions were supposed to be supported by 7th Royal Tank Regiment, but the Matilda tanks were late arriving and mistakenly all drove towards Butch, which was captured with the loss of 39 soldiers.

Without tank support, the Black Watch soldiers were exposed to the well-sited machine guns at Jill. After a series of near-suicidal dashes, B Company captured the post, but at a terrible cost. Of the five officers, three were dead, one was dying and the last was seriously wounded. All that remained from 100 soldiers were the company sergeant major and 10 men.

The battle for Tiger was worse. Rommel had brought forward his artillery in preparation for his own assault and together with the machine guns, they took a heavy toll on the advancing companies. Pipe Major Rab Roy "played in" the battalion with "Highland Laddie" and "Lawson's Men" and when he was wounded for the third time, Sergeant McNicol stepped forward to take his place.

And so it went on: as their forebears had in Flanders, so this generation of Highlanders defied the odds and marched into history. When a company commander fell, a platoon commander took his place; when a sergeant fell, a corporal stepped into the gap. All over the battlefield, a forest of rifles studded the ground with their bayonets marking the place where the dead and wounded lay.[13] Approaching the objective, 24 out of 32 officers and almost 500 men were stopped in their tracks.

Just as the Black Watch was running out of steam, Brigadier Willison's tanks caught up with them. By this time, Tiger was obscured by smoke and dust and the wire entanglements and minefields formed severe obstacles. However, with a final, desperate effort they advanced again and while the tanks destroyed enemy machine guns, the Highlanders repaid the favour by taking out the anti-tank guns. By

1015 hours, the position was captured together with 500 prisoners and the medics began the grim work of clearing the battlefield, while the survivors began preparing for the inevitable counter-attack that was repulsed later that afternoon.

Scobie now deployed 1st Battalion Bedfordshire and Hertfordshire Regiment, known for many years as the Peacemakers, to capture Tugan from the Italians on the west of the corridor and to consolidate the gains. To the south, the Royal Tank Regiment advanced towards Wolf and Freddie, but unfortunately, both these posts were strongly held and several Cruiser tanks were destroyed before the remainder limped back to the corridor after dark.

The ultimate objective for 70th Division, which was placed under command of General Godwin-Austen's XIII Corps, was El Duda, given the nickname Plum. This feature on the *Achenstrasse* was within sight of Sidi Rezegh and was the appointed location for the linkup with Eighth Army, but because they had not reached this point, Tobforce remained in the corridor, consolidating their impressive gains.[14] The British forces had taken on the might of Rommel's *Panzergruppe* and dispelled some of the myths about the German Army. They had captured hundreds of prisoners and established a protected corridor with three infantry battalions holding the lines.

During the night the magnificent work of the recovery team and artificers provided Brigadier Willison with good news as a trickle of repaired tanks re-joined the front line. In the morning, orders arrived to attack Plum, but these were soon rescinded. While Scobie waited for an update on Eighth Army's progress, the front-line troops identified another post named Lion that threatened the corridor. A battle group was formed around 2nd Battalion York and Lancaster Regiment, but the enemy abandoned the position before the attack went in.

As darkness descended on 22 November, icy rain fell like tears on the battlefield and the dug-in troops suffered another heavy bombardment. Brigadier Willison now had to confront two new challenges. The first was a demand to help XXX Corps, which was having difficulty in the east. Preparing for this, he identified a feature named Dalby Square and gave orders for an attack the next day. His second problem was a shortage of artillery ammunition. The overworked 1st Royal Horse Artillery had been firing continuously for two days, but Scobie's request for a resupply had been put on hold by Cairo, so the gallant gunners had to conserve whatever remained in the enclave.

Meanwhile, Rommel had launched a devastating counter-attack on XXX Corps and General Cunningham was making a hash of his first venture as an armoured commander. Although his plan had been to concentrate his armoured forces at Tobruk, after three days they remained dispersed and this allowed the Desert Fox to defeat individual units piecemeal.

The key battles occurred around Sidi Rezegh. During the morning of 21 November, 1st King's Royal Rifle Corps advanced in their Bren-carriers against a well-sited enemy position. They managed to seize the lip of the escarpment with the loss of 84 men and during this action a 23-year-old from Manchester, Rifleman John Beeley, won a posthumous Victoria Cross. His company "was pinned down by heavy fire at point-blank range from the front and flank on the flat and open ground of the aerodrome". All but one of the officers were killed or wounded, but on his own initiative, he rose to his feet and ran forward over open ground, firing his Bren gun. At 20 yards' range, he put an anti-tank gun and two machine guns out of action, but he was hit four times and fell dead across his gun. His self-sacrifice galvanised those with him "to reach their objective, which was eventually captured by them, together with 700 prisoners".[15]

Uniquely for the Western Desert Campaign, three Victoria Crosses were awarded to British soldiers for actions at Sidi Rezegh on that day. The second of these was earned by 29-year-old Second Lieutenant George Gunn of 3rd Royal Horse Artillery. He was a troop commander of four quick-firing anti-tank guns mounted on trucks in J Battery, commanded by Major Bernard Pinney.

When 60 panzers attacked the position from the rear, all but one of his guns were destroyed and this was on a burning truck with a dead crew except for the sergeant. While Pinney attempted to put out the flames, Gunn took over the aiming and firing with the surviving sergeant acting as his loader. Despite the danger of exploding ammunition on the vehicle, Gunn fired "between forty and fifty rounds" and set two enemy tanks on fire before he was shot through the head. His "utter disregard for extreme danger was an example which inspired all who saw it".[16]

The final award was made to Support Group's formidable commander, Brigadier Jock Campbell, who had lent his name to the successful raiding columns in Operation *Compass* and strangely had attended the same school (Sedbergh) as Gunn. His Victoria Cross was awarded for outstanding leadership under fire, when he effectively rescued Brigadier George Davey's 7th Armoured Brigade that was being annihilated by the combined might of two panzer divisions.

Campbell ignored the risks and moved to wherever the situation was most difficult and the fighting hardest. The South African test cricketer Bob Crisp, who commanded a squadron of M3 Stuarts (or Honeys as they were also known) in 3rd Royal Tank Regiment, described Campbell's bravery in his book *Brazen Chariots* and the journalist Alan Moorehead eulogised: "They say that Campbell won the VC half a dozen times that day. The men loved this Elizabethan figure. He was the reality of all the pirate yarns and tales of high adventure, and in the extremes of fear and courage of the battle he had only courage."[17]

The many acts of incredible bravery cannot disguise the careless handling of British armoured formations compared with the Afrika Korps. What is astonishing about the rout of 7th Armoured Brigade is the interpretation of events in Cairo, where a press statement was cabled that misled everyone who read it: "It is authoritatively stated that the Libyan battle, which was at its height this afternoon, is going extremely well."[18]

For years afterwards, military minds pondered what went wrong and the subject became a staple of Staff College and Royal Armoured Corps studies. Critics have blamed inadequate equipment, inaccurate reporting, scant training, confused communications, rash dogma and incoherent decision-making. There is no doubt that a poor plan was badly executed; however, what none of the detractors have been able to prove is that anyone else could have done any better if they had been placed in the same situation.

* * *

The following day, Rommel gave orders for his panzer divisions to press home their advantage. He assigned Oberstleutnant Gustav-Georg Knabe's battle group to drive the King's Royal Rifle Corps off the escarpment; he ordered Panzer Regiment 5 to hook round to the west; and he sent *Oberst* Marks' Rifle Regiment 115 south-east along the Trigh Capuzzo. The German approach began after the commander of 7th Armoured Division, Strafer Gott, informed his brigades that no attempt would be made that day to advance to Tobruk and his priority was to bring 5th South African Brigade into play and concentrate the division before a concerted effort on the besieged port began the next day.

Soon after Gott departed to meet the South African commander, the Afrika Korps appeared from the north. Brigadier Campbell's Support Group blunted the attack, but 22nd Armoured Brigade blundered straight into an 88mm killing zone and was virtually destroyed. While the battle continued on the airfield, Panzer Regiment 5's turning movement caught the riflemen in the flank and forced them off the high ground.

One of the officers of 2nd Royal Tank Regiment, Cyril Joly, described the battlefield scene that met his eyes: "I was appalled at the extent of the devastation and carnage, which seemed to spread as far as the eye could see. It was a frightening and awesome spectacle—the dead and dying strewn over the battlefield, in trucks and Bren-carriers, in trenches and toppled over the rails of their guns, some silent and grey in death, others vocal with pain and stained by red gashes of flowing blood or the dark marks of old congealed wounds. Trucks, guns, ammunition, odd bits of clothing were smouldering or burning with bright tongues of fire. Here and there ammunition had caught fire and was exploding with spurts of flame and black smoke…"[19]

Gott ordered a withdrawal to Point 178, but this was now held by *Oberst* Marks and the South African infantry had been unable to reach their objective due to Stuka attacks and a heavy concentration of fire. As the beaten elements of XXX Corps halted for the night, there was one final twist when 4th Armoured Brigade's headquarters was captured by 8th Panzer Regiment. This was a confidence-shattering blow to General Cunningham, only redeemed by the progress of Major General Freyberg's New Zealand Division along the Trigh Capuzzo.

Bernard Freyberg was a remarkable man who lived a charmed life. Winston Churchill gave him the nickname of Salamander due to his ability to survive fire. In World War I, he was awarded the Distinguished Service Order for swimming ashore at Gallipoli to create a diversion and the following year, he was awarded the Victoria Cross at the Somme. He was wounded nine times in France and in four years went from civilian to brigade commander, earning two bars to the DSO and the CMG in 1917. Twenty years later, the British Army declared him unfit for active service, so he joined the New Zealand Army and was appointed commander of 2nd Division at the outbreak of World War II.

Sunday 23 November was commemorated in Germany as *Totensonntag*, the equivalent of All Souls' Day. It began for the Allies with good news as Freyberg's division captured General Crüwell's headquarters, which more than compensated for the loss of 4th Armoured's command vehicles. However, Rommel had given orders to the Afrika Korps and Ariete Division to combine and destroy the remaining elements of XXX Corps. General Crüwell personally led the move to collect the Italian tanks, but this only served to alert the Allied forces to the oncoming onslaught and allowed them time to prepare their defences.

It was another day of chaos and confusion with intense fighting around Sidi Rezegh. The brunt of the assault was taken by 5th South African Brigade which fought to the death, but inflicted heavy casualties on the German and Italian divisions. Acts of courage abounded all over the battlefield, including Major Bob Crisp's tank charge that captured an artillery battery. There were also many acts of chivalry such as the careful way the German panzers avoided the South African Main Dressing Station as they passed within feet of the wounded men being treated on the ground.

* * *

Meanwhile, Tobforce was probing south from its corridor. A reconnaissance patrol, led by Lieutenant Beames, was knocked out close to Wolf and Captain Pip Gardner set out in two Matilda tanks to rescue the vehicles and crews. When he found Beames, he "dismounted in the face of intense anti-tank and machine-gun fire", but while he was attaching the tow-rope, his loader was shot through the head.

Lance Corporal Donald McTier now emerged from the gunner's seat and relayed instructions to the driver as Gardner lifted Beames, who was wounded in both legs and the arm, onto the car. In doing this, Gardner was hit in the leg and to add to the problem, the tow-rope snapped so he then had to carry Beames to the Matilda and lift him onto the rear of the tank still under fire. As he climbed up to join the casualty, he was hit again in the arm. McTier now took command and manoeuvred the tank back to the other Matilda, which gave covering fire as they withdrew to the corridor. For this selfless act of bravery Gardner was awarded the Victoria Cross[20] and McTier the Distinguished Conduct Medal.[21]

While this was happening, the York and Lancaster battalion attacked the well-defended position at Dalby Square. The Young and Lovelies, as they were known, came under heavy machine-gun and mortar fire and although they were supported by Lieutenant Colonel Walter O'Carroll's 4th Royal Tank Regiment, three Matildas were hit and disabled and the companies suffered heavy casualties. Responding to the crisis, Captain James Jackman brought up the Northumberland Fusiliers' machine guns and by knocking out the anti-tank guns, he allowed the battle group to capture the position with 100 prisoners.

That evening Scobie updated Eighth Army and confirmed that Tobforce had extended the corridor to an area five miles long and four miles wide and was waiting to be called forward to Plum. There are four Battle Honours awarded to regiments that fought in and around Tobruk in World War II.[22] Of all these "Tobruk Sortie 21 to 23 November 1941" is perhaps the most coveted because the casualties were so high and this battle was pivotal to the success of Operation *Crusader*.

Unfortunately, General Cunningham was not in a position to capitalise on Willison's achievements having lost 5th South African Brigade, as well as most of 7th Armoured Division. When the Auk arrived at his headquarters he was met by a hesitant man who didn't know what to do. Reluctantly, the Auk took control and ordered his subordinate "to continue to press the offensive against the enemy". According to Winston Churchill, this action "saved the battle and proved [Auchinleck's] outstanding qualities as a commander in the field".[23]

* * *

That night Rommel had the Allied forces at his mercy. He could have made a plan either to capture Tobruk, or to finish off XXX Corps at Sidi Rezegh. However, instead of tightening the noose around Cunningham's neck, he made a dash to the frontier with his divisions, believing that he could break through all the way to the Nile. However, the attrition he suffered from the Royal Air Force and the harsh desert conditions stopped him at the frontier, where 4th Indian Division under Major General Frank Messervy resolutely defended the Allied rear area. The sinking of two oil transports *en route* from Italy by HMS *Aurora* and HMS *Penelope* on 24 November didn't help his cause.

The reason he did not have any air support over this "dash" was because the Luftwaffe was continuing to prioritise Tobruk. The casual bravery established by the defenders during the summer continued throughout Operation *Crusader*. Eric Newby tells a story of how the Royal Navy officers drinking pink gins in the "excellent bar" in Navy House would drain their glasses and collect their Lewis guns from "a rack in the vestibule", just as if they were picking up an umbrella in a smart London club before going out in the rain. They would offer a spare to any guest and then take them to the caves in the cliffs "from where they would spray away at [the Stukas] as they came diving in."[24]

Newby was a member of the Special Boat Service, equipped with motor torpedo boats that could dart in and out of coves and land men behind enemy lines where they could raid supply camps and disrupt Rommel's support. The trouble with these noisy craft was that they carried cans of high-octane fuel, but they were extremely well armed and every afternoon when the Stukas came calling they joined the anti-aircraft defence with their twin Oerlikon guns.

* * *

Three momentous events occurred on 26 November. Having consulted Lyttleton and informed the prime minister, Auchinleck replaced Cunningham, who was clearly out of his depth, with one of the staff officers in Cairo, Neil Ritchie. This was a controversial move because he was junior to the corps commanders and unproven in battle. Churchill had suggested that Auchinleck take charge himself, but the Auk knew that answering the daily demands from London was just as important as supervising the corps commanders.

Meanwhile, in Tobruk, Brigadier Willison finally ordered Plum after hearing that General Freyberg's New Zealand Division had retaken Sidi Rezegh and was poised to link up. He had already attempted to capture Wolf, but the infantry could not hold on, so at first light, the York and Lancaster battalion, supported by 4th Royal Tank Regiment, finished the job and with this post in Allied hands, Willison personally came forward to lead the advance to El Duda.

The formation came under heavy fire from the Trieste Division, but by 1320 the majority of the 68 tanks had reached the objective. However, before the Essex soldiers joined them a "torrent of shells" rained down on the ridge. Coincidently, Major Robert Loder-Symonds arrived with the 25-pounders and Captain Jackman brought up his machine-gun platoons, which he rapidly sited around the tanks. Unfortunately, as 1st Essex were about to join the fray, they were hit by misguided Maryland airplanes dropping 250lb bombs that killed Major Colin Robinson and destroyed half the Bren-carrier Platoon.

Their commanding officer, Lieutenant Colonel John "Crasher" Nichols, rallied his men and established their position along the ridge just before the first counter-attack arrived at 1500 hours. Even though the Essex soldiers had a hard time that night, the gallantry awards went to the Northumberland Fusiliers after their commander, James Jackman, was killed by a mortar round. The 25-year-old Dubliner who for a second time "turned the tide of battle" was awarded the Victoria Cross when "his exemplary devotion to duty regardless of danger not only inspired his own men but clinched the determination of the tank crews never to relinquish the position which they had gained".[25]

The New Zealand Division still had to cross five miles of unfamiliar terrain in the dark. Herbert Yeo, commanding 44th Royal Tank Regiment, led the way in his Matildas with Lieutenant Colonel Sydney Hartnell of 19th Battalion in close support. At 1830, they were met by Willison and their symbolic handshake was welcomed in London as gratefully as Stanley's meeting with Livingstone. However, the brief union was also marked by tragedy for sadly Yeo's son, William, the adjutant of 1st Royal Tank Regiment, who had been eagerly waiting to meet his father, was killed by an exploding shell shortly before his arrival.

* * *

Responding to this development, 15th Panzer Division came charging back from Bardia to tackle the New Zealand division from the rear. General Godwin-Austen demanded that Tobforce hold onto El Duda, but warned that they would lose the support from XIII Corps. This gave Scobie a significant challenge because he was too thinly spread along the corridor to hold onto all the gains as well as Plum. However, bad weather and poor visibility conspired to prevent the German attacks on the following day.

By the time Rommel returned from the east, XXX Corps had been resuscitated and 22nd Armoured Brigade blocked the Trigh Capuzzo. There was a chance to strike a decisive blow when 4th Armoured Brigade attacked Rommel's exposed flank, but as dusk arrived, the tanks broke off the engagement and during the night, 15th Panzer Division escaped through the sleepy British lines.

The following day, Brigadier Willison was pulled in three directions at the same time. Scobie ordered him to relieve the Kiwis east of El Duda at the same time as he was attacking two posts astride the corridor in the north, Freddie and Walter. Meanwhile, the troops on El Duda identified enemy columns to the south and were in the process of repelling an attack. The chaos might have been an indication of poor planning in 70th Division, but it was more to do with the arrival of General Godwin-Austen's headquarters at the Fortress as anything else.

When the infantry at Freddie suffered 35 casualties, Scobie realised that he had to find some reinforcements to help the beleaguered front line. He turned to the commanding officer of the Australian 2nd/13th Battalion, Lieutenant Colonel Fred Burrows, known as "The Bull", who readily volunteered to help. Scobie added two troops of Polish artillery to his infantry and sent him forward to El Duda.

The toll was beginning to tell on the exhausted British troops and after a week of battle, "prepare to advance" changed to "prepare to defend". The fight began again at 1140 hours on 29 November and soon "enemy tanks were now appearing on all sides and it seemed that El Duda was being deliberately isolated".[26] Fierce fighting continued for three and a half hours, when Willison saw some 88mm guns being brought alongside the panzers. The Essex position was being hammered, so Willison ordered every tank in the corridor to move up to the ridge no matter what its condition. It was his last throw of the dice.

Meanwhile, another attack was launched by Italians on Dalby Square, but this was driven off by the York and Lancaster Regiment and an outflanking manoeuvre was thwarted by the Royal Horse Artillery. Then as light began to fade another thrust down the main road was repelled by the outnumbered Matilda tanks that had been in action all day.

After many hours of dogged resistance, Willison, who was hit by shrapnel, telephoned General Scobie, who said of El Duda at 2135: "The position must be held at all cost." Following the dictum "the best form of defence is attack", Major Jack Pritchard of 4th Royal Tank Regiment lined up half a dozen of his C Squadron tanks and with Bull Burrows' battalion advanced under intense fire to recapture El Duda. It was a pivotal moment watched ruefully by Rommel and Crüwell in the south.

Unfortunately, the reconstituted armoured brigades of XXX Corps did not exploit this success and remained cautiously to the east. The commanders were conscious of Auchinleck's directive to wear down the Axis forces, rather than destroy them in battle, and General Norrie had suddenly became much more reticent about using his own tanks, so they remained with the elusive 1st South African Brigade, out of the battle.

The result was that General Freyberg's force on the ridge was exposed to strong attacks by the Ariete and 21st Panzer divisions. The way they were abandoned by their flanking formations and higher command was scandalous. Some historians, such as the polymath Barrie Pitt, are circumspect about criticism of those responsible but Frank Harrison, who was with Tobforce, is more blunt and sums up the sacrifice of the New Zealand Division as a result of "self-interest, caution, weak leadership and poor tactics".[27]

* * *

At the height of the fight for El Duda, the Advance Repair Section continued to mend Willison's broken tanks and provide him with a trickle of replacements. The soldiers in this key support group were required to delouse the minefields to reach some of the Matildas and as a result, they too suffered serious casualties. While they offered this crucial help, the infantry strengthened the defences and the engineers sewed new minefields along the corridor.

The problems on the ridge forced Scobie to transfer the Bedfordshire and Hertfordshire battalion from the west to the east early on 1 December. Soon after they arrived at Leopard and Wolf, they began mining the area and welcomed the remnants of 20th New Zealand Brigade, who filtered in from Bel Hamed with five guns. Together with the Australians of 2nd/13th, Major Stephenson built a strong defensive position and with steely resolve the combined commonwealth force prepared to face the might of Rommel's panzers.

On 1 December, the Desert Fox attacked the corridor and once again, flame-throwers led the advance against Jill. While the Leicester Tigers defended the post, the Northumberland Fusiliers at Jack caught the enemy in the flank and gained the upper hand. There followed a confusing interlude when 70th Division sent a warning order to everyone outside the perimeter to withdraw into the Fortress, but Lieutenant Colonel O'Carroll and the other commanding officers "would not contemplate leaving a position for which their men had fought and died" and Scobie withdrew the order soon afterwards.

When the infantry of 15 Panzer Division eventually attacked the south-east section in the late evening, they overran the Bedfordshire and Hertfordshire's front company. However, the battalion sowed a new anti-tank minefield overnight and this helped them to repulse the heavy panzer attack that began at dawn on 2 December. Much of the credit for defeating the German tanks went to Loder-Symonds who was awarded the Distinguished Service Order to go with the Military Cross he earned during Operation *Compass*.[28]

The reward for 70th Division was to be asked to do even more. In this regard, Scobie shared the same situation as Rommel's divisional commanders, who desperately needed to rest their troops, but were only given new orders which stretched the imagination and "spread the jam" even more thinly across the battlefield. The Desert Fox's second dash to the frontier to take supplies to the garrison at Bardia was no more successful than the first, with the 5th Maori Brigade taking revenge for the Sidi Rezegh defeat and Allied air and artillery attacks further reducing the number of effective panzers in the Afrika Korps.

On 4 December, Rommel made his final play at the corridor, but Scobie had reinforced the front line with 4th Border Regiment and 1st Durham Light Infantry, which was released from its perimeter responsibilities. The Germans brought forward a battery of 88mm guns that destroyed 16 Matilda tanks and "Mikl Group" established a position between Trigh Capuzzo and the *Achenstrasse* ready for a major assault the following day.

However, Rommel suddenly realised that he was in danger of being cut off by Eighth Army advancing to the south-east on the Trigh El Abd. The Auk had launched 4th Indian Division along this approach and a fresh 11th Brigade, with a composite armoured brigade, were now attacking the Italian position at El Gubi. During the night, Rommel gave orders for his troops to withdraw west and to cover this move, entrusting Crüwell to respond to the new threat.

The Afrika Korps made one last successful attack which stalled XXX Corps. However, General Norrie's loss was Brigadier Willison's gain; on 8 December after a tricky night attack by the Faithful Durhams who put in a "magnificent bayonet charge" Willison had the privilege of capturing El Adem from the remnants of the Pavia troops that were left behind. This allowed General Auchinleck to inform Churchill on 10 December "El Adem is taken... and I think it now permissible to claim that the siege of Tobruk has been raised."[29]

Although Rommel managed to rescue most of his forces, there were some notable losses, including the gallant Pastor Bach at Sollum. What was worse for him and the German High Command was the death or capture of so many senior commanders, including Walter Neumann-Sylkow, of 15 Panzer Division, who died of his wounds on 9 December; 90 Light Division's Max Sümmermann, who died of wounds the following day; and General Johann von Ravenstein, the charming commander of 21 Panzer Division, who was taken prisoner by General Freyberg on 29 November.

While the final act of Operation *Crusader* played out in Cyrenaica, the war took a new twist on 7 December. At 4.55 p.m. London time, Japanese forces landed in Malaya and 95 minutes later 353 Imperial Japanese aircraft attacked the United States Fleet in Honolulu. At a moment of potential despondency, when the Royal Navy suffered grievous losses in the Mediterranean Sea and the Indian Ocean, the indefatigable prime minister was at his most combative.

In making a full statement to the House of Commons on 11 December, Churchill declared: "I said the other day that four-fifths of the human race were on our side. It may well be an understatement. Just those gangs and cliques of wicked men and their military or party organisations have been able to bring these hideous evils upon mankind. It would indeed bring shame upon our generation if we did not teach them a lesson which will not be forgotten in the records of a thousand years."[30] While the Members of Parliament contemplated these words, he set off for Washington to commiserate with President Roosevelt and plan for 1942.

CHAPTER 11

Rommel Returns

From the Sublime to the ridiculous is but a step.

NAPOLEON TO THE FRENCH AMBASSADOR IN WARSAW, 10 DECEMBER 1812[1]

When Brigadier Willison captured El Adem, Rommel withdrew to the Marsa Brega choke-point where he started in April. The Afrika Korps began their move south-west from the Gazala Line on 16 December, while the Italian infantry followed along the coastal route. The Eighth Army pursuit was not as effective as Richard O'Connor's at the beginning of the year and several opportunities were missed to cut off Axis columns before they reached Adjabaya on Boxing Day. At that stage, the Guards Brigade launched a frontal assault and a re-equipped 22nd Armoured Brigade attempted a turning movement, but both were defeated, and the year ended with another reverse at El Haseiat, where 65 British tanks were lost.[2]

It did not take long for Rommel to return to Cyrenaica. During the first three weeks of the new year, he was reinforced by sea convoys that slipped through the Allied cordon into Tripoli. With 84 panzers and 89 Italian tanks supported by General Albert Kesselring's 335 aircraft and sufficient fuel and supplies, he launched a stunning riposte on 21 January, code-named *Theseus*. The surprised Allied forces had been planning an advance to Tripoli, Operation *Acrobat*, but as the eminent military historian Liddell Hart observes, by the end of the month, they had completed "a string of somersaults backwards."[3]

Part of the problem was the overconfidence that stemmed from the top. General Auchinleck wrote to London: "There is no doubt that German morale is beginning to feel the strain... I am convinced the enemy is hard-pressed more than we dared think."[4] This might have been true of the prisoners the British were interrogating, but the German officers who were reorganising for battle "saw no signs of wilting morale among our rearguard troops" because there was a "staunch pride in being outnumbered, but successful".[5]

The second part of the problem was the perceived inferiority of British tanks. It is true that the Panzer Mark III was superior to the Cruiser, but the success of

Tobforce showed that the way tanks were handled was more important than the equipment itself and this was the crux of the third part of the problem: British tactical decision-making. Auchinleck acknowledged this in a note to Ritchie on 1 January: "I have a most uncomfortable feeling that the Germans outwit and outmanoeuvre us as well as outshoot us."[6]

Unfortunately, there was a fourth part of the problem, which was a repeat of the previous year, when battle-hardened troops (of 7th Armoured Division) were replaced by inexperienced novices (in 1st Armoured Division). This formation had arrived from England without proper training "and was in a highly unsatisfactory state".[7] The commander, Herbert Lumsden, had been wounded in an air attack, so Frank Messervy had taken over without knowing any of the staff or brigade commanders. The Afrika Korps's soldiers noticed the difference immediately and one commented: "We could not help feeling that we were not up against the tough and experienced opponents who had harried us so hard on the Trigh Capuzzo."[8]

Rommel's tactics were so astute that the British chain of command reacted in shock and made poor decisions. By 25 January, 1st Armoured Division was driven from the field of battle and the commander of Cyrenaica, Lieutenant General Godwin-Austen, ordered 7th Indian Brigade to evacuate Benghazi and fall back to Derna. However, Lieutenant General Ritchie, commanding Eighth Army, cancelled this order and took the Indian Division under direct command with a view to hit Rommel "really hard when he puts his neck out".[9]

Severe sandstorms limited everyone's movement the next day, which featured more squabbling between senior British generals. Rommel's intercept team briefed him on their plans and he decided to capture Benghazi, where the German forces "found an enormous stash of supplies."[10] The night before this attack, the Indian Brigade managed to escape through a daring move across the face of the enemy in diabolical weather, but this was not due to Ritchie's tactical acumen.

The defeated forces withdrew to a line between Gazala on the coast and Bir Hakeim, more than 50 miles to the south. Although Godwin-Austen proved to be right in his assessment, he resigned his command of Cyrenaica and handed over XIII Corps to William Gott. This led one sympathetic general to write, "We lost the wrong man."[11] He was not the only good officer that Auchinleck lost that month because soon after Jock Campbell assumed command of 7th Armoured Division and was awarded the Victoria Cross, he was killed when his staff car overturned on the wet road at Hellfire Pass. It seemed that whenever a budding star appeared in the British Army, he fell to earth like a tailing meteorite.

* * *

The speed of 1st Armoured Division's capitulation was as surprising to Auchinleck as the earlier defeats were to Wavell. However, his assessment was not as bad because the

British had not been pushed all the way back to Egypt and the situation elsewhere in the world was more promising. Germany's advance into Russia had been blunted and America had entered the war, so the industrial balance had swung towards the Allies. However, the prime minister was still impatient for success in Libya because there were more than half a million men "standing idle in the Middle East theatre while the Russians were fighting desperately and Malta, closer at hand, was being reduced to an extremity by Kesselring's sustained air attack".[12]

The commander-in-chief resisted Churchill's urgent demands. He was acutely aware of British deficiencies on the battlefield and spent the spring months reinforcing the defensive line, re-equipping Eighth Army and planning an offensive. This preparation included dealing with General Kesselring's air superiority in the Mediterranean and on 10 May, Operation *Bowery* delivered 61 Spitfires and 100 spare Merlin engines to Malta by American and British ships. These had an immediate effect on control of the skies and enabled Eighth Army to plan Operation *Buckshot*, targeting the installations around Benghazi.

Rommel pre-empted this mission with his own *Unternehmen Venezia* (Operation *Venice*) just as the Auk had done in November. The assault began on the clear, moonlit night of 26 May. At the time, the two sides were evenly matched in numbers of tanks and aircraft. Both had improved their holdings; Rommel with the Mark IV panzer and Auchinleck with American Grant tanks, although the majority of the divisions were made up of the same type of weaponry as they had in 1941.

A military "rule of thumb" is that an attacking force needs three times as many troops to seize a defended position, so the advantage lay with the British. However, yet again the Afrika Korps showed that tactical ingenuity and close tank-infantry-artillery co-operation could overcome a poorly co-ordinated, larger force. And Rommel's personal influence proved Napoleon's dictum that "in war, three quarters turns on personal character and relations", or as Liddell Hart adapted it: "The moral is to the material as three is to one."[13]

It began well enough for the Eighth Army. In the north, 1st South African Division held General Crüwell's initial push and at the southern bastion of Bir Hakeim, the 1st Free French Brigade, commanded by Brigadier Marie-Pierre Koenig, held the Italian XX Corps. However, beyond this point, the old hands in 15th and 21st Panzer Divisions made a long hook around the south and "one by one... the British formations offered themselves for destruction".[14]

By the afternoon of the first day, 3rd, 4th and 22nd British Brigades which all fought in isolation were put to the sword and 90th Light Division captured the headquarters of 7th Armoured Division. However, the rot stopped in the centre at an area named Knightsbridge where 50th Division's mobile reserve, commanded by Brigadier O'Carroll (who had been promoted after *Crusader*), together with Lieutenant Colonel Edward Cooke-Collis's 6th Green Howards and 201st Guards

Motor Brigade Group (previously 22nd Guards Brigade) held firm, with the Mark 3 Grant tanks making their presence felt for the first time in the Western Desert.

Rommel's supply route to his divisions was blocked by a thick belt of mines that had been transported from Tobruk. He desperately needed to clear lanes along the Trigh Capuzzo and Trigh El Abd, but these were overlooked by well-sited infantry in trenches, who prevented him from bringing fuel and supplies through to his forward troops. According to many historians, Ritchie now had an opportunity to strike a fatal blow on Rommel, who was forced to establish his own defensive position, known as the Cauldron. His troops were stuck between the mines and 150th Brigade and pummelled by the Royal Air Force. The British commander had Gott's two tank brigades and Norrie's four armoured brigades ready for a *coup de grâce* (tank brigades had Matildas and Valentines, armoured brigades had Cruisers, Grants and Stuarts), but the German anti-tank screen frightened the British and Ritchie never issued the orders.

The vacillation between the corps commanders in Libya and General Auchinleck in Cairo combined with a lack of tactical co-ordination to allow Rommel one last opportunity to link up with his forward divisions on 1 June. In his path lay 46-year-old Brigadier Cecil Haydon, commander of 150th Brigade with his East Yorkshire and Green Howards soldiers, as well as the divisional reserve on the edge of the Knightsbridge box.

* * *

The 50th Northumbrian Division, with its twin Ts insignia, was one of the few formations that had returned from France in 1940 with credit. Its three brigades, 69th, 150th and 151st, fought well at Arras, where their counter-stroke gave the British Expeditionary Force the time to evacuate from Dunkirk. Returning to England, they spent a year protecting the Dorset coast, before leaving for the Middle East on board the SS *Empress of Russia*,[15] on a voyage that took six weeks around Africa, reaching Egypt on 13 June 1941.

The division arrived too late to fight in Operation *Battleaxe* and so 53-year-old Major General William Ramsden found himself in Cyprus, preventing Hitler from using the island as a stepping stone into Syria. When this threat faded, the 69th and 151st Brigades drove to Iraq, without maps, across the Jordanian desert and dug in north of Kirkuk. The winter was miserable; the soldiers suffered under canvas from the torrents of rain and 12 degrees of frost and the conditions did not improve when they motored 700 miles to Syria in January.

As the situation eased, Ramsden was ordered to Libya to reunite with 150th Brigade, which had been sent forward when Rommel took Benghazi. This brigade held an important, but desolate position at Garet el Auda, nicknamed the Bloodiness, safeguarding Eighth Army's withdrawal to the Gazala Line. When the front stabilised,

Brigadier Haydon returned to his parent division, which had to look after 25 miles of the front line. To their north, 1st South African Division held the coastal area, but to the south, there was a 10-mile gap to Bir Hakeim, which was only denied to the enemy by mines and wire and occasional patrols.

The three brigades became like Wellington's squares at Waterloo; self-contained defensive fortresses. They were stocked with food and water to withstand a three-week siege and told to hold fast in the case of an enemy breakthrough and provide a manoeuvre point for the armoured brigades poised to the east. In spite of two months' preparation, there was a major problem with their equipment. Divisional headquarters had only five wireless sets and there was a dearth of working engines for the gunners' observation trucks. Tyres "were so scarce that many vehicles were permanently jacked up".[16]

The division was "blooded" in March, when it was ordered to attack the enemy air base at Martuba. The aim of this operation (*Full Size*) was to support the Royal Navy's MW10 relief convoy to Malta. It was led by Brigadier Crasher Nichols, who had been promoted after the siege of Tobruk to command 151st Brigade. Although his three columns suffered heavy casualties and lost 40 vehicles, the Durham Light Infantry captured 150 prisoners and more importantly, the convoy successfully passed Cyrenaica without interference.[17]

Back in 50th Division's area, 151st Brigade held the north, 69th Brigade was in the centre and 150th Brigade was six miles further south at Got el Ualab. This took the worst of Rommel's assault with the fighting as fierce as any previous battle in Libya. Every day there were magnificent deeds of gallantry. For example, at 5 p.m. on 27 May, the enemy launched a blistering attack in the east against the 5th Green Howards outpost, which had to withdraw in contact. It took the remnants of this group five hours to rejoin their battalion and during this time Sergeant Walter Burdett covered the move with his mortars, for which he was awarded the Military Medal.

The following day, 4th Green Howards was running out of officers, so the regimental sergeant major, Jim Exall, was given command of a post overlooking the Trigh Capuzzo. His location was bombarded with artillery all day and after this softening up, the enemy expected to overrun the position with ease. However, the men from Cleveland led by the warrant officer from Bermondsey held their ground with accurate shooting from their slit trenches.

As soon as the enemy withdrew, the shelling resumed and continued throughout the night. At dawn, another infantry attack developed, but Exall rallied the troops and repelled the enemy until at last the Brigade Reserve relieved him and his wounds could be treated at the dressing station. For his courage and leadership, Exall was awarded the Military Cross.[18]

When he returned to duty, he heard that the battalion had captured General Crüwell, who was forced down in his Feisler Storch aircraft.[19] This prize captive was escorted out of the area by Lieutenant Colonel Cooke-Collis, who earned a Distinguished Service Order for fighting his way back to 69th Brigade.

The chivalry that characterised the 1941 campaign continued at Gazala. Although the fighting at the front was fierce, it was not vicious and wounded men were helped by medics on both sides. The 150th Field Ambulance was overrun by the Afrika Korps, but the German soldiers followed the Geneva Convention and did not interfere with the personal belongings, or treatment of the wounded. In fact, the German doctors worked alongside British doctors, although the former would often operate without anaesthetic.[20]

One of the British officers treated by German doctors was Major Peter Fox, second in command of 5th Green Howards. On the morning of 30 May, he was moving between the company positions with two sections of Bren-carriers when an attack developed in front of D Company. He was the first to react and with his small group swept through the advancing German infantry, but unfortunately, his vehicle hit a mine and he was badly wounded and captured. For his courageous leadership in battle, he was awarded the Distinguished Service Order and Lance Sergeant Robert Cass, from Scarborough, who provided magnificent support with his mortar section, earned the Military Medal.

After three days of fighting, Brigadier Haydon's troops were desperately short of ammunition. Artillery rounds had been rationed since the second day and all efforts at relief were repulsed by the German cordon that completely surrounded the brigade. The Matilda tanks, which had blocked so many penetrations, were also short of shells, so he shortened the perimeter by adjusting the battalion positions. The 4th Green Howards defended the north-west, 5th Green Howards held the south and 4th East Yorkshire, the Hull Rifles, were in the east.

Rommel steadily wore down the North East's finest. Early on 30 May, he captured Point 174 that overlooked the whole of the brigade's area and brought accurate fire down anywhere he pleased. That day 4th Green Howards lost B Company's commander, 34-year-old Major Brian Jackson, as the gap widened with relentless shelling, Stuka raids and infantry assaults.

The next morning, the pressure fell on 4th East Yorkshire's position in the east. The enemy broke into the northern corner where B Company, under 35-year-old Captain Cyril Good and F Troop 286th Battery fought for six hours until they were eventually killed at their posts. In the southern sector, Major Jack Brewer gathered the men in battalion headquarters and repelled an incursion at the junction with 5th Green Howards, so earning a Military Cross.

Pressure built everywhere and everyone was called to arms, including the headquarters staff, who helped restore the front line in places where it was broken. After B Company of 4th Green Howards withstood a sustained attack by the enemy, which had cleared a path through the minefield, Captain Paul Watson bravely re-laid the "lifted" mines while under heavy fire, thereby earning the Distinguished Service Order.[21]

At the end of the fifth day Rommel was down to his "last cup of water" and Haydon knew that if he was not reinforced his brigade would be finished. While Rommel calculated and gave clear orders, Ritchie continued to sit on his hands and abandoned the men at the front. As a last desperate measure, Haydon organised two defensive areas around the Green Howards, where all the supporting arms assembled, knowing this would be their last stand.

The battalion padres went around the men helping with the wounded and offering comfort to the anguished. Captain The Reverend Henry Jamieson of 5th Green Howards witnessed the bravery of the men from Bridlington, Scarborough and Whitby, who had given everything, but now had to meet an uncertain future. What was particularly frustrating for them was that their sister battalions, 6th and 7th Green Howards and 5th East Yorkshire in 69th Brigade were relatively unscathed, but they were expressly forbidden to attempt a rescue mission.

History repeated itself and just as the New Zealand Division was sacrificed at Sidi Rezegh, so it happened with 150th Brigade on 1 June. It began with a heavy bombardment in the north against 4th Green Howards and continued with a co-ordinated all-arms attack. Platoon by platoon fought until they ran out of ammunition and then surrendered. Sergeant John Leng, from Middlesborough, who fired the last burst from his Bren gun, won a Distinguished Conduct Medal for his courage, but his resistance was in vain.

The story was the same in 5th Green Howards' area. Lieutenant Percy Bray, working the only serviceable anti-tank gun, was awarded the Military Cross for staving off an attack at 1100 hours. However, the platoons were steadily whittled down and the last to surrender was B Company commander Captain Bert Dennis, who held out until 1400 hours.

Some tried to escape, but very few slipped through the net. The gallant Cecil Haydon, urged on by General Ritchie, was sadly killed in action along with hundreds of his soldiers. He had commanded the brigade since 1940 in France where he was awarded the Distinguished Service Order to go with his Military Cross. From there, he built it "to that state of discipline and efficiency which resulted in the men of his Brigade fighting gloriously against the odds, until, with their last rounds of ammunition expended, they passed into captivity".[22] His best epitaph was written by Rommel: "Yard by yard the German-Italian units fought their way forward against the toughest British resistance imaginable. The British defence was conducted with considerable skill."[23] Given this endorsement, it is very surprising that Haydon received no recognition for his outstanding leadership and sacrifice.

* * *

The tragic loss of 150th Brigade was pivotal in the battle of Gazala. The Desert Fox now concentrated on eliminating the French at Bir Hakeim, but they fought as valiantly as their neighbours. While Rommel's 90th Division was occupied in the south, Ritchie attempted to regain ground in the Cauldron on 5 June with Operation *Aberdeen*. However, this was a complete failure because the artillery bombardment hit empty desert, the armoured brigades were picked off by well-sited German guns and the 5th Indian Division was thrown incoherently into the fray.

Rommel exploited the confusion in the British formations and sent 15th Panzer Division around the south into their flank. Despite the heroic stand of the South Nottinghamshire Hussars, whose gunners fought to the last round of their 25-pounders, desolation ensued as the Afrika Korps captured four regiments of artillery and the British tanks turned tail and retreated again.

The only highlight of that day was in the north at Alem Hamza, where Sergeant Quentin Smythe of the Royal Natal Carabineers was awarded the Victoria Cross. During an attack in 1st South African Division's area, he was hit in the head by shrapnel, but took charge of a platoon when his officer was wounded and captured an enemy strong point, which came under rapid machine-gun fire. "Realizing the threat to his position, Sergeant Smythe himself stalked and destroyed the nest with hand grenades, capturing the crew. Though weak from loss of blood, he continued to lead the advance, and on encountering an anti-tank gun position again attacked it single-handed and captured the crew."[24]

The next day was even more perilous as Rommel attempted to encircle 7th Armoured and 5th Indian Divisions. Lieutenant Colonel Normand Birley of the 17th/21st Lancers, commanding the Royal Gloucestershire Hussars, was killed in his tank, but Lieutenant Colonel Henry Foote, of 7th Royal Tank Regiment, rescued the situation. He earned the ninth and last Victoria Cross to be awarded for action in Libya for his outstanding gallantry. Leading his regiment, "which had been subjected to very heavy artillery fire, in pursuit of a superior force of enemy", he was wounded in the neck and had to change tanks after his was knocked out. When this second Matilda was disabled, "he continued on foot under intense fire, encouraging his men by his splendid example."[25]

This beacon of light did not change the course of the battle. The Desert Fox turned his keen eye back to Bir Hakeim, but the Desert Air Force provided outstanding support to the Free French, who made their fortifications virtually impregnable. The British contingent supporting Brigadier Koenig included 71-year-old Admiral Sir Walter "Tich" Cowan,[26] who was captured with the Indian cavalry on 27 May, and a group of 5th Green Howards led by the future *Spectator* correspondent, Joseph Huntrods, who was trapped when the position was surrounded. He was surprised to find that a multi-talented British nurse, Susan Travers, was also in the enclave. She had already served as an ambulance driver in Finland, Syria and Lebanon and now she was driving the brigade commander around the battlefield.

The weather brought some relief when choking sand storms and morning fog stopped the enemy's bombardment. However, dwindling ammunition and a dearth of supplies made it impossible for the valiant defenders to continue their "epic resistance". Koenig planned a break-out with the help of 7th Armoured Division's commander, Frank Messervy, and at 2030 hours on 10 June, he led his surviving soldiers along a cleared minefield lane. His car was driven by Travers, who later wrote that her main concern "remained that the engine would stall...".[27]

Their intention was to head west and then south to a rendezvous with British trucks five miles away, but the column was spotted by 90th Light Division and so Koenig ordered his men to charge through the minefield. As they scattered, some of the 3,600 men were caught, others were killed and many became lost; but about 2,700 were picked up by the Royal Army Service Corps and escorts from the King's Royal Rifle Corps and 2nd Rifle Brigade later that night and the following day. When Travers eventually arrived at the British lines, she found that her vehicle had "eleven clear bullet holes in the bonnet" and a broken shock absorber.

Meanwhile, the remaining brigades in 50th Division held on while its position was invested on three sides and the flanking formations were pulled out. On "Black Saturday", 13 June, a decisive action was fought south-west of Tobruk, which resulted in so many losses that Rommel "for the first time had a superiority in tank strength".[28] During this fateful day, Henry Foote again blocked the enemy advance and showed "outstanding courage and leadership" in protecting the withdrawal of the Guards Brigade from the Knightsbridge escarpment.

Ritchie's "readjustment" isolated the two divisions in the north. The 1st South African Division escaped along the coastal road to Tobruk, but a conventional withdrawal for 50th Division was impossible because the Afrika Korps held the ground to their east. After consulting his commanders, William Ramsden decided to fight through the Italian lines to their west and then head south and around Bir Hakeim on a 180-mile desert march to Fort Maddalena.

This was a high-stakes gamble. The risks of losing the only English infantry division in Libya were "odds-on", so planning was extremely thorough. Assembling in small columns, troops were instructed to scatter widely after they had broken through the Italian position. With insufficient trucks, they discarded any equipment that was not required to fight, or survive in the open desert.

A dust storm on the afternoon of 14 June masked their preparatory activity to establish bridgeheads 3,000 yards away. In 5th East Yorkshire's sector, Private Albert Robinson earned the Military Medal for crawling 200 yards and silencing two machine-gun posts and Warrant Officer Thomas Mattock was awarded the Distinguished Conduct Medal for establishing the battalion position on the ridge. A fierce Italian artillery bombardment caused most of the 50 casualties in 8th Durham Light Infantry, but the commanding officer, Maver Jackson, rallied his troops and with the help of Major Bob Lindsay's last six working tanks in 8th Royal Tank Regiment, they managed to reach their objective.[29]

The long march through the desert began. The divisional intelligence officer, Lieutenant Edward Moss, described the scene: "It was a black night, with brilliant stars, but not a wisp of moon. We started grinding and jolting off through the darkness at four or five miles an hour, nose to tail, with every now and then, strange unexplained halts, while we looked and listened and wondered what was happening. My own truck was spluttering and I had continually to ask for a push from the three-tonner behind me to get it started again."[30]

The division drove cautiously through the "exceptionally cold night" and all through the hottest day of the year. Many trucks broke down, but most of the passengers were picked up by other overloaded vehicles. It was not unusual "to see a troop carrier towing another, both grossly overladen with the crew of a third". As they passed Bir Hakeim and turned towards the frontier, they realised that this desert was completely different to the scrub they had experienced near the coast. With nowhere to hide when the sun was high, the soldiers came across the ominous power of the Sahara's hell-like heat.

Some of the stranded were picked up, but others were lost having gone mad with thirst. Moss came across four men from "the 69th Brigade whose carrier had given trouble, fallen back and eventually petered out". They had neither water nor compass but refused the offer of a lift because there was no room for their machine gun. Eventually, they managed to start the engine, so Moss accompanied them at their speed until they rejoined a convoy.

In an amazing feat of comradeship, 96 per cent of those who set out made it to the frontier and on to Mersa Matruh, including Bob Lindsay's remaining tanks. There they were joined by 9th Durham Light Infantry and other remnants of the division, who had taken the coast road after vehicle breakdowns had prevented them from joining the main force.

The coastal group of nearly 1,000 soldiers had caught up with the rear elements of 1st South African Division that fought their way to Tobruk. The second-in-command, Major John Slight, was awarded the Distinguished Service Order for clearing a strong enemy position comprising infantry, tanks and artillery that blocked "three or four hundred vehicles". Further back, Second Lieutenant Vince Evans of 7th Green Howards was awarded the Military Cross for capturing two positions and Sergeant Geoff Usher from Bridlington won the Military Medal for leading the carrier platoon, which fired over 15,000 rounds.[31]

* * *

There was little time for celebration as the remnants of the Eighth Army came streaming into Egypt from Libya and the prime minister sent exhortations to hold Tobruk, which had become the symbol of Allied resistance in 1941. His instruction was problematic because Ritchie had intended to evacuate the troops, so no preparation had been made for a siege. What made this worse was the fact that the Royal Navy did not have time to evacuate the huge amount of stores in the harbour area.

Rommel had learned the lessons of his previous failure to capture the port and paused his pursuit eastwards to seize this strategic prize. Early on 20 June, he struck with the full force of his three Afrika Korps divisions and General Kesselring's aircraft, which flew 588 sorties to add to 177 Italian flights. By 0830 hours, the first German tanks were across the ditch that had been defended so stoutly by the Australians in April 1941. The inexperienced Maharatta regiment called for help, but the response was slow and did not include the Coldstream Guards, who might have made a difference

By 1330, the Afrika Korps were overlooking the harbour. The 21st Panzer Division motored straight into the town, scattering the remaining tanks of Brigadier Willison's brigade, while 15th Panzer Division turned west and pushed the Guards Brigade into Fort Pilastrino.

The commander of Tobruk, Major General Hendrik Klopper, was a young South African who had not yet led a formation in battle.[32] At 1600 hours, as shells were falling around his headquarters, he panicked and ordered his staff to destroy wireless sets and all documents and disperse. When the immediate threat moved away, his hasty decision had "deprived him of the means of exercising command".[33]

At dawn on 21 June, he made the decision to surrender and at 0940 hours he met Rommel on the Via Balbia to agree terms. This was the second largest capitulation of Allied forces in the war after the Fall of Singapore, with more than 32,000 prisoners herded into unsanitary cages. The blame for the debacle initially landed on Klopper, but the official enquiry and subsequent studies revealed that the inexperienced South African commander was not the only culpable senior officer.

According to the official history, General Ritchie never intended to defend Tobruk, so the mines that blunted Rommel in 1941 were lifted and re-laid at Gazala. Sand filled the trenches and the wire and communication lines fell into disrepair. Additionally, neither Auchinleck nor Ritchie realised "the extent of the Eighth Army's defeat. Had they done so, they would scarcely have attempted to carry out three simultaneous policies—to continue the battle in the Tobruk area, to organise the defence of the frontier, and to prepare for a counter-offensive."[34]

The prime minister heard the news in Washington. Churchill had left Stranraer on the night of 17 June for a meeting with President Roosevelt, having written to the king recommending that Anthony Eden form a government if his aircraft was shot down on the journey. On 21 June, he was at a morning meeting with the president, who passed a telegram to him that read: "Tobruk has surrendered, with 25,000 men taken prisoners." A few minutes later, General Ismay brought a longer message from Admiral Harwood at Alexandria: "Tobruk has fallen, and situation deteriorated so much that there is a possibility of heavy air attack on Alexandria in near future, and in view of approaching full moon period I am sending all Eastern Fleet units south of the Canal to await events."[35]

Churchill did not attempt to hide his shock when he wrote: "It was a bitter moment. Defeat is one thing; disgrace is another." Fortunately, Roosevelt offered to help and instructed General George Marshall to send 300 Sherman tanks to Suez. After lunch Churchill met General Eisenhower for the first time to discuss the planned invasion of Europe set for 1943, but before leaving America, he wrote to General Auchinleck with news of the Sherman tanks and exhorting him to keep fighting: "You have my full confidence, and I share your responsibilities to the full… You have 700,000 men on your ration strength in the Middle East. Every fit male should be made to fight and die for victory."[36]

On returning to London, Churchill found his government under immense pressure from the media and malcontents on both sides of the House of Commons, who were aggrieved at the way the war was being conducted. A vote of censure was set for 1 July and the fractious debate continued into the next day. In response, Churchill delivered a resounding speech that highlighted contradictions in his opponents' arguments and rallied the MPs: "All over the world, throughout the United States, as I can testify, in Russia, far away in China, and throughout every subjugated country, all our friends are waiting to know whether there is a strong, solid Government in Britain…"[37] He won the vote by a huge majority.

Churchill quickly realised that the Eighth Army commander was more culpable than General Klopper. He was aghast that Ritchie had neither saved Tobruk, nor held firm at Sollum, and was "glad" when General Auchinleck took command himself on 2 June. However, the major military influence on the Middle East commander was now the maverick staff officer, Major General Eric Dorman-Smith, who was not trusted for command, but held the appointment of deputy chief of the General Staff in Cairo.

In this role, Dorman-Smith advised Auchinleck to abandon Mersa Matruh and most of the Egyptian coast and establish a strong position at El Alamein, which would force the enemy to squeeze through a 35-mile gap between the Mediterranean and the impassable Qattara Depression. It was a stroke of genius, but before the Afrika Korps came up against this formidable obstacle, there was much more pain inflicted on the Eighth Army.

Meanwhile, Rommel, who was promoted to field marshal after capturing Tobruk, broke an agreement with General Kesselring to attack Malta. He appealed directly to his political masters, who agreed for him to continue his advance into Egypt, code-named Operation Aïda. On the night of 24 June, he crossed the frontier and reached Sidi Barrani and Mersa Matruh, where the Allied forces had fought the Sanussi a quarter of a century before.

As part of the Allied defensive plan, the Auk brought forward X Corps under Lieutenant General William Holmes and added 50th Division to hold the town, while Norrie's XXX Corps prepared the main defensive position at El Alamein. He assigned XIII Corps under Gott to cover the desert and prevent Rommel from outflanking Holmes.

However, the wily Desert Fox did not pause to allow the defenders to fortify Matruh. Although he was outnumbered by 60 tanks to 160 he sent 15th Panzer against 1st Armoured Division and audaciously advanced into the gap between the two corps that was covered by a minefield. At daylight on 27 June, two of his divisions reached more than 10 miles beyond the British position, so Gott had to order a withdrawal before he was outflanked.

The hasty departure of 1st Armoured Division left the infantry divisions in a pickle. The 2nd New Zealand Division succeeded in breaking through the enemy that night, but the soldiers of 50th Northumbrian Division again had to display incredible bravery. In 69th Brigade, two commanding officers earned Distinguished Service Orders for their leadership.[38] However, the worst fighting was in 151st Brigade's area, where Private Adam Wakenshaw of 9th Durham Light Infantry was awarded the only Victoria Cross in this battle.

Soon after dawn on 27 June, he was firing a two-pounder when it was hit by a pair of tracked light guns. He was the only survivor of the team, but his left arm had been blown off at the shoulder. Crawling back to his gun under intense fire, "he loaded the gun with one arm and fired five more rounds, setting the tractor on fire and damaging the light gun. A direct hit on the ammunition finally killed him and destroyed the gun, but his conspicuous gallantry allowed his fellow soldiers to withdraw safely."[39]

For a second time, 50th Division had to fight its way out after the German net closed around it. The daring escape on the night of 29 June was even more fraught than at Gazala because the route took the troops in overloaded trucks and carriers up blind wadis and through the enemy position to the south, before turning east to El Alamein. There, they took up a position on the famous Ruweisat Ridge, where they managed to repel Rommel's attack on 1 July.

Three days later, the division withdrew to refit having earned a heroic reputation. Between Gazala and El Alamein, it had suffered 8,875 casualties. Apart from the Victoria Cross, there were numerous awards for gallantry and medals and for his outstanding leadership, William Ramsden was promoted to command XXX Corps.

After Rommel captured Matruh on 28 June, he intended to sweep through to the Nile Delta, but now the Desert Air Force had superiority and he began to lose momentum with the heavy air raids. Nevertheless, by the evening of 30 June, he had closed up to El Alamein. In theory, he should have run out of supplies, but the vast amount of stores that he captured at Tobruk and Matruh enabled him to establish a strong position right up against the British front. This created panic in Cairo and Alexandria, where thousands of British citizens fled to Palestine.

General Auchinleck held his nerve and managed to blunt Rommel's advance on Wednesday 1 July. Liddell Hart suggests that this day "was the most dangerous moment of the struggle in Africa. It was more truly the turning point than the repulse of Rommel's renewed attack at the end of August, or the October battle that ended in Rommel's retreat."[40]

The fight in July swayed back and forth, but the Auk weathered the storm. Although the Eighth Army suffered 13,000 casualties, it captured over 7,000 prisoners and with the damage inflicted by the Desert Air Force, Rommel was far harder hit than the Allied commander. The critical battleground was in the centre at Ruweisat Ridge, where Rommel was twice repelled. More displays of outstanding bravery earned Victoria Crosses for three Antipodean soldiers[41] and ensured Egypt was secure, but this success was not enough to save Auchinleck his job.

* * *

The chief of the Imperial General Staff, General Sir Alan Brooke, had planned to visit North Africa for some time. Before he set off from London, he had a conversation with the prime minister after dinner on 28 July, when he tried to explain why Auchinleck had not been able to defeat Rommel. Two days later, Churchill informed him that he would follow him to Egypt.[42]

They arrived in Cairo on the morning of 3 August and were met by the chief of staff, Lieutenant General Thomas Corbett, who made a poor impression on them both. Visiting the front line, they met the senior commanders, and all the while discussed the need to bring fresh minds to the Western Desert. Churchill wrote to the deputy prime minister on 5 August: "Wherever the fault may lie for the serious situation which exists, it is certainly not with the troops, and only to a minor extent with their equipment."[43]

Churchill asked Brooke to take over from Auchinleck, but he resisted the offer and instead they decided on Sir Harold Alexander who was earmarked for the Anglo-American invasion of French Africa. They promoted Strafer Gott to command the Eighth Army, but sadly, he was killed when his plane was shot down on 7 August. It was therefore agreed to bring Lieutenant General Bernard Montgomery to Egypt.

The prime minister informed Auchinleck that he was replacing him by letter on 8 August and stayed in Cairo for two more days at the residence of Ambassador Sir Miles Lampson.[44] Meanwhile the chief of the Imperial General Staff replaced Corbett with Richard McCreery. Churchill managed to speak at length to Alexander, who flew immediately from England. His directive was straightforward: "Your prime and main duty will be to take or destroy at the earliest opportunity the German-Italian

Army commanded by Field-Marshal Rommel, together with all its supplies and establishments in Egypt and Libya."[45]

For the vast majority of Allied forces in the Middle East, the focus of the next three months was the defence of Egypt. However, for a small number of men involved in raiding Rommel's supply lines, the focal point remained in Libya. They were to make an important contribution and establish the foundations of British Special Forces that are revered by so many to this day.

The Australian Memorial at Tobruk. Major General Leslie Morshead's inspirational 9th Division set the standard in World War II by inflicting the first defeat on the German military machine. Their heroic resistance at Tobruk was as great a symbol of defiance for the Allies as the Blitz and the Battle of Britain. (Picture courtesy of The Hon Philippa Weatherly)

The Knightsbridge Commonwealth War Cemetery at Acroma. Rommel's victory at Gazala saw some of the most intense fighting of the Desert War. Among those buried at Acroma was 44-year-old Lieutenant Colonel Normand Birley, of the 17th/21st Lancers, who was killed in action on 6 June, while commanding the Royal Gloucestershire Hussars. (Picture courtesy of The Hon. Philippa Weatherly)

The Commonwealth War Cemetery at Benghazi is the resting place for 1,063 casualties including the commander of 3rd Armoured Brigade, Reggie Rimmington, who died during Rommel's first advance in Cyrenaica in April 1941. (Author)

The Commonwealth War Cemetery at Tripoli is the resting place for 1,242 casualties, including The Hon. Patrick Hore-Ruthven of the Rifle Brigade and SAS, son of the Earl of Gowrie, who was killed on Christmas Eve 1942, following a raid behind enemy lines. (Author)

Geoffrey Keyes was awarded a posthumous Victoria Cross for his role in the failed attempt at assassinating Rommel in November 1941. Of the nine VCs earned for gallantry in Libya, this was the most contentious. (Picture courtesy of Anthony Layden)

William "Strafer" Gott was the commanding officer of 1st King's Royal Rifle Corps at the beginning of the war in North Africa. He went on to command Support Group as a Brigadier and then 7th Armoured Division during Operation *Crusader*. In early 1942, he was promoted to acting lieutenant general to command XIII Corps and after Churchill sacked General Auchinleck, the prime minister selected Gott to take over the Eighth Army. But he was killed six days before his 45th birthday when his transport plane was shot down in the desert. (Reproduced with kind permission of The Royal Green Jackets (Rifles) Museum, Winchester)

General (later Field Marshal) Montgomery inspecting the Sherwood Rangers Yeomanry in the desert. The commanding officer, Lieutenant Colonel Flash Kellett, MP for Birmingham Aston, is standing on the right with Lieutenant General Herbert Lumsden between them. (Crown copyright)

Captain Patrick McCraith, who raised the first Yeomanry Patrol of the Long Range Desert Group, wearing the distinctive Arab head-dress of a sand-coloured Gutrah and black-corded Igal. (Picture courtesy of The Hon Philippa Weatherly)

Members of the Yeomanry Patrol, Long Range Desert Group, 1941. (Picture courtesy of The Hon Philippa Weatherly)

CHAPTER 12

Special Forces Agreement

Next in importance after the port at Tripoli comes the 400-mile coastal road… Every feasible method of harassing constantly this section of the route is to be attempted, the necessary losses being faced.

CHURCHILL'S MIDDLE EAST DIRECTIVE, 14 APRIL 1941

The change of command in Egypt made little difference to Rommel in the short term. What mattered more was that the Allied base on Malta was still interfering with his supply line in Libya. His diary and letters provide a litany of complaints "castigating Italian and German administrators as far back as Tripoli and across the whole expanse of Europe, for failing to meet his demands".[1] The capture of Tobruk helped the supply line of reinforcements arriving from Crete, but his food and fuel still had to travel 300 miles along a road that was easily attacked by Allied aircraft and raiding parties.

Rommel assumed that Montgomery would not be ready until mid-September and planned another assault at the end of August. However, calculations on both sides were compromised by security breaches. German plans were decoded at Bletchley Park and British plans were forwarded to Rommel by the Italian Secret Service, which had broken the State Department's Black Code, used by their ebullient military attaché in Cairo, Bonner Fellers.

Fortunately, the breach was discovered in June 1942 and Fellers changed to a new code, so this source of information dried up. However, Cairo was a hotbed of gossip and there were many officers who carelessly discussed military plans in the bars and night clubs frequented after work. They were overheard by waiters and barmen and later in the evening, "lovely dark Syrian heads on crumpled pillows listened carefully to their blond bed-fellows".[2]

Belly-dancers, such as Hekmet Fahmy, sold precious information to the highest bidder and Italian spies collected useful intelligence from unwitting helpers, who "loved to impress their friends with a knowledge of our future operations".[3] These indiscretions led to the failure of the largest commando attack in September 1942, which involved four simultaneous raids by Special Forces. As a result, the new chief of staff in Cairo, Richard McCreery, decided "to set up a co-ordinating section of the General Staff to control raiding operations".[4]

This team was run by Lieutenant Colonel Shan Hackett, who was aghast when he discovered the range of "private armies" operating in Libya. Pre-eminent among these was the Long Range Desert Group, which had been formed in 1940 by the renowned explorer Ralph Bagnold. He was supported by a fellow recipient of the Royal Geographical Society Founder's Medal and now head of civil-military affairs, Major General Francis Rodd, whose father had been the British ambassador to Italy during World War I (see chapters 5 and 6). The proposal to form "a unit capable of carrying out reconnaissance deep into Libyan territory"[5] had found favour with General Wavell, who needed "eyes and ears" in Libya and protection along his line of communication between Cairo and Khartoum.

Bagnold might have thought of Machiavelli's advice that "there is nothing more difficult to plan, more doubtful of success, nor more dangerous to manage than a new venture" when he worked through the red tape in Cairo. It was a struggle to pull together the people, vehicles, training, equipment, supplies and wireless sets for his pioneering unit. However, he did have a loyal group of friends who shared his love of the Sahara and his first task was to discover whether any of them would become founding fathers in his new enterprise.

They did not let him down. This core of explorers included Pat Clayton, previously with the Egyptian Government Survey Department, who arrived from Tanganyika and threw himself into the new venture. They were also joined by Bill Kennedy-Shaw from the Colonial Service in Palestine; and Teddy Mitford, who was serving in 6th Royal Tank Regiment.

For the majority of recruits, Bagnold turned to Bernard Freyberg's New Zealand division that was digging ditches at Mersa Matruh. About 100 independently minded farmers transferred from the cavalry regiment and these were joined later by Rhodesians and Guardsmen, who were attracted by the freedom of action and autonomous lifestyle. The British yeomanry also provided a patrol that was raised by Patrick McCraith of the Sherwood Rangers Yeomanry.

The vehicles were another concern, but at least Bagnold knew what worked best in the desert. Assembling a fleet of Chevrolet trucks, he instructed the workshops to strip them of doors, windscreens and unnecessary superstructure, so they could carry three tonnes of fuel, water, ammunition and supplies. These had to have effective firepower, so mountings for heavy machine guns were welded to the base by technicians working secretly in Alexandria.

The biggest challenge was navigation because map-reading in the desert was such a difficult skill to master. During his pre-war expeditions, Bagnold had invented a sun compass, but not many were manufactured, so the time-consuming oil-based compass was used by some of the sections. Maps were less of a problem because "men like Lyons, Ball, Murray, Clayton and Walpole, four of them distinguished medallists of [the Royal Geographical] Society, had produced maps of a quality not easily matched".[6]

The first patrol led by Pat Clayton in August 1940 established the route south west into Libya and made new discoveries around Kufra, which was held by a strong Italian garrison and guarded by their Italian equivalent, *Compagnia Autosahariana*. Thereafter, they spent the summer months establishing supply dumps and training new recruits in survival techniques, such as inspecting boots for scorpions before pulling them on in the morning. This eight-legged arachnid became such a mascot that it was placed at the centre of the regiment's cap badge.[7]

In September, Bagnold established contact with the French in Chad and discovered they were loyal to De Gaulle. He also learned they were anxious to recover military prestige after the fall of France and were willing to help in the Sahara. A plan was hatched with Colonel Jacques Leclerc for a joint attack against the Italian garrisons at Murzuk in the south-west of Libya and Kufra in the south-east. Meanwhile, Teddy Mitford was awarded an immediate Military Cross for leading a spirited attack on an Italian outpost at Ain Dua.

Building on its early successes, the Long Range Desert Group came of age during the patrol that left Cairo on Boxing Day 1940 and returned on 9 February 1941. While General O'Connor was besieging Bardia, Pat Clayton set off with 76 men in 23 vehicles. *En route*, he collected a revered veteran of the Libyan insurgency, Sheikh Abd el Galil Saif al Nasr.

They took two days to cross the Great Sand Sea 300 miles south of the coast. The 500-foot peaks that characterise this force of nature may seem like a wonder of the world when at rest in the evening, but in the midday sun, when the metal was hot enough to "fry an egg", the excruciating effort of climbing their crests was described by Kennedy-Shaw as being "as good an imitation of Hell as one could devise".[8]

Once they were in Libya, there was the Kalansho Sand Sea to cross before they reached the Jalo road to Kufra. Very often trucks would become stuck in the soft sand and the only way out was the hard labour "of digging out under the wheels to get sand-channels or canvas strips under the tyres, the gentle and ever hopeful letting in of the clutch to see if the wheels would grip and not just tear the channels or strip back under the tyres, while 20 cursing men tugged and shoved and rocked the truck to get it moving back just the two-yard length of the mat; then to start all over again."[9]

After 10 days, they arrived at their rendezvous and together with the future chief of French Forces in Germany, Jacques Massu, the patrol attacked the fort and airfield at Murzuk. The Italians defended their territory tenaciously. In the action around the hangar, a French colonel was killed and Clayton was pinned down in his truck, but Kennedy-Shaw arrived with a Bofors to outgun the enemy.

While Clayton blew up four aircraft in the hangar, the other half of the patrol vanquished the garrison at the fort and wrecked their communications. Within two hours, the patrol was back in the desert heading south towards French-held territory. Unfortunately, one New Zealand sergeant was killed and five soldiers wounded, including Massu, who cauterised the bullet holes in his calf with his cigarette.

This raid was merely an appetiser for the big event. Travelling south of the Tibesti mountains into Chad, Clayton met Leclerc at Faya to co-ordinate the attack on Kufra. The sweet water in this ancient oasis, which links the caravan routes between Chad, Sudan and Egypt, flows 1,000 miles from the equatorial rain belt before it wells up and irrigates palm-groves and gardens of millet. It is hugely symbolic to many Libyans as it was the final enclave captured by Graziani.

The plan was more complex than the raid on Murzuk because the oasis was protected by a strong garrison with Italian Special Forces patrolling the desert. A major challenge was posed by the 350-mile distance from the last well at Tekro, in Chad. Fully aware of the logistic constraints, Clayton left on 26 January and took four days to reach Jebel Sharif, 60 miles south of the objective. As he carefully drove through the narrow gully, he was ambushed by the *Compagnia Autosahariana* with supporting Caproni aircraft. Three British trucks were destroyed, one man was killed, and Clayton was taken prisoner with two other soldiers.

The remainder of the patrol withdrew to Tekro and reported to Leclerc. That would have been the end of it, but what was to follow would establish the reputation of the Long Range Desert Group forever. Unbeknown to anyone, four soldiers reported missing believed killed, set out on foot from the ambush site towards Chad with a leaking two-gallon container of water. The group was led by 25-year-old Trooper Ronald "Skin" Moore, a farm hand from New Zealand, who had a shell splinter in his right foot. He was accompanied by two Scots Guardsmen, John Easton from Edinburgh and Alexander Winchester from Glasgow. The fourth soldier was Private Alf Tighe from Salford, a mechanical fitter with the Royal Army Ordnance Corps.

For four days, they retraced their route in the relentless heat. On the fifth day, Tighe, who was suffering from an old injury, began to lag and the others left him to follow at his slower pace with his share of the water. At Sarra, the Italians had sealed the well, but there were mud huts which offered some protection from the freezing nights, fierce sandstorms and unyielding heat. When he arrived after the others, Tighe sensibly decided to stay and was discovered by a French patrol on 9 February. The following morning, they found the other soldiers spread over a 20-mile area. John Easton, who was wounded in the throat, sadly died that night, but Alexander Winchester, although delirious when he was picked up, survived to tell the tale.

The final soldier to be picked up, Ronald Moore, seemed to be irritated that he could not finish his trek. By then, he had hobbled more than 200 miles in 10 days on a wounded foot with little food and water. It was no wonder that the newspapers headlined his return as "Moore's March" and the king awarded him the Distinguished Conduct Medal for his leadership and determination. As a sad postscript, Alf Tighe, who later received the Military Medal, was killed in Greece in the last year of the war.[10]

The capture of Clayton changed the plan of attack. Leclerc released the Long Range Desert Group apart from one truck to help the French with their navigation. Captain Bruce Ballantyne led the remainder of the patrol back to Cairo having travelled 4,300 miles, mostly behind enemy lines.

Meanwhile, the French began their attack at Kufra on 18 February and fought a close battle of manoeuvre with Clayton's captors. When the *Compagnia Autosahariana* finally withdrew north, the French invested the fortress, but allowed local inhabitants to come and go as they pleased. After 10 days, the Italian garrison surrendered, and the Free French had their first victory of the war.

This was a huge benefit to General Wavell's Middle East Command because it secured the southern flank of Egypt and also provided the Long Range Desert Group with a forward operating base for their patrols to watch the *Strada Litoranea*. It also became a vital Royal Air Force landing site for 216 Bomber Squadron, providing air support for the disparate raiding parties interfering with Rommel's lines of communication.

After the loss of Clayton, Teddy Mitford was promoted to major and took command of A Squadron, comprising the Guards and Yeomanry Patrols. In March, he led his troops into Cyrenaica to work with Eighth Army. The squadron's main task was to report along the southern flank and deceive the enemy about the strength of Allied forces.

On the way to establish a new base at Siwa, the squadron came upon a track which was the enemy's main axis of advance on Tobruk. As the trucks started to cross it, one of them hit a thermos bomb that blew off a wheel and before the repair was finished, an enemy column appeared. The patrol managed to escape with only minutes to spare, the men picking their way through the minefield, as one of them said afterwards, "like bare-legged children stepping through stinging nettles".[11]

Bagnold continued to recruit intrepid soldiers including Lieutenant Colonel Eric Wilson, who had been awarded a (posthumous) Victoria Cross in British Somaliland in August 1940, thus becoming the first soldier in Africa to be awarded the highest gallantry medal in World War II. The Long Range Desert Group also benefited from the disbandment of Orde Wingate's Gideon Force in Abyssinia, but the total number of soldiers never exceeded 350. Although they undertook some more combat missions and acted as guides for other Special Forces, they were mainly used for intelligence work because they became masters of stealth, with their distinctive Arab head-dress of a sand-coloured *Gutrah* and black-corded *Igal*.

Another arrival on 1 July was Captain Ken Lazarus of the East African Engineers, who brought with him Sapper Griffiths and Sapper McKenzie to survey unexplored areas. Lieutenant Colonel Guy Prendergast took over from Bagnold as commanding officer a month later, but according to Vladimir Peniakoff, who formed his own private army, he "had the unapproachable quality of the commander-in-chief", whereas his successor Jake Easonsmith was a "model commander".[12]

Clayton, who was awarded the Distinguished Service Order for his leadership of the Murzuk patrol, was taken to a prisoner-of-war camp in the Abruzzo region of Italy. There he was visited by László Almásy, who had previously accompanied him on a desert expedition to Libya in 1932 and whose name became famous with the publication of Michael Ondaatje's prize-winning book *The English Patient*.

Almásy had been educated in England and spent four years exploring the Sahara at the same time as Bagnold and Clayton. However, as a Hungarian by birth, he was recruited by Germany at the outbreak of the war and eventually placed in charge of a commando unit in Libya. In this role, he managed to infiltrate two German agents into Egypt under the noses of the Long Range Desert Group, when Eighth Army was at Gazala.

This extraordinary operation in May 1942, code-named *Salam*, transported the two spies to Asyut, via Jalu. From there, it was easy for them to catch a train to Cairo, where they rented a houseboat on the Nile. They lived an opulent life, but their reporting of British movements was a failure. Not only was the plan discovered at Bletchley Park, but their forged money was identified by British security and their radio contacts in Rommel's headquarters were captured by the Eighth Army.

The interrogation of these agents was very helpful to the commander-in-chief because he concluded that "it was not practicable to pass a force through the desert south of the Qattara Depression to reach the Nile Valley through the Fayum". In his official despatch on the conquest of Libya, General Alexander specifically mentions Almásy's reconnaissance as the source of this information, which allowed him to concentrate on the El Alamein position without worrying about a turning movement to the south.[13]

* * *

The second Special Forces group comprised the coastal raiders of Layforce, named after their founder, Robert "Lucky" Laycock, whose father had accompanied the Duke of Westminster on his rescue mission into Libya in 1916. This *ad hoc* group, sent by Churchill in 1941 with three assault ships, included 2,000 commandos who were originally earmarked to capture Rhodes.[14] Laycock arrived in Cairo in March, but had difficulty fitting into the chain of command. When Rhodes dropped off the agenda in April, Layforce was assigned to Operation *Addition*, a raid on Bardia one week after it was captured by Rommel.

Unfortunately, this was not a success. The folding kayak section, which should have lit the landing site, was delayed by friendly fire. With no lights on the beaches, the landing craft set the men down in the wrong place. Faulty intelligence meant that the targets were missed and on their return, 70 men were captured after they mistakenly arrived at the wrong pick-up point. To add to the woes, the only commando to die was an officer shot by his own sentry, when he failed to give the correct password.

It was no better at sea, where one of the landing craft could not find its mother ship HMS *Glengyle* and continued along the coast in the wrong direction until it arrived in Tobruk. In his memoir, Jan Yindrich describes how "a bunch of commandos arrived at [his] camp" on Friday 25 April after blowing up "a bridge and several ammunition and supply dumps on the western approach to Bardia".[15]

One of the ships used in this operation was HMS *Aphis*, another Yangtse river boat that provided such outstanding support during the siege that it was adopted by the people of Warminster and Westbury. The ship was commanded by Frank Bethell; however, he was not the most senior naval officer on board because 69-year-old Admiral Sir Walter Cowan was serving as a commando. Six weeks before his 70th birthday, he was on deck firing his machine gun at enemy aircraft, but his extraordinary individual courage could not prevent the failure of the mission.

The cost of this operation, in terms of both lost men and equipment and the demands it placed on the hard-pressed Mediterranean Fleet, did not help Laycock in Cairo, where sentiment towards the commandos verged on being obstructive. Layforce was subsequently used in Crete, but it lost 600 men and Laycock and his intelligence officer, Evelyn Waugh, only escaped on the last ship to leave the island.

The commandos' reputation was repaired slightly when a team sent to Tobruk carried out a successful raid on 17 July against an Italian position known as the Two Pimples. However, the loss of so many men on Crete, as well as the operational hitches and the failure of Laycock to garner support in Cairo, led to their disbandment soon afterwards.

Laycock immediately travelled to London and appealed to Churchill, who was a family friend. On 23 July, the prime minister wrote a curt letter to the Chiefs of Staff:

> I wish the commandos in the Middle East to be reconstituted as soon as possible. Instead of being governed by a committee of officers without much authority, Brigadier Laycock should be appointed Director of Combined Operations. The three Glen ships and the DCO with his forces, should be placed directly under Admiral Cunningham, who should be charged with all combined operations involving sea transport and not exceeding one brigade. The Middle East Command have indeed maltreated and thrown away this invaluable force.[16]

After a flurry of signals, he amended this so that "The DCO and the commandos will be under the direct command of General Auchinleck".[17]

When he returned to Cairo, Laycock found his new command included six troops. These included the embryonic Special Air Service formed by David Stirling and a troop of the Special Boat Section under Roger Courtney. The remainder were provided by 11 (Scottish) Commando and 51 (Palestinian) Commando.

Their first raids took place as preludes to Operation *Crusader*. On the night of 13 November, in a howling gale, the Scottish Commando, led by Lieutenant Colonel Geoffrey Keyes of The Royal Scots Greys, was landed by submarine 20 miles west of Marsa Susa (Apollonia) to undertake Operation *Flipper*. Their problems began immediately when one of the submarines touched ground and as a result, men and landing boats were swept overboard.

In the morning, Robert Laycock, who was technically there as an observer, reduced the mission to two attacks: one on the telegraph system at Cyrene and the other on a house at Beda Littoria, wrongly identified as Rommel's headquarters. Leading the second raid, Geoffrey Keyes was hindered by torrential rain and it took three days for him to reach the cave where he made his final reconnaissance and gave orders for the attack.

Unfortunately, Keyes was shot dead in the dark and his deputy, Robin Campbell, was wounded. Their explosives failed to detonate and the subsequent pick-up by HMS *Torbay* never happened because the Royal Navy could not read the commando signals. According to Vladimir Peniakoff, "someone had carelessly dropped a map with the rendezvous"[18] and as a result everyone in the group was captured apart from Laycock and Sergeant Terry, who were eventually picked up by Eighth Army during Operation *Crusader*.

For his "magnificent leadership and outstanding gallantry" as well as setting "an example of supreme self-sacrifice and devotion to duty",[19] Geoffrey Keyes was awarded Britain's highest gallantry medal. Of the nine Victoria Crosses earned in Libya between April 1941 and June 1942, this was the most contentious award. The post-mortem showed that Keyes was shot by his own soldiers, as was his second-in-command. More recently, his motivation has been questioned by the iconoclastic Michael Asher, who claims in a forensic study that Laycock's citation was a fabrication because he did not see the attack for himself. It is certainly true that the details on Keyes's gravestone in Benghazi do not correspond with the memoirs of contemporaries, such as Vladimir Peniakoff,[20] but perhaps this merely demonstrates how chaotic operations behind enemy lines were in the early days of Britain's Special Forces.

There is one further thought on this. A few years later, Laycock wrote: "More than once [David Stirling] would have won the highest military honour the sovereign can bestow, were it not for the rule that a senior officer must be present to vouch for the circumstances of the citation—and senior officers were never well placed to witness Stirling's raids behind the lines."[21] Perhaps this provides the answer to the questions posed by the eminent Desert War historian, Barrie Pitt: "Why should a party of maximum sixty men be commanded by a Lieutenant Colonel, however young?" and "Why was a full colonel accompanying the party?"[22]

There is a huge irony that while Laycock was with Keyes on the night of 16 November, Stirling was parachuting into Gazala with his Special Air Service. Unfortunately, this operation to attack the new Messerschmitt 109F aircraft fared no better than Keyes' effort. A low cloud base and high winds conspired to spoil the plan as many soldiers were dragged along the boulder-strewn ground by their canopies and broke their backs. The dispersal of equipment and explosives over a wide area prevented the group from continuing and the surviving soldiers only just managed to reach their rendezvous with the Long Range Desert Group.

These operations foundered on the jagged rocks of poor preparation, inadequate training and inauspicious weather. However, their failure did not stop Laycock and Stirling, who learned hard lessons and continued to develop ideas for surprise attacks. Although there were more calamities, the strategic shock of these raids forced Rommel to increase the guards on his supply dumps and communication sites, which ultimately benefited the Eighth Army.

* * *

Other specialist teams included the deception department established in Cairo by General Wavell that was titled Advanced Headquarters A Force. In 1940, he sent for a friend from his time in Palestine, Dudley Clarke, who was running the MI9 department for escape and evasion in London. Clarke's crucial contributions included Operation *Cascade*, which created three bogus formations, and Operation *Bertram*, which deceived Rommel about the timing and location of General Alexander's attack in 1942.

The idea of raiding behind enemy lines attracted a certain breed of intrepid volunteer, epitomised by the explorer Wilfred Thesiger. Captain of the Oxford University Boxing Team and treasurer of the Oxford University Exploration Club, fluent in Arabic and familiar with the desert, he earned the Distinguished Service Order with the Sudan Defence Force for his role in capturing Agibar in Abyssinia and also served with the Special Air Service in Libya and the Special Operations Executive (SOE).

Directed by Brigadier Colin Gubbins in London, the SOE had become expert at espionage and sabotage. The Cairo branch was responsible for covert operations in the Middle East and the Balkans. Hermione, Countess of Ranfurly, who worked in the office at Rue Kasr el-Nil, became suspicious that "some of our actions are quite contrary to the direction and regulations we receive".[23] She informed the foreign secretary, Anthony Eden, during his visit in March and provided decisive evidence to General Wavell's headquarters that resulted in the branch's re-organisation.

Not all the work of the Cairo SOE was counter-productive and one of the successes was a "research" section named G(R) that employed Arabs and Libyans to foment sedition behind enemy lines. It also established a training school (STS-102) at Mount Carmel, close to Haifa, where mavens ran commando and parachute courses and prepared individuals for capture with counter-interrogation techniques, unarmed combat lessons and desert navigation skills.

The Special Interrogation Group, another of the "armies" spawned from Layforce, was trained by these instructors. The SIG, as it was known, crossed the line between soldiers and spies. Individuals were selected for their fluency in German and many of them had served in 51 (Palestinian) Commando. The unit was the brainchild of Captain Herbert Buck, who had escaped across Libya using German uniform and put forward a proposal which was agreed by the Director of Military Intelligence, Colonel Terence Airey, in March 1942.

After two months' training, which included learning *Wehrmacht* marching songs, SIG was tasked to deploy alongside the Special Air Service and attack the Derna and Martuba airfields that threatened the Royal Navy convoys from Alexandria to Malta. They had already infiltrated the German positions to prove their role in May and were given fake identities with forged pay books and documents.

Their raid was planned on the night of 13 June 1942. The Martuba attack was successful with 20 aircraft destroyed. However, the Derna group was betrayed by a double agent named Herbert Brückner, who alerted the German garrison. All but one of the group were captured or killed, but despite this setback, the SIG was included in the plans for the multiple raid in September that involved all the main Special Forces in Middle East Command.

This daring plan for independent, but simultaneous attacks in north-east Libya began on the night of Sunday 13 September. Four operational names were allocated, but the floral code-words offered by Bill Kennedy-Shaw in his memoir seem more apposite. Operation *Snowdrop* (*Bigamy*) was commanded by David Stirling with 200 men from the SAS, whose objective was to release thousands of prisoners of war in Benghazi, before attacking Benina airfield. Operation *Hyacinth* (*Caravan*) had the Long Range Desert Group attacking the airfield at Barce and Operation *Tulip* (*Nicety*) saw the Sudan Defence Force raid Jalu. However, the most fanciful idea was Operation *Daffodil* (*Agreement*), which was John Haselden's scheme to drive into Tobruk with 80 commandos and the SIG acting as German guards. He planned to capture the coastal batteries and link with Royal Navy ships and motor torpedo boats to seize the port.

There is no doubt that Haselden was a talented and brave officer. Half Scot and half Greek, but born in Egypt, he was fluent in Arabic, French and Italian. At the beginning of the war, he joined the Libyan Arab Force and was commissioned into the Intelligence Corps as a 37-year-old second lieutenant. In the space of six weeks in 1941, he earned two Military Crosses. The first was when he swam ashore from a submarine and spent nine days behind enemy lines reconnoitring enemy positions before he was picked up by Jake Easonsmith on 19 October. A month later, he was dropped at Slonta and walked 100 miles through enemy territory to guide Geoffrey Keyes's party onto the beach and escort them to their objective before returning to a rendezvous with the Long Range Desert Group.[24]

According to Kennedy-Shaw: "Haselden was the outstanding personality of the men who worked with the tribes in Cyrenaica behind the Axis lines. Untiring, strong, courageous, never without some new scheme for outwitting the enemy, yet with a slow and easy-going way of setting about a job which was far more successful with the Arabs than the usual European insistence on precision and punctuality, which they neither like nor understand."[25]

In 1942, his promotion was accelerated to lieutenant colonel in preparation for the raid on Tobruk. However, his brilliance at languages, communication and disguise did not translate into competence at hard-nosed planning and co-ordination. He invited Vladimir Peniakoff, an expert in demolitions, to join his team, but "Popski" found that there was "ten per cent planning, ninety per cent wishful thinking" and when he asked about the detail, discovered that "he relied for ammunition and supplies on what he would find in Tobruq [sic]".[26]

Popski preferred to join the Barce raid, which was the only operation to succeed. Travelling 1,000 miles with B Squadron, Long Range Desert Group led by Jake Easonsmith, he helped to destroy 35 aircraft together with fuel dumps and other vital installations. For this achievement, Easonsmith earned the Distinguished Service Order and Popski was awarded the Military Cross.

Unfortunately, all the other schemes failed. It was not just poor planning that caused the fiasco. The plans had been around since Churchill's visit and too many people knew about the details. In Cairo, loose tongues wagged in the bars and night clubs and bedtime revelations were converted into military intelligence and passed to enemy command in Cyrenaica, who alerted all the garrisons to the forthcoming operation.

Arriving in Benghazi, David Stirling realised the operation was compromised when he was stopped by an Italian reconnaissance unit at a road block. He immediately aborted the mission and decided to withdraw to Kufra. However, the next morning, enemy aircraft decimated his convoy when it was caught in the open along with some of Easonsmith's vehicles that were travelling from Barce.

At Tobruk, the Italians were also alert after the Royal Air Force bombed the harbour. Nevertheless, the ruse with SIG succeeded and Haselden's group passed a number of enemy convoys and guard posts before reaching their objective close to the beaches allocated as landing sites. Before the amphibious forces arrived, Haselden began to destroy the coastal guns, hoping to be reinforced from the sea, but unfortunately, the elaborate plan unravelled as the Italian artillery engaged the Royal Navy's ships in a fierce fire-fight.

Two destroyers, a cruiser and several patrol boats were sunk; more importantly, the ships were unable to land the 400 commandos, 180 Argyll and Sutherland Highlanders and the machine-gun platoon of the Royal Northumberland Fusiliers, that were crucial to Haselden's operation. Without these reinforcements, the Italian garrison surrounded Haselden and during an attempt to break out, he was killed by a hand grenade, along with several of his men. Eventually, six of his party made it back to Egypt, which was a slightly different outcome to the ending of the 1967 Oscar-nominated Hollywood film that this operation inspired (*Tobruk*), with the three tragic actors, Rock Hudson, Nigel Green and George Peppard.[27]

The final raid by the Sudan Defence Force on Jalu occurred the following night. By then, knowledge about the attacks had spread widely and the Italian garrison was reinforced and ready. When the lightly armed troops approached the oasis, they were easily repelled and had to withdraw with the other groups to Kufra.

The loss of 200 soldiers and sailors killed and 576 men captured from the sunken ships compared badly to the Axis losses of 16 killed and 44 wounded. Blame for the debacle was laid on the fleet commander, but in reality the over-elaborate plan was never fit for purpose. General Alexander felt the ignominy of defeat for the first time and as a result, his chief of staff pulled Shan Hackett out of 7th Armoured Division after the battle of Alem el Halfa and installed him behind a desk in General Headquarters, with instructions to tighten control of the disparate raiding parties in North Africa.

Hackett had a huge influence on the quality of planning by the Special Forces. His eye for detail and intellectual rigour went hand in hand with a creative mind that encouraged imagination. Perhaps his greatest contribution was the "invention" of Popski's Private Army.[28] Its formal name was Number 1 Long Range Demolition Squadron and its war establishment allowed for three officers, 18 soldiers and six vehicles. It was the smallest independent unit in the British Army, but had one of the smartest cap badges, an astrolabe cut by hand in silver and brass at a shop in El Manakh Street, Cairo.

The commanding officer, Vladimir Peniakoff, was a polyglot who had studied mathematics at St John's College, Cambridge. At the beginning of the war he joined the Libyan Arab Force, but was assigned to garrison duties, which he hated. After 18 months, he took a Sanussi battalion to Tobruk (the LAF was composed almost exclusively of Sa'ada tribesmen, hand-picked by the Sanussi leadership)[29] and established strong relations with local tribal leaders in Jebel Akhdar. However, in March 1942, this force was sent back to Egypt.

Popski, as he was known to everyone, now knew what he wanted, which was to work behind enemy lines providing intelligence and destroying German and Italian fuel dumps. As part of his team, he selected a British sergeant and a Libyan officer, Lieutenant Sa'ad Ali Rahouna, who became the only Libyan to earn the Military Cross for his leadership and demolitions work. Twenty-two other Libyans volunteered for this new force, which returned to Jebel Akhdar via Siwa and Jaghbub. They worked closely with the Obeidat tribe as Popski won the friendship of Sheikh Ali bu Hamed el Obeidi, who helped him to inflict severe damage on Rommel's supply line.

The world of "behind enemy lines" operators was small in 1942. Everyone knew everyone and reputations were won and lost in the blink of an eye. There was always a demand for talented individuals like Popski, Thesiger and Maurice "Tiffen" Tiefenbrunner, who moved seamlessly between 51 Commando, SIG and the Special Air Service. Their work to degrade Rommel's supplies was important, but perhaps their most valuable contribution, in the long term, was the strength of their relationship with the Libyan tribes.

It is to Shan Hackett's great credit that after he took control of Special Forces operations, there were no more disasters. That is not to say that there were no mishaps in the desert, but losses on the scale of Operations *Flipper* and *Agreement* did not recur. Credit also has to be given to the improved intelligence analysis provided by officers such as Captain Tony Peck, who was awarded the MBE for his top secret work that "entailed very long hours and tremendous concentration and accuracy".[30]

Hackett's tight control meant that patrols were run on the "solid basis of a railway service". Commanders reported their positions twice a day by radio and troops were coordinated so that chances of a "blue on blue" incident receded. The amateur approach to planning eschewed by Popski became a thing of the past as Special Forces now played a supportive role in Eighth Army's operations to free Libya of its brutal overlords. Little did they know that their endeavours would be repeated by British Special Forces in Libya 70 years later.

PART 4

FREEDOM IS NOT JUST ANOTHER WORD
(1942–2021)

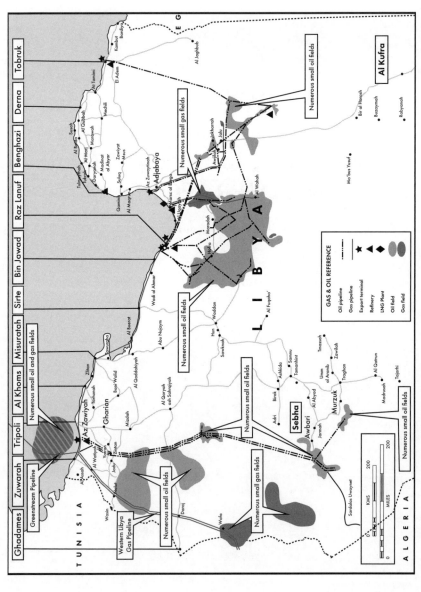

Libya's oil and gas lines. When oil was discovered in Libya in the late 1950s, the geostrategic importance of the country changed overnight. From a standing start, Libya became one of the biggest oil producers in the world in less than ten years. Exports jumped from $11 million in 1960 to $1.168 billion in 1967. This wealth generated a raft of security problems and arguably is the main cause of the current fighting. (Author)

CHAPTER 13

Advance to Tripoli

Lay the coin on my tongue and I will sing of what the others never set eyes on.

KEITH DOUGLAS[1]

When Monty took over at El Alamein after Strafer Gott was killed, the Eighth Army had just blunted Rommel's first attack in July 1942. There is no doubt that he benefited from Auchinleck's decision to save the formation from destruction in Libya and Dorman-Smith's advice to establish an impregnable position "barely sixty miles from Alexandria". Two years of stern fighting had toughened the Allied army, but there was still much to do to overcome Rommel's Panzer Army Africa.

The new commander had to address three glaring deficiencies: technical, tactical and training. Churchill helped with the first by delivering 300 of the latest Sherman tanks. Montgomery addressed the tactical failings by shifting the balance from mobility to attrition and increasing his artillery (as Churchill recommended). However, the most important change that was needed was to improve the co-ordination of infantry and tanks and the synchronisation of the sappers, gunners and close air support. The only way to accomplish this was by training and rehearsals, which in turn instilled a fighting spirit and belief that victory could be achieved.

The Eighth Army was a conglomerate of multicultural Allies. In the northern sector of the front line, there were Australian, Indian, New Zealand, South African and Highland divisions. Further south, Greek and French brigades sat astride two English foot divisions (44th Home Counties and 50th Northumbrian). There were also three British armoured divisions, 1st, 7th and 10th, making a total of nearly 200,000 men with new equipment, facing about 100,000 Germans and Italians in Rommel's army.

This wide diversity might have been a weakness, or a strength. Among the Australians, there was a perception that they had borne more than their share at Tobruk and many of the New Zealanders were still aggrieved about the way they had been abandoned at Matruh. Arguably, General Montgomery's greatest achievement was the way he made the disparate elements of his force more than the sum of its parts. Symbolic hats and badges played a part, but his insistence that the mother country carried the heaviest burden at the battle of Alem El Halfa in September was arguably the most important step in this process (the British contingent suffered 984 casualties, compared with 766 European and commonwealth soldiers).

This confrontation was not the first action after Churchill appointed General Alexander as commander-in-chief because the pivotal island of Malta held centre stage in the prime minister's mind. The Allied bases there had been under severe pressure since Hitler sent the 335 aircraft of Fliegerkorps II from Russia to Sicily in December 1941. The Fuehrer's Directive 38 gave General Kesselring the task of "paralysing Allied traffic through the Mediterranean and preventing British supplies reaching Tobruk and Malta".

Kesselring had supported Rommel faithfully at Gazala by taking command of General Crüwell's group when he was captured, but the Desert Fox did not return the favour after capturing Tobruk. His subsequent complaints about supplies not reaching him from Italy must have sounded rather hollow to the air commander because the newly promoted field marshal pursued his own goals with single-minded determination, rather than supporting Operation *Herkules*, the plan to destroy the British bases on Malta.

By the time Churchill visited Cairo the situation on the island was critical. Everything depended on a relief convoy of 50 ships, code-named Operation *Pedestal*, passing through the Strait of Gibraltar. First reports revealed that Axis forces had decimated this convoy and only five of 14 merchant ships survived. However, these brought sufficient food and supplies to last until December and equally as important, the American carrier USS *Ohio*, with four months' aviation fuel, arrived safely at Grand Harbour on 15 August. The Spitfires were now able to protect the Maltese airspace, while the British bombers and naval forces took a heavy toll on Rommel's supply line, sinking one third of the Axis supply ships in the following month.

Meanwhile, Montgomery purged the old guard, who he believed were not fit for the forthcoming battles. He summoned Brian Horrocks, who was famously played by Edward Fox in the film *A Bridge Too Far*, from England to command XIII Corps. "Jorrocks", as he was known, had come to Monty's attention as an energetic leader of 2nd Middlesex during the withdrawal to Dunkirk in 1940, but had remained in England, where he was commanding a home defence division. When he received the call, he was slightly worried that "command in the desert was regarded as an almost certain prelude to a bowler hat"[2] since so many generals had been sacked for poor performance in Libya.

He need not have worried. Monty had full confidence in him and gave him a masterful briefing when he arrived on 18 August:

> We have two corps in the line; 30 Corps on the right and 13 Corps on the left. The position of the former is strongly held in depth and protected by mine-fields. I do not anticipate any penetration in this part of the front. I haven't sufficient troops to hold the whole 35 miles in

depth, so 13 Corps on the left is rather thin on the ground. This has been done purposely in order to tempt Rommel wide out into the desert where he will use more petrol. And it is against 13 Corps that he will undoubtedly launch his main attack. You, Jorrocks, are to take over command of this corps—13—and you will defeat Rommel and repel his attack without getting unduly mauled in the process.[3]

About a week later, Horrocks hosted the prime minister wearing a blue boiler suit and topee. Churchill was perturbed that this new young commander was so defensive minded. "Why don't you attack? That's the way to win battles, not by sitting down in defence." Afterwards, he instructed Monty to "get rid of [Horrocks]", but the commander of Eighth Army responded curtly: "Look here, sir, you stick to your sphere and I'll stick to mine."[4]

On 30 August, Rommel launched his last desperate offensive, but Horrocks successfully blocked him at the Alem el Halfa ridge. Monty's counter-attacks, Operations *Game Birds* and *Beresford*, petered out after a few days as the Allies suffered 1,750 casualties (which was nearly 1,200 less than Rommel). This meant that by 6 September, the lines were more or less where they were at the start, with both sides constructing large minefields and strong defensive positions along the front, in order to prevent any incursions by enemy tanks.

Captain Patrick Hore-Ruthven, whose father was the governor general of Australia, was commanding a company in the Rifle Brigade and wrote a letter to the Countess of Ranfurly on his 29th birthday during the battle, in which he concluded sombrely: "Armoured horrors in their death agonies are not beautiful. It is all so impersonal when tank encounters tank that human fear and courage play little part. It is the mighty machines which overawe us… Man has created something in the devil's own image and now must bow before it as he can no longer control it."[5]

The result of Alem el Halfa was no more than Auchinleck achieved in July and with Churchill's pressure from London, Montgomery might have worried, had he not been reinforced with the Sherman tanks that arrived at Suez on 3 September. The Americans were given credit for these tanks, but in reality, they were the product of British design improvements on the Grant tank that had been criticised by British soldiers for its limited arc of fire. The arrival of these new tanks was welcomed by the soldiers in the three armoured divisions because it now put them on an equal footing with Rommel's panzer divisions.

The failure of the Special Forces operation in September was embarrassing for General Alexander, but he subsequently wrote that this "had no effect on the plans and preparations for the great offensive which was shortly to be launched against the enemy's main forces".[6] More important to him were the elaborate deception operations, planned by Brigadier Dudley Clarke, that confused the Germans about the location of Eighth Army's main thrust.

Alexander's hardest challenge was informing Churchill that the date of the offensive was delayed until the full moon at the end of October. This upset Churchill so much that he immediately contacted General Brooke, who was shooting grouse in Yorkshire. On 19 September, the chief of the Imperial General Staff had to drive 30 miles to a secure telephone to return the call of the prime minister, who immediately asked: "What do you think of [General Alexander's] message?"

Brooke replied "I have not seen it."

"You have not seen it? Do you mean to say you are out of touch with the strategic situation?"

"I told you I was going grouse shooting today, and I have not yet solved how I am to remain in touch with the strategic situation whilst in a grouse butt."

"Well, what are you going to do about it now?"

"If you want to know what I think of Alex's wire, I shall have to have it sent up here tonight and shall let you know tomorrow."

"How? Will you send a telegram? Have you a cipher officer with you?"

"No, I do not take a cipher officer to load for me when I go grouse shooting! I shall come back here tomorrow evening and continue this conversation with you on the scrambler when I have read Alex's wire."[7]

Unsurprisingly, Brooke fully supported Alexander's decision, but Churchill "continued to brood over the unpalatable delay".[8] When he returned to London, Brooke was summoned again and on 23 September had to stop the prime minister sending a curt telegram to Alexander, changing the message to "helpful support".

* * *

Montgomery made a key change to his senior leadership team after Alem el Halfa by replacing William Ramsden as commander of XXX Corps with Oliver Leese. Ramsden had been promoted after saving 50th Division at Gazala, but he was wounded in an air attack soon afterwards. Leese had earned the Distinguished Service Order as a young Coldstream Guards officer at the battle of the Somme in 1916 and had impressed Montgomery at Staff College. He had already commanded three divisions in the war, including the Guards Armoured Division, and was known to have an energetic and forceful character.

As part of the build-up to the main offensive, Montgomery launched Operation *Braganza* on 29 September. This was a small-scale manoeuvre involving two Surrey battalions to capture an area for use as an artillery site.[9] Although this was a tactical failure as the Italian Folgore Division repelled the British force, it did provide the Eighth Army with important information about the terrain and dispositions of the enemy.

Meanwhile, Rommel left Africa to recuperate from the physical and mental exhaustion he was suffering after 18 months of continuous campaigning in the desert. He was still in Austria when General Alexander launched the decisive offensive, Operation *Lightfoot*, on 23 October and his absence made a huge difference because his replacement, General Georg Stumme, made several critical errors with the use of his artillery and reserves.

The second battle of El Alamein is widely considered to be one of the finest British victories, ranking alongside Agincourt, Quebec, Waterloo and Trafalgar (although unlike each of these, it was not concluded in a day). Its intensity was comparable to the great offensives of World War I, but whereas the Somme and Passchendaele gained little territory, the victory at El Alamein opened the way into Libya. If Auchinleck laid the foundations of this victory and Montgomery was the architect, it was the field commanders and ordinary soldiers who deserve the real plaudits. According to Field Marshal Carver, who served in 7th Armoured Division during the battle, the tactical decisions "lay at the level of the battalion or company commander... His superiors at brigade, division or corps, no longer had any say and, in the case of infantry attacks, little power to control events."[10]

Friday 23 October was a fearful day. The front-line infantry had to spend it crouched in their slit trenches and were not even allowed to leave them for calls of nature. Veterans of previous battles coped better than those faced with their first combat. Many wrote a letter home, which they knew might be their last. The sense of nervous anticipation was palpable, but the enemy had no inkling what was about to happen.

A breathtaking artillery barrage broke the silence as the full moon shone at 9.40 p.m. The brunt of the fighting on the first night fell to Leese's XXX Corps, which was required to break into the enemy minefields and create two corridors for Lumsden's X Corps. The main burden fell to General Morshead's 9th Australian Division in the northern sector. Three Victoria Crosses were awarded at El Alamein and it is a testament to the role played by the Aussies that they earned two of the highest medals for valour.

Both these soldiers were members of 2nd/48th Battalion, commanded by the indomitable Lieutenant Colonel Heathcote "Sledge" Hammer. His battalion suffered 344 casualties in the following two weeks, with 98 men killed in action, or dying of their injuries. He was wounded when a bullet pierced his right cheek and exited through the other side, but this did not stop him leading his soldiers in the attack because the bullet did not touch any bones, or teeth.

The first Victoria Cross was won by Private Percy Gratwick. On 25 October, with both his platoon commander and sergeant dead and only seven men remaining, he single-handedly charged two enemy positions on Miteirya Ridge. He put the first mortar position out of action, but was shot whilst attacking the second post with his bayonet.[11]

The second award went to Sergeant Bill Kibby, who was actually British since he was born in County Durham. For seven days, this 5-foot 6-inch pocket-of-fire rode his luck after his platoon commander was killed. Finally, on 31 October, he led his platoon to "Ring Contour" where he "went forward alone throwing grenades to destroy the enemy position at the final enemy" until he too "was killed by a burst of machine-gun fire".[12]

Miteirya Ridge was the scene of the first crisis point of the battle. After Leese's XXX Corps created the "corridors", the engineer task forces in Lumsden's X Corps began to clear routes for the armoured brigades to break out. While this was happening, Horrocks's XIII Corps occupied 21st Panzer Division in the south and attempted to fool Stumme into believing this was the location of Monty's main thrust.

Unfortunately, Montgomery's plan did not go well. Although Leese's corps did their bit, the clearance of five miles of minefields was not feasible in the time allotted under the conditions of constant enemy fire and blinding dust. For security reasons, the sappers had been prevented from reconnoitring the minefields beforehand and this created more confusion in the heat of the battle when they discovered new minefields on the reverse slope.

No man's land resembled a badly organised car park as Major General Gatehouse's 10th Armoured Division packed nose to tail on the ridge. The Staffordshire Yeomanry was leading the 8th Armoured Brigade advance on route Bottle, with the Sherwood Rangers Yeomanry on Boat and 3rd Royal Tank Regiment on Hat. These regiments had been itching to engage the enemy and take retribution for what happened at Gazala. There was a sense of steely determination among the officers and on the eve of the advance, the commanding officer of the Sherwood Rangers, Flash Kellett, said to Pat McCraith, who had returned to his regiment after commanding the Yeomanry Patrol in the Long Range Desert Group: "Put on your white flannels. You're batting first for England."[13]

As regimental navigator, McCraith led the column through a British minefield. However, he could not continue because the engineers had not cleared the enemy minefields by dawn and there was an anti-tank screen waiting for them on the other side. As recently as Alem el Halfa, this regiment had met a German 88mm gun position, dug-in on a reverse slope, which decimated their Grant tanks when they charged forward without infantry in close support.

The congestion provided the enemy artillery with a prime target and the casualties began mounting up. The carnage was horrific. A troop leader jumped from his tank to aid a wounded man but was killed when a shell exploded next to him. Another officer crouching on Arthur Reddish's tank was blown 20 yards away when he was hit by a tank round. He lay on the ground "like a rag doll, with arms and legs at grotesque angles... The tank turret was crimson from blood and bits of flesh, bone and clothing were splattered all over the right side of the vehicle."[14]

The Regimental padre, Captain George Hales, received a Military Cross for his "fearlessness and selfless devotion to duty" as he "made several trips into the minefield... to bring back the wounded"[15] and later, he restored order and offered comfort in the regimental aid post after it received a direct hit by an enemy shell.

There were also Military Medals for Sergeant Major Hutchinson and Trooper McDonald for collecting injured men from the front line, until they too were wounded by shellfire.

That night, as the Sherwood Rangers were assembling for another push, a German plane dropped flares over their position and the Luftwaffe attacked. The first stick of bombs landed on a lorry containing fuel which set light to other vehicles. "The conflagration attracted enemy artillery, mortar and machine gun fire and more bombers."[16] McCraith felt a searing pain in his back as he was hit by white-hot shell splinters and had to be evacuated to hospital.[17]

The tension boiled over at 3.30 a.m. on 25 October when General Lumsden had a heated argument with Montgomery about the plan, which was causing the wasteful destruction of so many British men and tanks. This flaw had been known for some time[18] and had caused friction between the senior officers, but now it came to a head at the worst possible time. Ironically this dispute about cavalry advancing against well-sited gun positions took place on the 88th anniversary of the Charge of the Light Brigade.

Herbert Lumsden had been promoted to lead X Corps after earning a second Distinguished Service Order commanding 1st Armoured Division at Gazala. It was well known that he did not get on well with the new Eighth Army commander, but Alexander over-ruled Montgomery's request to replace him. Monty had in fact offered X Corps to Brian Horrocks, but the newcomer had sensibly turned it down because it was "composed largely of the real old desert sweats, and... I was still very much a foreigner from the UK".[19]

As a result of Lumsden's intervention, Montgomery did amend his plan, but not in time to save the Staffordshire Yeomanry, which lost all but 15 of its tanks when they were "picked off like sitting ducks". Lumsden was proved right, but Montgomery had marked his card and after he later captured Tobruk, Derna and Benghazi, Montgomery replaced him with Horrocks, who had been mopping up in Egypt with the salvage units of XIII Corps.

* * *

The situation in the air compensated for the lack of progress through the enemy minefields. Air Marshal Arthur Coningham quickly established complete supremacy over the battlefield, prompting Montgomery to point to a squadron of medium bombers and say to Horrocks: "They are winning this battle for me; the RAF are doing a wonderful job."[20] The close air support was matched by the aircraft attacking the enemy's rear area. At Tobruk on 26 October, three Wellington night bombers destroyed the tanker *Tergestea*, carrying 1,000 tons of fuel and an equal weight of ammunition, and Beaufort torpedo bombers sank the *Proserpina*, carrying 4,500 tons of fuel.

On the ground, the fierce fighting continued with another Victoria Cross earned on 27 October by the commander of the Rifle Brigade, Lieutenant Colonel Victor Turner. His soldiers had spent two nights with little sleep in the Minefields Task Force and had suffered heavy casualties. They were joined by half a dozen gun teams from 76th Anti-Tank Battery and 16 sappers from 7th Field Squadron on a two-mile night-time advance and captured what proved to be a pivotal position close to Kidney Ridge. Unbeknownst to him, this was on the axis of a massive counter-attack, so the next day this isolated battle group had to repel a constant stream of tanks from 15 Panzer Division. Fortunately, they had time to dig-in the guns before the first assault and this concealment saved many lives.

In the morning, they were joined for a short time by some tanks of 24 Brigade, but the position was a death-trap and so these Shermans withdrew to hull-down positions on ridge a mile back from Turner's position. Alone, cut-off and with virtually no hope of relief, the battalion, which was made up mainly of cockney Londoners, braced themselves for the forthcoming test. As the temperature rose and the sweat ran down the soldiers' faces, the terrible stench increased and flies swarmed in black clouds around the dead bodies and excreta.

Early in the afternoon, an Italian assault began on the south-western sector, where there was a solitary six-pounder manned by Sergeant Charles Calistan. Seeing the predicament, Turner and Lieutenant Jack Toms acted as loader and Number One against the advancing tanks. While doing this, a shell splinter penetrated Turner's steel helmet and wounded him severely in the skull, "but he refused all aid until the last tank was destroyed".[21]

Calistan's incredible skill in laying the gun so accurately was matched by his coolness in the heat. After destroying eight tanks and a self-propelled field gun, he poured some water into a billy-can, which he set on the bonnet of a burning jeep and brewed up some tea, which Turner said was "as good a cup as I've ever tasted".[22] The heroic sergeant was put forward for a Victoria Cross, but this was downgraded to a Distinguished Conduct Medal; he was later commissioned, but sadly killed in Italy.

The day continued in this vein, with the adept gunners destroying the advancing panzers and the resolute riflemen picking off the dismounted soldiers. As the sun turned crimson, and the shadows lengthened, the scene of desolation around the position bore witness to an extraordinary triumph against the odds. The destruction or immobilization of "37 panzers and self-propelled guns"[23] was more than any previous single action and crippled Rommel's plans. The site became so famous that a special committee of investigation examined the ground a month later to analyse the performance of every single gun, but the victory was not without its cost in terms of human life, with 72 riflemen and gunners killed or wounded.

Many of the seriously wounded ended up in hospitals in Jerusalem and Cairo where the Countess of Ranfurly helped the nurses, in between working for the High Commissioner for Palestine. She described the terrible scenes in the leg ward, the smell of rotting flesh in the dark corridors and the silence "in the long ward where the burn cases lie so still".[24] When she transcribed their letters home, she sat with her back to the patients so they could not see the tears in her eyes.

Across the battlefield, the German commander, General Stumme, was killed during a visit to the front line, but Rommel arrived shortly afterwards on 25 October. When his sure hands grasped the reins, Montgomery already held the advantage of numbers and with his shorter supply lines, began to "crumble" away the German and Italian defences. However, it took another week of dour fighting before the turning-point arrived on 2 November after the transfer of a brigade from XIII Corps in the south and the launch of Operation *Supercharge.*

Up to this point, the 50th Northumberland Division, under Major General Crasher Nichols, had played a successful part in Horrocks's battle, taking command of the Greek Brigade and later the 1st French Brigade. On 28 October, Nichols was instructed to send 151st Brigade, comprising three battalions of Durham Light Infantry, to Tel el Eisa. When this brigade arrived, it was joined by 152nd Brigade from 51st Highland Division and 28th Maori Battalion from the New Zealand Division and was ordered to advance through the Australian front-line positions and attack objectives held by German and Italian divisions along the Sidi Rahman Road.

The approach march "was particularly long and dusty and the night seemed warm and sticky".[25] After midnight the air turned cold, but visibility was little more than 50 yards through the dust and smoke. After a seven-hour artillery barrage the infantry advanced and the "leading companies invariably increased their pace as each small post was rushed". The enemy was "stunned" and "offered little resistance"[26] as the infantry punched a hole through the battered line. Once they achieved their objective, the plan had 9th Armoured Brigade exploiting through their position and at dawn, they appeared as expected.

Unfortunately, the tanks were silhouetted by the rising sun and they made an easy target for the German anti-tank guns to the west. The brigade commander, John Currie, knew when he was given orders by General Freyberg to spearhead this attack that he was facing another Balaklava. He predicted that his three regiments, 3rd The King's Own Hussars, the Royal Wiltshire Yeomanry[27] and the Warwickshire Yeomanry, would lose half their tanks, but the result was worse as they lost 102 out of 128 tanks and 229 soldiers, of whom 31 were officers.

Currie desperately called for help from the leading formation of 1st Armoured Division, but Brigadier Arthur Fisher's 2nd Armoured Brigade was "enveloped in clouds of dust… along tracks congested with masses of vehicles which should have been cleared…"[28] Currie must have felt let down, but he didn't give up and by drawing in Rommel's reserves, his brigade's action at Tel el Aqqaqir was the decisive point of the battle.

For his "courageous leadership", he was awarded a second Distinguished Service Order to the one he earned in Libya. The DSOs for Guy Jackson, commanding the

Warwickshire Yeomanry and Major Martin Gibbs of the Royal Wiltshire Yeomanry, as well as many other gallantry awards for officers and soldiers, are testament to the importance of this action.[29] Montgomery later wrote: "If the British armour owed any debt to the infantry of the Eighth Army, the debt was paid on November 2 by 9th Armoured Brigade in heroism and blood."[30] There was still much hard fighting to do for 1st Armoured Division as they battered away at 15th and 21st Panzer Divisions, but gaps now appeared in the Axis lines and Montgomery showed great skill in directing his troops through these breaches.

It was now just a matter of time. By 5 November, the battle was won and Montgomery had launched *Guillotine*, the operation to drive Rommel out of Egypt and Libya. Some critics suggest that he missed an opportunity to cut off the Afrika Korps after capturing Sidi Barrani, but the rain made the desert impassable and so Rommel managed to preserve his most precious troops.

* * *

The victory at El Alamein was achieved "in time to precede [Operation *Torch*] Eisenhower's landings at the other end of the Mediterranean".[31] A delighted prime minister summed up the situation during his speech at the Lord Mayor's reception on 10 November: "Now this is not the end. It is not even the beginning of the end. But it is, perhaps, the end of the beginning." The next day Rommel's remnants left Egypt for the final time, possessing "neither the strength to hold a feature nor the armoured force to cover its flank… Speed—its surviving asset—alone could save it in association with tight traffic control."[32]

Two days later, an Italian Morse-code signal was intercepted at the secret listening base at Winchester, HMS *Flowerdown*. The Wren who recorded "Tobruk Gone" was Betty Howard and she knew immediately what this meant. She alerted her supervisor and the message was sent straight to London, where Churchill celebrated by authorising the mass ringing of church bells on Sunday 15 November. These had not been heard for more than two years and brought cheer to the British people.

The prime minister's focus now turned to the political difficulties of smoothing De Gaulle's aspirations and America's ascendancy. Montgomery was left unhindered to pursue Rommel and liberate Libya, with many of the towns in Cyrenaica changing hands for the fifth time in two years. Derna (more pleasant than Tobruk according to Stanley Christopherson of the Sherwood Rangers Yeomanry) and Benghazi fell in quick succession with the Desert Air Force harassing the retreating German troops under Operation *Chocolate*. The Royal Navy also played their part by clearing the north coast with three minesweepers and reopening the port at Benghazi to supply Eighth Army, through Operation *Pike*.

This resulted in a strange incident when a petty officer in the Royal Naval Volunteer Reserve was ordered to open up a petrol point north of Marsa Brega.

Setting off unarmed in a truck loaded with a boat, he outstripped the Allied air cover and bumped into General Montgomery, who was "up behind the leading elements of the leading armoured cars" where the enemy still "strafed the road". Monty stopped the lorry and exclaimed: "What are you doing here? Do you realize that you are right up with the most forward elements…You must turn round and go back at once."

The petty officer knew exactly who he was talking to and pleaded: "Don't send me back, sir. If the armoured cars don't get their petrol, they will have to halt and you will lose touch with the Germans. Couldn't I go on with you? I would then be quite safe." Impressed with his sense of duty, the Eighth Army commander escorted the sailor to his destination and became his first customer for fuel. Later he wrote: "Britain will never lose her wars so long as the Royal Navy can count on men like him."[33]

Rommel made a brief stand between Marsa Brega and El Agheila, but on 11 December, Montgomery launched another deliberate attack. The Afrika Korps held him for a week, but then withdrew to a position they had prepared on the other side of Sirte at Buerat. The Eighth Army now advanced over some of the most inhospitable country in the world and captured Sirte on Christmas Day, unaware that it had been explored by the Beechey brothers 121 years before, or that it would become the last stand of Colonel Gadhafi 70 years later.

Although Montgomery has been criticised for the slowness of his pursuit at this stage of the advance, the reality is that he was hindered by treacherous weather and cruel booby-traps that cut short lives, while giving Rommel time to withdraw intact. In the New Year, a violent three-day storm "wrought havoc at Benghazi harbour. The outer breakwater was smashed and heavy seas poured into the inner harbour."[34] Four ships were sunk, and the loss of ammunition and fuel created "a great petrol shortage".[35] Monty had already disbanded 44th Division and he now had to "retire" 50th Division from the front line. The storm also affected conditions in the desert. "What had once been firm, fine sand suddenly became a morass. Hundreds of vehicles became bogged in the area of Msus…"[36]

The Afrika Korps mined the route with spiteful abandon, blowing the bridges and scattering mines in the rubble. When a soldier stepped on one of the dreaded three prongs of the S-Mine that protruded from the sand, a metal ball sprang to the height of his waist and ejected shot in all directions. Sometimes, anti-tank mines were laid on top of each other to target unwitting soldiers sent to remove them. To add to the difficulty, trip-wires were placed where troops might take refuge in the scrub, or close to overturned vehicles, and booby-trapped pens were left for unsuspecting soldiers to pick up.

Knowledge about the enemy's dispositions was vitally important. The leading formations depended on the Long Range Desert Group to provide up-to-date reports about the best routes. One of the patrol leaders was Captain Tony Browne, who had been awarded a Distinguished Conduct Medal for his role in Pat Clayton's raid on Murzuk and earned high praise from David Stirling for his assistance to the Special Air Service during the raid on Benghazi.[37] Browne had emigrated to New Zealand after Cambridge University and was the perfect guide for navigating General Freyberg's division around El Agheila.

Unfortunately, he was badly wounded when his jeep was blown up in an unmarked minefield, while checking three wadis west of Sirte, so Lieutenant Paddy McLauchlan replaced him as patrol leader. On Christmas Day, when Eighth Army soldiers enjoyed a rest, he led another mission to recce the proposed lines of advance. His first patrol was ambushed close to Qaryat Abu Nujaym, but the second managed to identify a suitable route to Bani Walid for an armoured division, avoiding the impassable upper reaches of Wadi Sawfajjin.

While the Long Range Desert Group found new routes, the SAS attacked the enemy's logistics bases near to Tripoli. Sadly, Major Patrick Hore-Ruthven died on Christmas Eve in Misuratah hospital after he was severely wounded during a raid on a fuel dump. He had foretold his own death in a poem, inscribed to a young man who died:

> *Oh, he died,*
> *Yes, he died,*
> *As other brave men died,*
> *But for valiant quenched vitality*
> *Deeds spring to immortality:*
> *A young man lingers lightly*
> *Where he dies.*[38]

"Advance to Tripoli" is a Battle Honour that is not sewn onto many regimental colours because it is considered an easier engagement than Tobruk, Gazala and El Alamein. However, for the Special Forces and other soldiers who died in Libya, the terrain and conditions were as bad as any they met and prompted General Alexander to describe the country as "very difficult".[39]

Much of the burden fell on the yeomanry. Churchill was a great supporter of this distinguished branch of the British Army. He visited them on 8 August and wrote:

> These fine troops, hitherto wasted and never yet effectively engaged with the enemy... For two years they had served in the Middle East, mainly in Palestine, and I had not been able to have them equipped and worked up to the high quality of which they were capable. Now at this moment in their career, it had been necessary to take all their tanks from them in order to feed and rearm the fighting line... It was my task to go from brigade to brigade and explain to all the officers gathered together, two or three hundred at a time, why they must suffer this mutilation after all their zeal and toil. But I had good news as well. The 300 Shermans were already approaching through the Red Sea, and in a fortnight the division would begin to be armed with the most powerful armoured vehicles current at that time.[40]

With the new tanks, they did indeed show their quality and the gallantry awards followed in abundance. At the pinnacle stood the Sherwood Rangers Yeomanry, about which General Brian Horrocks wrote: "No Armoured Regiment can show a finer record of hard fighting."[41] In 1941, the regiment had suffered from the same flawed strategy as 50th Division that was split between Iraq and Egypt. In the Sherwood Yeomanry's case, their commanding officer had to send B Squadron to Crete and change the regiment's role to coastal gunners and before he received the tanks promised by Churchill, the regiment also had a stint as an *ad hoc* strike force in Bren-carriers.

On 10 January, Montgomery assembled his commanders for a conference on the final phase of the Libyan campaign. His plan, code-named *Fire Eater*, began with an attack around the south-west of Buerat, using the route discovered by Paddy McLauchlan. Three days before Leese's XXX Corps launched their advance, the Western Desert Air Force began an intense bombardment of Rommel's strong points. The British and American aircraft flew 770 sorties with some reaching the port and air bases at Tripoli.

Early on 15 January, under the cover of darkness, the leading troops of 8th Armoured Brigade under Brigadier Edward Custance approached the Abu Nujaym road (now the A3) and crossed the front line. However, Rommel had mounted his anti-tank guns to the west of a three-pronged valley known as Wadi Zem Zem and "seemed to have every inch of it well covered". As C Squadron of the Sherwood Rangers Yeomanry advanced on the right, they met a deadly ambush and lost 11 tanks. To their left, Major Stanley Christopherson's A Squadron "was perched on the forward slope, spotting for [the] guns..."[42]

All day long, the fighting continued as 14 of the regiment were killed in action, including Lieutenant Ken Graves, whose witty description of the life of a tank commander is still so apt: "The '75 is jammed. The '37 is firing but is traversed the wrong way. I'm saying: 'Driver, reverse' on the radio; and the driver, who can't hear me, is advancing. As I look up over the turret and see 12 enemy tanks 50 yards away, someone hands me a cheese sandwich."[43]

One of the troop leaders was the brilliant war poet Keith Douglas, who immortalised this ferocious battle in his poignant memoir, *Alamein to Zem Zem*, but made light of the wounds he received when his tank was knocked out and he stepped on a land mine. That night, while the shelling continued, Christopherson drove back into the battle zone in a Dingo Scout Car with Michael Laycock to recover the casualties. They returned with four badly wounded men, including their artillery officer, Captain Burrows, who was taken to the regimental aid post where his foot was amputated by the new medical officer, Hilda Young.

Early the next morning, they discovered that the Afrika Korps had withdrawn after Rommel ordered "movement red" to a new line centred on As Sedadah. Colonel Kellett ordered an immediate pursuit, while the dependable padre buried the bodies of those who had been killed. Approaching the new German position, Michael Laycock's B Squadron "fought a brilliant action, destroying three enemy tanks, knocking out several 50mm anti-tank guns and taking the crews prisoner".[44]

German Stukas and treacherous going slowed the advance on 17 January and the regiment was still 20 miles from Bani Walid when the sun set. Meanwhile, Major General "Tam" Waverley's 51st Highland Division was making swifter progress along the flat terrain of the coastal road, fighting a series of short actions against the depleted 90th Light Division. Montgomery decided to make this easier approach his main effort for the final phase and moved 22nd Armoured Brigade forward to support the Highlanders.

Further north, news of the Allied success had spread rapidly among the Italian population, who had started streaming back to Italy soon after Montgomery entered Libya. A Savoia Marchetti S74 with 24 passengers had made the last flight from what later became Tripoli International Airport on 7 January. Now the only way to reach Italy was on board one of the small ferries that continued to leave Tripoli for another week. These were hindered by the Axis work to deny the use of the port to the Allies by mining and scuttling ships in the harbour.

Special operations were launched from Malta to prevent this from happening. On the night of 18 January, a "chariot" human torpedo, launched from HMS *Thunderbolt*, reached the port, but the crew was captured. Two days later, the Royal Navy sent motor torpedo boats on Operation *Childhood* to harass the Italian officials and protect the mole from further damage.

That day, Rommel had a "stormy" row with the Axis command. While he was fighting his way to the coast, he received a message that: "The Duce is not in favour of the steps at present being taken, because they are not in accordance with his instructions to hold the Tarhuna—Homs positions for at least three weeks." Rommel later wrote: "We gasped when we received this signal. A position which has been broken through or outflanked is valueless unless there are mobile forces available to throw back the enemy outflanking column."[45]

The final actions in Libya took place on 22 January when XXX Corps closed on Tripoli. Night attacks on the coast by 51st Highland Division and at Tarhuna by 7th Armoured Division left 15th Panzer Division holding the high ground south of al-Aziziyah, where the Royal Scots Greys engaged the enemy from hull-down positions. Meanwhile, radio intercepts reported Rommel's intention to save his army and abandon Tripoli that night.

Sure enough, the front line was clear in the morning and while the Long Range Desert Group followed Rommel into Tunisia, the forward elements of Eighth Army entered Tripoli. At 5 a.m. on 23 January, the 11th Hussars cautiously drove into the Libyan capital and declared it free from enemy troops. Meanwhile, the New

Zealanders and Highlanders met in the main square at al-Aziziyah and amicably agreed to split the responsibilities.[46]

The capture of Tripoli was something of an anti-climax. Many troops were not allowed into the centre of the city and were disabused of the view that this was the end of the North African campaign. For two and a half years Tripoli had been the carrot that had motivated the donkey, but now Donkey was denied its reward and sent instead to the Mareth Line in Tunisia.

For those who were allowed into this iconic city, the priority was to restore the harbour into service under Operation *Trundle* and prepare for a VIP arrival. On 4 February 1943, a jubilant Winston Churchill arrived for a celebratory visit. He had already met President Roosevelt at the Casablanca Conference to discuss the Allied strategy for the next phase of the war and had attempted to woo Turkey at a meeting with President Inönü at Adana.

The prime minister, whose code-name was Mr. Bullfinch, spent two nights in the Libyan capital and when he witnessed the "magnificent entry" of the Eighth Army, "tears were rolling down his cheeks."[47] Churchill described the pipers of the 51st Highland Division under Pipe Major Anderson as "spick and span", but many had "a great flair for finding alcohol" and several search parties had to be sent out by the company sergeant majors to ensure the pipers arrived on parade at the right time.

After reviewing 40,000 troops and speaking to 2,000 officers and men, the prime minister flew to Algiers to meet the American and French commanders in his Liberator aircraft named "Commando". General Alexander had already sent the following message to Churchill: "The orders you gave me on August [10] 1942 have been fulfilled. His Majesty's enemies, together with their impediments, have been completely eliminated from Egypt, Cyrenaica, Libya and Tripolitania. I now await your further instructions."[48] His dubious reward was to be put under the command of General Eisenhower in Tunisia, an appointment that drew criticism in the British press for the fact that "British commanders and troops had been unfairly ignored for the sake of some move in international politics."[49]

The victors arranged a conference on 15 February that was attended by 100 British and American generals from England and Tunisia, including General Eisenhower. Monty "told them how to win battles" and Flash Kellett, who had been awarded a DSO at El Alamein, performed a demonstration of tactics with dummy tanks on stage that drew the commander's approval: "I have nothing to add to a completely superb demonstration, the best I have ever seen." After two days of brilliant but boastful presentations, Myles Hildyard believed that the attendees "went home hating Eighth Army."[50]

Meanwhile, the Americans took over the other airfield in Tripoli, next to the Grand Prix circuit at Mitiga, for operations in support of Tunisia. The US Ninth

Army Air Force also flew from Soluch Airfield at Benghazi. Here they operated B-24 Liberators, which flew all the way to Italy.

One of these aircraft, famously named "Lady Be Good", failed to return after its first mission over Naples on 4 April. It was believed the aircraft crashed into the Mediterranean. However, the crew overshot the airfield and continued flying for two hours before they all parachuted from the aircraft and allowed it to crash in the desert near to Kufra. Tragically, they died of thirst in the desert, but their remains were not found until 1960. It is no wonder that Libyans say that the desert cannot be claimed by anyone.[51]

CHAPTER 14

Kingdom to Jamahiriya

Libya is extremely poor and lacking in most natural resources.
FOREIGN RELATIONS OF THE USA 1952–1954

On 19 June 1943, King George VI visited Libya and met the Tripoli base commander, Major General Brian Robertson,[1] before boarding HMS *Aurora* for passage
to Malta, where he presented a field marshal baton to Viscount Gort for his work
during the siege. The royal visit under the cover plan of Operation *Loader* was low
key compared with the prime minister's triumphant parade in February because
the difficult questions about the country's future were yet to be answered and the
priority for Robertson was supporting Eighth Army in Tunisia. There was also a
deep awareness of the harsh conditions prevailing in Libya, with widespread poverty
and shortages of food.

The immediate problem of providing humanitarian relief was accomplished
by "friendly young Englishmen in khaki shirts and shorts… dashing about the
countryside in dilapidated 15-hundredweight trucks [who] distributed food supplies
and helped the tribal and urban leaders to re-establish their affairs on Arab lines".[2]
However, delivering aid and repairing infrastructure were relatively straightforward
tasks compared with the thorny problem of what form of government should be
put in place when the occupation ended.

As an interim solution, the country returned to the Ottoman structure and was
geographically split into three autonomous regions, or *Muhafazat*. Cyrenaica and
Tripolitania were run by the British, but in the south, the Free French looked after
the lightly populated Fezzan. Initially, the administrations retained the Italian legal
system,[3] (albeit interpreted slightly differently in each region) while a new civil
service was recruited, and the diaspora slowly returned from their self-imposed exile.

The arrival of a "Red Fez" cohort of Syrians, Palestinians and Egyptians in Tripoli
was not welcomed by everyone. There were many families that had benefited from
the Italian regime and held positions of influence in running the state's commerce.
Their loss of power and wealth pushed them into the arms of Britain's rivals and
increased political dissent.

Britain held no colonial aspirations in Libya but did wish to see a benign regime that was friendly to Egypt and took account of the long-standing relationship that dated back to the colourful consuls, who had helped Britain become the partner of choice in the 19th century. Unfortunately, there was scant agreement among the Allies because France wished to annex Fezzan, while the Americans favoured a republican state and the Italians, who joined the Allies in 1943, maintained their claim on Tripolitania.

Responsibility for nation-building fell to a group of Oxbridge-educated Arabists who had served as officials in Egypt and Sudan. Duncan Cumming (Caius, Cambridge) was the chief administrator of Cyrenaica and Travers Blackley (Worcester, Oxford), his counterpart in Tripoli.[4] These scholarly pro-consuls were heavily influenced by Lord Rodd (Balliol, Oxford) and Edward Evans-Pritchard (Exeter, Oxford), who were both experts on the tribes of the region[5] and Professor Sir Norman Anderson (Trinity, Cambridge), who served with the Libyan Arab Force and became political officer for Sanussi affairs.

The administrators encouraged eminent archaeologists to join them in Libya. Theodore Burton Brown was the resident antiquities officer in Cyrenaica and became the first Briton in the 20th century to excavate in the necropolis at Cyrene. His counterpart in Tripolitania was Richard Goodchild, who helped preserve the heritage on a very tight budget and worked with John Ward-Perkins, who was assigned to protect Leptis Magna and Sabratha. These academics did not just concentrate on classical antiquity and in 1948, Charles McBurney discovered a karstic cave that was once occupied by Neolithic people.

The governing principles were based on the "Activist Arabist" notion of kinship that stemmed from the writings of men like Rennell Rodd, who noted: "The Briton and the Bedouin not infrequently find in one another a certain kinship of instinct that compels mutual regard."[6] The state the administrators conceived was based on a model that continues to serve Britain well in Jordan. The focal point was the Sanussi and its sagacious head, Idris al-Sanussi, who had lived in self-imposed exile in Egypt since December 1922.[7]

The former Emir of Cyrenaica, who had established a special bond with Britain through the diplomacy of Milo Talbot in 1916 and supported the Allies in World War II, seemed to be a natural leader, whose cautious approach might unify the country and ensure Libya co-existed peacefully with its neighbours. The discovery that leading tribes in the Sanussi Order could trace their lineage back to the 11th century, when the Ibn Hillal and Ibn Salim migrations brought 200,000 Arabs into Libya, provided the administrators with a hereditary nobility. However, promoting the "pure" Arab tribes, who provided the "upper level functionaries" of the Sanussi, came at the expense of the sophisticated urban elite, including many Berber families that pre-dated the Arab invasion.

This distortion of society was not supported by every British administrator. Peter Synge, who looked after the important town of Ajdebaya and held posts in Benghazi and Tobruk, was not seduced by the elite "Oxbridge Orientalism".[8] His assessment that the Sanussi were ill-suited for creating a modern state structure cost him promotion when Idris returned to live in Cyrenaica and for "speaking truth to power",[9] he was transferred to Eritrea in October 1947.

Idris had visited briefly in 1944 but declined the offer of a permanent homecoming until the threat of foreign control was removed. This question was resolved at the Potsdam Peace Conference in 1945, when Churchill, Roosevelt and Stalin agreed that the Italian colonies seized during the war should not be returned to the new government in Rome. Italy reluctantly relinquished its claim to Libya on 10 February 1947 and this paved the way for the arrival of Idris, who took up residence in a house at Benghazi, close to "Lethe's Grotto". The Sanussi leader was fully aware that Britain needed him to mediate with a dissenting population, since the liberators were now viewed by many as occupiers and in danger of becoming part of the problem, rather than the solution. Idris's presence was the key to governing Cyrenaica and so his frequent requests for money were tolerated by the proponents of the Sanussi project.

The political challenges that faced Travers Blackley in Tripolitania were even more demanding. By raising the Bedouin over the city dwellers and creating an artificial hierarchy based on tribal relationships, the British pro-consuls alienated many of the urban population. The disaffected and dispossessed were ripe for sedition and the tension on the streets led to a major security crisis when the State of Israel was proclaimed in 1948.

The Tripoli riots were not the first occasion that the Jewish community was targeted in Libya. At the beginning of the Italian occupation, the Jewish population stood at 40,000. However, after Mussolini signed his pact with Hitler, their situation deteriorated and over 2,500 were transported to a concentration camp in the Jebel Nafusa, where about 600 died of typhus and malnutrition. Others were sent to labour camps in Cyrenaica, but the most unfortunate were those with dual nationality because they were transported to Belsen in Germany.

General O'Connor's defeat of the Italian Tenth Army in February 1941 was "a cause of rejoicing" for the Jews in Benghazi.[10] Some of the men were able to join the Allies, but the families left behind suffered retaliatory attacks after Axis troops recaptured Cyrenaica two months later. When Montgomery drove Rommel out of Libya, the freed Jews welcomed the British again and were looked after by the Palestinian Regiment, which provided food and restarted schools. However, their allegiance was tested when more than 140 were killed during three days and nights of rioting and looting in Tripoli beginning on 4 November 1945.

After quelling this violence, the chief administrator did his best to improve relations between the Arab and Jewish communities, but anti-Semitism was not the only cause of tension on the streets. Libyan nationalists impatient for independence called on their brothers to overthrow the authorities. On the advice of the police commissioner, Alan Saunders, Blackley had to deploy troops again in February 1948 and impose a curfew after the political activist Fiki Hassan was arrested for inciting violence.[11]

Three months later, the State of Israel was proclaimed, and this caused a resurgence of tension, despite the efforts of the Arab-Jewish Pacification Committee. On the night of 12 June, angry rioters attacked families living among cosmopolitan communities. Fourteen were killed, but the number of casualties was much lower than in 1945 because paramilitaries had organised a self-defence group, which protected the Jewish quarter and counter-attacked the mob.

Reluctantly, Blackley had to deploy the British Army for a second time in the thankless role of Arab-Jewish peacekeeping. Allegedly this new violence was instigated by Tunisians passing through Tripoli. Whether this was the case or not, more incidents of anti-Semitism were recorded in both the east and west of Libya during the following year and the palpable sense of insecurity was played on by those who wished to increase the Jewish population in Israel.[12]

As independence neared, negotiations with the government resulted in mass emigrations. However, the Jews' departure did not end the demonstrations, which switched to nationalist grievances. As the protests increased, Idris played an expert hand, knowing there was little alternative to his leadership because any of the other choices would result in civil war. In 1949, he proclaimed Cyrenaica to be an independent emirate and introduced a distinctive black flag with a white star and crescent (this reappeared in Benghazi after the fall of Colonel Gadhafi). However, the United Nations refused to recognise this state and passed a resolution in November 1949, directing Britain and France to prepare the whole country for independence.

The popular Dutch diplomat, Adriaan Pelt, served as high commissioner for Libya during the United Nations Administration that began on 10 December. He had to deal with the intense distrust between regional leaders, but managed to successfully draft a new constitution and mentored the government of 60 tribal leaders from the three autonomous regions that was put in place nine months before the Kingdom of Libya was formally established.

The new country created on 24 December 1951 retained the provinces from the British Administration. In the west, there were 800,000 "sedentary" Tripolitanians and in the south about 50,000 Fezzanese lived in the desert oases. In the east there were 300,000 semi-nomadic Cyrenaicans alongside their cousins in the cities. In addition, about 46,000 Italians in Tripolitania still played "a leading role in the economy".[13]

Prime minister Mahmud al Muntasir, from Misuratah, faced an immediate challenge about the foreign military bases in Libya. He approached Egypt, which was still under King Farouk's rule, but their terms for $1,000,000 included ceding

Jaghbub oasis, whereas London offered nearly three times as much to retain their bases, so the prime minister signed the Treaty of Friendship and Alliance in 1953 that permitted British military barracks to remain at Tripoli, Benghazi, Barce, Derna, Tobruk and El Adem.

This quelled the anxious security situation and apart from the odd alert for overseas deployment,[14] the garrisons settled into a comfortable existence, with servicemen and women living with their families in insular messes and restricted clubs. They were joined by intrepid workers, such as the pioneering nurses Mary Benson and Anne Withers, who began training Libyan medics and midwives at Benghazi civilian hospital in 1952.[15]

Washington's anti-imperialist position did not stop American forces from helping the new nation. As Britain mentored the Libyan Army and Navy, America built the Libyan Air Force and retained their base at Mitiga, which they renamed in honour of Lieutenant Richard Wheelus, who was killed in Iran. This became the focus of a famous humanitarian operation in August 1952.

The world was alerted to the crisis by media reports of thousands of starving pilgrims caught without transport in Lebanon on their way to the Hajj. For four days and nights, 41st Air Transport Squadron from Wheelus, together with a squadron from Germany, airlifted 3,763 devotees from Beirut to Jeddah in their C-54 Skymasters. It was a generous gesture that demonstrated America's support to the Muslim world.

Two years later, Washington signed a concession to permanently station American forces at Wheelus. Sadly, this meant the destruction of the old racing circuit. The huge grandstand from where the excited spectators had watched the Tripoli Grands Prix and the iconic control tower were demolished and the start-finish area was converted into a new runway.[16]

While America was helping in the west, Her Majesty, Queen Elizabeth II paid an official visit in the east. She had previously touched down at El Adem in February 1952, when the plane taking her from Nairobi refueled on its way to London, but she did not meet King Idris because her father had just died. The two sovereigns did rendezvous on 1 May 1954, at the end of her world tour, when she also met Queen Fatima as-Sanussi (daughter of the third Grand Sanussi and wife of King Idris) and paid her respects at the war cemetery before meeting British families.

By then, the garrisons were basking in the aftermath of the war. Life was self-contained with welfare and education provided by British hospitals, cinemas and schools in Tripoli and Benghazi. Fourteen-year-old Mick Kiernan "only had lessons until 1 p.m." and spent most of the afternoons at the British sailing club, where there was a swimming pool "formed with pontoons anchored in the sea", or playing among the battlefield sites and ancient ruins.[17]

British boys and girls met other children, but friendships "tended to be rather less deep than England as service families moved from posting to posting". In August 1953, Kiernan spent a fortnight camping at Ras al Hillal, avoiding the spiders and other biting creatures. On the way home, his bus crossed the Bailey Bridge over Wadi el Kouf, named after the dramatic caves in the cliff face, and passed a column of armed horsemen on their way to Derna where they "shot up the local police station". His limited contact with Arab boys came either when he bought peanuts and chewing-gum, carried in wicker bowls balanced on their heads, or when they threw stones at each other after school.[18]

At the end of the royal visit, the queen and Prince Philip boarded RMS *Britannia* at Tobruk, where their patient young children, Princess Anne and Prince Charles, waited eagerly, having sailed from Portsmouth in the royal yacht's maiden voyage that began on 14 April. An enthusiastic prince rushed up to Her Majesty when she was piped aboard, but she meticulously stuck to protocol and said: "No, not you, dear," as she greeted dignitaries first, then shook the five-year-old's extended hand before privately sharing a "warm and affectionate" reunion in her cabin.[19]

* * *

The queen left behind a fragile state. Although Tobruk, Benghazi and Tripoli were all thriving, the economy remained almost wholly dependent on foreign aid and the budget deficit, which fluctuated between three and five million dollars, was mainly underwritten by the British government. The new prime minister, Mustafa Ben Halim, a brilliant 33-year-old who had been the minister of public works in the first government, had his hands full due to the widening gap between east and west, with the majority of Tripolitanians displaying "increasing distaste for their shepherd chieftains".[20]

By then, many Libyans were looking admiringly at Egypt where Gamal Abdel Nasser's Revolutionary Command Council had abolished the monarchy and instigated a programme of Arab socialism. As Nasser brought mass nationalisation and land reform to the country, he squeezed the Muslim Brotherhood out of political life in Egypt and was courted both by Moscow and Washington. President Eisenhower sent the Texan lawyer and former secretary of the Navy, Robert Anderson, to negotiate a peace deal between Egypt and Israel in 1956. At this time, the Soviet Union was selling unlimited arms to Nasser, while France was dealing similarly with David Ben-Gurion in Israel. Anderson failed in his attempts to broker a deal partly because Nasser wished to remain neutral in the Cold War and partly because he sought leadership of the Arab world, which meant promoting Egypt as an anti-Zionist state.

Libya's other North African neighbours were also fighting for their freedom from colonial rule. Both Tunisia and Morocco became constitutional kingdoms in the first half of 1956, but the war in Algeria that began on 1 November 1954 continued unabated. The convergence of the Cold War, anti-colonialism, Arab-Israeli conflicts and the struggle for leadership in the Arab world all combined into a single crisis that was to change the face of the Middle East and become a watershed moment in history.

The crisis began in July 1956, when Nasser nationalised the Suez Canal Company, which was not due to revert to Egyptian ownership until 1968. In response, Britain and France signed a secret agreement with Israel, known as the Protocol of Sèvres, to protect their interests in what by then was the main highway for oil arriving in Europe. After Israel invaded Sinai in October, French and British commandos and parachutist troops landed as part of Operation *Musketeer* and achieved their military objectives. However, President Eisenhower and First Secretary Khrushchev, together with the United Nations General Assembly, supported President Nasser over Prime Ministers Eden and Mollet. Huge political and economic pressure was put on the British and French governments, and this eventually resulted in their demeaning withdrawal from the Canal Zone by the end of the year.

Britain's humiliation might have provided a catalyst for political violence in Libya. However, the effective diplomacy of the British ambassador, Walter Graham, and a package of generous economic support, placated the ruling elite. The ascetic King Idris was no friend of Nasser and played a careful hand to ensure the population did not rise up against his government, or his British allies.

At the height of the Suez Crisis, British dependents were evacuated from Tripoli as the perceived threat to them increased. One of these was 12-year-old Janine McQuillan, the daughter of a Royal Engineers officer. She left the army school in Aziziyah Barracks and excitedly boarded a Handley Page Hermes passenger aircraft with her mother after lunch on 5 November. The Britavia pilot, Captain Connor, and his crew had little rest before flying the aircraft (G-ALDJ) all the way to Blackbush airport. Just before midnight he began his approach in foggy conditions, but unfortunately, he misjudged the height and undershot the runway, hitting a beech tree before the plane burst into flames. Both pilots and the radio operator died on impact and four children were burned to death in the tragedy.[21] This traumatic event affected everyone's stay in England and when it was time to return to Libya, Janine and her mother took the option of a sea passage in the SS *Syrian Prince*.

In some ways, Libya was a net beneficiary of the Suez Crisis as it became a safer tourist destination than Egypt. The intrepid Barbara Toy, described as a "woman of remarkable courage" by *The Spectator*,[22] had already paved the way for others by driving across Libya in her Series 1 canvas-topped Land Rover named "Pollyanna" in 1951 and 1952. Her adventures included diving at Benghazi, searching for war casualties in the desert and motoring to Kufra with the same guide who had accompanied Rosita Forbes in 1921.[23] Her popular book, *A Fool In The Desert: Journey In Libya*, which was launched at the beginning of 1956, brought the possibility of desert travel to a much wider audience.

As the risks in Egypt increased, the British film industry also preferred Libya for their locations. Producers of the award-winning *Ice Cold in Alex* changed their film set to Tripoli and began work in September 1957. The lead actress, Sylvia Syms, suggested that the desert conditions in Libya were so difficult that "there was very little acting. It was horrible. We became those people... we were those people."[24]

This was not the first major production in the Libyan desert. Two years earlier, Donald Sinden had worked on *The Black Tent* at Sabratha and Ghadames. During the filming, the daily British Overseas Air Corporation (BOAC) C-4 Argonaut flying 40 passengers from London via Rome struck the top of some trees on its approach to Tripoli International Airport in poor visibility. Fifteen passengers and crew died, and many others were injured in the worst civilian air accident in Libya up to that time. The facilities at the airport could not cope, so the US Air Force picked up the injured in helicopters and took them to Wheelus. During a break in filming, one of the cast escorted a survivor named Rosemarie to the American air base but was arrested for taking a photograph of her in a restricted area.[25]

The British Army provided assistance to many of the films. The tanks of the Queen's Bays, which had earned six Libyan Battle Honours in 1942, appeared in one of Cubby Broccoli's early films, *No Time To Die* with Victor Mature and Anthony Newly.[26] Many of the extras in the wartime adventure *Sea of Sand*, in which Michael Craig was nominated for the Best Actor prize at the BAFTAs, were British Army personnel serving in Libya. Their autograph books filled up when Richard Burton, Nigel Green and Christopher Lee featured in *Bitter Victory*, a war film typical of the genre that portrayed the clash of classes and ranks. However, the most famous cast appeared in the *Legend of the Lost*, filmed at Leptis Magna and Ghadames, which starred John Wayne and Sophia Loren.

* * *

The Anglo-Libyan relationship changed complexion in 1959 with the discovery of huge oil reserves in all three provinces. This resulted in an enormous expansion of government services and improvements to the standard of living in Cyrenaica and Tripolitania, albeit that the Bedouin, whose home was the desert, received few of the benefits.

In 1960, there were still more than 10,000 British service personnel with their families living in barracks along the east and west coast that had been established in 1943. Armoured cars patrolled the desert from Kufra to Sebha, while garrison life continued oblivious to the changes in Libyan society. The British military hospitals at Benghazi and Tripoli were particularly busy with bouts of dysentery, bites and stings, burns and diseases, births and deaths. Road traffic accidents were the biggest cause of casualties, but there were also the tragic losses of children and babies, such as Paul Hughes, who was buried in the Benghazi garrison cemetery before his first birthday.[27]

In March 1963, King Idris assigned Mohieddin Fikini to form a new cabinet. His government replaced the federal system in Libya with a central administration and gave women the right to vote. However, Fikini didn't last long, despite being the son of a famous resistance leader. In January 1964, police in Benghazi shot and killed young protesters. The prime minister asked the king to remove the chief of police, who refused to punish his officers, but Idris would not remove a loyal officer who had fought in the Libyan Arab Force during World War II, so Fikini resigned before the end of the month.

British autonomy ended on 27 April 1963, shortly after King Idris awarded Sir Winston Churchill the Grand Sash of the High Order of Sayed Muhammad ibn Ali as-Sanussi. In London, the Labour government that was elected in October 1964 decided to withdraw its military contingents in Tripoli and Benghazi (other small barracks in places such as Derna had already closed), but retain the Tobruk-El Adem staging post and overflight rights.[28] This allowed Britain's Vulcan bombers carrying nuclear weapons to fly from Cyprus to the Indian Ocean, where they were on standby to attack the Soviet Union in the event of World War III.

Roderick Sarell took over as ambassador in 1964 and strengthened the ties between Britain and Libya, despite increasing evidence of corruption in the administration.[29] Opaque government processes meant that negotiations to develop oil pipelines in tribal areas were desperately slow. The BP general manager, John Haines, pleaded with King Idris: "Your Majesty, during the War I was a prisoner in Tobruk, a prisoner of the Germans. I spent a great deal of time and effort trying to find ways of getting out of Tobruk. I never dreamed that, all these years later, I would be equally frustrated trying to find ways in again."[30]

Sarell was keen to retain the British garrison at Benghazi,[31] but as Labour idealists such as Roy Jenkins gained influence in London, the Wilson government decided in a strategic defence review to abandon Britain's military role east of Suez and to concentrate on Europe and NATO. At a high-powered meeting in Washington in January 1966, the secretary of state for defence, Denis Healey, and the foreign secretary, Michael Stewart, tried to persuade their American counterparts Robert McNamara and Dean Rusk to compensate for British reductions by increasing their military commitment in Libya.[32] However, America was bogged down in Vietnam and President Johnson was unwilling to make any further commitment than the "Letter of Interest in the Territorial Integrity of Libya" that he had already written to King Idris.

The Tripoli garrison, which included the British military hospital and British Forces Broadcasting Service, closed in February 1966. Two months later, the general officer commanding in Malta and Libya, Major General Johnny Frost, who was famously played by Anthony Hopkins in the film *A Bridge Too Far*, submitted another plea to retain the garrison in Benghazi. This was supported strongly by the British ambassador (and by Washington) because three strategic changes had complicated the situation since the original decision.

The first concern stemmed from Algeria, where a new nationalist regime had added a threat of a combined Egypt-Algeria attack on the desert oil fields. Security officials in Libya felt that a strong British military presence at Benghazi and Benina airport had a much greater deterrent effect than hidden away at El Adem. The second development was the reduced requirement for Libyan overflights. Both Washington and London were in the process of changing their nuclear arsenal from air-delivered bombs to inter-continental ballistic missiles, with the Polaris-armed HMS *Resolution* launched in September 1966. Together with the decision to withdraw from Aden, this lessened the need for a landing site at El Adem. Third, British oil companies were lobbying the government because they were increasing their presence and were very concerned about nationalist saboteurs attacking their sites.

These defence and security arguments led the chiefs of staff to recommend that the armoured regiment at Wavell Barracks in Benghazi should be retained. However, by the end of the year, the economic crisis in Britain had become so severe that they changed this recommendation to an unaccompanied infantry company at Tobruk and an unaccompanied armoured car squadron at El Adem "housed and administered on a shoestring basis".[33]

While the British economy failed, Libya prospered on the back of the oil industry. From a standing start, Libya became one of the biggest producers in the world in less than 10 years. Exports jumped from $11 million in 1960 to $1.168 billion in 1967. Among the beneficiaries of this wealth was the archaeological community with a resurgence of important projects funded by the government. Professor Sandro Stucchi became the leading Italian authority in Cyrenaica and collaborated with Richard Goodchild to restore precious sites, including the Severan Arch at Leptis Magna. Another ambitious project was the excavation of Apollonia by the University of Michigan.[34]

Everything changed on 5 June 1967 when Israel launched a pre-emptive air attack and invasion of the Sinai Peninsula after Nasser closed the Straits of Tiran to Israeli vessels. In Benghazi, the hysterical mood replicated the situation faced by the Beechey brothers in 1822 (see page 18). Young Arabs, stirred by Egyptian propaganda, attacked British, American and Jewish businesses and homes. British soldiers had to rescue vulnerable citizens and provide refuge for threatened expatriates as angry mobs burned the NAAFI club and British Reading Room. However, they did not intervene in the riots; as the consul, Peter Wakefield, explained, "it was questionable how effective they could have been".[35]

The American consul, John Kormann, barricaded himself with his staff of nine in the consulate and began to destroy secret documents. After 10 hours trapped in the building, soldiers of the 5th Inniskilling Dragoon Guards from Wavell Barracks rescued him and his wife and three children from their besieged quarters. The troops ignored the petrol bombs thrown at them and brought the rescued civilians to D'Aosta Barracks, where they joined thousands of other families evacuated from the city.[36]

In one block of flats the wives on the bottom floor joined those above and spent an anxious day watching the plumes of smoke and gangs of raging Libyan students. At 9 p.m., Janet Baker, who was looking after her 18-month-old daughter and was pregnant with her second child, was collected by the army and climbed on board a three-ton truck with a water cannon that was used against the mob as they drove back to D'Aosta. The Royal Electrical and Mechanical Engineers camp, which was only designed for 400, now had to cope with 3,000 people including oil workers, who came in from the desert. Janet had to live in a hangar with a towel hung up for privacy for three weeks before she was allowed to return home.[37]

The garrison troops were reinforced by 1st Battalion Dorset Regiment, which was in the middle of Exercise *Ballotage*, a three-week field-firing manoeuvre in the middle of the desert "on a scale unimaginable in Germany". The commanding officer, Lieutenant Colonel John Archer, who later became commander-in-chief of land forces, had just finished the second battle run of the day when he received orders to move his troops to Benghazi and Tobruk. His important intervention helped to defuse the volatile situation and restore order in Cyrenaica.

In Tripoli, Ambassador Sarell had to work hard to counter the "Big Lie" broadcast from Cairo by the popular Voice of the Arabs radio station. In a blatant propaganda attack on America, Egyptian reporters claimed that US Air Force planes from Wheelus had joined in the Israeli attack. The British embassy was caught up in the anti-Western sentiment and was besieged by student activists and hard-line Arab nationalists, who criticised the Libyan government for failing to help Egypt. Stung into action, Hussein Maziq, who had been prime minister for two years, suspended oil exports to the United States, Great Britain and West Germany and requested the withdrawal of British troops on 15 June.

However, when Sarell met King Idris a week later, the sovereign asked whether the British would maintain their facilities at El Adem in case he was forced to flee in the event of a revolution. The government in London was tempted to withdraw completely, but the Foreign Office understood that "the treaty, the presence of British bases in Libya and the existence of a substantial Libyan market for our exports must all be regarded as part of a whole. Without the treaty, we could not expect Libya to look to Britain as she now does as a major source of imports."[38] In the end, Prime Minister Harold Wilson considered the oil business, export trade and overseas training benefits outweighed the cost savings and agreed to maintain the Tobruk-El Adem staging post for the foreseeable future.

Meanwhile, the Six Day War marked another deterioration in Libya's relationship with its Jewish community. Many of those who had remained through the 1950s had been denied citizenship permits and the right to vote in a 1961 law and now lived in a state of uncertainty. They looked to King Idris for protection, but he could not prevent a rising tide of physical assaults and a media campaign that spilled into the sermons preached in mosques. The anti-Jewish riots and the burning of the Bet El Synagogue were the catalyst for the Italian and American governments to begin an airlift from Tripoli on 11 June, which eventually rescued 6,000 refugees, who were forced to leave their homes, businesses and possessions.[39]

On 1 July, King Idris replaced Hussein Maziq with the housing minister, Abdul Qadir al Badri. The new prime minister ended the oil embargo and acted as a stop gap until a young reformer, Abdul Hamid al-Bakkoush, succeeded him on 25 October. He immediately encouraged greater citizen participation in society; however, he also put on trial political dissenters, such as Mahmud Suleiman Maghribi, who had gained a US PhD in petroleum law at George Washington University and initiated a strike among the Libyan oil workers, for which he was sentenced to four years' imprisonment and stripped of his Libyan nationality.

As the situation in Libya calmed, a succession of financial crises hit Britain and these finally led to the devaluation of the pound in November 1967. At the end of that month, British forces withdrew from Aden after a four-year insurgency, but thanks to the work of the embassy staff in Tripoli and Benghazi, there was a major upswing in official Anglo-Libyan relations. By the end of the year, the Foreign Office claimed: "The market for British goods and particularly services such as consultancy is excellent; the Libyans [are] well disposed to us and the demand [is] expanding."[40]

This was only partly true. Although influence with King Idris and his government remained healthy, to many Libyans who listened to Egyptian broadcasts, the British were pro-Israeli and this generated a level of hostility that was always close to the surface. On the key issue, whether Britain would intervene militarily in the case of an Egyptian-backed revolution, the Foreign Office considered it would only be possible with the support of Washington.[41]

The closure of the British garrison at Benghazi, code-named Operation *Bordon*, was completed when the last units left for Malta on the *Empire Gull* on 3 February 1968 and with the sale of British property to the Libyan government for "rather more than £250,000".[42] This left 400 soldiers and 785 RAF personnel at El Adem, with 22 Royal Navy mentors at Tripoli and 45 military advisors to the Libyan Army.[43] The removal of troops from Benghazi did not solve the government's problems, but it did allow British troops to concentrate on their desert training. Battle groups from Germany, Cyprus and Malta rotated through the desolate tented camp named Chatham and the coastal camp at Timini, 30 miles west of Tobruk.[44]

British strategy now concentrated on bolstering Idris and preventing the Soviet Union from establishing any bases in Libya. The Army's strategic commander, Lieutenant General Sir John Mogg, visited in March to assess the requirements to rearm and retrain the Libyan Army. His report led to a £46.8 million contract to provide 180 of the latest Chieftain battle tanks and 20 Abbott self-propelled artillery. Six tanks were to be delivered in December 1969 with a further 40 in 1970 and the remainder arriving in stages up to 1973. The package included a large British training team to help reorganise the Libyan Army.

The contract was signed in September 1968, when the Italian-trained lawyer, Wannis al-Qaddafi, became Idris' 10th prime minister. He had been recruited after the war to help run Cyrenaica, but was described as "indecisive" by the British administrators.[45] At the Libyan National Assembly, he emphasised "stability, prosperity and progress", but 79-year-old King Idris' health was not good and his heir, Sayed Hasan ar-Rida as-Sanussi, was unpopular with young Libyan nationalists.

By 1969, the last British garrison in Libya was located 18 miles south of the busy port of Tobruk at Royal Air Force El Adem. This comprised a large airfield and a transit camp for visiting regiments. In June, the unaccompanied armoured squadron provided by 3rd Carabiniers (known as the Old Canaries for their yellow facings) was relieved by 106 officers and soldiers of the 17th/21st Lancers, who began a nine-month unaccompanied tour of duty.

The Death or Glory Boys were led by Major Johnny Hills, who had soldiers from the 4th/7th Dragoon Guards and Queen's Royal Irish Hussars attached, together with a Sioux helicopter flight. Each armoured troop comprised two Saladin armoured cars carrying a 76mm gun and two Ferret Scout Cars, which had replaced the much-loved Daimler Dingo. They were supported by a pale quartermaster who hated the desert, Jimmy Lund, and a diligent young orderly room sergeant, John Hodges.

The troops rapidly familiarised themselves with the desert terrain, which had changed little from the time of the famous siege of Tobruk. Rommel's tank tracks had hardened to cement and the old trenches were filled partially with sand. The flies were as bad as ever and checking for scorpions and camel-spiders became second nature. The triple dannert-wire barrier still ran along the border and the active mines and other remnants of war provided dangerous obstacles, which were cleared by Support Troop.

Lieutenant Richard Wilkin, who had recently completed a posting in the Gulf, took his troop into the Sahara to improve the military skills needed in the desert. Navigation was still notoriously difficult. He used the sun compass developed by Ralph Bagnold during the day and the North Star by night. At midday, he had to halt the vehicles because the petrol in the Saladin fuel tanks began to boil. Stopping in one particular wadi that was 100 feet deep, his soldiers became aware of a melancholy presence and quickly asked to move on; later, he discovered that the Long Range Desert Group had been ambushed there during the war and suffered several casualties.

The facilities at El Adem were tired and needed refurbishment, but the Treasury baulked at the £2 million cost. Living in the sergeants' mess with 200 itinerant members turned the squadron's senior soldiers into fine athletes. To use one of the two small washing machines a sergeant needed to be able to sprint 80 yards in seven seconds, otherwise he would have to wait for the next cycle. Queues for meals started 30 minutes earlier than normal and the key agility tests involved finding a basin with a plug and a lavatory with a seat.

Relations with the Cyrenaica Defence Force[46] remained close and cordial because the British mechanics assisted Sayed Abdallah Abed al Sanussi, known as the Black Prince, with his Ferret Scout Cars. The Royal Military Police continued with their joint patrols to reassure local communities; however, they had little to do with the Libyan Army, which had been at loggerheads with the Cyrenaica Defence Force for years.

In July, some of the squadron ran a desert rescue exercise while the Air Troop was in Jebel Akhdar. Their very high frequency Larkspur C-42 radios had difficulty with the link back to El Adem, but they managed to listen to President Nixon talking to Neil Armstrong walking on the moon, while looking at it through their binoculars. As the worst of the summer heat arrived in August, half the squadron travelled to Cyprus to conduct a training exercise with their sister squadron, little realising that a group of young men in the Libyan Army, calling themselves the Free Officers Movement, was in the latter stages of planning a *coup d'état*.

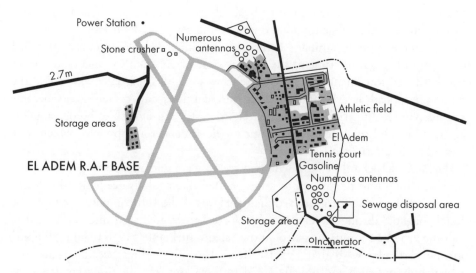

Royal Air Force El Adem. The town changed hands five times during World War II. Her Majesty Queen Elizabeth II landed here on the way from Kenya to London after her father died in February 1952. As Britain's last permanent base in Libya, it was handed over to Colonel Gadhafi on 23 March 1970.

Bir Hakeim. Captain Richard Wilkin with soldiers of B Squadron, 17th/21st Lancers, the last British Army combat unit to be based in Libya that was evacuated in March 1970. (Crown copyright)

FV601 Saracen of 17th/21st Lancers patrolling the perimeter of the Royal Air Force Station at El Adem, which was renamed Gamal Abdel Nasser Airbase by Colonel Gadhafi. This highly capable light tank had a Rolls-Royce petrol engine and 76mm gun as its main armament. It continued to be used on operations by the British Army in Cyprus until after the First Gulf War in 1991. (Crown copyright)

CHAPTER 15

Line of Death

Who would tell the lion that his breath stinks?

LIBYAN PROVERB

After King Idris flew with sacks rumoured to be filled with over £4,000,000, from the Royal Air Force base at El Adem to holiday in Greece and Turkey in August 1969,[1] the Free Officers Movement seized power and proclaimed the Libyan Arab Republic on 1 September 1969. The 80-year-old sovereign had already abdicated in favour of his brother's son, Hasan, who was due to be enthroned on the day after the coup. However, the Crown Prince was arrested in Benghazi and renounced his claim in favour of the 12 young officers in the Revolutionary Command Council. The RCC, as it was known, was made up of earnest acolytes of Egypt's nationalist leader, Gamal Abdel Nasser, and their first decree was to abolish the monarchy and end the Senussi's prominence in Libya's government.

The newly arrived British ambassador, Donald Maitland, was a diminutive, silver-haired Arabist (who was later knighted for his role as prime minister Edward Heath's chief press secretary). He placed British forces on high alert when he was asked for help by Idris's advisor, Omar el Shelhi, while declaring that the coup "would not harm Britain's good relations with Libya".[2] However, after the king decided to retire to Egypt with his wife,[3] London officially recognised the new government (on 6 September) and Maitland began negotiations with the RCC to save the jobs of 5,000 British workers in the Libyan oil industry.

Meeting the new head of state, Muammar Gadhafi (who was rapidly promoted from captain to colonel), Maitland described the 27-year-old as "exceedingly courteous" but full of "misconceptions" derived from the Voice of the Arabs broadcast from Cairo.[4] The ambassador's assignments with the RCC, which were normally held at 9 p.m., were extremely positive and the members of the RCC were impressed with the way he understood their culture and mastered their language.[5]

The new leaders were too young to remember Britain's role in freeing Libya from colonial rule and were unaware of the full extent of financial support that Britain had given to their country before the discovery of oil. Some had been imprisoned by Idris's government, including the first prime minister after the revolution, Mahmud Suleiman Maghribi, who was released from his four-year sentence immediately after the coup. These nationalists preferred to believe Egypt's propaganda that Western governments had "treated Libya like a prostitute" and as a result, Gadhafi set his own price for Libya's most valuable commodity. According to Maitland, this later "led directly to the oil crisis of 1973".[6]

The other big question was what would happen to Britain's military bases at Tobruk and El Adem after the RCC demanded their closure on 29 October.[7] Immediately after the coup, the infantry battle group training in the desert, 3rd Battalion, The Parachute Regiment, was dragooned into helping to guard the perimeter and this allowed B Squadron, 17th/21st Lancers to deal with the rogue vehicles that attempted to break into camp. Weapons were loaded and orders issued to open fire, but fortunately they did not have to be used in anger.

In theory, the 17th/21st Lancers were confined to the British base. However, they were soon asked for help by the Cyrenaica Defence Force, which had a number of broken-down scout cars. The request was passed to the Near East Land Forces headquarters, which authorised Sergeant Smails and Lance Corporal Corney from the Royal Electrical and Mechanical Engineers fitters section to travel to the Libyan base and repair these vehicles.[8]

This released the tension and as a result, the Lancers extended their patrols to the tented desert camp 80 miles west of El Adem and to the magnificent mosque at Jaghbub 200 miles to the south. They continued to practise their driving in the Great Sand Sea dunes that rose 500 feet from the stone desert and to shoot sand grouse in 150-degree heat. One group even managed to secure a pass to visit the ancient site at Cyrene and to trek through the rugged gorges full of large cobwebs, hanging from the shrubs and trees.

Camping at the favourite British site at Ras al Hillal, close to where Geoffrey Keyes earned his Victoria Cross, they met the redoubtable Royal Beekeeper, Olive Brittan. She had earned an MBE in 1959 for modernising apiculture in Libya[9] and was held in high regard by the British women and men who met her during their postings to Libya. Living alone in Rommel's old mess with no electricity, looking after herself with a paraffin heater and cooker, she carried on regardless of the revolution. When the British *chargé d'affaires* in Benghazi, Peter Wakefield, eventually informed her that she must evacuate her home, she insisted on a formal diplomatic ceremony with a salute to the Union flag as it was lowered for the last time on Bee Hill.[10]

* * *

The British ambassador needed the help of the commander of British Forces Cyprus, Air Chief Marshal Sir Denis Smallwood, and Major General Philip Goddard to persuade the prime minister, Harold Wilson, to agree to the evacuation of all British military personnel and equipment by the end of March 1970. With this concession, Maitland earned Gadhafi's confidence and was able to arrange the sale of British installations to the new government. Gadhafi also agreed to fulfil the arms deals, including the Bloodhound anti-aircraft missiles and Chieftain battle-tanks for which the Treasury had already received £10 million.

In London, there were second thoughts about this deal due to the competing relationship with Israel. Beginning in 1958, the government had completed a number of tank deals with Golda Meir's government, so that by 1967, the Israeli Defence Force operated 250 Centurion tanks that proved decisive in the Six Day War. British policy in the Middle East mirrored that of the French and was dominated by concerns about an Arab-Israeli conflict escalating into World War III. Both countries attempted to play a fine line between supporting Israel against Nasser, while at the same time providing assistance to long-standing Arab friends, including in Britain's case the Hashemite king of Jordan and the Sanussi king in Libya.

Before the coup in Libya, there was an intense debate in Whitehall about a proposal to sell a further 200 Centurions as well as 250 new Chieftain tanks to Israel. The defence secretary, Denis Healey, was a strong advocate for the sale, whereas the foreign secretary Michael Stewart suggested that it would be better to sell only the less capable Centurions. The Defence and Overseas Committee was lobbied by British ambassadors in Tel Aviv and Kuwait who argued for and against the deal. At the time, British investments in the Arab world were £166 million and exports £211 million, whereas investments in Israel only amounted to £2.5 million and exports to £64 million. More importantly, there was a possibility of losing up to £500 million worth of orders to Arab countries if Britain sided with Israel.[11]

It all came to a head after the coup. The future use of El Adem training facilities (where Britain conducted its major overseas manoeuvres) and the £155 million Bloodhound contract were at stake, so the decision was taken on 16 October to delay the Israeli Chieftain deal, while continuing to supply them with Centurions. However, rumours continued to circulate in Tripoli that Britain was diverting the tanks destined for Libya to Israel. The British embassy was attacked on the anniversary of the Balfour Declaration and Maitland warned London that many expatriates had contacted him because they were "concerned about their safety".[12]

The foreign secretary heeded this advice and declared "it would be wrong to introduce into the Middle East a powerful new weapon held by no other Middle Eastern country, and which is not being supplied to Israel".[13] The government's hesitation about selling arms contrasted with the French, who agreed to sell Mirage fighters on the basis that these would act as a catalyst for a benign relationship and keep the Soviet Union out (this position was supported by Washington). When he heard about this change in policy, Maitland criticised London's lack of "political will", which effectively ruined the long-standing partnership that his predecessors had built over many years.[14]

Washington was also cautious about the new regime in Libya, but this did not stop the US government from authorising three Sikorsky HH-3E Jolly Green Giant helicopters flying from Wheelus into flood-ravaged Tunisia in November where they saved the lives of at least 433 people trapped in high waters.[15]

Meanwhile, on 2 January 1970, the port and maritime squadron at Tobruk, led by Major Robin Barton,[16] began loading hundreds of vehicles onto a succession of Royal Fleet Auxiliary landing ships.[17] The 17th/21st Lancers squadron was the one unit feared by the RCC, so it remained operational until the end of February. It was therefore present when Colonel Gadhafi, who had taken over as prime minister on 16 January, visited with sacks of Libyan pounds[18] to pay for the British installation.

On 5 March the final 45 vehicles were saluted by the air base commander, Group Captain Peter Terry, as they drove to the port where they were loaded onto RFA *Sir Tristram*. Three days later, the soldiers boarded a VC-10 in one of the worst sandstorms of the winter. Flying to Brize Norton, there was no respite because they landed in snow and were subjected to a two-hour delay as their bags were searched for contraband. From there, they flew to Northern Ireland, where they were soon patrolling the border and responding to riots.[19]

On 23 March Peter Terry handed over El Adem ahead of schedule to thwart any planned demonstrations. Five days later RFA *Empire Gull* ended the British military presence in Libya, when it ferried the last 78 passengers and 42 vehicles from Tobruk to Cyprus, prompting Gadhafi to claim:

> The raising of the flag of the Libyan Arab Republic instead of the British flag is a victory for the Arab nation as a whole and not only for the Libyan people. What increases my pleasure and that of members of the revolutionary command council is the sight of the British troops withdrawing from the Tobruk base and retracing their steps in all sorrow and distress while we see the sight of Libyans delighted to enter today the base from which they have been barred for long years.[20]

By then, the Defence and Overseas Committee had decided to cancel the arms sales. This perceived slight enraged Gadhafi and led to a serious deterioration in relations as training concessions ended, foreign oil companies were expelled, and the remaining Jews were persecuted. After the Americans handed over Wheelus in June, Russian tanks appeared in Tripoli as Gadhafi turned to the Soviet Union for equipment and modelled his rule on Nasser's authoritarianism, imposing tough restrictions on liberty, while distributing some of the oil wealth to the population through improved education and health care.

By the end of July, the British military advisory mission in Benghazi had closed and all that was left was an unsecured administrative presence. Michael Hannam, who worked in the British embassy on defence sales, met with the 25-year-old RCC deputy chairman, Major Abdessalam Jalloud. He was a classmate of Gadhafi and equally as impatient for immediate responses and ignorant of international protocols. Although London wished to re-engage in the Libyan market, the new regime conducted a series of show trials of the king (in his absence) and government officials, which generated suspicion and mistrust. Erratic responses provided little confidence about how the arms would be used and so the relationship withered, and Libya was lost to the West.

* * *

Gadhafi's strident anti-Israel foreign policy was aggravated when a Libyan Airlines Boeing 727 passenger aircraft flying from Tripoli to Cairo was shot down over the Sinai Peninsula on 21 February 1973. The 42-year-old French pilot, Jacques Bourges, had lost his bearings due to bad weather and faulty instruments and had turned back towards Egyptian airspace when the Israeli Phantom jets fired their cannons at the airliner. Only five of the 113 passengers and crew survived the attack.

The following day, a mob attacked the US embassy in Tripoli, but Washington had withdrawn its ambassador three months earlier. Libyan-US relations deteriorated further after Gadhafi breached the international convention on the Law of the Sea in 1973, when he arbitrarily claimed the whole of the Gulf of Sirte to be within Libyan internal waters and declared the latitude at 32 degrees, 30 minutes between Benghazi and Misuratah as a "Line of Death". His resolve was tested when a Lockheed C-130 flew across this line one month after the Sinai incident, on 21 March. The Libyan Air Force launched a pair of Mirage fighters, which intercepted and fired at the American transport plane, but the Hercules escaped by flying into thick cloud.

Gadhafi's relations with his eastern neighbour collapsed about the same time. After Nasser died on 28 September 1970, he initially supported his successor Anwar Sadat and provided him with troops and funds for the 1973 Yom Kippur War. However, when Sadat agreed a peace settlement with Israel, Gadhafi began to undermine him, and this culminated in a short war with Egypt in 1977.

By then Gadhafi had reformed Libya's government and constitution after several of the original members of the RCC had become disillusioned and attempted to overthrow him in August 1975.[21] Gadhafi realised that any coup would depend on the support of the Libyan Army and so he refused to allow standing formations larger than a battalion and promoted loyalists over competent officers. This resulted in a low-grade army with poor operational standards, compared with the well-trained Egyptian Army.

Gadhafi dissolved the RCC and created the General People's Congress (GPC), which adopted the "Declaration of the Establishment of the People's Authority" on 2 March 1977 and proclaimed the Socialist People's Libyan Arab Jamahiriya with its distinctive green flag. He divided the state between the GPC, which administered the country, and the Revolution, which ruled the people. He had no role in the former, but as supreme commander of the armed forces and "Brotherly Leader of the Revolution", he maintained tight control of the country with a brutal national intelligence service, *Mukhabarat el-Jamahiriya*, that organised frequent public executions of dissidents.

This move aligned him closer to the Soviet Union and further away from Sadat's Egypt, which increasingly sided with Washington. As the rhetoric and subversion intensified, the border between the two countries became the focus of another Cold War conflict. Tension increased throughout the summer months[22] and on 21 July, the Libyan 9th Tank Battalion crossed the frontier and attacked Sollum just as the Sanussi, Italians and Rommel had done earlier in the century.

However, the Egyptian Defence Force was ready and within three days their aircraft, tanks, artillery and commandos made serious inroads into Libya, raiding the El Adem air base, ironically renamed in honour of Nasser, and logistics sites in the desert. This crisis was mediated by the odd combination of Washington and the leader of the Palestinian Liberation Organization, Yasser Arafat.

Sadat conformed to American pressure and after achieving his goals on 24 July, he declared a self-imposed ceasefire. Tensions remained high during the following days, but this did not prevent an exchange of prisoners in August. Slowly, the frontier returned to normal as both sides withdrew troops, despite the personal relationship worsening as the leaders traded insults and plotted the other's downfall.

After the failure of his army in this short war, Gadhafi realised he needed to modernise his forces and complete his political reforms. However, this did not prevent another disastrous performance at the battle of Lukaya, when the Libyan Army, which fought beside President Idi Amin's loyal forces, was defeated by Tanzanian troops and Ugandan rebels in March 1979.

This tumultuous year in world affairs also witnessed the fall of the genocidal Pol Pot regime in Cambodia, the return of Ayatollah Khomeni to Iran and the Soviet invasion of Afghanistan along with numerous international terrorist attacks. On 20 November, 16 days after Iranian students took over the American embassy in Teheran, Saudi Arabia's holiest mosque in Mecca was seized by an Islamic fanatic group, led by Juhayman al-Otaybi, who denounced the Westernisation of Saudi Arabia. For two weeks he held hundreds of worshippers hostage. When Saudi troops ended the siege, Muslim leaders falsely claimed that American forces had entered the Holy Shrine, and this resulted in a mob in Tripoli burning the US embassy on 2 December.

Meanwhile, Gadhafi continued to pursue an aggressive foreign policy, instigating a campaign to assassinate dissidents overseas, attempting to become a nuclear power and sponsoring international terrorism. In this respect, he became one of the main providers of weapons and explosives to the Provisional IRA at a time when it was supported by the Irish American organisation NORAID. However, this association did not placate the Brotherly Leader's animosity towards Washington, or his virulent anti-Zionism. In March 1981, he warned America of "war in the full sense of the word" if US forces again entered the Gulf of Sirte. However, his bluster did not deter the new president, Ronald Reagan, who responded by authorising the Sixth Fleet to conduct maritime exercises in the contested zone during the summer.

This antagonism culminated in a dogfight on 19 August, when two Libyan Sukhoi Su-22 fighters attacked two Navy F-14 Tomcats from the USS *Nimitz* over the Gulf of Sirte. Both Libyan aircraft were shot down 60 nautical miles from the coast and this incident caused Washington to advise all Americans to leave Libya as their passports were being invalidated. Adversarial relations deepened and the following spring, the United States announced a ban on imports of Libyan oil.

Americans were not the only people to leave Libya as its better educated and enterprising citizens, who were dispossessed by Gadhafi's socialism, sought opportunities abroad. Many of the Brotherly Leader's opponents moved to England and in April 1984, a crowd of 75 dissidents, organised by a leading opposition group, the National Front for the Salvation of Libya, protested outside the Libyan People's Bureau in St James's Square, London about the public execution of two students at the University of Tripoli.

Overnight, the Libyan diplomats received a message from Colonel Gadhafi to open fire on the protesters and at 10.18 a.m. two men sprayed bursts of machine-gun fire from the first floor of the building. Eleven protesters were wounded and a 22-year-old policewoman, Yvonne Fletcher, was killed. She was among a group of police standing in the street between the protesters and counter-protesters. The bullet that passed through her, entered from her right side, cut across her lungs, liver and gall bladder and exited from the left side of her body.

While she was taken to Westminster Hospital, a cordon was formed around the building, but the gunmen escaped through the garage before the police could seal it. Obstructing the investigation, Gadhafi refused access to the Bureau, so it was effectively placed under siege. The British public was outraged not only by the murder but also by the response from Libya where the British ambassador, Oliver Miles, was detained, and this sense of disgust increased when Gadhafi instructed his agents to begin a campaign of bombing in London.

The prime minister, Margaret Thatcher, responded by breaking diplomatic relations with Libya on 22 April 1984. Five days later, at the same time as Yvonne Fletcher's funeral was taking place in Salisbury Cathedral, the remaining 30 staff in the Libyan Bureau were deported and that evening, Oliver Miles returned to London from Tripoli with the British embassy staff.

The failure to admit responsibility hung like a dark cloud over what had once been a flourishing relationship between the two countries. It was not the amount of trade that mattered because imports and exports had reduced to about a quarter of a million pounds in 1983. It was the oil and construction industries that suffered because there were still 8,000 British workers in Libya.

While British affairs in Libya were handled by the Italian embassy, Gadhafi chose the Royal Embassy of Saudi Arabia to look after Libyan relations in London. The effect on Libya of his behaviour was dramatic. There is no doubt that internally Libya had made progress in the 14 years of Gadhafi rule. The gross domestic product per person was higher than in the United States and the European Union and significant improvements had been made to education, health, housing and gender equality.

Gadhafi supported archaeological restoration projects and paid for the addition of Cyrene, Sabratha and Leptis to the World Heritage List in 1982 (these were joined later by the cave paintings of Tadrart Acacus and the old town of Ghadames). More importantly, he had begun the creation of a network of water pipes known as the Great Man Made River, bringing water from prehistoric aquifers deep in the desert, thousands of miles to the coastal cities.

Global endorsements and economic growth ended with his refusal to show remorse for the murder of Yvonne Fletcher. He became further isolated in August 1984 when America forbade members of Libya's mission to the UN from traveling outside New York City without special permission and later expelled an *attaché* for involvement in attacks on Libyan exiles in the United States.

His continuing support for international terrorism led President Reagan to impose sanctions on 7 January 1986. Another incident in the Gulf of Sirte followed in March when six missiles were fired at American aircraft, which responded by sinking two Libyan patrol craft. Gadhafi retaliated by bombing *La Belle* discotheque in West Berlin on 5 April, killing two American sergeants and a Turkish woman, as well as wounding 230 people, of whom 79 were American servicemen and women.

Ten days later, President Reagan, with support from Prime Minister Thatcher, launched Operation *El Dorado Canyon*. American bombers flew from four Royal Air Force bases in England (Mildenhall, Fairford, Lakenheath and Upper Heyford) and from two carriers in the Mediterranean (USS *America* and USS *Coral Sea*). While Gadhafi's air defence systems were suppressed with jamming and missiles, 18 F-111Fs attacked targets in Tripoli and 14 A-6 Intruders attacked military bases at Benghazi.

The Brotherly Leader's residence at al-Aziziyah was included in the target list, but the Italian prime minister alerted him to the danger, so he escaped with his family just before it was hit by the American bombs. During the raid, the Libyans suffered about 60 casualties, but Gadhafi claimed a "spectacular victory" by surviving the assassination attempt and shooting down one F-111F with the loss of two American pilots. More importantly, he was the victor in the court of international opinion with the United Nations General Assembly adopting a resolution which condemned "the military attack perpetrated against the Socialist People's Libyan Arab Jamahiriya on 15 April 1986, which constitutes a violation of the Charter of the United Nations and of international law".[23]

In response, Gadhafi provided a haven for the infamous terrorist Abu Nidal and announced that the eighth most spoken language in the world, Russian, would replace the English language in schools. This denied a generation of young Libyans the opportunity of learning the leading language of international affairs, which proved crucial when the new government in 2011 needed people with these skills to re-engage with the Western world.

There were other examples of his mercurial approach to foreign relations in the 1980s. For several years, he had supported Iran in its war against Iraq, but when sanctions began to bite, he offered to swap sides to secure financial support from Saudi Arabia for the Great Man Made River project. However, he was not able to retain Saudi support for long.

His capricious behaviour also played out with a southern neighbour. Ever since 1973, he had claimed and occupied a large area south of the border with Chad, known as the Aouzou Strip. This was full of minerals, including uranium deposits used in his nuclear programme. In 1987, the Chadian government, with military assistance from France and the United States, launched an offensive to recapture this land. By the end of September, Gadhafi's troops were routed with more than 7,000 Libyans killed in what was named the Toyota War after the vehicles that were predominantly used in the conflict.

This was another blow to the Brotherly Leader's prestige and in revenge, he sponsored his most despicable acts, downing Pan Am Flight 103 on 21 December 1988 and Union de Transports Aériens Flight 772 on 19 September 1989. The former was a Boeing 747 which was destroyed when a bomb exploded in its fuselage as it flew over the Scottish village of Lockerbie; all 259 passengers and crew (from 21 countries) were killed along with 11 residents of Sherwood Crescent. The latter was a French DC-10 that was flying from Brazzaville in the People's Republic of the Congo to Paris; all 170 passengers and crew (from 18 countries) were killed when a suitcase bomb exploded over the Niger desert.

Much of the sympathy and goodwill Gadhafi had gained from the bombing of Tripoli was eroded by these acts of international terrorism. As the tide of opinion turned, Ronald Reagan made one of his final decisions before handing over as president to George H. W. Bush, when he authorised an incursion into the Gulf of Sirte. This prompted another Libyan retaliation and on 4 January 1989, two MiG-23 Floggers attacked two Navy F-14s from the USS *John F. Kennedy*, but both Libyan fighters were shot down by the superior American aircraft.

Gadhafi's international support dwindled to a few revolutionary socialists, such as his apologist, George Galloway. However, the Brotherly Leader did not change his fickle behaviour, which was consistently inconsistent. Having supported Shiite Persians against predominantly Sunni Arabs during the Iran-Iraq war, he changed his allegiance and backed Saddam Hussein when he invaded Kuwait in August 1990. At the meeting of the Arab League which condemned the illegal invasion, Gadhafi was the only head of state to vote with Iraq.

Falling out with other Arab leaders and facing political isolation, his focus turned to pan-Africanism, a movement he had supported since the 1970s. His munificence bought friends among several corrupt countries and helped brutal despots such as Charles Taylor, who he trained and sponsored to become president of Liberia.[24] He also supported other pariah regimes, such as Slobodan Milosovic's genocidal government in Serbia. The irony of the Brotherly Leader aligning himself with Orthodox Serbs against Balkan Muslims was not lost on the world, who increasingly viewed him as a complete maverick.

One change he did make in 1994 was to reap enormous benefits during the following decade. Gadhafi's brother-in-law Abdullah Sanussi had been the feared head of Libyan intelligence and throughout the 1980s had been responsible for much of the repression and many of the executions of opponents. Easing him aside, Gadhafi brought in the deputy head of foreign affairs, Musa Kusa, who had completed his degree in Sociology at Michigan State University. This urbane diplomat had cultivated cordial relations with world leaders in the 1980s and now he turned his intellectual acumen to the weighty obstacle that divided Libya from the West.

* * *

When Tony Blair became prime minister in May 1997, Britain's relationship with Libya was at an all-time low, disrupted by the two unresolved terrorist crimes. Investigators of the Lockerbie bombing had reconstructed the aircraft and understood how the device had been planted. Their evidence had led the Scottish lord advocate and the American attorney general to indict two Libyans, Abdelbaset al-Magrahi and Lamin Khalifah Fhimah, for the crime in 1991. However, Gadhafi's offer to try them in a court in Libya and Nelson Mandela's proposal to host a trial in South Africa (through the diplomacy of Musa Kusa) were both rejected by the British and American governments, which continued to place economic pressure on Libya through international sanctions.

Behind the scenes, a series of diplomatic engagements between the director of the Middle East and North Africa section in the Foreign and Commonwealth Office and the Libyan ambassador in Rome paved the way for a rapprochement. A formula for a trial was mapped out by Professor Robert Black of Edinburgh University and this was used by the foreign secretary, Robin Cook, to move forward on the issue of justice for the Lockerbie victims. The scheme was based on the concept of establishing a Scottish tribunal in a neutral country and on 5 April 1999, the two suspects were escorted to the Netherlands, where they were placed under arrest at a US base in Utrecht.

This breakthrough helped Britain to reopen diplomatic relations with Libya in July 1999. An accomplished Arabist, Richard Dalton, who had been *de facto* ambassador to the Palestinian Authority during the Middle East peace process, became the first British ambassador in Tripoli for 15 years. He handled the delicate negotiations while the specially convened Scottish court conducted a 36-week trial and eventually found al-Magrahi guilty of murder on 31 January 2000. The judges' verdict on Fhimah's case was not proven, which was a uniquely Scottish outcome that acknowledged his possible involvement in the crime, whilst recognising the technical weakness of the evidence.

As relations began to improve, the next priority for Britain and the United States was Gadhafi's weapons of mass destruction. Due to public sensitivities, responsibility was handed to MI6 to conduct clandestine work to unravel a network run by Abdul-Qadeer Khan, a Pakistani scientist, who supplied Libya with nuclear material.[25]

Ever since the humiliation of Suez, MI6 had done its utmost to keep as close as possible to American intelligence services. Although relations were occasionally strained, as when the American secretary of state, Dean Rusk, pleaded with Britain to be heavily engaged in Vietnam,[26] or during the Falklands War, when America remained neutral, the two countries shared a huge amount of secret material during and after the Cold War. In 2000, the relationship was still flourishing because the governments were aligned towards many global security challenges, such as the Balkan wars, the Middle East peace process, the fragile state of Russia and the inadequacy of the United Nations.[27]

The well-established protocols were used extensively after the attacks in America that killed 2,977 people, including 67 British citizens, on 11 September 2001. British officers were allowed access to secret US computer systems as the United Kingdom became the leading partner in America's Global War on Terror. The *quid pro quo* was to provide America with intelligence acquired by GCHQ and to assist US operations, including the highly controversial extraordinary renditions. Dozens of Al Qa'eda prisoners captured in Afghanistan were transported to a British Indian Ocean Territory, Diego Garcia, where they were "processed" before their onward journey to the US detention camp at Guantanamo Bay in Cuba.

In the aftermath of the 9/11 attacks, Colonel Gadhafi expressed sympathy for the victims and called for Libyan involvement in the war on terror against militant Islamism. His head of intelligence, Musa Kusa, had been the first to unravel the Al Qa'eda network and five months before their 1998 attack on the US embassy in Nairobi, he had alerted Interpol by issuing an arrest warrant for Usama bin Laden. He had also urged Gadhafi to reconcile his relations with the Arab League and this led to an invitation to the summit at the Red Sea resort of Sharm el-Sheikh in March 2003, shortly before the invasion of Iraq.

The Brotherly Leader was now serious about restoring friendly relations with the West. He sent his son, Saif al-Islam, to London as emissary to negotiate on his behalf to decommission Libya's chemical and nuclear weapons and subsequently renounce its possession of weapons of mass destruction. Gadhafi also agreed to donate $1 billion towards the compensation fund for the families affected by Lockerbie and this resulted in the United Nations lifting sanctions on Libya on 12 September 2003.

An imperturbable Scot, Anthony Layden, had taken over as British ambassador in 2002 and witnessed significant developments during his time in Tripoli. Gadhafi allowed key elements of his nuclear programme, including centrifuge parts and missile guidance systems, to be flown out of the country and in February 2004, he signed the Chemical Weapons Convention. Sealing this reconciliation, the British prime minister visited in March and claimed: "Libya's voluntary and open implementation of that decision [to dismantle WMD] gives us real hope that we can build a new relationship with it, one for the modern world."[28]

Separately, MI6's counter-terrorism unit in London controlled the flow of intelligence and negotiated a rendition partnership with Libya and the United States. There was a price to pay for this, which would come back to haunt the British government. Musa Kusa asked whether the US-UK would deliver a Libyan dissident named Abdelhakim Bel Haj, who was known to have fought with the Mujahidin against the Soviet Union in Afghanistan. Tracked by the CIA after a tip-off from MI6, Bel Haj was arrested with his pregnant wife, Fatima, in Kuala Lumpur airport in 2004. They were then transferred to Bangkok and flown in the CIA's Boeing 737 rendition aircraft, N313P, to Tripoli where they claimed they were tortured in Abu Salim jail.[29]

The political co-operation achieved in the early part of the millennium paved the way for another bilateral security framework that was signed in 2005 (Deportation with Assurances). British anti-terrorist police also visited Tripoli with a view to solving the murder of Yvonne Fletcher. However, it was difficult to avoid an atmosphere of suspicion in the joint enquiry between the Metropolitan Police investigating officers and the Libyan officials.

Economic benefits followed the security and intelligence co-operation. Before handing over as ambassador to Sir Vincent Fean, Anthony Layden expedited a breakthrough for Shell, which allowed them to return to Libya after 20 years. Further progress was made when Washington permitted American commercial and academic activity to resume and opened an official liaison office in Tripoli.

When the European Union ended their sanctions, the number of British companies re-entering Libya increased dramatically and the Libyan British Business Council was formed to nurture trade relationships. Washington cautiously followed London's lead and in June 2006, the US government formally rescinded Libya's designation as a state sponsor of terrorism. A year later, Gadhafi's international reintegration progressed when the United Nations General Assembly elected Libya onto the Security Council for the first time in four decades.

In 2007, President Bush nominated Gene Cretz as the first US ambassador to Libya since 1972, but the Senate hesitated at the decision and so two retired diplomats were sent as *chargés d'affaires* to Tripoli. The reports written after each of their six-month assignments convinced the US government to reinstate the post, but the patient Cretz had to wait until 27 December 2008 to be sworn in as ambassador.

By then, Britain was benefitting from the commercial opportunities flowing from Gadhafi's new approval. Vincent Fean had to host a trade mission almost every month and agreed UK visas for hundreds of Libyan post-graduate students. Another important development saw the opening of Libya's World Heritage sites for international tourism. These tempted many of the British children who had grown up in Cyrenaica to visit their old haunts. Ted Jones, who returned in 2008 with others who helped build the bridge at Wadi el Kouf, described his trip as the "highlight of his life".[30]

Gadhafi's trusted son Saif, who was perceived by British diplomats as "making efforts" to end human rights abuses, was the driving force for greater interaction with the West. Heading the grandly named Green Mountain Conservation and Development Authority, he developed a plan for Cyrenaica that included creating a national park around the ancient ruins with three hotels designed by a British architect. However, there was a huge outcry from the hardliners when he suggested ending the ban on alcohol and as a result the proposal was shelved.[31]

Many accounts of this era emphasise the importance of Western influence in the humanitarian, social and political domains in Libya.[32] It was certainly the case that Anthony Layden worked hard in areas such as international assistance to the hundreds of children who were victims of the HIV scandal caused by contaminated needles. The subsequent release of the Bulgarian nurses who had been tortured and sentenced for murder was a moment of personal satisfaction for those involved in securing their liberty.

Perhaps the most welcome project was the reform of prisons. Two past governors of British jails were sponsored by the International Centre for Prison Studies to visit Libya and through a "well-judged and nuanced approach", won the confidence of the prison authorities. They were allowed access to all the prisons in the country, including the infamous Abu Salim jail. Their recommendations were acted on, and significant improvements were made that led the ambassador to observe this was "the best project I have been privileged to witness".[33]

However, the key point is that the new relationship with Libya was based, as it was during the time of King Idris, primarily on defence and security interests. British Special Forces were invited to train Libyan Special Forces. The *Mukhabarat el-Jamahiriya* shared human intelligence (HUMINT) gathered from interrogations with MI6.[34] The two countries saw eye to eye in their mutual opposition to Al-Qaeda and Libya agreed to Britain's nuclear weapons demands. These were the connections that opened the door for multi-million-pound commercial contracts and social improvements that made life better for the Libyan people.

Anglo-Libyan relations improved so much that families of veterans who had fought in the Western Desert travelled to pay homage at the beautifully maintained Commonwealth War Cemeteries. His Royal Highness, Prince Edward, Duke of Kent, had led the way in November 2004 and was flown to El Adem by the Royal

Air Force, the first time they had landed at the former British air base in many decades.

The widow of Patrick McCraith, the first yeomanry commander in the Long Range Desert Group, also journeyed along the Libyan coast with nine companions and managed to see some of the ancient sites as well as the deeply emotional memorials, such as the cave hospital where so many soldiers were treated during the siege of Tobruk. She was treated with great consideration by the Libyan guides, but she sensed they trusted few in their government and knew little of the outside world.[35]

It was clear that a deliberate policy existed to disconnect parts of the country that might pose a serious threat to the regime. In the south, the disenfranchised Tuareg and the Tebu tribes that "owned the desert and the valleys"[36] were constantly at loggerheads with the sedentary administrators living in the flourishing oases. Other regional tensions existed, but the deepest division lay between Cyrenaica and Tripolitania; the everlasting rivalry between east and west that dated to antiquity. This enduring tension that pre-dated Gadhafi remained as taut as it was in the time of King Idris, or the Qaramanlis. It needed only a spark to ignite the population into a new revolution.

Weapons of Mass Destruction. Centrifuge parts, missile guidance systems and drums of uranium ready to be loaded onto the CIA's C-17 at Mitiga Airport. This cargo was flown to Oregon, where it was shown to the American media. (Picture courtesy of Anthony Layden)

HRH The Duke of Kent welcomed by Group Captain Sa'aqr of the Libyan Air Force at Gamal Abdel Nasser Airbase in 2004 (now Tobruk International Airport). The Group Captain was selected to be the first Chief of the Air Staff after the Revolution. (Picture courtesy of Anthony Layden)

Foreign minister Musa Kusa divided opinions among Libyans; however, he was welcomed to America by Secretary of State Hillary Clinton in September 2010 and thanked for his contribution to the fight against Al Qa'eda.

CHAPTER 16

Arab Winter

The Pan Islam movement, though it may still want the cohesion and organisation necessary for vigorous action, is a force with which Europe will have to reckon.

GEORGE ABBOTT, 1912

Visits to pay homage to the Desert Rats were not the only benefit of the rapprochement with Libya. Tony Blair's second meeting with Colonel Gadhafi in May 2007 sealed a £450,000,000 energy exploration agreement that marked BP's return to Libya after three decades.[1] This deal was highly controversial because the oil company's special adviser, Mark Allen, had been head of the MI6 unit involved in Bel Haj's rendition and was given the Cabinet Office's special approval to take up his commercial appointment.

Soon afterwards, the Scottish Criminal Cases Review Commission granted permission for al-Magrahi to make a new appeal on the grounds that there might have been a miscarriage of justice when he was jailed for the Lockerbie bombing. However, the 57-year-old prisoner dropped his application after he was diagnosed with terminal cancer and when his doctors declared that he only had three months to live, he was permitted to return home for compassionate reasons.

Arriving at Tripoli airport in one of Gadhafi's personal jets on 20 August 2009, he was fêted as a hero. However, much to the annoyance of the US administration[2] and the sense of injustice felt by many of the families of the victims, al-Magrahi survived much longer than expected and did not die until 20 May 2012.

After the convicted murderer left Scotland, the Labour government that smoothed up to Colonel Gadhafi was replaced by an historic coalition, led by 43-year-old David Cameron. Inheriting the consequences of the global financial crisis, the new prime minister faced economic meltdown as bad debt combined with rampant overspending to endanger the country's future prosperity. The team he assembled to deal with this colossal challenge included a generation of politicians and advisors who had never served in government and were heavily influenced by the profligacy of their predecessors.

They also took over an interminable war in Afghanistan that had lost the support of the population. In October 2006, "64 per cent of the [British] public believed that there was no clear strategy guiding the use of British troops in Afghanistan".[3] Together with the widely held view that the invasion of Iraq was illegal and the MPs' expenses scandal that emerged in 2009, public trust in parliament was at its lowest ebb when David Cameron and Nick Clegg agreed their priority of reducing the budget deficit in their programme for government.

* * *

Seven months later, Tarek el-Tayeb Mohammed Bouazizi set himself on fire in protest at the loss of his work as a street vendor in Tunisia. He probably didn't foresee the chain of events that would follow his immolation, but this act of desperation led to mass demonstrations that spread rapidly through the region, with protesters complaining about high unemployment and repressive systems of government. President Ben Ali of Tunisia was the first to be deposed and he was quickly followed by Egypt's president, Hosni Mubarak, who resigned on 11 February 2011.

The protests were not confined to presidential republics, as the kingdoms of Bahrain, Jordan and Morocco also witnessed political violence on their streets. The response of the international community during 2011 was inconsistent. Some authoritarian regimes, such as Syria, were propped up because they were at the forefront of the fight against Islamic terrorism, while others, such as Libya, were targeted for change.

The people of Benghazi claim that their demonstrations on 17 February following the arrest of the human rights lawyer Fathi Terbal began the uprising, but in fact there were earlier protests in Misuratah, which also claims to be the source of the insurrection. The reality is that the journey from sporadic civil protest to outright revolution was not straightforward and the outcome was far from certain in the early stages because the opposition was so fragmented.

After ruling Libya for more than 40 years, Muammar Gadhafi had made many enemies at home and abroad. Within the country, his opponents included tribes that lost out when he came to power and those who complained about his radical reforms, as well as business owners who suffered from his programme of nationalisation. Internationally, the large diaspora included exiled academics, who disagreed with his policies and brutality, as well as the descendants of Jewish families that he had expelled from Libya.

Despite ending sanctions when Gadhafi gave up his nuclear ambitions, America was less willing to forgive his previous support for international terrorism. In the years preceding the Arab Spring, the CIA had actively fomented revolution and trained many of the dissidents, such as Mohammed Bashir,[4] in the political skills of campaigning and public information. At the same time, the UK and US intelligence communities benefited enormously from Libyan information in their fight against Al Qa'eda.

However, Gadhafi was not totally isolated. Several sub-Saharan countries that benefited from his largesse continued to see him as an African champion and back his regime. South Africa's deep loyalty dated to when the Brotherly Leader was one of the few heads of state to support Nelson Mandela. China had sold some of their latest weapons to him, as had Russia, which provided the bulk of his military equipment, including the latest anti-tank missile system, code-named Chrysanthemum.[5]

Britain's position hardened when Gadhafi broadcast a terrifying speech on 22 February. Referring to the demonstrators as "cockroaches", he conjured images of the fateful genocide in Rwanda and confirmed his intentions when he announced that he would "cleanse Libya inch by inch... until the country is rid of the dirt and scum". His track record of brutal repression and well-known military capabilities made this threat highly credible and so his chilling forecast became the biggest test of the United Nations since 9/11.

Fortunately, at the 2005 World Summit, all member states had endorsed the Responsibility to Protect (R2P); an agreement based on a recommendation by the International Commission on Intervention and State Sovereignty.[6] This document provided a framework of measures to deal with potential mass atrocities and on 26 February 2011, the Security Council unanimously adopted Resolution 1970, citing R2P and demanding an end to the violence in Libya. They also imposed a new series of international sanctions that included seizing Gadhafi's assets abroad.

By then, the British armed forces were already involved in Libya. The first troops were sent when the Foreign and Commonwealth Office asked the Ministry of Defence to evacuate more than 600 British nationals from across the country. It took the personal authorisation of the prime minister for the Royal Air Force to launch what was known in military circles as a NEO (non-combatant evacuation operation), with the code-word *Deference* on 24 February.

The airlift of the majority of British citizens living in the coastal cities was a well-rehearsed operation run by the Permanent Joint Headquarters at Northwood. The problems lay further into the desert where the crews of the C-130 aircraft needed help and guidance to pick up the oil and gas workers. Embassy staff relied on the skills of former Special Forces soldiers, who now worked for private security firms, to organise the evacuation from isolated locations such as Jalu and Ghadames.

Not every country evacuated their civilians. North Korea, Malaysia and Ukraine all retained medics in hospitals and several African countries continued to provide economic and military support to the Libyan government throughout the crisis.

Emboldened by his friends, Gadhafi ordered a large force to destroy the nascent revolution. At the same time, the British government overstepped the mark, when a team of MI6 officials and SAS soldiers landed in a helicopter near to Benghazi on 3 March and were promptly arrested by local militia. The embarrassed foreign secretary, William Hague, had to apologise in parliament and explain what had happened, lifting the veil from Britain's intelligence agency and Special Forces.[7] The botched plan had serious ramifications for intelligence gathering because MI6's movements in Libya were constrained thereafter.

On 17 March, the Security Council adopted its second resolution (1973) demanding an immediate ceasefire, including an end to ongoing attacks against civilians, which might constitute "crimes against humanity". The UN froze the assets of seven individuals and five entities, including the Central Bank of Libya and the National Oil Corporation. Condemning the flow of mercenaries arriving from the Sahel, it established a "no-fly zone", authorising member states to take "all necessary measures" to protect civilians under threat of attack, while excluding a foreign occupation force of any form on any part of Libyan territory.

This made it difficult for anyone using air-launched missiles because they are most effective when guided to their targets by soldiers on the ground. Nevertheless, David Cameron and the French president, Nicolas Sarkozy, were keen to protect the threatened civilians, but needed help from US forces to neutralise Gadhafi's anti-aircraft systems. The American president, Barack Obama, was reluctant to commit to this enterprise. In *A Promised Land*, he describes his irritation that "Sarkozy and Cameron had jammed me on the issue" and his scorn at the "Arab League's hypocrisy".[8]

At a national security meeting on 15 March in Washington, the secretary of defense, Robert Gates, said, "Can I just finish the two wars I am in before you go looking for a third?"[9] However, secretary of state Hillary Clinton, who was attending the G8 meeting in Paris, and Susan Rice at the United Nations were more hawkish in their advice to the president.

According to David Cameron, "the world's great superpower was dithering while Benghazi was about to burn".[10] However, two days after the Security Council passed its new resolution, the president authorised the use of Tomahawk cruise missiles to launch the international military response. By then, the British prime minister had already allowed HMS *Triumph* to fire its cruise missiles, but the most important strike was by French Mirage and Rafale aircraft, which destroyed a large convoy of tanks approaching Benghazi from the south.

It was a seminal moment that turned a civil protest movement into an internationally backed insurrection. Several revolutionary leaders admitted that "the revolution would probably have been crushed at that time without this foreign intervention".[11] It was also a ringing endorsement for the government's unanimous agreement and parliament's overwhelming approval to continue military action to prevent a humanitarian atrocity (by 557 votes to 13).

Unfortunately, this early success led to overconfidence in the Western capitals. Government officials underestimated the resilience of the forces controlled by Gadhafi's sons and overestimated the military capabilities of the opposition. The

French foreign minister Alain Juppé claimed: "the destruction of [Gadhafi's] military capacity is a matter of days or weeks, certainly not months".[12]

This did not reflect the reality on the ground. Ever since army officers from Misuratah had tried to overthrow Gadhafi in the 1990s, he had neutered any potential source of internal threat and concentrated power in the Special Forces led by members of his family. He still had a strong power base and paid handsomely for the loyalty of his army, so the outcome depended completely on external support.

Gadhafi also made a critical decision to reject the advice of Musa Kusa, whose guidance had been so vital for his recent diplomatic successes. Instead, he looked to his brother-in-law, Abdullah Sanussi, a hard-liner who had no qualms about conducting a brutal repression. In turn, Musa Kusa left the country on 28 March and travelled to London where he resigned his post as minister of foreign affairs.

One of the key developments that emboldened the international community was the appearance of a credible alternative government. The Interim Transitional National Council, or NTC as it became known, included renowned academics and former government officials, who had gone into exile after disagreeing with Gadhafi. They were joined by young activists who helped draft a vision of democratic Libya that was published on 29 March.[13]

The head of the council was Mahmoud Jibril who had been trained in America and spent many years out of Libya, so he did not have the full support of the revolutionary leaders in Benghazi. However, his two-page vision that espoused the principles of political democracy and made a commitment to build a "state which will join the international community in rejecting and denouncing racism, discrimination and terrorism while strongly supporting peace, democracy and freedom" appealed to Western allies, who promoted the NTC as the government-in-waiting and eventually gave it Libya's seat at the United Nations.

* * *

A week after the first attack, NATO took over command of the operation from the United States of America, even though only eight members of the Alliance agreed to participate in the air strikes and Germany's leader, Angela Merkel, was highly sceptical. However, an effective diplomatic dialogue helped to widen participation to 33 countries, including many nations from the Arab League and African Union. The US withdrawal was understandable given the fact that they were coincidentally planning Operation *Neptune's Spear*, the raid on Abbottabad that led to the death of Usama bin Laden.

By now, British military involvement included a Type 42 destroyer, HMS *Liverpool*, as well as the Tornado and Typhoon aircraft flying precision attack missions from Gioia del Colle air base in Italy and surveillance aircraft from RAF Akrotiri in

Cyprus. However, information from the ground was sketchy and so it was decided to make another attempt to insert Special Forces into Libya.

This time, they drove for 14 hours from Egypt along the well-worn coastal road that Richard O'Connor had used 70 years before. On 9 April 2011, a British team of seven men, headed by a colonel who had served in the Special Air Service and the Royal Green Jackets, began their work in Benghazi. They quickly realised the scale of the task and called for reinforcements to help the rebel leaders. This second United Kingdom Mentoring Team arrived on 22 April and was headed by a Royal Marine. They increased the number of British troops on the ground to 18 and extended the mission from liaison and intelligence work to active participation.

Until this deployment, the operation could be described legitimately as a humanitarian intervention. However, the regime had not collapsed under economic pressure and in April, Gadhafi demonstrated that he would not concede victory when his sons recaptured Marsa Brega in the east and Zawiyah in the west. Reports of atrocities by his "mercenaries" hardened the resolve of the international community. As a result, the mission controversially morphed into "regime change" on the grounds that UN Resolution 1973 could not be fulfilled while Gadhafi remained in power.

The British government never described its policy as regime change because this is illegal in international law. However, David Cameron suggests that by May "the war had sunk into stalemate and needed a renewed focus".[14] During this impasse, several organisations, such as Amnesty International, unhelpfully raised the spectre of a humanitarian disaster. It was certainly true that the flow of migrants across the Mediterranean increased that month, with dozens of refugees drowning after their overloaded craft sank *en route* to Italy.

Taking the initiative, the prime minister used economic levers to support the rebels in Benghazi, but this still left a military problem caused by a shortage of available capabilities. The chief of defence staff, Sir David Richards, had never been totally supportive of the Libya operation for two reasons. In his previous role as head of the Army, he had promoted the operation in Afghanistan and ensured it remained the main effort in the Ministry of Defence (MoD) throughout the Libyan campaign. In this respect, he held the same attitude as General Robertson, chief of the Imperial General Staff in 1916, who relegated the Sanussi campaign to "side-show" status.

The second reason for the shortage of weapons was the reduction caused by the 2010 Strategic Defence and Security Review. The deep antagonism between the chiefs and the prime minister was epitomised by the sale of the iconic Harrier jump jets that left British carriers without any aircraft. David Cameron's creative solution was to use Apache helicopters. These aircraft had never been designed to operate at sea, but they had flown from amphibious landing ships at events such as the 2005 International Fleet Review.

The MoD reluctantly agreed to send four to the Mediterranean and on 26 May, the prime minister announced the decision to deploy them onboard HMS *Ocean*.[15]

These highly capable helicopters with a range of nearly 300 miles and a top speed of 205 miles per hour made a huge difference. Their laser-guided Hellfire missiles became a key battle-winning capability for the rebels. Their use was applauded by some in the media[16] although critics again accused the government of "mission creep".

Detractors were divided into two broad camps; those who were against all war and those who were against this war. The Stop the War Coalition that protested in London comprised many CND activists and people who had objected whenever the British military had been used since the Cold War. However, these anti-war appeasers lost credibility because they were never able to provide a credible alternative to the challenge of preventing genocide.

The second group was more insidious. In June, the head of the Royal Navy said: "The British military intervention in Libya is unsustainable" and that "the campaign would have been more effective without the Government's defence cuts".[17] Journalists were provided with MoD briefings that undermined the prime minister's authority. As Ramadan approached, Con Coughlin wrote:

> The advice Mr Cameron received from both his military chiefs and senior officials was to stay clear. Again and again, he was warned that never in the 100-year history of air power had a campaign been won by bombing alone. But Mr Cameron imagined he could replicate Tony Blair's achievements in taking on and defeating rogue dictators. So he ignored the advice—and is now discovering the hard way that being a wartime leader can be a very lonely business.[18]

NATO's secretary general, Anders Fogh Rasmussen, was also having difficulty. At the beginning of June, the tally of strike sorties totalled 3,584, but their effect was less than predicted. Political and military credibility was at stake and so, unsurprisingly, Rasmussen announced an extension of 90 days of military operations while the United Kingdom deployed the enhanced 2,000lb Paveway III to escalate their air strikes against the regime's bunkers.

The media continued to highlight the divisions and tensions in the plans. They accused the French of breaching UN resolutions by supplying arms to the rebels and they raised concerns about the fractured opposition after the murder of the charismatic general Abdul Fatteh Younes al-Obeidi in Benghazi. However, they missed the key point, which was that up to this time, Russia and China had continued to support Gadhafi. In June, they shifted their position and this meant that the dictator was increasingly isolated and his regime could not recover.

In July, more British troops deployed to Libya, including a joint MoD and Department for International Development team that assessed the challenges of reconstruction. The colonel in charge described the front line as fluid with "large tracts of disputed land frequently changing hands and half-hearted battles that quickly lost intensity because Libyans did not really wish to fight each other". He suggested that the post-war division of the country would be unlike Iraq and Afghanistan because the families of the martyrs, who had given their lives to the revolution, would have the loudest voices. Finally, he reaffirmed that the Libyan people remained highly suspicious of international involvement because they knew they were sitting on 187 billion dollars of assets with some of the largest oil and gas reserves in the world.

On 26 July, the chairman of the United States Joint Chiefs of Staff, Admiral Mike Mullen, acknowledged that the military mission in Libya had again stalled. Gadhafi held the eastern revolutionaries from strong defensive positions around the Brega oil terminal and he contained the rebels in the port of Misuratah with mercenaries from Chad. These soldiers of fortune lived in Tawergha, a new town built by Gadhafi, 20 miles along the coast. Tripoli remained his centre of gravity with vital supply routes open to Tunisia. The committed support for the regime in the capital was estimated as 70 per cent but shrinking rapidly as the extensive secret police network loosened its grip on the oppressed population.

The breakthrough arrived in the middle of August. It was the rebel forces from Jebel Nafusa, known as the Zintan Brigade, which made the difference. They secured the key terrain overlooking Tripoli and then stormed the last working oil refinery at Zawiyah before tightening the noose around Tripoli by approaching from the south and west. The head of the Zintan Military Council was Usama Juwayli, who was assisted by British Special Forces throughout the advance on Tripoli. He was extremely grateful to his two British advisors, who also marked targets for the NATO bombers when they attacked Gadhafi's stubborn defenders.

Their deployment had been authorised by the prime minister after he formed a contact group with France, Qatar and the United Arab Emirates, which also deployed their Special Forces. These "Four Amigos" steered the campaign from a secret cell in Paris, providing training and equipment as well as mentors, who guided the militias through the final phase of the war.[19]

By the end of August, most of Tripoli was in the hands of the rebels and the NTC began arriving in the capital city amid the chaos. The focus of the main fighting now shifted to the heart of Gadhafi's tribal support area around Sirte. Many people believed the dictator had escaped through the Fezzan in the south-west, while his son remained in Bani Walid marshalling defences. A number of Tuareg soldiers who managed to cross the frontier reported confusion everywhere as many officials in the regime fled to neighbouring Niger.

An important moment for British influence occurred when Tripoli fell on 28 August. The British special representative to the National Transitional Council, Sir John Jenkins, always believed the key to military victory was not the eastern front at Ajdebaya but the western axis of Misuratah, the Jebel Nafusa and the internal resistance in Tripoli.[20] Leaving a small team behind in Benghazi, he took his key personnel, flew to Misuratah in the dark and drove at dawn through a series of anxious checkpoints into a sleepy capital to establish a new office in the Radisson hotel.

Conditions were bad and people were regularly ill. Jenkins was evacuated with bronchial emphysema just as the British prime minister and French president paid a joint visit on 15 September. The two leaders were welcomed wholeheartedly in Tripoli and Benghazi by ordinary citizens, who recognised the part they had played in freeing Libya from a brutal regime and continually chanted *Libya Hurrah!*

The National Transitional Council attempted valiantly to restore order and establish a democratic process with all the associated architecture. They wished to change Libya for the better and there were no doubts about their aspirations, but it became clear very quickly that the baseline they inherited was rock-bottom. They needed help, but they did not know how to frame their requests to the international community and there were many distractions to divert them from the hard work of post-conflict reconstruction.

The primary diversion was the continued presence of Gadhafi in the country. His final stronghold was in his home town of Sirte, where he moved from hideout to hideout in an ever-shrinking pocket held by a dwindling group of loyalist fighters. He swung from rage to despair over his loss of power and finally he made his fatal dash for freedom on 20 October. It was an ignominious ending, which he could have avoided by handing over power six months earlier. After his body was left on public display in Misuratah for four days, he was buried secretly with his son Mutassim and Abu-Bakr Younis Jabr, an original member of the RCC and former head of the army, who was with Gadhafi when he was killed in Sirte.

Before the NATO mission ended on 31 October, Britain deployed more military teams into Libya. These groups included: a Special Forces section that hunted the indicted members of Gadhafi's entourage; a joint Royal Air Force and Army group searching for 25,000 Man Portable Air Defence Systems (MANPADS) that Gadhafi had bought from the Eastern Bloc; intelligence teams in Benghazi and Tripoli that reported on the rival militias and potential Islamic terrorists; and advisors to the new ambassador Dominic Asquith, whose father had been the Libyan prime minister's *chef de cabinet* at independence.

* * *

Responsibility for reconstruction fell to the United Nations. However, their Support Mission in Libya (UNSMIL) focused on political issues and neglected the immediate security challenge facing the country; what to do with the *Thuwaar*, the young "guardians of the revolution", who felt unappreciated after the NTC formed the new government in Tripoli. The UN staff also made totally unrealistic demands on the new government, which needed a helping hand, not a nagging lecture. Their only telling contribution in the security sector in 2011 was to facilitate the removal of the remaining nuclear material from Sebha and the chemical weapons stored in desert bunkers at Wadden.

The European Union also failed in their main responsibility, which was border security. In the immediate aftermath of the fighting, there was a tremendous opportunity to deal with the flow of migrants entering Libya through the porous Saharan frontier. However, this required a dynamic mobile force equipped with modern communications systems and a joined-up process for dealing with the diverse people, depending on whether they were fleeing persecution or seeking economic opportunities. Brussels, for all their bragging about leading the way, made no meaningful contribution to this well-financed, vital programme.

Of course, international organisations are only as good as their individual members allow them to be. In this respect, the leading lights of the multinational coalition that supported the revolution must also take some responsibility for the failure to prevent Libya falling back into the abyss and becoming a "crucible for terror".

However, the chief blame lies with the NTC. Their message in November and December was that they could manage without outside interference. They rejected Qatari, British, French and Canadian offers of help and when the head of United States African Command, on 11 December, showed their leaders evidence that Mokhtar Bel Mokhtar, leader of Al Qa'eda in the Islamic Maghreb (AQIM), was in Tripoli buying weapons, including surface to air missiles, and shipping them to his bases in Mali, they refused to take action, or allow the Americans to deal with the threat.

One of the key documents that any country has to sign if it wishes to integrate with the international community is a memorandum of understanding, or exchange of letters, that confirms the legal status of people working in embassies. On 5 November 2011, David Cameron telephoned the new prime minister, Abdurrahim el Keib, and after congratulating him on his appointment, asked him to sign the document to allow the United Kingdom to continue to provide support to Libya.[21] Although he received reassurances that this would be "taken care of", this letter and those with Libya's other close friends were never signed and this blocked further help in dealing with issues such as disarmament and the reform of the security sector.

There were so many positive advantages for the country at this time. The population of 6.5 million was about the same as the metropolitan area of Nairobi and less than half that of Cairo. There was no sectarian divide as in Iraq, or Syria. There was plenty of land and vast reserves of oil and gas, making it one of the richest countries in Africa. The people were hard-working, polite and respectful. Families took care of their widely-spread dependents. The senior official in Ghadames, Dr. Kassim Almana, who had been tortured by Gadhafi's police in Abu Salim jail, was regularly in touch with his two brothers in government and his sister, who was married to the head of the Tobruk council.

When the United Nations released the frozen assets belonging to Libya in December, the new government reassured the international community that it could cope. Libya was categorised as a job well done and the world's leaders focused on other countries that were in a much worse state, including Egypt, Yemen, Syria and Iran, where the Green Path of Hope struggled to keep their dreams alive.

British advisers in Libya realised early in 2012 that there was a tremendous opportunity to seal a special relationship similar to that established by the great consuls of the 19th century and the admirable administrators in the period after World War II. The British ambassador formed a very strong relationship with the new government and identified exactly where to direct help and "what we might usefully do".

Unfortunately, the Foreign and Commonwealth Office had, in the words of David Cameron, "lost a sense of can-do"[22] and the chief of Defence Staff continued to minimise the support to the troops on the ground. In February, the British embassy staff drafted a credible strategy for Libya. However, when this document was received in Whitehall, it was turned into an incoherent and uncoordinated list of pet projects with the focus changing from conditions to process. The new paper made the same mistake as the United Nations, emphasising "advice" rather than "assistance". It also stripped out the vital aspects of counter-terrorism and capacity building at a time when AQIM and other violent extremist organisations were establishing a foothold in the country.[23]

Worse was to follow when instructions arrived from London to evacuate the British military team in Benghazi. There were two reasons why this was a fatal mistake. The first centred on the political rivalry between east and west. Ever since the NTC established their government in Tripoli, the people of Cyrenaica had felt aggrieved about being left behind. A movement to split the country emerged in January as the Cyrenaica black flag with white star and crescent, adopted in 1947, increasingly appeared at protest gatherings in Benghazi. This culminated in the appointment of Ahmed al-Sanussi as leader of the self-declared Cyrenaica Transitional Council on 6 March.

The British team in Benghazi had been tracking the rise of this organisation and mapping parallel security structures for six months. They had nurtured hard-earned confidence with Libyan leaders in the manner of Milo Talbot and Eric de Candole and discovered the truth behind many of the frequent outbreaks of violence by groups such as the Obaydah bin Jarrah and the 17 February Martyrs Brigade, which together formed Ansar al-Sharia later that year. A measure of their success was seen when they secured a helpful response after an Islamic group vandalised about 150 gravestones in the Commonwealth War Cemetery.[24]

This relationship was lost when the British team flew out of the country in April and no one from the international community filled the vacuum. It provided further evidence to people in Cyrenaica that the founders of the revolution were being ignored not only by the NTC, but also their former international partners. The eastern political leaders railed at the perceived insult and their diminished status. Extremist organisations capitalised and increased their violence while General

Khalifa Haftar, who had also been snubbed by the NTC over the chief of defence appointment, responded in kind with his Cyrenaica Military Command.

The second reason why the removal of the British military team in Benghazi was a fatal error was the increase of attacks on foreign diplomats. Up to this time, a French arms dealer who had been a friend of Ghadafi's regime was the only European killed in Libya after the revolution. However, soon after the British soldiers' departure from Benghazi, the attacks against foreigners increased in scale and importance with a bomb exploding close to the convoy taking the British head of the UN Mission, Ian Martin, to a Supreme Security Committee meeting in April.[25]

In separate incidents, another bomb exploded outside an empty American office and a rocket-propelled grenade was fired at the British ambassador when he visited Benghazi on 11 June.[26] Two close protection officers were wounded in this attack, which alerted the world to a new threat in Libya. It was therefore astonishing that America did not protect its new ambassador, Christopher Stevens, who was murdered on 11 September in Benghazi in a totally avoidable incident that brought memories of the events of June 1967 (see pages 190–192).

* * *

It was also surprising how Britain forgot its close historical ties to Libya. There are several million people in Britain whose relations fought to free Libya or worked in the country before 1969. The shared history goes back more than 200 years to when Nancy Dornbush wrote about the customs and manners of the Berbers in Tripoli. British surveyors, diplomats, archaeologists and journalists have made significant contributions to Libya's independence and freedom. More importantly, the people of Libya repeatedly said that they wished to renew the close trading relationship that existed before Gadhafi seized power.

Unfortunately, these strong roots were suffocated by the dire events that cast their shadow on public perceptions: the murder of PC Yvonne Fletcher; the bombing of Pan Am Flight 103; and Gadhafi's support for terrorists in Northern Ireland. The continued campaign by lawyers seeking financial profit[27] from these dreadful actions and the characterisation of Libya as a pariah state by the British media did nothing to encourage re-engagement on the scale required to lift the country out of its mess.

There were other "missteps" in 2012. The absence of MI6, due to their botched operation, reduced Britain's knowledge and understanding. The failure to apologise to Abdelhakim Bel Haj for his rendition in 2004 badly damaged Britain's reputation.[28] However, these paled into insignificance when compared to the pusillanimous response by the United Nations and Western governments after the murder of Ambassador Stevens.

All the good work which had culminated in the successful elections on 7 July, when over 62 per cent of the population exercised their democratic right to vote with 30 seats won by women, was undone when the Western capitals pulled their diplomatic missions out of the country. Only one month into its term of office, the General National Congress (GNC) was abandoned by its fair-weather friends and as a result, it made three catastrophic mistakes.

The first was to purge Gadhafi-era officials from the government. This not only reduced the number of competent administrators, but also added to the anti-democracy movement. The second mistake was to lose control of the allocation of oil revenues; the main source of income for the government. Finally, the GNC undermined the police and army by allowing local militias to exercise more power and earn more pay than the state's security forces.

The problem for countries where political violence becomes a successful way to change public policy is that the threshold for peace is low. In stable countries, where governance is well established, disagreements are settled in the debating chamber. However, in countries such as Libya, where there are "thousands of individual grievances" and state institutions that have been "deliberately weakened"[29] it becomes easy to reach for the gun to settle disputes. In the first National Survey after the war conducted by Oxford researchers at the end of 2011, 16 per cent of those asked said they were ready to use violence for political ends. This represented 630,000 potential fighters, which when viewed against the 280,000 who took up arms against Gadhafi, was a significant increase.[30]

The British government was alerted to the risks several times by their ambassador in 2012. There were also warnings about what needed to be done "to prevent a further conflict and to ensure that Libya does not become another Afghanistan, facing a decade of internal security conflict."[31] At the end of 2012, the government's annual report to parliament described a mixed picture that had "changed significantly over the last year."[32]

The political, economic and security situation continued to deteriorate in 2013,[33] as Libya descended into what President Obama claimed was a "mess" and newspaper editors described as "anarchy". Political assassinations, oil blockades, a civil war between east and west and tribal disputes added to the sense of chaos. With a failing United Nations mission and the absence of Western diplomats, other menaces emerged, including Islamic State, which established control in places that had been neglected by the NTC and GNC, such as Sirte and Derna. More relevant to Britain and Europe, the migrant crisis grew as tens of thousands of sub-Saharan Africans attempted to cross the Mediterranean in flimsy boats.

By the anniversary of the successful elections, the Libyan narrative was very different. Instead of an exemplary model of humanitarian intervention, it had become a fragile state, and this was to have a dire effect in the following month when parliament voted on a humanitarian motion to intervene in Syria. After compelling evidence appeared in the media, which showed that President Assad had used poison gas on his own people, Britain stood ready to act. The American president had already established a red line for such an occasion, based on the Responsibility to Protect, and was planning to strike against carefully selected military targets, in order to deter Assad from continuing to flout international law.

It all came down to a vote in the House of Commons on 29 August 2013. The arguments not to intervene were rehearsed by the usual suspects of appeasers and anti-war activists. They were bolstered by an odd alliance of MPs: those who felt parliament had been deceived over the invasion of Iraq and those who believed Islamic State was a worse threat to the world than President Assad's regime.

In this finely balanced debate, it might have been very helpful for those who argued from a moral standpoint, if they could point to Libya and say, "look how we made it better". Instead of a good news story, the chaotic situation in Libya allowed those who had voiced their doubts about British involvement in 2011 to argue persuasively that it would have been better to do nothing.

The result was close (272–285), but the defeat for the government had serious ramifications. First, President Obama changed his mind and did not act against Assad.[34] Second, it led to Britain losing its position as one of the leading actors on the world stage. Third, it meant that the government became even more focused on the domestic agenda. And finally, it made it very difficult to envisage a future situation where Britain would intervene in another R2P scenario.

* * *

Without meaningful help from its leading partner in the international community, the situation in Libya worsened. A disputed election in 2014 split the country between two rival governments, the Islamic-leaning GNC in Tripoli and the House of Representatives in Tobruk, where the international airport at El Adem re-opened in 2013.

What was needed was an experienced and diplomatic leader, who could bring the sides together. The 65-year-old Musa Kusa, who had not been involved in the revolution, might have fitted this specification, although he would have been totally unacceptable to some who had suffered under his authority and anyway, the government had decreed that those who were previously involved in Gadhafi's regime were banned from holding public office.

The interminable struggle for political control allowed Islamic State to tighten its grip in Sirte and Derna. Libya became a haven for terrorists on the Mediterranean shore and in the end, President Obama had to take action to defeat this menace, along with European Special Forces. This opened the door for the head of the UN-backed Government of National Accord (GNA), Fayez Mustafa al-Sarraj, to arrive by boat in Tripoli on 30 March 2016.

British involvement had reduced significantly by then. A training programme which had begun very well in 2012 with English language courses at Jansur had ended ignominiously when five Libyan soldiers were jailed after they attacked and raped men and women in Cambridge in 2014.[35] After these shameful incidents, Britain's main contribution switched to the Royal Navy's participation in Operation *Sophia*, the European Union's naval force in the Mediterranean dealing with people-trafficking and the migrant crisis.[36]

A renewed effort was made to help in April, when the foreign secretary, Philip Hammond (who had been defence secretary during the 2011 revolution), visited al-Sarraj to discuss the possibility of deploying a European-led stabilisation force with 1,000 British troops.[37] There was no doubt about the pressing need to help the country, but the plan was ill-conceived because no British brigade had been trained for the specific challenges, they would face in Libya despite having had three years to prepare. In the end, the proposal was dropped due to the reluctance of the GNA to support the deployment of foreign troops in their country.

Since then, instability has continued with a bitter civil war fought between east and west. On one side is Field Marshal Haftar, who is supported by Egypt, the United Arab Emirates and the Russian private military company, Wagner. On the other side, Sarraj is backed by Turkey and the West. France has a foot in both camps. With a huge diplomatic effort, the United Nations created the Libyan Political Dialogue Forum and brought the two sides together on 19 January 2020, with Chancellor Angela Merkel hosting the Berlin International Conference on Libya.

The talks made little progress because the chief protagonists refused to be in the same room together. However, the peace process continued with virtual meetings during the Covid pandemic and at the beginning of 2021 a date was agreed for national elections on the 70th anniversary of independence. This focus on politics is understandable, but the fact that the draft constitution still needs to be approved in a national referendum is one of several challenges that cause government officials to question whether the United Nations can achieve its goal.[38]

In the meantime, Libya's reputation in Britain incurred further damage when a 22-year-old student blew himself up on 22 May 2017 after a concert at the Manchester Arena, killing 22 innocent civilians and injuring 800 others. The irony that the bomber had been rescued by the Royal Navy during the 2014 civil war and that his father had been supported by Britain when he was fighting against Gadhafi was not lost on those who investigated this crime.

The Manchester Arena attack demonstrates clearly that those who advocate a policy of disengagement are misguided if they believe that "doing nothing" will bring about global peace. There remains a huge amount at stake in the 16th largest country in the world, which is geographically closer to Britain than parts of Europe. The car bomb that killed three United Nations workers in Benghazi in August 2019[39] is evidence that foreigners will constantly be at risk, but with Britain's help, Libya could one day fulfil a leading role in North Africa and the Mediterranean. It is in no one's best interests if it is abandoned by the West or taken over by another ruthless dictator.

17 February Revolution. The weapon of choice of the *thuwaar* (revolutionary militias) was a pick-up truck with a mounting welded to the base that could support a heavy machine gun or rocket-propelled launcher, similar to the Chevrolet trucks adapted by the Long Range Desert Group in 1940. (Author)

Benina Airbase: copying David Stirling's raids during World War II, the revolutionaries sabotaged Colonel Gadhafi's Sukhoi aircraft at Benina Airbase. (Author)

Tobruk. Early in the revolution, the Tobruk council sided with the opponents of Colonel Gadhafi. The Mig-21s at Gamal Abdel Nasser Airbase played no part once NATO established air supremacy. (Author)

Misuratah suffered some of the worst of Gadhafi's atrocities during the Revolution. A Soviet T-55 tank can be seen to the right of the picture. (Author)

Tripoli Intelligence Headquarters after NATO's attack in 2011. It was here that investigative journalists found the papers incriminating the British Government's role in the CIA rendition of Abdelhakim Bel Haj and his pregnant wife from Kuala Lumpur. (Author)

Tripoli Intelligence Headquarters. Unfortunately, not all the NATO bombs detonated successfully. Remnants of War found in 2012 included a US Tomahawk missile, a French 2,000 lb bomb and this British Mark 20 that was discovered close to the intelligence building. The bomb was defused because it was located too close to a residential area to be blown up. (Author)

The British Ambassador's Residence in Tripoli (owned by Queen Fatima) before the Revolution. (Picture courtesy of Anthony Layden)

The British Ambassador's Residence after it was burned during the Revolution. (Author)

Zawiyah. The huge refinery on the coast, which was fed from the numerous oil fields in the Fezzan, was captured in August 2011 by the Zintan Brigade, commanded by the first Defence Minister, Usama Juwayli. The author was hosted at this post-war celebration at Zawiyah by Salahedin Ali, a 31 year-old Libyan army officer who returned from a university degree course in Malaysia to fight with the rebels in the Western Military Council. (Author)

In response to the burning of the Koran by American soldiers in Afghanistan, an Islamic militia entered the Benghazi War Cemetery in February 2012 and attacked dozens of Commonwealth graves with sledgehammers. Interestingly the large section of Muslim graves was not disturbed. (Author)

Storm Shadow. The UK Ministry of Defence claimed that no Storm Shadow cruise missiles failed to detonate until one was discovered by the Bedouin in the desert. The outer parts were retrieved and flown to England in 2012, while the explosive was blown up where it was found. (Author)

Afterword

By Jason Pack

The bond between two nations is a product of their shared enemies, joint participation in multi-national organisations, mutual investments, and trading relationship. But it is also about so much more. First and foremost, nations are bound together by person-to-person ties and their linked historical narratives. Those personal relationships and narratives are strongest when they have involved fighting and dying for each other.

Libya and the United Kingdom are not that similar when it comes to language, creed, ancestry, form of government, or level of economic development. In fact, they are highly dissimilar. Yet, they are more closely intertwined than is traditionally understood. Libyans and Britons have fought and died over the last century on the same side of many armed conflicts. In fact, Britons have been involved on the winning side of *all* of Libya's major armed conflicts over the last century and a half. In those experiences, many Britons and Libyans have forged deep personal ties. These Anglo-Libyan links cannot be quantified in barrels of crude lifted, in the size of BP's offshore concessions, in the number of British-educated and British-domiciled Libyans, or in the extent of Libyan Letters of Credit that flow through London.

Simply put, a shared imaginary exists between certain Britons and certain Libyans—especially the tens of thousands of British families whose relations' formative wartime experiences in Libya still carry sentimental meaning for them and the plethora of Libyans who have worked closely with British colleagues. As such, the Anglo-Libyan relationship has a human breadth and depth that the Russo-Libyan, Sino-Libyan, and American-Libyan relationships lack.

I appreciate this more than most people. I was the Executive Director of the U.S.-Libya Business Association and am currently a board member of the American Chamber of Commerce in Tripoli. I deeply value the interpersonal connections between Americans and Libyans. Yet, the UK-based Society for Libyan Studies and the Libyan British Business Council operate on a different plane than their American counterparts. It is not because of their larger membership or more frequent events; it is because of the intangibles that lie behind the Anglo-Libyan relationship. Many British archaeologists, businesspeople, diplomats, soldiers, and amateur historians involved in the Libya field have had deep personal or familial connections with the country, frequently during World War II and its aftermath.

I know the handful of native-born Americans whose lives are fundamentally intertwined with Libya—we are professionals in diplomacy, archaeology, oil, business, and journalism. We are a small and committed bunch, respected by our Libyan counterparts. Yet in the UK, tens of thousands of Brits have close personal and familial stories connecting them to Libya. When British-educated Libyans or Anglo-Libyan dual citizens are added to the picture, we are talking about an elite of tens of thousands with the requisite human capital to meaningfully shape Libya's future trajectory.

Today, when I want to meet my closest Libyan colleagues in the most convivial setting, I travel to London, Nottingham, or Leicester. When I need to employ talent to analyse the Libyan economy, I hire it from British universities. I see the Anglo-Libyan relationship as a source of good in the world. Its unique dynamics cannot be substituted with another bilateral relationship. They are based on specific historical experiences that come from blood, sweat, patience, laughter, and more than a few Victoria Crosses.

Personally, I aspire to foster the cultural, economic, and diplomatic aspects of this special Anglo-Libyan relationship. A fourth-generation New Yorker, I am in the process of becoming a British citizen to add to these ties. I have put my money where my mouth is and have become an actor in this story rather than just an impartial academic commentator sitting on the side lines.

Rupert Wieloch is also a partisan of the Anglo-Libyan relationship. His *Liberating Libya* illustrates this truth as his artful historical narrative uncovers hidden connections across the centuries, linking seemingly discrete episodes of Britons and Libyans whose lives were intertwined.

Human relationships are always a bit messy, however. As explained in the Prologue and detailed via the unadulterated quotations in the body of the manuscript, sometimes prejudices, pettiness, romanticism, and ignorance clouded Anglo-Libyan ties. But frequently, those were overcome, and a sense of duty and shared destiny was forged.

* * *

Probing the dense mysteries of the Anglo-Libyan relationship, Rupert Wieloch's work is an engaging romp through two millennia of Libyan history with extra emphasis placed on recent kinetic engagements. As such, *Liberating Libya* has brought to a new public a range of first-hand accounts from British diplomats, desert explorers, military personnel, and civilians. It gives the reader a flavour of the seminal events of Libyan history through distinctly British-hued glasses. Wieloch conveys key themes that have eluded earlier historians, especially the very existence of a unique "Anglo-Libyan relationship" rooted in the enduring geostrategic importance that Libya's territory has held for British policymakers and cemented through the sympathetic bonds that have united specific British diplomats and officers to their Libyan counterparts.

He shows that early in World War II and during the aftermath of the Arab Spring when British statesmen have unfortunately ignored Libya's geostrategic centrality, profound problems have arisen—causing dangerous externalities. Conversely, when they have invested resources in freeing Libya from hostile external forces and promoting coherent administrative structures, Libyans and Brits were able to build hope for the future and to reap prosperity together.

Britons have on multiple occasions been Libya's liberators (or have tried to be so) and many Libyans would like them to play that role again by increasing their presence in the country's healthcare, training, construction, oil field services, and electricity sectors. As shown in the Foreword, many opportunities have been missed over the past decade. A happy ending to this story will require making up for lost time with bold initiatives emanating from both Whitehall and the private sector.

Although it points to the future and contains policy prescriptions, *Liberating Libya* reads as old-school history: organised around a central narrative, attributing blame and praise where the author feels it is due (in truly Polybian fashion), highlighting forgotten anecdotes that strike the author as representative, and expressing unfiltered views about personalities, cultures, and causation. The book is a highly welcome addition to the tragically sparse literature about Libya. It highlights how many more stories need to be unearthed to convey the multifaceted importance of Libya—combining issues of human sacrifice, energy security, migration, climate change, jihadism, and globalisation.

Given its multifaceted importance—cultural, sentimental, political, economic, and military–Libya has left a profound imprint on those individuals, officers, firms, and nations who have interacted with it in a sustained way over the centuries. Wieloch's narrative puts forth a compelling case that Libya will always have an oversized importance on the global stage and that Britain's unique history with the country—several times playing the role of liberator and principal diplomatic partner—uniquely positions mid-21st-century Britain to eclipse Italy, France, and Turkey in forging bonds of friendship, cultural exchange, and mutual commercial interest with Libya.

If the Libyan populace was polled about what foreign nation they would choose to play the paramount role in mediating their peace conferences, boxing out destabilising external actors, fixing their pipelines, staffing their training colleges, repairing their electrical grid, and imbedding experts in their ministries—the top choices would almost certainly be Britain and America. But America is not a realistic contender as she is withdrawing from such international engagements and her post-Benghazi political discourse prevents her from occupying a paramount role in Libya's reconstruction.

* * *

Wieloch's message about the depths of the Anglo-Libyan connection couldn't come at a more propitious time. To modernize Dean Acheson's famous aphorism: Britain long ago lost its empire and is currently in the process of losing its mediating role between the US and EU. As such, her policymakers are struggling frantically to carve out an indispensable global role in the wake of Brexit. There are few remaining theatres outside the Commonwealth where the UK can punch above her weight as the dominant convening and cultural power. Libya is one such geostrategically and economically crucial arena.

As Christopher Donnelly articulated so clearly in his Foreword, Libya's geography has undergirded its destiny. It bestrides the African, Mediterranean, and Middle Eastern systems. Its sweet crude is the closest to Europe of any major exporting country, sub-Saharan migrants travel through it to get onto dinghies to reach EU territorial waters, jihadis based there are able to proliferate arms and fighters throughout Europe and the Middle East.

And yet, Libya could be a beacon of hope, stability, and prosperity. Libya has the natural resources, human capital, and geostrategic alliances to be a major success story. History suggests that Britons and Anglo-Libyans can play a pivotal role in improving the country's trajectory throughout the mid-21st century.

* * *

Libya as a country and as a concept has been meaningfully shaped and formed by its interactions with the United Kingdom. Many historians see the state of Libya as three disparate provinces united by their being the last Ottoman possessions in North Africa that were then cobbled together into an administrative unit by the Italians after their conquest. Rupert Wieloch's novel presentation of this history hints at a deeper truth. As he shows, Britons have worked together with Libyans over the last two centuries to help create and then defend, reconquer, and liberate an entity called Libya.

Did the British ever colonise Libya? Difficult to say. Either way, it was a part of Britain's informal empire as the term was used by Ronald Robinson and Jack Gallagher in their ground-breaking 1953 *Economic History Review* article, "The Imperialism of Free Trade". Furthermore, as Wm. Roger Louis demonstrated in "Libya: The Creation of a Client State", in Louis and Gifford (ed.) *Decolonization and African Independence: The Transfers of Power 1960–80* (London, 1988), Libya's decolonization was a struggle in which Britain and the Sanussiyya leveraged American assistance to best their rivals and shape the contours of the Libyan state.

The Italian conquest of Libya was "allowed" and facilitated by the British since the secret 1902 Anglo-Italian and Anglo-French concordats on the future of Ottoman North Africa insulated the territory from larger geopolitical rivalries and destined it as a buffer between the French and British Imperial spheres. As example, Britain was always an internal actor inside Italian colonial Libya. British correspondents wrote the articles through which the world found out about the Libyans' anti-Italian struggle, while British officials controlled the Egyptian border, either allowing or forbidding, resistance fighters, charity monies, and arms to flow into the country.

From 1882 until 1969, the personal aspect of the British role in Libya was mediated through the Anglo-Sanussi relationship. My historical work focuses on detailing the personal and sentimental logic of this relationship. I sketch its origins in "The Antecedents and Implications of the so-called Anglo-Sanussi War (1915–17)" in Fraser (ed.), *The First World War and its Aftermath: The Shaping of the Middle East*, (Ginkgo Library, 2015). I illustrate how it culminated in the structures of the Libyan State. In particular, the British Military Administration (1942–51) reinvented and reinforced the Ottoman-era distinctions among Cyrenaica, Fezzan, and Tripolitania—cementing their institutional and cultural separateness, as it was seen to foster British interests by giving added strength to the Sanussiyya and those tribal Cyrenaican and Fezzanese allies, who had close person-to-person ties with Britain.

When Libya became a monarchy, its protector and patron was initially the UK. As British power waned in the Middle East, America was never willing to fully step into the void. This was as clear when Qadhafi was "allowed" to come to power, as when he was overthrown. Even the Anglo-Libyan relationship has been weak—and Britons were not willing to fight and die defending Libya—it has never been replaced by an equally committed American-Libyan one.

Given this history, as well as Britain's ongoing clout and perception of neutrality inside Libya, the will to bold action to coordinate a unified international community response to the Wars of Post-Qadhafi Succession must be found in Westminster and Whitehall, or it will not be found anywhere.

* * *

Libya is a wealthy, sparsely populated country, with a civically minded populace. I am always amazed at how hard my Libyan colleagues work and how much they are committed to working for their communities. Unfortunately, militias take this positive impulse and sinisterly manipulate it—pitting one community against others. But in my experience, unlike in other Arab oil states, an elite cadre of largely British-educated Libyans is ready to choose civic engagement over making money.

Another striking Libyan trait is a profound aversion to killing their countrymen. Libya's decade of Wars of Post-Qadhafi Succession have caused fewer cumulative casualties than the bloodiest single month in either the Yemeni or Syrian civil wars. This is not only because of the absence of sectarian cleavages, but because of the inherent value Libyans place on their countrymen's lives. This comes from Libya's tribal social contract, which has yet to be fully subverted.

Libya is filled with economic opportunities as the Libyan people need a whole range of goods and services. At present these economic needs are manipulated by status quo stakeholders to enable corruption. These needs could be turned into great opportunities to release the productive capacity of the Libyan people and to connect Libya with the Western private sector.

To my mind, only one actor has the diplomatic clout, historical ties, perception of neutrality, and the technical skills to supervise the peace making and economic reform phase needed to end the Wars for Post-Qadhafi Succession. As Rupert Wieloch's *Liberating Libya* has aptly demonstrated, that actor is the United Kingdom.

Jason Pack is president of Libya-Analysis LLC, author of
Libya and the Global Enduring Disorder (Hurst, 2021),
and a recipient in 2020 of the UK Global Talent Visa.

Bibliography

Abbott, George. *The Holy War in Tripoli*. Edward Arnold, 1912.

Africanus, Leo. *The Fifth Book of the History and Description*. London Haklyut Society, 1896. (Published in 1550 by the Venetian Giovanni Ramusio, translated by John Pory in 1600).

Agar-Hamilton, J. A. I. and Turner, L. C. F. *The Sidi Rezeg Battles 1941*. Cape Town: Oxford University Press, 1957.

Alanbrooke, Field Marshal Lord (edited by Alex Danchev and Daniel Todman). *War Diaries 1939–1945*. Weidenfeld & Nicolson, 2001.

Al Magariaf, Mohamed. *Libia men al Shar'iya ad Dustouriya elal Shar'iya ath Thawriya*. Libya, 2008.

Anderson, Lisa. "The Tripoli Republic 1918–1922." In *Social and Economic Development of Libya* (pp. 43–65) edited by George Joffe and Keith McLachlan. Menas Press, 1982.

Anthon, Charles. *A Classical Dictionary*. Harper & Brothers, 1841.

Asad, Muhammed. The Road to Mecca. Simon and Schuster, 1954.

Badaglio, Pietro. *L'Italia Nella Seconda Guerra Mondiale*. Mondadori, 1946.

Baldinetti, Anna. *The Origins of the Libyan Nation: Colonial Legacy, Exile and the Emergence of a New Nation-State*. Routledge, 2013.

Barclay, Sir Thomas. *The Turco-Italian War and Its Problems*. Constable, 1912.

Barth, Heinrich. *Wanderungen durch das Punische und Kyrenäische Küstenland*. Berlin, 1849.

Beechey, F. W. and Beechey, H. W. *Proceedings of the Expedition to Explore the Northern Coast of Africa from Tripoly Eastwards 1821–1822*, John Murray, 1828. Retrieved from www.biodiversitylibrary.org/item/216106#page/7/mode/1up.

Bennett, Ernest. *With the Turks in Tripoli*. Methuen, 1912.

Blundy, D. and Lycett, A. *Qaddafi and The Libyan Revolution*. Little, Brown and Co., 1987.

Braddock, D. W. *The Campaign in Egypt and Libya 1940–42*. British Army Staff College, 1964,

Bromley, David and Janet. *Wellington's Men Remembered, Volume 2*. Praetorian Press, 2012.

Buckingham, William F. *Tobruk: The Great Siege 1941–42*. Tempus, 2008.

Byron, Lord George. "Don Juan". In *The Works of Lord Byron*. John Murray, 1838.

Cameron, David. *For The Record*. Collins, 2019.

Carver, M. *El Alamein*. Batsford, 1962.

Carver, M. *Tobruk*. Batsford, 1964.

Carver, M. *Dilemmas of the Desert War: a new look at the Libyan campaign 1940–42*. Batsford, 1985.

Christopherson, Stanley (edited by James Holland). *An Englishman at War*. Bantam, 2014.

Churchill, Randolph. *Winston S. Churchill, Volume II*. Heinemann, 1967.

Churchill, Winston. *The Gathering Storm*. Cassell, 1948.

Churchill, Winston. *The Grand Alliance*. Cassell, 1948.

Churchill, Winston. *The Hinge of Fate*. Cassell, 1951.

Churchill, Winston. *The River War (Volumes I and II)*. Longmans, 1899.

Ciano, G. (edited by Hugh Gibson). *The Ciano Diaries 1939–1943*. Doubleday & Co, 1945.

Clark, C. *The Sleepwalkers: How Europe Went to War in 1914*. Harper Collins, 2013.

Clay, Ewart. *The Path of the 50th: The Story of the 50th Northumbrian Division in the Second World War 1939–45.* Gale & Polden, 1950.

Connell, John. *Auchinleck: A Critical Biography.* Cassell, 1959.

Connell, John. *Wavell, Scholar and Soldier.* Collins, 1964.

Cricco, Massimiliano. "The United Kingdom and the Italo-Turkish War in British Documents". In L. Micheletta and A. Ungari (edited), *The Libyan War 1911–1912.* Cambridge Scholars Publishing, 2013.

Crisp, Robert. *Brazen Chariots.* Corgi Paperback, 1960.

Cumpston, JS *The Rats Remain: The Siege of Tobruk 1941,* Grayflower 1966

De Candole, Eric. *The Life and Times of King Idris of Libya.* Ben Ghalbon, 1990.

De Felice, Renzo (translated by Judith Roumani). *Jews In an Arab Land: Libya 1835–1970.* University of Texas Press, 1985. (First published Bologna, 1978).

De Grummond, N. T. *Encyclopedia of the History of Classical Archaeology.* Routledge, 1996.

Del Boca, Angelo. *Mohamed Fekini and the Fight to Free Libya.* Palgrave Macmillan, 2011.

Della Cella, Paolo. *Narrative of an Expedition from Tripoli in Barbary, to the Western Frontier with Egypt, in 1817.* Marotta and Van Spanduch, 1830.

De Pradt, Dominique-Georges, *Histoire de l'Ambassade dans le Grand Duché de Varsovie en 1812.* Paris, 1815.

Dickson, William. *The Life of Major General Murdoch Smith.* Blackwell, 1901.

Douglas, Keith. *Alamein to Zem Zem.* Faber and Faber 1992. (First published 1946).

Duvevrier, Henri. *The Fortresses and the Army of the Religious Orders of Sidi and Senoussi.* Paris, 1888.

Evans-Pritchard, E. E. "The Senusi of Cyrenaica". *Journal of the International African Institute* Volume 15, Number 2 (April 1945): 61–79.

Fergusson, Bernard. *The Black Watch and the King's Enemies.* Collins, 1950.

Field, Leslie. *Bendor: The Golden Duke of Westminster.* Weidenfield and Nicolson, 1983.

FitzSimmons, Peter. *Tobruk.* Australian Harper Collins, 2006.

Fortna, Benjamin C. *The Circassian: A Life of Esref Bey, Late Ottoman Insurgent and Special Agent.* Hurst, 2016.

Gawrych, G. *The Young Atatürk: From Ottoman Soldier to Statesman of Turkey.* Tauris, 2013.

Gibbon, Edward. *The Decline and Fall of the Roman Empire Volume III.* Frederick Warne & Co., Verbatim Reprint, 1880.

Glennon, John (editor). *Foreign Relations of the USA 1952–54, Volume XI Africa and South Asia.* US Government Printing Office, 1983.

Glubb, J. B. *The Great Arab Conquests.* Hodder and Stoughton, 1963.

Goddard, Farley Brewer. "Researches in the Cyrenaica". *American Journal of Philology* Volume 5, Number 1 (1884): 31–53.

Goldberg, Harvey. *Jewish Life in Muslim Libya.* University of Chicago Press, 1990.

Goodchild, R. G., et al. *Apollonia, The Port of Cyrene: Excavations by the University of Michigan 1965–67.* Tripoli, 1976.

Greenhalgh, Martin. *The Military and Colonial Destruction of the Roman Landscape of North Africa, 1830–1900.* Brill, 2014.

Grey, Viscount. *Twenty Five Years 1892–1916 (Volumes I and II).* Hodder and Stoughton, 1925.

Guthrie, William. *A New Geographical, Historical and Commercial Grammar.* London, 1774.

Gwatkins-Williams, R. S. *Prisoners of the Red Desert.* Thornton Butterworth, 1919.

Hadaway, Stuart. *Pyramids and Fleshpots: The Egyptian, Senussi and Eastern Mediterranean Campaigns 1914–16.* History Press, 2014.

Hamilton, James. *Wanderings in North Africa.* John Murray, 1856.

Harrison, Frank. *The Great Siege Reassessed.* Arms and Armour, 1996.

Hart, Peter. *To The Last Round: The South Notts Hussars: The Western Desert 1939–1942.* Leo Cooper, 1996.

Heckstall-Smith, Anthony. *Tobruk: The Story of a Siege.* Blond, 1959.

Hess, Andrew C. "The Ottoman Conquest of Egypt (1517) and the Beginning of the Sixteenth Century World War". *International Journal of Middle East Studies*, Volume 4, Number 1 (1973): 55–76.

Hildyard, Myles. *It Is Bliss Here: Letters From 1939–1945*. Bloomsbury, 2005.

Holmes, Richard. *Bir Hacheim: Desert Citadel*. Ballentine Books, 1971.

Horgan, John. "The Irishness of Francis McCullagh". In Kevin Rafter, *Irish Journalism Before Independence*, Manchester University Press, 2011, pp. 106–109.

Horrocks, Brian. *A Full Life*. Collins, 1960.

Huff, Elizabeth. "First Barbary War". In *Thomas Jefferson Encyclopedia 2011*. Retrieved from: www. monticello.org/site/research-and-collections/first-barbary-war.

Jefferson, David. *Tobruk: A Raid Too Far*. Robert Hale, 2013.

Johnson, Adrian (editor). *Wars In Peace: British Military Operations Since 1991*. RUSI, 2014.

Joly, Cyril. *Take These Men*. Constable, 1955.

Keegan, J. *A History of Warfare*. Hutchinson, 1993.

Kelly, Saul. "A Succession of Crises: SOE in the Middle East, 1940–1945". *Intelligence and National Security* Volume 20, Issue 1 (2005): 121–46.

Kennedy-Shaw, W. B. "Desert Navigation: Some Experiences of the Long Range Desert Group". *The Geographical Journal* Volume 102, Number 5/6 (November 1943): 253–8.

Kennedy-Shaw, W. B. *Long Range Desert Group*. Collins, 1945.

Kenny, Peter. *We Who Proudly Serve*. Xlibris, 2015.

Kilmeade, Brian and Yaeger, Don. *Thomas Jefferson and the Tripoli Pirates*. Sentinel, 2015.

Kingsberry, W. H. "The Cyrenaica Defence Force". *RUSI Journal*, Volume 88 Issue 551 (1943): 210–14.

Lacher, Wolfram. *Libya's Fragmentation: Structure and Process in Violent Conflict*. Bloomsbury, 2020.

Landsborough, Gordon. *Tobruk Commando*. Cassell, 1956.

Latimer, John. *Tobruk 1941: Rommel's Opening Move*. Osprey, 2001.

Leiner, Frederick. *The End of the Barbary Terror*. Oxford University Press (US), 2007.

Liddell Hart, B. H. *History of the Second World War*. Cassell & Co, 1970.

Liddell Hart, B. H. *The Tanks, Volume 2*. Cassell & Co, 1959.

Lindsay, T. M. *Sherwood Rangers*. Burrop, Mathieson & Co., 1952.

Long, Gavin. *To Benghazi: Australia in the War of 1939–45*. Canberra, 1952.

Lucan (Marcus Annaeus Lucanus). *Pharsalia: Dramatic Episodes of the Civil Wars*. https://www. gutenberg.org/ebooks/602.

Lyman, Robert. *The Longest Siege: Tobruk, The Battle That Saved North Africa*. MacMillan, 2009.

Macksey, Kenneth. *Armoured Crusader: Major General Sir Percy Hobart*. Hutchinson, 1967.

Macksey, Kenneth. *Afrika Corps*. MacDonald & Co, 1968.

Malcolm, James. *Born of the Desert: With the SAS in North Africa*. Collins, 1945.

Massey, William. *The Desert Campaigns*. Constable, 1918.

Matar, Nabil. *British Captives from the Mediterranean to the Atlantic 1563–1760*. Brill, 2014.

Mattingly, D. J. *The Laguatan: A Libyan Tribal Confederation in the late Roman Empire*. Society for Libyan Studies, 1983.

Mazard, Béatrice. *Libya*. Darf, 2006.

McClure, W. K. *Italy in North Africa: An Account of the Tripoli Enterprise*. Constable, 1913.

McCollum, Jonathan. *The Anti-Colonial Empire: Ottoman Mobilization and Resistance in the Italo-Turkish War, 1911–1912*. UCLA, 2018. https://escholarship.org/content/qt5341c962/qt5341c962. pdf?t=pfnubl.

McCullagh, Francis. *Italy's War for A Desert*. Herbert & Daniel May, 1912.

McGregor, Andrew. "The Libyan Battle for the Heritage of Omar al-Mukhtar, the Lion of the Desert". *Terrorism Monitor*, Volume 9, Issue 10 (2011): https://www.refworld.org/docid/4d7a29de2.html

McGuirk, Russell. *The Sanusi's Little War: The Amazing Story of a Forgotten Conflict in the Western Desert, 1915–1917*. Arabian Publishing, 2007.

McLaren, Brian. *Architecture and Tourism in Italian Colonial Libya: An Ambivalent Modernism*. University of Washington Press, 2006.

McNamara, James. "The Monstrosity of Cato in Lucan's Civil War". In Giulia Maria Chesi and Francesca Speigal (editors), *Classical Literature and Posthumanism*. Bloomsbury, 2019.

Metz, H. C. *Libya: A Country Study*. Washington GPO for the Library of Congress, 1987.

Mileham, Patrick. *The Yeomanry Regiments*. Spellmount, 2003.

Mitcham, Samuel W. *Rommel's Greatest Victory: The Desert Fox and The Fall of Tobruk Spring 1942*. Presido, 1998.

Mitchellhill-Green, D. *Tobruk 1942: Rommel and the Defeat of the Allies*. History Press, 2016.

Montgomery, Field Marshal the Viscount. *Memoirs*. Collins, 1958.

Moorehead, Alan. *The Desert War: The North African Campaign 1940–1943*. Hamish Hamilton, 1965.

Newby, Eric. *On the Shores of the Mediterranean*. Picador, 1985.

Nicolson, Harold. *King George the Fifth: His Life and Reign*. Doubleday & Co., 1953.

Obama, Barack. *A Promised Land*. Viking, 2020.

O'Byrne, William. *A Naval biographical Dictionary*. John Murray, 1849. https://en.wikisource.org/wiki/A_Naval_Biographical_Dictionary.

Ostler, Alan. *The Arabs in Tripoli*. John Murray, 1912.

Pacho, Jean-Raymond, *Voyage dans la Marmarique, la Cyrenaique, et les Oasis d'Audjelah et de Maradèh*. Firmin Didot, Paris, 1828. Extracts in *The Foreign Quarterly Review* Volume V (November 1829 and February 1830).

Pack, Jason. *The 2011 Libyan Uprisings and the Struggle for the Post-Qadhafi Future*. Palgrave Macmillan, 2013.

Pack, Jason. "Engagement in Libya was and remains the Right Answer". *The Spectator*, 30 January 2013.

Pack, Jason. "The Antecedents and Implications of the so-Called Anglo-Sanussi War 1915–1917". In T. G. Fraser (editor), *The First World War and its Aftermath: The Shaping of the Modern Middle East*. Gingko London, 2015.

Peniakoff, Vladimir. *Popski's Private Army*. Pan, 1957. (First published by Jonathan Cape, 1950).

Pitt, Barrie. *The Crucible of War: Western Desert 1941*. Jonathan Cape, 1980.

Playfair, Ian. *Official History of the Second World War: The Mediterranean and Middle East*. HMSO, 1960.

Playfair, Lambert. *Handbook to the Mediterranean*. John Murray, 1890.

Pollack, K. M. *Arabs at War: Military Effectiveness 1948–1991*. University of Nebraska Press, 2004.

Ranfurly, Hermione. *To War with Whitaker: The Wartime Diaries of the Countess of Ranfurly 1939–45*. Mandarin Paperback, 1995.

Reddish, Arthur. *El Alamein: A Tank Soldier's Story*. 1992.

Rennell, James. *The Geographical System of Herodotus*. Bulmer & Co., 1800.

Richardson, James. *Travels into the Great Desert of Sahara*. London, 1849.

Roberts, J. M. *Europe 1880–1945, Second Edition*. Longman, 1989.

Robertson, E. M. *The Origins of the Second World War*. Macmillan, 1971.

Rohlfs, Gerhard. *Von Tripolis nach Alexandrien 1879*. https://www.gutenberg.org/ebooks/17599.

Rose, Andrew. *The Prince, the Princess and the Perfect Murder*. Coronet, 2013.

Rosselli, Alberto. *Le Operazioni Militari in Libia E Nel Sahara 1914–1918*. https://www.arsmilitaris.org/pubblicazioni/Libia.pdf.

Sadler, J. *Operation Agreement: Jewish Commandos and the Raid on Tobruk*. Osprey, 2016.

Schmidt, Heinz Werner. *With Rommel in The Desert*. Harrap, 1951.

Schurtz, Heinrich. *Mediterranean North Africa*. London, 1908.

Simon, Rachel. *Libya between Ottomanism and Nationalism: The Ottoman Involvement in Libya during the War with Italy (1911–1919)*. Berlin: Klaus Schwarz Verlag, 1987.

Simons, Geoffrey. *Libya: The Struggle for Survival*. Palgrave MacMillan, 1993.

Small, Peter C. *Massacre at Tobruk; The British Assault on Rommel*. Kimber, 1987; Stackpole Reprint, 2008.

Smith, Robert Murdoch and Porcher, Edwin Augustus. *History of the Recent Discoveries at Cyrene, Made During an Expedition to the Cyrenaica in 1860–61*; Day & Son, 1864.

Smith, Simon. "Centurions and Chieftains: Tank Sales and British Policy Towards Israel in the Aftermath of the Six Day War". *Contemporary British History* 28(2) (2014): 219–239. https://doi.org/10.10 80/13619462.2014.930348.

Smyth, William Henry. *The Mediterranean: A Memoir Physical, Historical, and Nautical.* Parker & Son, 1854.

St John, Ronald Bruce. *Libya and the United States: Two Centuries of Strife.* University of Pennsylvania Press, 2002.

Steiner, Zara. *The Lights That Failed: European International History 1919–1933.* Oxford University Press, 2005.

Stephenson, Charles. *A Box of Sand: The Italo-Ottoman War 1911–1912.* Tattered Flag Press, 2014.

Stevens, W. G. *Official History of New Zealand in the Second World War 1939–45: Bardia to Enfidaville.* Department of Internal Affairs, New Zealand, 1962.

Strachan, Hew. *The First World War: Volume I: To Arms.* Oxford University Press, 2001.

Straw, Sean. *Anglo Libyan Relations and the British Military Facilities 1964–1970.* PhD Thesis, University of Nottingham, 2011.

Stucchi, Sandro. *L'Agorà di Cirene.* Rome, 1965.

Sundberg, V. "Siege of Tobruk: The Struggle to maintain the Coastal Supply Lines 1941". *RUSI Journal*, February 2009

Synge, Richard. *Operation Idris.* Silphium Press, 2015.

Synge, W. A. T. *The Story of the Green Howards 1939–1945.* The Green Howards, 1950.

Taylor, A. J. P. *English History 1914–1945.* Oxford University Press, 1965.

Thompson, Julian. *The Imperial War Museum Book of War Behind Enemy Lines.* Sidgwick and Jackson, 1998.

Thorn, James Copeland. *The Necropolis of Cyrene: Two hundred Years of Exploration.* Lerma di Bretschneider. 2005.

Torrey, Charles (editor). *The History of the Conquests of Egypt, North Africa, and Spain.* Yale University Press, 1922.

Toy, Barbara. *A Fool in The Desert: Journey In Libya.* John Murray, 1956.

Travers, Susan and Holden, Wendy. *Tomorrow To Be Brave: A Memoir of the Only Woman Ever to Serve in the French Foreign Legion.* New York Free Press, 2001.

Tuker, Francis. *Approach to Battle, A Commentary: Eighth Army, November 1941 to May 1943.* Cassell, 1963.

Tully, Richard. *Narrative of a Ten Years' Residence at Tripoli in Africa.* Henry Colburn, 1816.

Vandewalle, Dirk. *A History of Modern Libya.* Cambridge, 2006.

Williams, Claud (edited by Russell McGuirk). *Light Car Patrols 1916–19: War and Exploration in Egypt and Libya with the Model T Ford.* Silphium Press, 2013.

Williams, Gwyn. *Green Mountain: An Informal Guide to Cyrenaica and Jebel Akhdar.* Faber & Faber, 1963.

Willison, A. C. *The Relief of Tobruk: A Tribute to the British Soldier.* Leagrave Press, 1949.

Wilmot, Chester. *Tobruk.* Angus and Robertson, 1944.

Wingate, Reginald. "Libya in the Last War: The Talbot Mission and the Agreements of 1917". *Journal of the Royal African Society* Volume 40, Number 159 (April 1941): 128–131.

Wombwell, James. *The Long War Against Piracy: Historical Trends.* Occasional Paper Number 32, Combat Studies Institute, Fort Leavenworth, 2010. www.hsdl.org/?view&did=23760.

Wright, John. *A History of Libya.* Hurst, 2014.

Yindrich, Jan. *Fortress Tobruk.* Ernest Benn, 1951.

Young, Desmond. *Rommel.* Collins, 1950.

Notes

Prologue

1   See Rod Liddle in *The Spectator*, 16 January 2021, page 15, and also Charles Moore on 5 June 2021, page 12).

Chapter 1

1   Establishing the colony of Cyrenaica in 631 BC, King Battus I founded a dynasty that lasted until 450 BC when it became a republic under the suzerainty of Persia. He named his capital Cyrene after a flourishing spring of water (Kyre) and oversaw the construction of four other cities that together came to be known as Pentapolis: Apollonia (now Marsa Susa), the main port, 12 miles from Cyrene; Ptolemais (now Tolmeita), the second port, which had its heyday in the 1st century BC; Taucheira (later Arsinoe, now Tocra); and Euesperides (later Berenice, now Benghazi). After Persian rule, a period of decline followed when Alexandria took over as the centre of African Hellenic culture. Cyrenaica's resurgence occurred when Magas, whose widowed mother had married Ptolemy I, became governor in 300 BC.

2   Silphium, or silphion, was a plant used in classical antiquity as a seasoning, perfume, aphrodisiac or medicine. The plant's resin was also used as a contraceptive by ancient Greeks and Romans. It was such an essential item of trade for Cyrene that coins carried an image of the plant on the obverse. The Greek "father of Botany", Theophrastus, described it as about 48 centimetres tall with a hollow stalk and golden leaves like honey.

3   *Pharsalia* Book IX. Pallas was the daughter of Triton, messenger of the seas. She was killed accidentally by the goddess Athena, who was born from Zeus' forehead and took Pallas's name as a mark of remorse for her friend. The story of their relationship inspired a yearly festival in Libya dedicated to the goddess.

4   The colourful Amazigh flag is still seen in many places in Libya, especially in the Jebel Nafusa. However, for this book, I have used the more familiar word, Berber.

5   The airfield at Barce was raided by the Long Range Desert Group on 13 September 1942; it is now named Al-Marj or Merj.

6   Gibbon, Chapter 51, p. 223.

7   The story of Queen Dihya reminds us that powerful African women have often played leading roles in the history of the continent. From Cleopatra to Asantewaa, who led 5,000 Ashanti against British colonialism in 1900, Africa has a strong tradition of producing iconic women, who have fought for freedom against invading foreigners.

8   Gibbon, p. 225.

9   Several important lessons can be drawn from the ebb and flow of the Arab advance across Libya in the 7th century. The problems of dispersal of forces and overextending supply lines were as old as warfare itself, but the unforgiving conditions of the desert magnified their effect and made

the consequences more fatal. These lessons would have to be relearned in the 19th century by opposing armies in the Western Desert.

10 Genoa secured the rights of traffic along the Cyrenaican coast in 1216.

Chapter 2

1 Hess, p. 55.
2 This alliance lasted from 1536 until Napoleon invaded Egypt in 1798.
3 Not to be confused with the Tripoli Eyalet in what is now Lebanon and Syria.
4 Africanus, p. 738.
5 Pashas with three tails were the highest ranking of the three grades of Ottoman pasha, sometimes anglicised to bashaw. Only the sultan could carry four tails. A pasha with two tails is a governor of a province and *sanjak* is a pasha with one tail. Pashas were deemed to be higher than beys, which were district administrators and sons of pashas. *Efendi* was equivalent to sir, or an appointment such as a physician, or an educated gentleman.
6 Nabil Matar, p. 48.
7 Ibid., p. 168.
8 Tully was appointed as secretary at the British Consulate in Tripoli in 1768 and married Catherine Dornbush in St Paul's Church, Covent Garden, on 30 June, before travelling to Libya. In 1782, he was appointed consul general and brought his family back to North Africa, after they had returned to England due to his low pay as secretary. This entourage included his sister-in-law Miss Dornbush and two daughters, Anne and Louisa.
9 "Don Juan", Canto III Verse LXVII.
10 Tully, p. 337.
11 Goddard, p. 35.
12 Wombwell, p. 67.
13 Pacho, *Voyage dans la Marmarique*.
14 USS *Argus* was a brig with 20 guns that had been part of the Tripoli blockade since 1804. USS *Nautilus*, captained by Oliver Perry, was a schooner converted into a brigantine with 14 guns, whereas USS *Hornet*, captained by Samuel Evans, was converted from a merchant ship into a sloop-of-war with 10 guns by the American Navy in April 1805.
15 St John, p. 29.

Chapter 3

1 Smith and Porcher, p. 85.
2 "Memoire d'un Voyage dans les Montagnes de Derne", in *Voyages de Paul Lucas 1712*, Volume II, pp. 85–123.
3 Martha W. Baldwin Bowsky in the *Encyclopedia of the History of Classical Archaeology* lists other international explorers, including: a French surgeon named Granger in 1733; an Italian doctor, Augustin Cervelli, who was scared away by Berber tribes in 1812; an Apostolic priest, Father Pacifico, in 1819; and a Swiss soldier, Heinrich von Minutoli, who led a German scientific expedition from Egypt, but failed to reach beyond Hellfire Pass.
4 Greenhalgh, p. 172.
5 In 1854, Admiral Smyth was awarded the Royal Geographical Society's Founder's Medal for his valuable maritime surveys that included the coast of Libya. He had commissioned HMS *Aid* as a survey ship in 1817 and renamed it in 1821.

6 Hanmer Warrington retired as a lieutenant colonel in the 1st Dragoons in 1812 and took up his diplomatic appointment at Tripoli two years later. He served as the British consul general for 32 years and his son, Frederick, was a vice-consul at Misuratah in 1854 after serving in the 77th (East Middlesex) Regiment of Foot (known as the pot-hooks).

7 The Beechey report gives spellings of Tyndal and Tindall, but the *Naval Biographical Dictionary* for 1821 indicates that this name is spelled Tyndale.

8 Beechey also references Thomas Shaw's *Travels in Barbary and the Levant* published in 1738, but this mainly covers Algiers and Tunis. For a full dissertation on the archaeological surveys and expeditions to Cyrenaica between 1700 and 1870, see Farley Goddard's article "Researches in the Cyrenaica" in the *American Journal of Philology* (1844).

9 Having reached his objective and gone beyond, Dr. Oudney sadly died on the expedition in January 1824 in Northern Nigeria. Clapperton, who was joined by Major Dixon Denham, returned to a hero's welcome and was soon commissioned to lead another expedition to Africa via Benin. However, he too died in Northern Nigeria in April 1827.

10 Beechey, p. 293.

11 Ibid., p. 304.

12 In fact, *sahab* means cloud; it is more likely they were called the courtesy title of *sahib* (friend). Ally in Arabic is *halif.*

13 Thorn, p. 24.

14 Ibid., p. 28.

15 Frederick Beechey wasn't awarded a medal by the Royal Geographic Society, but he was elected as its president in 1855 after being promoted to rear admiral in the Royal Navy.

16 The other four are strung out in a loop parallel to the Nile: Bahariya; Dakhlah; Farafrah; and the largest at Khargah. The semi-oasis at Fayum is not included in the big five.

17 Pacho, *Voyage dans la Marmarique.*

18 Details of Pacho's suicide are taken from an obituary provided by Pacho's friend, M. Larenaudière, published in "Pacho's Travels in Marmarica and Cyrenaica", Article VII, *Foreign Quarterly Review* Volume V November 1829 and February 1830, pp. 191–207.

19 Goddard, pp. 42–3.

20 Ibid., p. 40.

21 Barth, *Wanderungen durch das Punische und Kyrenäische Küstenland.*

22 Memorial tablet, St Mary's Church, Alton Barnes, Wiltshire.

23 Hamilton's book was not published until 1856.

24 Herman was a member of the royal and military Order of St Ferdinand. His medals, which came up for auction at Baldwin's, included: the Carlist Medal; Iron Cross; Order of Carol III; Order of Carlos III; Order of St Ferdinand; and the Order of Isabella the Catholic.

25 The first Carlist War 1833–40 was a war of succession between the constitutional monarchy and those who wished to return Spain to an absolutist monarchy under the late king's brother, who refused to recognise a female sovereign. Britain, France and Portugal all sided with the liberal regency against the forces of Carlos de Borbón and the Basques.

26 Smith and Porcher reveal Herman's role in the campaign on page 11 of their book. Herman was also known as a technical officer and had written a paper on Samuel Warner's claim to have invented an invisible gun, published in the 1844 *Polytechnic Review and Magazine.*

27 Yale Centre for British Art; https://collections.britishart.yale.edu/vufind/Record/3731169.

28 Smith and Porcher, p. 7.

29 Ibid., p. 59; the sheikh's name is given as Bou Bakr Ben Hadood.

30 Dickson, p. 170.

31 Smith and Porcher, p. 55.

32 Ibid., p. 54.

33 Ibid., p. 85.

34 Unappreciated as a self-educated man, Dennis nevertheless published a 1,000-page book on the Etruscan civilisation in 1848 that remains an indispensable reference volume to this day. Farley Goddard describes him merely as an "able vase-hunter".

35 *Von Tripolis nach Alexandrien 1879*. Bismarck, who had created the German Empire with a series of short, victorious wars against Denmark, Austria and France between 1864 and 1871, was not keen on the idea of colonies.

Chapter 4

1 The redeemer of the Islamic faith; part messenger, part messiah.

2 Winston Churchill was not the only cavalryman to join the 21st Lancers, or Egyptian cavalry, in the campaign. Kitchener mentions officers and soldiers from nine other regiments in his official despatch.

3 *London Gazette*, 15 November 1898.

4 Churchill, *The River War, Volume II*, p. 140.

5 Churchill was later awarded a Nobel Prize for his mastery of historical and biographical description as well as for brilliant oratory in defending exalted human values.

6 Churchill, *The River War, Volume I*, p. 25.

7 A *zawiya* is an organisational centre for a Sufi sheikh and shrine.

8 The Hejaz is the western region of Saudi Arabia (previously a kingdom) that includes the most important Muslim spiritual cities of Mecca and Medina as well as Jeddah. This is where Lawrence of Arabia was sent by Allenby to meet with King Faisal and where all pilgrims travel for the Haj.

9 Grey, Volume I, p. 105.

10 Ibid., pp. 123–6.

11 Ibid., p. 131.

12 Ibid., p. 225 and Nicolson, p. 188.

13 This confirmed the progress of the Haldane Reforms after the French had asked whether, in the event of a war, Britain could send a force of 100,000 men to protect their left flank.

14 Grey, Volume I, p. 260.

15 Royal Archives, M230 IB and Nicolson, p. 191.

16 Grey, Volume II, Appendix C, p. 292.

17 Bennett, p. 83.

18 Full details can be found in the *Encyclopedia of the History of Classical Archaeology*.

19 McCullagh, p. 34.

20 Bennett, p. 83.

21 Ibid., p. 16.

22 See Stephenson, *A Box of Sand*.

23 Bennett, p. 159.

24 John Horgan, *The Irishness of Francis McCullagh*.

25 Two each of Blériot, Farman and Etrich, plus three Nieuports.

26 Stephenson, Chapter 6.

27 McCullagh, p. 206.

28 Horgan, *The Irishness of Francis McCullagh*.

29 Bennett, p. 307.

30 McCullagh, p. 165.

31 James Rennell Rodd, *Social and Diplomatic Memories*, Third Series, Chapter 6: https://wwi.lib.byu.edu/index.php/CHAPTER_VI:_ROME,_1910–1911.

32 In fact, Alvarez was a natural-born British subject and had served in various posts in the Near East and Mediterranean since 1877. See Hansard: https://hansard.parliament.uk/Commons/1911-12-05/debates/704d918c-a44b-425d-aa83-6b3d13da0d12/BritishConsul-GeneralAtTripoli

33 Cricco, p. 138.

34 Ibid., p. 139

35 Stephenson, p. 85.

36 Ibid., p. 88.

37 Ibid., p. 82.

38 Ibid.

39 Bennett, p. 90.

40 For more on the Red Crescent's humanitarian work in the Italo-Ottoman War, see McCollum 2018.

41 Montagu was reinstated as a lieutenant with the Royal Munster Fusiliers at the outbreak of World War I. In 1915, he landed at Suvla Bay and fought against the Turkish Army. He was wounded at Kislagh Dagh and invalided out of the Army, only to re-enlist as a private soldier in the Oxfordshire and Buckinghamshire Light Infantry the following year. Deploying to France for the latter stages of the battle of the Somme, he was killed in action at Moquet Farm near Thiepval on 25 November 1916, whilst waiting to be recommissioned for the third time. https://oxfordshireandbuckinghamshirelightinfantry.wordpress.com/tag/kislag-dagh/

42 McCullagh, p. 25.

43 Bennett, p. 20.

44 See ADM 116/3493, WO 106/214 and WO 106/218 at The National Archives for details of the Admiralty and War Office assessment and direction on the Western Frontier of Egypt and the Mediterranean, including the port of Sollum and the oases of Siwa and Jaghbub.

45 Kemal complained about the difficulties of dealing with tribesmen. Long preliminary conversations had to be held with the elders and heads of Sufi lodges before proposing a course of action. Decisions were slow and promised numbers were not always delivered, but he did recognise the bravery of these warriors.

46 Gawrych, p. 26.

47 Bennett, p. 239.

48 Abbott, p. 262.

49 Ibid., p. 263.

50 Randolph Churchill, p. 580.

51 Letter to Lord Haldane dated 6 May 1912, in Randolph Churchill, p. 588.

52 Churchill Memorandum, Naval Situation in the Mediterranean, dated 5 June 1912.

53 Randolph Churchill, p. 594.

54 McCollum, p. iv.

55 Fortna, p. 79.

56 Clark, p. 242.

57 David Buel's review of Italy in North Africa in *Bulletin of the American Geographical Society* 1915, Volume 47–6, p. 456.

58 Ostler, p. 60.

59 The Italian aviation commander, General Giulio Douhet, wrote a report about the use of aircraft and lessons learned in Libya that was used by all the Great Powers. He was the first theorist to advance the proposition that wars might be won by air-power alone.

Chapter 5

1   With 194 ships and 453,716 gross tons, Perière is the most successful submarine captain ever. During his career he fired 74 torpedoes, hitting 39 times, and after commanding the *U-35*, he transferred to the brand new *U-139*, which he surrendered in France after the Armistice.

2   Apcar, also known as Thomas Arratoon, was a member of the family that owned a famous shipping line in Calcutta. At the beginning of the war, he was an ambulance driver in France, but then took a commission in the Indian Cavalry on 29 May 1915. He joined HMT *Moorina* at Bombay with 548 horses bound for the 32nd Lancers in France. His grandson, Staff Sergeant Charles Seth Apcar, died tragically while on operations in Northern Ireland in 1974, shortly after being awarded the BEM.

3   Gwatkins-Williams, p. 6.

4   These were: Sub-Lieutenant Griffith Hugh Roberts; Engineer Sub-Lieutenant Richard Phillips; Leading Stoker Robert Phillips; Leading Stoker William Jones; Leading Stoker Thomas Jones; Fireman John Ellis Jones; Seaman James McKinven; Warrant Electrician James Hutton; Electrical Light Attendant John Parry; Steward Frederick Barber.

5   Gwatkins-Williams, p. 26.

6   William Thomas' body was never found so he was not re-interred, but his name is commemorated on the Chatby Memorial in Alexandria and the Holyhead War Memorial.

7   Gwatkins-Williams, p. 72.

8   Ibid., pp. 101–2.

9   The gay activist Peter Tatchell has alleged that Fitzgerald and Kitchener were lovers; see the Imperial War Museum website: livesofthefirstworldwar.iwm.org.uk/story/57182

10   WO 106/218 Report on Sollum and Western Frontier of Egypt by Captain O Fitzgerald.

11   CAB 44/14 Telegram from Viscount Kitchener in Cairo to Sir Edward Grey January 31, 1913, received 2:45 p.m.

12   For more on Royle's career in the Egyptian Coastguard, see McGuirk, *The Sanusi's Little War*.

13   McGuirk, p. 38.

14   Ibid., p. 85.

15   Nicolson, p. 268.

16   Rosselli, *Le Operazioni Militari In Libia E Nel Sahara 1914–1918*.

17   Rome telegram No. 1042 Oct 23 D 9.30pm R Oct 24 10.20 am, in "Precis of documents and proceedings connected with the political and military developments in the Balkan Peninsula October 21–25 1915" for the 40th meeting of the Committee of Imperial Defence (Secret G-26).

18   The *muhafizia* were the Sufi equivalent of the Sunni *mujahidin* that became famous in Afghanistan in the 1980s war against the Soviet Union.

19   Despatch Number 3 from Cairo dated 1 March 1916.

20   McGuirk, p. 149.

21   An excellent potted history of the Sikhs' involvement, published in the *Journal of the Indian Military Historical Society*, can be found at: http://www.kaiserscross.com/188001/297622.html.

22   The story of the Australian Light Horse in this campaign is told in meticulous detail by Steve Becker in *The History of the Composite Light Horse Regiment*, available at: https://www.greatwarforum.org/topic/76521-senussi-campaign/?tab=comments#comment-700110.

23   Another helpful website with details of the Western Frontier Force is The Long, Long Trail: https://www.longlongtrail.co.uk/battles/western-frontier-force-and-the-campaign-in-the-western-desert–1915–1916/.

24   The author is grateful to Andrew French, curator of the *Berkshire Yeomanry* Museum, for providing these quotes from Bill Cox's correspondence and details of the casualties.

25 French, Berkshire Yeomanry, unpublished pdf.

26 The 17 dead were initially buried at Matruh and subsequently re-interred at Chatby in Alexandria.

27 Massey, p. 4.

28 Hungerford Virtual Museum: https://www.hungerfordvirtualmuseum.co.uk/index.php/20-themes/war-memorial-1st-world-war/556-fredrick-john-north

29 Joseph Laycock earned a DSO with the Nottinghamshire Royal Horse Artillery in the Boer War where he befriended Winston Churchill. He competed with the Duke of Westminster in the 1908 Olympics at water motorsport and was later knighted and became the lord lieutenant of Nottinghamshire.

30 Newbold Archive 577/1/61, diary entry for 29 December 1915.

31 Despatch Number 3 from Cairo, dated 1 March 1916.

32 For his command in this campaign, Colonel Gordon was made a CB. The regiment earned the Battle Honour "Egypt 1915–1917". Captain Charles Hughes was awarded the Military Cross and Jemadar Basant Singh received the Indian Order of Merit for gallantry at Halazin.

33 Despatch Number 3 from Cairo, dated 1 March 1916.

34 Sources for this story are official despatches and Lieutenant Blaksley's letters to his home.

35 The list of those who died on 26 February can be found on the Commonwealth War Graves website and the memorial at Thornford, near Sherborne.

36 The prisoners who died at Bir Hakeim were re-interred at Alexandria Hadra War Memorial along with Thomas Pritchard, who died at Alexandria having survived the ordeal in Libya.

37 Gwatkins-Williams, p. 259.

38 Authors such as S. C. Rolls claim that during the rescue, some of the Duke of Westminster's troops went beyond the bounds of the Geneva Convention by unnecessarily killing some of the guards and their families.

39 Leopold Victor Arnold Royle, whose father was clerk to the robes of Queen Victoria, was later awarded a silver medal for military valour as an honorary *kaimakam* (lieutenant colonel) from the government of Italy (LG 31 Aug 1917). Sadly, he was killed in air operations over Palestine on 17 August 1918.

40 See Andrew Rose, *The Prince, The Princess and The Perfect Murder*.

41 John Leslie briefly played for Worcestershire and his father played in Ivo Bligh's team that regained the Ashes in Australia in 1882. After serving in Libya, he earned a DSO as a Tank Corps squadron commander during the final year of the war in France.

42 Two other rescuers awarded the Military Cross were Captains Charlie Amphlett and Arthur Protheroe, who transferred from the Royal Naval Reserve to the Motor Machine Gun Service.

43 The source for this quote is David Tattersfield and Captain C. A. Parr, curator of the Military Museum of Devon and Dorset. Further details can be found at: http://www.westernfrontassociation.com/world-war-i-articles/the-vc-that-never-was-colonel-souters-gallantry-against-the-senussi–1916/

44 Strachan, *The First World War: Volume I: To Arms*.

Chapter 6

1 Despite his glittering diplomatic career, Wingate was refused a peerage because he was made a scapegoat for the nationalist riots after the end of World War I in Egypt.

2 General Murray's first despatch to Lord Kitchener, dated 1 June 1916.

3 Ibid.

4 General Maxwell's third despatch to Lord Kitchener, dated 1 March 1916.

5 *The Geographical Journal*, Volume 79 Number 1 (January 1932): 78–9.

6   Wingate, pp. 128–31.
7   For more details on the disputed frontier between Egypt and Libya see Matthew Ellis, *Desert Borderland: The Making of Modern Egypt and Libya*, Stanford University Press, 2018.
8   Arab Bulletin Number 43, dated 28 February, p. 100.
9   Lloyd George, p. 508.
10 Colonel The Hon. Milo George Talbot CB. late Royal Engineers. *A Memoir 1931*. British Library General Reference Collection 10814.c.14 UIN BLL01003823579.
11 General Murray's despatch to the secretary of state for war, dated 1 March 1917; Supplement to *The London Gazette* of 6 July 1917, p. 6761.
12 Major Kinahan Cornwallis stepped up from his post as deputy director to take over from Lieutenant Commander David Hogarth as director of the Arab Bureau in 1916. This analysis is in Arab Bulletin Number 43, dated 28 February 1917, p. 101.
13 Secret Eastern Report Number, dated 15 March 1917 for the War Cabinet, p. 4. Between 26 February and 8 March, Talbot sent several important letters and telegrams to Wingate, updating him on the release of the prisoners.
14 Ibid.
15 Secret Eastern Report Number 10, 4 April 1917, p. 3.
16 Ibid.
17 Ibid.
18 Wingate, pp. 128–31.
19 Arab Bulletin Number 65 dated 8 October 1917, p. 404.
20 Williams, p. 96.
21 Arab Bulletin Number 43 dated 28 February, p. 101.
22 The Italians made extensive use of colonial troops (*savari*) and mounted police (*spahi*) who were recruited from the Arab-Berber population and formed part of the *Regio Corpo Truppe Coloniali della Libia* (Royal Corps of Libyan Colonial Troops).
23 Anderson, p. 51.
24 Evans-Pritchard, p. 149.
25 Introduction to Mohammed Fekini's biography.

Chapter 7

1   Douglas Murray, "A Question of Tolerance". *The Spectator*, 13 June 2020, p. 12.
2   Steiner, p. 316.
3   Ibid., p. 323.
4   Del Boca, p. 134.
5   Ibid., p. 4.
6   Ian Thompson in *The Telegraph*, 29 September 2007, reviewing *The Force of Destiny: A History of Italy since 1796* by Christopher Duggan.
7   Andrew McGregor, "The Libyan Battle for the Heritage of Omar al-Mukhtar, the Lion of the Desert".
8   Asad, p. 359.
9   Baldinetti, p. 97
10 McLaren, p. 60.
11 Ibid., p. 50.
12 Bowsky in *Encyclopedia of the History of Classical Archaeology*, p. 346.
13 http://www.rsssf.com/tablesl/libkoloniehist.html.

14 Dennis David: http://www.grandprixhistory.org/track.htm.

15 https://www.rgs.org/about/medals-award/history-and-past-recipients/.

16 Winston Churchill, *The Gathering Storm*, p. 129.

17 See D. C. Watt, "The Secret Laval-Mussolini Agreement of 1935 on Ethiopia", *The Middle East Journal*, Winter 1961.

18 Winston Churchill, *The Gathering Storm*, p. 135.

19 Ibid., p. 141.

20 Ibid., p. 130.

21 Roberts, p. 512.

22 Winston Churchill, *The Gathering Storm*, p. 133.

23 Taylor, p. 381.

24 Ibid., p. 385.

25 Roberts, p. 515.

26 Robertson, p. 20.

Chapter 8

1 Badoglio, p. 37.

2 Ciano, p. 139.

3 British troops landed in Norway on 9 April, after a successful naval engagement, but these forces were outmaneuvered by the Wehrmacht, supported by the Luftwaffe. On 30 April, the German columns linked up close to Hjerkin. The Norwegian Army covered the evacuation of British troops from Namsos on 2 May, but unfortunately two rescue ships were sunk by dive-bombers. Norwegian military resistance in central and southern Norway ceased on 5 May. King Haakon and his parliament had already evacuated to Tromso, which became the *de facto* capital for the remaining weeks of the campaign. General Auchinleck took command on 13 May, but after Germany invaded France, London withdrew all the British troops.

4 Churchill, *The Gathering Storm*, p. 521.

5 Ibid., p. 526.

6 Ciano, p. 248.

7 Ibid.

8 Alfa Romeo took the first three places in the race. When racing began again after the war, Nino Farina won the first official Formula One world driver's title in 1950, driving for Alfa Romeo. Remarkably, Ascari, who was 9th at Tripoli and won the 1952 and 1953 Formula One Championship with Scuderia Ferrari, was the last Italian Formula One champion.

9 Churchill, *Their Finest Hour*, p. 15.

10 Ibid., p. 376.

11 Pitt, p. 64.

12 https://warfarehistorynetwork.com/2018/12/28/general-percy-hobart-britains-genius-tanker/.

13 Macksey, p. 170.

14 Moorehead, p. 31.

15 Kennedy-Shaw, *Long Range Desert Group*, p. 42.

16 Ciano, p. 283.

17 Churchill, *Their Finest Hour*, p. 393.

18 Ibid., p. 399; Operation *Hats* was a convoy mission from Alexandria to Malta, completed between 30 August and 5 September 1940.

19 Connell, p. 288.

20 Savory wrote a diary about his life in Vladivostok, which the author used in his book, *Churchill's Abandoned Prisoners*. He described the Canadian Mounted Police weeping when they had to give up their horses for the Jaeger artillery brigade and the Bolshevik train attack which killed 18 horses. Savory commanded the British base at Vladivostok in October 1919 and supervised the evacuation of troops following the defeat of the White Army.

21 Liddell Hart, p. 50.

22 Ciano, pp. 321–2.

23 Churchill, *Their Finest Hour*, p. 543. The prime minister sent a further message two days later on 18 December, quoting St Matthew, chapter vii, verse 7: "Ask and it shall be given you; seek, and you shall find; knock and it shall be opened unto you." He was then driven to Harrow School for his first visit since his departure in 1891, where he sang songs with the boys, who gave him a rapturous ovation.

24 Ibid., p. 548.

25 *The Times*, 9 January 1942.

26 Wilmot, p. 37.

27 Long, p. 239.

Chapter 9

1 Churchill, *Their Finest Hour*, p. 543.

2 Churchill, *The Grand Alliance*, p. 14.

3 Ibid., p. 17.

4 The British Army designed their ubiquitous 25-pounder in the 1930s for suppressive fire, rather than destroying the enemy. It replaced the 18-pounder gun and 4.5-inch howitzer and was considered to be one of the best artillery designs in World War II.

5 Churchill, *The Grand Alliance*, p. 58.

6 J. W. B. Judge. *Airfield Creation for the Western Desert Campaign*, Chapter 40. https://www.laetusinpraesens.org/guests/jwbj/jwb2.htm#23.

7 Private papers of Patrick McCraith.

8 Ranfurly, p. 87.

9 Churchill, *The Grand Alliance*, p. 183.

10 WO 201/353 Diary of Leutnant Schorm, Panzer Regiment 5.

11 The pilots killed in action were Flight Lieutenant Smith, Pilot Officers Lamb, Goodman and Mills and Flight Sergeant Webster, who was tragically blown out of the sky by a British Bofors when he was on the tail of a ME 109.

12 Heckstall-Smith, p. 90.

13 Yindrich, p. 178.

14 Ibid., pp. 147–53.

15 Harrison, p. 103.

16 Ibid., p. 108.

17 Yindrich, p. 94.

18 Ibid., p. 192.

19 Harrison, p. 140.

20 Yindrich, p. 159.

21 Ibid., pp. 177–8.

22 Churchill, *The Grand Alliance*, p. 309–10.

23 Pitt, p. 310.

Chapter 10

1 Ciano, p. 325.

2 Churchill, *The Grand Alliance*, p. 369. Churchill agreed with Auchinleck, stating in the cable to Lyttleton of 18 September 1941: "I particularly stimulated Auchinleck when he was at home not to prejudice defence of Tobruk by making a needless relief."

3 Apart from the original constituents, 16th and 23rd Brigades, Auchinleck added 14th Brigade, 32nd Tank Brigade, 1st Polish Carpathian Brigade as well as artillery and machine gunners.

4 Harrison, p. 109.

5 Wilmot, p. 200; many eye-witness accounts suggest that the Afrika Korps's soldiers were not fans of the Nazi Party.

6 HMS *Latona* was built in 1940 as the latest minelayer with a crew of 242. Four officers, 16 ratings and seven soldiers were killed when she sank after being hit by the Luftwaffe north of Bardia on 25 October 1941.

7 Scobie played centre in all the Scotland matches in the 1914 Five Nations; the result of the Calcutta Cup was 15–16 to England.

8 Scobie oversaw a huge amount of engineering work in East Africa from the headquarters in Sudan. This included the clearance of the port of Masaawa and all railway and ropeway transportation in Eritrea, organised by Major Leonard Vining, who was awarded an MBE for his efforts. Vining had previously earned fame leading the last British prisoners of war out of Russia in 1920; further details can be found in *Churchill's Abandoned Prisoners*.

9 Macksey, p. 43.

10 Churchill, *The Grand Alliance*, p. 493.

11 Agar-Hamilton and Turner, pp. 199–200.

12 This was one of four gallant actions between 19 November and 30 December 1941 described in Cameron's citation dated 3 January 1942. He ended up as the most highly decorated officer in his regiment, earning another MC at El Alamein and two DSOs in Tunisia and Italy. The citations can be read on the Kent and Sharpshooters Yeomanry website: https://www.ksymuseum.org.uk/stories/ViewStory/30

13 A full account of the battles for Jill https://www.ksymuseum.org.uk/stories/ViewStory/30 and Tiger can be found in Bernard Fergusson's regimental history, *The Black Watch and the King's Enemies*.

14 Frank Harrison, who was Brigadier Willison's signaller, makes it clear in his book *The Great Siege Reassessed* that contrary to many historical reports of this battle, Rommel did not stop the sortie from Tobruk. The reason Tobforce did not continue to El Duda was because Eighth Army had not called the code-word "Pop".

15 Second Supplement to *The London Gazette* of Friday 17 April 1942.

16 Ibid.

17 Moorehead, p. 61.

18 Pitt, p. 387.

19 Joly, p. 199.

20 *The London Gazette*, Friday 6 February 1942.

21 McTier was not awarded the DCM until 25 September 1947.

22 These are: "Defence of Tobruk April to December 1941"; "Tobruk 18 November to 10 December 1941"; "Tobruk Sortie 21 to 23 November 1941"; and "Relief of Tobruk 7 to 10 December 1941".

23 Churchill, *The Grand Alliance*, p. 505.

24 Newby, pp. 309–10.

25 *The London Gazette*, 27 March 1942.

26 All quotes concerning the El Duda battle are from Pitt, *The Crucible of War* and Harrison, *The Great Siege Reassessed*.

27 Harrison, p. 276.

28 Sadly Loder-Symonds was killed later in the war when he was posted to the Far East. Details can be found at: www.pegasusarchive.org/arnhem/robert_loder_symonds.htm

29 Churchill, *The Grand Alliance*, p. 511.

30 Ibid., p. 552.

Chapter 11

1 Abbé de Pradt, p. 214.

2 Liddell Hart, *History of the Second World War*, p. 206.

3 Ibid., p. 78.

4 Connell, pp. 423–4.

5 Macksey, p. 57.

6 Connell, p. 420.

7 Pitt, p. 469.

8 Schmidt, p. 126.

9 Pitt, *The Crucible of War*.

10 Ibid., p. 476.

11 Tuker, p. 81.

12 Liddell Hart, p. 280.

13 Ibid., p. 289—taken from Napoleon's 1808 *Observations on Spanish Affairs*.

14 Macksey, p. 73.

15 The *Empress of Russia* had a distinguished record as an armed merchant cruiser and troop ship during World War I. Her guns were used to rescue diplomats in Yemen and in April 1917 she brought 2,000 members of the Chinese Labour Corps to help in France. After transporting American troops in the final year of the war, she left Liverpool on 12 January 1919 with 30 volunteers for the Siberian campaign.

16 Clay, p. 55.

17 Ibid., p. 53. The convoy of four ships was escorted by an aircraft carrier, 18 destroyers and four light cruisers, including the old warhorse HMS *Carlisle*. Although the ships successfully passed Cyrenaica, they had to fight the second battle of Sirte against a heavier Italian fleet and were delayed from arriving at Malta during the dark and so a large part of the supplies were lost to enemy air attacks.

18 Synge, p. 97. https://www.yorkpress.co.uk/news/10932981.memories-of-wartime-hero-jim-exall/.

19 Some historians suggest that Crüwell's pilot landed in error, but Clay claims the plane was shot down (p. 59).

20 Clay, p. 61.

21 Supplement to *The London Gazette* of 8 November 1945. https://www.thegazette.co.uk/London/issue/37340/supplement/5432/data.pdf.

22 Synge, p. 104.

23 Young, p. 267.

24 Supplement to *The London Gazette* of 11 September 1942.

25 Supplement to *The London Gazette* of 16 May 1944.

26 Admiral Sir Walter Cowan commanded HMS *Princess Royal* during the battle of Jutland. At the beginning of World War II, he came out of retirement and volunteered to serve as a commando.

27 Travers, p. 180.

28 Liddell Hart, p. 286.

29 Jackson and Lindsay were awarded DSOs for their outstanding leadership; see Clay, p. 67 and Synge, p. 117 and Supplement to *The London Gazette* of 22 September 1945. https://www.thegazette.co.uk/London/issue/35715/supplement/4155.

30 Clay, p. 70.

31 Evans was captured at Matruh, but escaped and trekked 100 miles across the desert to return to the division. Usher was commissioned into the regiment, but later killed in Sicily in July 1943.

32 Klopper took over 3rd South African Brigade from Brigadier Cliff Borain, when the latter was blown up by a mine. Klopper was awarded a Distinguished Service Order for his role as a battalion commander in the capture of Bardia and Sollum, but he did not command the brigade until after this operation.

33 Ian Playfair, p. 270.

34 Ibid., p. 275.

35 Churchill, *The Hinge of Fate*, p. 343.

36 Ibid., p. 349.

37 Ibid., p. 366.

38 Lieutenant Colonel Francis Macdonnel commanding 7th Green Howards and Guy Stansfield commanding 5th East Yorkshire.

39 Supplement to *The London Gazette* of 8 September 1942.

40 Liddell Hart, p. 294.

41 Two New Zealanders earned their medals for deeds at Ruweisat Ridge on 14 and 15 July. Captain Charles Upham won a Bar to his Victoria Cross and Sergeant Keith Elliott was awarded the medal for leading the survivors of B Company. Despite being wounded four times, he destroyed five machine guns and one anti-tank gun, and captured 130 prisoners. The Australian Private Stan Gurney was posthumously awarded a Victoria Cross for taking three machine-gun posts at El Alamein on 22 July.

42 Alanbrooke, p. 287.

43 Churchill, *The Hinge of Fate*, p. 415.

44 Lampson had been the British High Commissioner in Siberia when Admiral Kolchak was executed in January 1920 (see *Churchill's Abandoned Prisoners*). In 1934 he moved from Shanghai to Cairo, where he became ambassador to Egypt and high commissioner for the Sudan. He was particularly kind to Hermione Ranfurly when her husband was captured (see *To War with Whitaker*) and was raised to the peerage as Baron Killearn in May 1943.

45 Churchill, *The Hinge of Fate*, p. 424.

Chapter 12

1 Macksey, p. 104.

2 Peniakoff, p. 174.

3 Ibid.

4 Ibid., p. xiii.

5 Pitt, p. 224.

6 Kennedy-Shaw, *Desert Navigation*, p. 256.

7 http://maltacommand.com/unit%20history%20LRDG.html.

8 Kennedy-Shaw, *Long Range Desert Group*, p. 37.

9 Pitt, p. 232.

10 https://salfordwarmemorials.proboards.com/thread/1498/private-alfred-tighes-remarkable-journey.
11 https://www.telegraph.co.uk/news/obituaries/1405654/Brigadier-Teddy-Mitford.html.
12 Peniakoff, p. 205.
13 Supplement to *The London Gazette* of 3 February 1948. https://www.thegazette.co.uk/London/issue/38196/supplement/839.
14 Churchill, *The Grand Alliance*, p. 238.
15 Yindrich, p. 115.
16 Churchill, *The Grand Alliance*, p. 721.
17 Ibid., pp. 725–6.
18 Peniakoff, p. 121.
19 https://www.thegazette.co.uk/London/issue/35600/supplement/2699.
20 Peniakoff, p. 62.
21 Laycock, *Commando Extraordinary*, pp. v–vi.
22 Pitt, p. 352.
23 Ranfurly, p. 77.
24 Citations dated 12 February 1942 and 18 February 1943.
25 http://www.hambo.org/kingscanterbury/view_man.php?id=273.
26 Peniakoff, p. 173.
27 Hudson died of Aids aged 59; Green died of an overdose of sleeping pills aged 47; and Peppard was an alcoholic with lung cancer, when he died aged 65.
28 Peniakoff, p. xi.
29 Email, Jason Pack 8 July 2021.
30 Citation written by the director of Special Operations and Military Intelligence, approved by General Alexander.

Chapter 13

1 Taken from the poem, *Desert Flowers*. Douglas is considered to be one of the finest poets of World War II. He served in Libya with the Sherwood Rangers and was wounded at Wadi Zem Zem and later killed in action in Normandy.
2 Horrocks, p. 104.
3 Ibid., p. 108.
4 Ibid., p. 119.
5 Ranfurly, pp. 143–6.
6 *The African Campaign from El Alamein to Tunis*; Supplement to *The London Gazette* of Tuesday 3 February 1948, p. 848.
7 Alanbrooke, p. 323.
8 Carver, *El Alamein*, p. 86.
9 https://codenames.info/operation/braganza/.
10 Carver, *El Alamein*, p. 203.
11 Supplement to *The London Gazette* of Tuesday 26 January 1943. https://www.thegazette.co.uk/London/issue/35879/supplement/523.
12 Ibid.
13 Reddish, p. 12.
14 Ibid., p. 17.
15 Lindsay, p. 175.
16 Reddish, p. 18.

17 Private papers of Patrick McCraith.

18 Carver, *El Alamein*, p. 96.

19 Horrocks, p. 130.

20 Ibid., p. 139.

21 Supplement to The London Gazette of 17th November 1942. https://www.thegazette.co.uk/London/issue/35790/supplement/5023.

22 Bryant, p. 394.

23 Carver, *El Alamein*, p. 150.

24 Ranfurly, pp. 150–1.

25 Clay, p. 100.

26 Ibid., p. 101.

27 The Royal Wiltshire Yeomanry was the senior of 55 Yeomanry Regiment according to the order of precedence in the Army List of 1914. The Warwickshire Yeomanry was second, Yorkshire Hussars third and the Sherwood Rangers Yeomanry fourth. The senior Scottish regiment was the Ayrshire Yeomanry (seventh) and the senior Welsh regiment was the Denbighshire Yeomanry (sixteenth).

28 Carver, *El Alamein*, p. 166.

29 Supplement to *The London Gazette* of 28 January 1943.

30 *The Times*, 11 May 1967.

31 Carver, *El Alamein*, p. 195.

32 Macksey, p. 122.

33 Montgomery, p. 145.

34 Lindsay, p. 60.

35 Holland, p. 302.

36 Clay, p. 110.

37 http://www.lrdg.org/LRDG-Photo-gallery(Trooper%20Section).htm#Tony%20Brown.

38 Bryant, p. 409.

39 Supplement to *The London Gazette* of Tuesday 3 February 1948, p. 839.

40 Churchill, *The Hinge of Fate*, p. 421.

41 Lindsay, p. 181.

42 Christopherson earned a Military Cross at El Alamein and later became commanding officer of the regiment after D Day. His wartime diaries were published in 2014.

43 Lindsay (*Regimental History of the Sherwood Rangers Yeomanry*).

44 Lindsay, p. 63.

45 Liddell Hart, B. H. *The Rommel Papers*. Collins,1953, pp. 388–9.

46 Stevens, p. 116. http://tothosewhoserved.org/nz/army/nzarmy06/chapter06.html.

47 Lindsay, p. 68.

48 Churchill, *The Hinge of Fate*, p. 646.

49 Ibid., p. 649.

50 Hildyard, p. 217.

51 This was not the only tragedy of this kind. Before the battle of Gazala in May 1942, 11 out of 12 South African crewmen died next to their three Bristol Blenheims when serious navigational errors had forced them to land in the desert. After eight days, a rescue party that had been hampered by a two-day sandstorm arrived, but by then there was only one man alive, Air Mechanic Noel Juul.

Chapter 14

1 General Robertson was the son of the chief of the Imperial General Staff, who famously became the first and only soldier to be promoted from Private all the way to Field Marshal. In his own

right, his son became Baron Robertson of Oakridge and was known as the best logistician in WWII, later earning fame for his part in the relief of Berlin, when he was military governor of the British zone.

2   De Candole, p. 73.
3   Metz, p. 25.
4   The chief administrators were in fact a Scot and an Irishman. Cumming, who played rugby for England despite his Scottish heritage, was later knighted and became president of the Society of Libyan Studies. Blackley was born in County Cavan, served in the Royal Artillery and accompanied the Highlanders through Libya.
5   Cumming took over in Cyrenaica from Stephen Longrigg (Oriel, Oxford) and handed over to Peter Acland in 1945. Acland had also followed a similar path; Christ Church, Oxford, followed by service with the Sudan Political Service and Sudan Defence Force, with whom he earned a Military Cross and fought in the Western Desert. The final incumbent, Eric de Candole (Worcester, Oxford), oversaw the transition on 1 March 1949.
6   Rodd; *Introduction to The Lost Oases* by A. M. Hassanein Bey (1925), p. 14.
7   For more on this aspect of the Anglo-Sanussi relationship, see Jason Pack's 2015 chapter in *The First World War and Its Aftermath*, pp. 41–62.
8   For more on the Orientalist and Arabist ideas that dominated the "official minds" in Libya, see Richard Synge's *Operation Idris*, Silphium Press 2015.
9   Jason Pack in Synge, p. 13.
10 Benjamin Doron interview, Yad Vashem testimony: https://www.yadvashem.org/articles/interviews/doron.html.
11 *The Daily Examiner*, 19 February 1948: https://trove.nla.gov.au/newspaper/article/195760762.
12 *Arab-Jewish Disturbances Tripoli*, Brigadier Blackley FO 160/98 18/B/16/6, 23 June 1948.
13 Glennon, p. 139.
14 The King's Royal Rifle Corps at Derna were warned to deploy to the Gulf in March 1956.
15 See "British Nurses in Libya", *American Journal of Nursing*, Volume 52 Issue 4 (April 1952): 423.
16 Ironically the US Air Force bombed Wheelus, renamed Mitiga Airport, on 15 April 1986, in retaliation for the bombing of the *La Belle* discotheque in Berlin, 10 days earlier.
17 The Army Children Archive: archhistory.co.uk/taca/schooling.html.
18 The British bridge, which linked Marj to Bayda, was replaced by the largest steel cable bridge in Libya. This was designed by the Italian Riccardo Morandi and built between 1965 and 1971 at a cost of $5,300,000.
19 https://www.vanityfair.com/style/society/2012/01/queen-elizabeth-201201https://www.vanityfair.com/style/society/2012/01/queen-elizabeth-201201.
20 Glennon, p. 139.
21 Statement by the Secretary of State for Air, Mr. Nigel Birch; Hansard, 7 November 1956.
22 *The Spectator*, 29 April 1955, p. 557.
23 Toy, pp. 145–6.
24 Sylvia Syms interview in Blu-Ray DVD Release 2015.
25 https://www.imdb.com/title/tt0049014/trivia/?ref_=tt_trv_trv.
26 The 2nd Dragoon Guards (Queen's Bays) were in action for 19 days during the Cauldron battle at Gazala.
27 The Benghazi military cemetery should not be confused with the War Cemetery. The former is a mile from the latter and contains 314 burials, which took place after the war. The Tripoli garrison cemetery contains 239 post-war graves. The four War Cemeteries in Libya hold 8,783 casualties. For more on the British military hospitals see the army nursing website: https://www.qaranc.co.uk/bmh-benghazi.php.

28 FO/371/178883 Libyan Treaty, 16 December 1964.
29 Vandewalle, p. 71.
30 British Diplomatic Oral History Project: Interview with The Hon. Ivor Lucas, first secretary and head of Chancery, Tripoli; 25 January 2005, by Malcolm McBain. Available at: http://www.chu.cam.ac.uk/archives/collections/BDOHP/Lucas.pdf.
31 FO 371/184231-184232; R. Sarell to R. Scrivener 25 June 1965 and Draft Libya Present position of the treaty review 30 September 1965; FO/371/190489 UK Proposals for Defence of Libya, January 1966.
32 FO 371/190785; Record of a meeting Stewart and Healey with US Counterparts at the State Department 27 January 1966.
33 FO 371/190495; Memorandum, 10 November 1966.
34 Goodchild et al.
35 FCO 39/120; Wakefield Memorandum 9 February 1968.
36 Kormann Lowe, Andrea. "Mercy Is Its Own Reward". *Foreign Service Journal*, October 2017.
37 "Barkston Couple Reunited with Army Veterans Caught Up In Riots In Libya 50 Years Ago". *Grantham Journal*, 21 July 2017.
38 FCO 39/118; Libyan bases, 29 June 1967.
39 Roumani, M. "Final Exodus of Libyan Jews in 1967". January 2007 at Researchgate.com.
40 FCO 39/344; Libya: Annual Review for 1967, January 1968.
41 FCO 39/121; D. J. Speares to ambassador in Tripoli, suspended draft letter, January 1968.
42 FO 371/178883; Confidential memorandum by P. G. A. Wakefield as annex to the UK Ambassador's Tripoli despatch dated 17 February 1968.
43 Straw, p. 136.
44 See https://bfg-locations.editboard.com/t2293-major-exercise–1967-libya.
45 DEFE 11/632; Tripoli to FCO, 5 September 1968.
46 The Libyan Arab Force (Sanussi) that fought in World War II, was re-designated as The Cyrenaica Defence Force in 1943.

Chapter 15

1 *The White Lancer and The Vedette* 1970, p. 15.
2 http://news.bbc.co.uk/onthisday/hi/dates/stories/september/1/newsid_3911000/3911587.stm.
3 Queen Fatima wrote two letters to Eric De Candole describing their journey from Turkey to Egypt via Greece. King Idris died peacefully in Cairo at the age of 94 in May 1983. Queen Fatima lived until 2009, when she was 98.
4 Sir Donald Maitland transcript 1997; British Diplomatic Oral History Programme, Churchill College, Cambridge; p. 15: https://www.chu.cam.ac.uk/media/uploads/files/Maitland.pdf.
5 Cyrenaican dialect is influenced by Egypt, whereas Western Libyan Arabic is closer to Maghrebi. Other Libyan languages include Tamazight (Berber), Tamahaq (Tuareg) and Nilo-Saharan (Tebu).
6 Maitland, p. 17.
7 Vandewalle, p. 75.
8 "The Coup and Us". *The White Lancer and The Vedette*, January 1970, p. 13.
9 https://www.thegazette.co.uk/London/issue/41589/supplement/21 For more on Olive Brittan's beekeeping, see Showler, Karl, "Beekeeper to The King of Libya" in *Bee World* Volume 88 Issue 2 (2011).
10 https://www.independent.co.uk/news/obituaries/sir-peter-wakefield-diplomat-who-went-found-asia-house-2184107.html.

11   For a full understanding of the government's decisions about these tank sales, see Simon Smith's meticulously researched *Centurions and Chieftains: Tank Sales and British Policy Towards Israel in the Aftermath of the Six Day War*.

12   Maitland, p. 41.

13   CAB 148/110; Minutes of the Defence and Oversea Policy Committee Meeting on 25 March 1970.

14   FCO 39/634; Maitland to Hayman, 19 February 1970.

15   https://www.airforcemag.com/article/0108wheelus/.

16   For further details on the evacuation, see: http://www.historicalrfa.org/archived-stories68/1487-the-army-and-raf-withdrawal-from-libya.

17   During this operation, the landing ships were transferred to the Royal Fleet Auxiliary. Three of the ships were later involved in the Falklands War. RFA *Sir Geraint* landed cargo at San Carlos Water and Fitzroy Sound. RFA *Sir Tristam* was attacked by Argentine Skyhawks and RFA *Sir Percivale* was the first ship to re-enter Stanley Harbour.

18   *The White Lancer and The Vedette*, 1971.

19   The Libyan pound was introduced in 1951. Previously, the currency had been the Ottoman qirsh, the Italian lira and after the war, a combination of the Tripoli lira and Algerian franc. In 1971, Gadhafi replaced the pound with the dinar.

20   *The White Lancer and The Vedette*, 1971, p. 32.

21   Al Magariaf, p. 228 (the plotters included Umar Muhayshi, Bashir Hawady, Abdul el Houni and Awad Hamza).

22   Pollack, p. 134.

23   UN Resolution A/RES/41/38 dated 20 November 1986. "Declaration of the Assembly of Heads of State and Government of the Organization of African Unity on the aerial and naval military attack against the Socialist People's Libyan Arab Jamahiriya by the present United States Administration in April 1986."

24   In May 2012, Taylor was sentenced to 50 years in prison by an international court in The Hague for "planning some of the most heinous and brutal crimes in recorded human history".

25   Fidler, Stephen, "The Human Factor: All is not well in the clandestine intelligence collection". *The Financial Times*, 7 July 2004.

26   Maitland, p. 15.

27   This refers specifically to the failure of the UN peacekeeping forces deployed in Rwanda and Srebrenica to prevent the genocides that took place in 1994 and 1995.

28   Mark Oliver, "Blair Meets Gadafy". The *Guardian*, 25 March 2004. https://www.theguardian.com/world/2004/mar/25/libya.politics.

29   "Iain Cobain's Special Report: Rendition Ordeal That Raises New Questions About Secret Trials". *The Guardian*, 8 April 2008.

30   Several internet chat boards have sections dedicated to veterans' life in Libya. Ted Jones' story is told on https://libocolors.wordpress.com/2010/03/01/a-story-of-two-bridges/ American and British stories can be found on: https://www.forcesreunited.co.uk/and military vehicles on: https://hmvf.co.uk/topic/35098-libya-tripolitania-vehicles-barracks–1950s-to–1966.

31   The author was informed about the proposal to end the ban on alcohol by a minister in the National Transitional Council in 2012.

32   Distinguished academics who have concentrated on social relationships during this period include Lisa Anderson, Ethan Chorin and Dirk Vandewalle.

33   The prison project straddled the time of two British ambassadors, who provided the quotes in this paragraph.

34   Jason Pack emphasises the importance of counter-terrorism intelligence sharing in: https://www.spectator.co.uk/article/engagement-in-libya-was-and-remains-the-right-answer.

35 Discussion and emails Wieloch–Weatherly, 12/13 March 2021.
36 From a conversation between the author and the leader of the Tuareg community in Ghadames, Sheikh Musa Ama; see Wieloch, R. *Belfast to Benghazi*, Mereo, 2016, p. 286.

Chapter 16

1 Woodward, Will, "First Stop of Blair's Farewell Africa Tour: Gadafy's Tent". The *Guardian*, 30 May 2007.
2 Bolger, Andrew, "US Hits at Decision to Free Lockerbie Bomber". *The Financial Times*, 21 August 2009.
3 Joel Faulkner Rogers and Jonathan Eyal in Johnson, *Wars in Peace*, p. 171.
4 Bashir was a former Libyan Air Force pilot who was appointed the head of the Bani Walid council after the revolution.
5 The best Russian equipment was issued to the brigades commanded by Gadhafi's sons. The Chrysanthemum was mounted on the latest BMP chassis and was photographed by British troops serving in Libya during the revolution.
6 The International Commission on Intervention and State Sovereignty was set up by the Canadian government; its initial report was published in 2001.
7 Patrick Wintour, "William Hague approved botched Libya mission, PM's office says". The *Guardian*, 7 March 2011.
8 Obama, p. 658.
9 Philip Collins, *Prospect Magazine*, 30 March 2016: https://www.prospectmagazine.co.uk/world/inside-obamas-white-house-reminds-us-that-politics-can-be-a-deeply-tragic-affair.
10 Cameron, p. 276.
11 Wieloch, *Belfast to Benghazi*, p. 240.
12 "Air Strikes Take Toll on Ghadaffi's Defences". *Jane's Defence Weekly*, 30 March 2011.
13 A Vision of A Democratic Libya, 29 March 2011. See for example https://www.theguardian.com/commentisfree/2011/mar/29/vision-democratic-libya-interim-national-council.
14 Cameron, p. 282.
15 Defence Internal Brief, dated 27 May 2011.
16 Patrick Hennessy, "Britain to step up attacks in Libya". *The Sunday Telegraph*, 5 June 2011.
17 James Kirkup, "Navy Chief: We cannot keep up Libya role". *The Daily Telegraph*, 14 June 2011.
18 Con Coughlin. "The Libyan Campaign is running into the sand". *The Daily Telegraph*, 26 July 2011.
19 Cameron, p. 284.
20 Parting Thoughts Letter from the British ambassador dated 3 November 2011 (Sir John Jenkins took over from Christopher Prentice on 13 May and handed over to Sir Dominic Asquith on 3 November).
21 10 Downing Street letter, dated 6 November 2011.
22 Cameron, p. 276.
23 Country Strategy Libya dated 22 February 2012; Revised AP-CP Strategy for Final Inputs 5 April 2012; Emails Tripoli-London dated 12 April 2012.
24 *Observer*, 4 March 2012 ("British war graves in Libya desecrated by Islamist militants") and *The Daily Telegraph*, 5 March 2012 ("Families' shock as Libyans smash British war graves").
25 Mohammed al-Tommy and Hadeel al-Shalchi; Reuters 10 April 2012.
26 *The Daily Telegraph*, 12 June 2012.
27 Libya: Victims/Transitional Justice/Militia Contract; Letter from McCue & Partners seeking $421m in liquidated parity damages.

28 The British prime minister eventually extended an apology in 2018 and awarded £500,000 compensation to Bel Haj. The author spoke with him after sharing a platform at the International Disarmament Conference held in Tripoli on 25 December 2012. See also "Abdul-Hakim Bel Haj torture case against UK rejected", BBC News, 20 December 2013 and "Rendition Victim Gets £500,000 compensation as May apologises 'unreservedly' for UK's conduct", The *Guardian*, 10 May 2018.

29 See Lacher, "Families, Tribes and Cities in the Libyan Revolution" (*Middle East Policy Council Journal* Volume XVIII Number 4, Winter 2011, pp. 140–54) for more on the effect of Gadhafi deliberately weakening state institutions.

30 Oxford Research International openanthropology.org/libya/firstnationalsurveysummary.pdf

31 Wieloch; "Defence Diplomacy and Defence Assistance in Post-conflict Situations in The British Army 2012", Newsdesk Media.

32 Annual Report to Parliament on NSS and SDSR, dated 28 November 2012.

33 Libya: Two Years On; A Libya Working Group discussion at Chatham House on 13 February 2013.

34 The degree to which the vote in the Houses of Parliament affected President Obama's decision not to intervene militarily in Syria was recorded in the documentary *Inside Obama's White House: Don't Screw It Up*, released in 2016.

35 "Bassingbourn Libyan Soldiers Jailed for Cambridge Women Attacks", BBC News, 18 May 2015.

36 According to the Royal Navy website, a destroyer, a frigate and two survey ships were involved in Operation *Sophia*.

37 *The Daily Telegraph* Editorial, 19 April 2016.

38 The Outlook for the Government of National Unity; Chatham House Webinar 4 March 2021.

39 See UN announcement at https://news.un.org/en/story/2019/08/1044111.

Index